DOOM GUY

LIFE IN
FIRST PERSON

JOHN ROMERO

ABRAMS PRESS, NEW YORK

Library of Congress Control Number: 2022933914

ISBN: 978-1-4197-5811-9
eISBN: 978-1-64700-536-8

Printed and bound in the United States
10 9 8 7 6 5 4 3 2

The events and descriptions depicted herein are remembered to the best of my ability, and while my memory is good, it is not infallible. If I left anyone out or remembered things incorrectly, I am sorry.

Abrams books are available at special discounts when purchased in quantity for premiums and promotions as well as fundraising or educational use. Special editions can also be created to specification. For details, contact specialsales@abramsbooks.com or the address below.

Abrams Press® is a registered trademark of Harry N. Abrams, Inc.

ABRAMS The Art of Books
195 Broadway, New York, NY 10007
abramsbooks.com

I dedicate this book to everyone who has played my games. This book would not exist if not for you. Thank you for allowing me to fulfill a childhood dream, and thank you so much for playing my games.

Of these players, I wish to call out one specifically: my wife, Brenda. She is my best friend and love of my life. She has played all my games, is my number one fan, and supports my need to code and create. This book is for you.

CONTENTS

EPISODE ONE

PROTOTYPING

CHAPTER 1

The Talk

"That was not at all what I expected."

After the talk, I heard this line again and again. People came up to meet me and to shake my hand. Some asked me to sign their games or told me about their experiences playing *DOOM* or *Quake* or *Wolfenstein 3-D*. A few people, having seen themselves in the talk I'd given, shared stories of growing up in homes like the one I grew up in. They didn't have to tell me much, because when you grow up like I grew up, you just know.

The talk itself was at a private event, a conference for a game company in eastern Canada. The three hundred people in attendance represented the complete spectrum of game development. There were programmers of every type, game designers, level designers, artists and animators, musicians, and audio engineers. I recognized some of the biz people from other game-dev conferences.

I remember when the HR and Events team first reached out to me about giving this talk. They told me they wanted something different. "People know a lot about your games. We wonder if you could talk about something new."

I was puzzled by their request, though. What might I talk about to a room of game developers if not my games?

"We have an idea," the Events person said. "We wondered if you could talk about yourself, your story. You know, everything that made you make the games you made. Where you come from, your background. We think people would enjoy that, and it could be inspiring, particularly to our junior team members."

My story? My *personal* story? My life story was not something I had shared before. Of course, my family knows it. My wife, Brenda, knows it, but not even my kids know all of it. I wasn't sure where to start.

"I suppose I could do that," I said.

"That's great. We'll see you in November, then. Feel free to send along any materials or requirements you have in advance."

A few days later, I was staring at a blank slide deck. I typed "My Life" on the first slide. It was going to be a forty-five-minute talk with fifteen minutes for questions. I had a lot of slides to go. Exactly what parts of my life did they want to know about?

Everything that made you make the games you made.

Everything.

So I put it all in there, the whole story—or what you could tell in about an hour, anyway.

Once I proofed and practiced it, I sent it off. Then I headed from my home in Galway, Ireland, to Canada to deliver the talk.

By the time I got to the slides about my family's involvement in the drug trade, I could tell by the looks on people's faces that this was not the story they expected to hear. Two first cousins were murdered. Two uncles ran drugs for a well-known cartel. My father and one uncle died from their addictions to everything from cocaine to alcohol. The rest of that generation managed to sober up before their addictions could claim them (my amazing Aunt Yoly miraculously escaped all of it).

From my position on the stage behind the podium, I saw mouths agape. At the word "murdered" there were more than a few audible gasps. Perhaps they expected something different—a middle-class, bright kid who grew up in a stable home in the 1970s and '80s with lots of electronic toys like Mattel's *Electronic Football* or *Simon* to inspire me. My reality was a lot different than that, but I liked my reality all the same. It was all that I knew, and it made me grateful for the good in my life, and there *was* a lot of good around me.

My talk started with 1972. I was a scrappy, impish-looking five-year-old with dark, wavy, unruly hair and thick glasses, which I've had forever, and nightmarish teeth that came in splayed and overlapping. We lived in a small house on South Oregon Drive in a low-income barrio in Tucson, Arizona. My parents, Alfonso and Ginny Romero, were young, both of them twenty-two. My father was five feet eight with jet-black hair, brown eyes, and sepia-toned skin. My mother was the same height as my father, hazel-eyed, and fair-skinned with blond hair that she wore pinned on the top of her head. My mom took care of me and my three-year-old brother, Ralph, and she sewed clothes for the family and others to earn extra money. My dad fought rock for a living in the Pima County copper mines that surrounded Tucson. As couples go, they were equipped with energy, love, laughter, and flashes of rage. There was always beer around.

"While my family is now known for programming and design," I told the audience, mentioning with pride that my son and two stepchildren also worked in games, "my family has also known tremendous success in dealing drugs and drinking vast amounts of alcohol."

I laughed, and a few others did, too.

My father grew up in the barrio in South Tucson in a house beside his father Alfredo's junkyard. My grandparents' house always felt like home to me. Walking in the front door, the first thing to hit you was the smell of my grandmother's cooking. My grandma Socorro (we called her Suki) was a nurturing machine: She hugged and fed everyone, and constantly pressed out tortillas made from flour, Sonoran style. I loved everything about her food, especially the heaping dishes of frijoles, crispy tacos dorados, and Spanish rice seasoned with tomatoes, peas, carrots, green onions, cilantro, and whatever else she happened to throw in. Food is so central to Mexican culture, and no one makes it better than a Mexican grandmother. When my grandma passed in 2007, the surviving children and grandchildren spontaneously started exchanging her recipes—recipes we'd gathered over the years—and my cousin Trisha put them all into a binder, which was shared with the family. Every one of us treasures it. If you walked in the door of my grandma's house, you were going to be fed. It was the way she welcomed you and told you that she loved you.

It was always the same when I walked through the front door.

"Hola, mijo," she'd say before she turned and walked into the kitchen to get a plate. I'd sit at the table, and her food would appear in front of me. To this day, I still cook on my grandma's comal, a flat, cast-iron griddle my grandfather made for her from the top of an iron barrel. Inside my grandparents' house, it was a picture of domestic bliss. Outside the house in the backyard, it was often a party that went on late into the night. My father, aunts, uncles, and their friends were drinking, singing, and having a great time. My cousins added to the fun. It was a constant, chaotic family gathering with all of us running around. There was a lot of love, music, and food, and a whole lot of beer. Everyone spoke Spanish except the kids. In the 1970s, parents wanted their children to fit in and assimilate, so they didn't teach us Spanish. It was a misguided hope that we would escape some of the racism our parents experienced, and it came at a cultural cost.

In addition to being Mexican American, I'm Yaqui on my father's side and Cherokee on my mother's side. There was a family at the end of South Oregon Drive who lived in an adobe hut with an actual tepee next to it. They had a rug for a door and dirt floors. I went to school with the boy who lived in the adobe hut, and we sometimes played together. No one else I knew had a house like his, particularly with the tepee (I would learn later in life that they were used by the Plains tribes and not the Yaqui). When I asked my parents about my friend's home, they let me know that we were two of a kind, even if we didn't live in houses that looked the same.

My mother's family, in contrast, lived in the Glenheather suburb of east Tucson on East 17th Street. There was a shiny new school with a big field I could see from their back fence, and everything was paved and nicely landscaped, unlike the dirt alleys and random cacti near our place. My maternal grandparents, John and Ann Marshall, spoke only English. My grandmother was a small woman with mousy brown hair and a preference for polyester clothing. Grandpa John, who I'm named after, was a tall man, around six feet, with light-brown skin and gray hair. He loved game shows and had a habit of verbally assaulting the contestants on the TV. If those contestants were non-white? Watch out. He would unleash streams of racist curses and insults. As a little kid, I didn't know any better, and I thought it was hilarious. He laughed, so I did, too. He didn't know these people, but he spewed out naughty words that I knew you weren't supposed to say. Though my mom always told me that Grandpa John was Cherokee, it wasn't until later that I processed this and realized his behavior made no sense. He was a virulent bigot who hated non-whites even though he was non-white himself.

When my grandpa wasn't yelling at the TV, their home was a quiet and docile environment. My grandmother read while my grandfather painted. My mom often left me with my grandparents while she ran errands, particularly if my father was nowhere to be found. That happened a fair bit.

I don't remember my father without a beer. I didn't know what he did when he was at work down in the mines, but when I saw him aboveground, there was always a bottle or a can in his hand and a cigarette in his mouth. They were there when he got out of the truck after work, and more followed when he was talking to friends who stopped by the house. Working on the engine of his car, he'd sit a cold one on top of the fender. When he went to the drag races, he'd come back with two beers, one in each hand. Sometimes, he'd take us out to the Sonoran Desert to scavenge for mesquite wood to cook carne asada, and he'd have a beer between his legs as he drove and a cooler in the back that carried still more. My father was the life of any party—people tell me that to this day. He had a great laugh and a welcoming demeanor that made you want to be his friend. He was a mariachi with a beautiful voice who performed with Mariachi Cobre for a time. He loved to sing "Cucurrucucú Paloma" and "Malagueña Salerosa."

Just a fair warning before you read further: The following events contain descriptions of domestic abuse and aren't easy to hear about.

If my father didn't have alcohol, bad things happened—he was irritable and easily angered, and things could shift in a split second. We walked on eggshells to avoid provoking him. If he did have alcohol, he might be loving and kind, or he might turn into a monster. I remember my dad walked in the front door one morning, hungry and looking for food. He'd been out all night at the bars. He stormed into the bedroom where my mother was still sleeping, grabbed her by the hair, and dragged her out of bed and down the hallway, her feet trailing behind her. She yelled his name, begging for him to stop. I sat paralyzed in front of the TV where I was watching Saturday-morning cartoons, unsure what to do. I can't remember what happened, but it still pains me to this day to think of it. My father was incredibly strong. He didn't just make his living fighting rock—he beat it. He battered the earth down in the mines and won.

Aboveground, the battering continued. Sometimes, it was my mom. Sometimes, it was me or Ralph. When the beatings came, I felt like I deserved them, because, inevitably, I'd done something wrong. I didn't always know what I'd done, and sometimes, it didn't matter. Oftentimes, what I did "wrong" was to be in the wrong place at the wrong time.

Sometimes, it was others who took a beating.

There's an oft-told story in my family about a hitchhiker who tried to rob my dad. It ended with a pipe wrench and that hitchhiker on the side of the road in the desert between Phoenix and Tucson. A lesser-told story involves my dad and his brothers getting into a bar fight with some cops. Many of my father's fights took place in bars, but I suspect that one ended in arrests. Anything could set my father off, even when he did have beer. He wasn't afraid of action. If he even suspected a fight was coming, he'd start it. I left many of these finer details out of the talk I gave that day in Canada for obvious reasons.

"We didn't have much money," I continued, "so we got by however we could."

My mother used food stamps to purchase bulk rice, flour, and powdered milk. Sometimes, "however we could" involved my grandma Suki feeding us. Other times, my father came up with his own solutions.

"My mom told me how my dad once held up a Circle K to steal my diapers at gunpoint," I told the audience. Everyone laughed, and it was funny in a weird kind of way—my father committing a felony for diapers of all things, not to mention its similarity to a scene in *Raising Arizona*. My mother had no idea he was doing this, of course. She only found out a few years later during a quick stop at that same store. The cashier spotted him, and they made a hasty exit.

At the conference, I advanced to a slide showing the Sonoran Desert. Behind me, a giant saguaro cactus was projected on a screen thirty feet across and twenty feet tall.

"It's another day, and my mom was hanging laundry outside. I wandered into the kitchen and unscrewed a jar of rice and another of beans. When there are no toys, you make your own fun," I told them.

"The rice and beans became ammunition. I was throwing them at my brother, and he was throwing them at me. We were having a massive food fight! Making a mess, flinging things at each other. We were having a ball. My mom came in the door and yelled, 'Stop that right now!' She was furious, but she was not a hitter. 'Get out of here!' And so we did. We went outside."

We played in the yard, in the dirt with rocks and twigs, building little forts and looking out for scorpions and tarantulas. When my dad came home, he went inside. From outside, we could hear the fight brewing.

"Que pasó?" My dad wanted to know what the hell had happened.

"What happened? Look at this place. Your damn dinner is on the floor."

"It's just rice and beans. They must have been having fun."

My dad was unpredictable. Something like this could set off his temper or make him laugh. My mother was having none of it.

"*Fun?* I'm an expert in fun. Fun is being here all day long with two little boys while *you're* out drinking. Fun is going to your mother to ask for chicken so that we have something to eat. Fun is you working all night and coming home six beers into the day and me trying to keep these kids quiet so you can sleep."

The fridge door opened and shut, and we heard my father crack open a new beer.

"Get rid of them!" My mom yelled. "I've had enough for today."

My dad slammed the door and headed back toward the driveway. "Mijos!" he called. "Get in the truck!"

I opened the passenger door to the cab and helped Ralph climb in. He was four, and I was six. I could tell dad was angry, so I didn't ask questions. I just sat there while he drove us into the nearby desert.

I came this way all the time with my dad. It was our source of firewood for the barbecues. My dad used a plumber's wrench to knock dead branches off mesquite trees, and I dragged them to the truck. The desert was also a source of pride for my dad. He told stories about its history, plants, and animals. He told me about discovering pecan groves, how he would sneak in, climb the trees, shake the branches, and then scour the ground to harvest as many pecans as possible. The farmer spotted him and grabbed a gun. Sometimes he shot rock salt, which would sting like hell. Once, my dad caught a BB pellet in the neck. It remained there for the rest of his life, embedded in his right side.

The truck veered off the highway and onto a dirt road. We drove into the Sonoran Desert, the hottest terrain, day in, day out, in the entire country, where the sun baked the ground so hot it seemed to ripple on the horizon and the saguaros looked like they were dancing. He pulled the truck to a stop and said, "Get out."

I got out first and then helped Ralph climb down. I looked at the cab, waiting for my father to join us, but that didn't happen. Instead, he leaned over, grabbed the door, and slammed it shut. We waited for his instructions, but there were none. My dad put the truck in gear and pulled a U-turn. He was not looking at me. His eyes were on the road, and he was driving away. I watched the pickup vanish out of sight.

Get rid of them.

I repeated my mother's words in my head. She hadn't meant that literally, but he took it that way, or he was punishing her for blowing up at him. Either way, it was bad news for Ralph and me. Had he really left us out here? There was nothing but bone-dry desert and the dry bed of the Santa Cruz River. We couldn't even see the highway. I looked around. I had been close to here before. The pecan groves were somewhere nearby.

Ralph started to cry, so I grabbed his hand and told him, "I think I know the way."

We started to walk back toward the highway. It was hot, but being six, I was blessed with naivety. It's only when I got older that I realized just how many ways this could have gone wrong. I hoped a police car would come by or one of our uncles or our grandpas. They could drive us home. I knew where to go, to the highway. I hoped Ralph could keep up. He had to.

"This is the right way," I reassured Ralph. The larger saguaros were like landmarks.

We walked for thirty minutes.

I scanned ahead, and then, rocketing down the highway, I saw a familiar sight: Dad's pickup.

It screeched as it braked to make the turn-off and headed our way.

The truck stopped, the passenger door swung open, and my mother ran toward us. She was crying, yelling our names. She dropped down to her knees and pulled us close.

My dad said, "Get in."

I helped Ralph into the cab and then climbed in myself. Our mother got in behind us. Dad put the truck in gear. He didn't look at me. His eyes remained on the road the whole way home. He didn't say a single word. Neither did we. We knew better.

Years later, my wife, Brenda, asked my mother about this incident, and my mom drew in a shocked breath.

"Oh my god," she said. Tears started to well in her eyes. "You remember that, Johnny?"

I had never discussed it with her. In my family, when something bad happened and was over, you didn't bring it up again.

"I do," I said.

She was crying, which, of course, made me tear up, too.

"Tell me you're okay? Did it affect you?"

"I'm okay," I said. "I'm okay. It didn't affect me."

"Does Ralphie remember?"

I nodded that he did. Ralph and I had talked about it before.

She put her head in her hands.

"It wasn't your fault, Mom."

She told us the story of him arriving home without us and her asking him where we were.

"I got rid of them," he said.

"You what?" she cried.

"You got what you wanted."

She screamed at him to get in the truck, screamed all the way. "How could you? What's wrong with you? Where are they?"

The truck tore up the road, past the edge of town, out by the pecan trees. That's when she saw us walking. All these years, she'd kept the story to herself, hoping we didn't remember, hoping it hadn't affected us.

Most of the time, my father was fun—blasting music, singing, working on cars, laughing, cooking. We camped and explored in the desert. My love for our traditional food and my sense of humor come from him. He told me that he loved me every night before I went to bed. *I love you, mijo.*

When he passed away, in the same house in which he was born, he was ill from a lifetime of drinking and drugs. I tried to help him many times. I bought him a house and sent him to rehab. At the end of his life, he had just a few possessions, including a folder that contained the things most important to him: his GED and a photocopied magazine article about me, his son, *mi hijo*, who made computer games.

I told the audience all these things—how growing up in this family made me take nothing for granted, how my mom ended up finding happiness, how that happiness led to my first computer, and how that first computer led to the games everyone knew: *Wolfenstein 3-D*, *DOOM*, and *Quake*.

When the talk was done, I thanked everyone and stepped off the stage. The crowd of game developers applauded, and the chorus of "That wasn't what I expected" commenced.

CHAPTER 2

More ROM than RAM

I have hyperthymesia. Neuroscientists and researchers call this condition "highly superior autobiographical memory," and pop-culture fans and journalists frequently apply the phrase "total recall"—taken from the movie adaptation of "We Can Remember It for You Wholesale," a classic Philip K. Dick story about implanted memories—to describe it.

Based on what I've read about hyperthymesia, many people with the condition regard it as a curse. It's easy to imagine painful scenarios, as if straight out of a Stephen King novel or *Groundhog Day*, that involve reliving the past's disasters and humiliations in a vivid, never-ending loop.

I actually can see scenes from the past—images, often fully realized—in my mind's eye. I can home in on distinctive details. Sometimes, the setting activates other specifics tied to the scene—the song that was playing, the weather that day—that are not part of the visual. I can relive encounters with people, recalling actual conversations, reactions, laughter, anger, sorrow, and I can tap into how I was feeling at this time—my own internal life.

You can see how this condition could be a real challenge for some people, but I am fortunate. While I experience the past events in my life—both the good and the bad—I am an analyzer, not a ruminator. Escaping into my memory and imagination is something I enjoy, as I think this book will attest, and it's an incredibly useful skill when creating and playing immersive games. Even as a small boy, I could get lost in playing make-believe, inventing simple games, like throwing rocks at a target or drawing pictures. Consciously or not, my personality traits have conspired to turn my condition into an asset, a gift.

I am primarily self-taught. From the age of twelve, I worked at odd jobs whenever I could because money was tight in my family. Being short on cash also meant being short on time. Having the ability to absorb massive amounts of detail and retain that information was a great advantage. I didn't realize it was even a "condition" when I was a kid. It was just the way I was. My teachers called me gifted, but neither my parents nor I knew what that meant, and even if we did, I'm not sure there was anything we could do about it. This "gift" only extended to things I really cared about. The rest, which included some subjects at school, was forgotten.

I get the impression some experts view the origins of hyperthymesia as sort of a chicken-or-egg condition. Does it lie dormant and then present itself, or do those who have it create it? There is an argument to be made that I sharpened my memory, that I created my condition due to my obsession with programming and games. As a teenage boy in the 1980s, I realized information on programming was hard to come by, so I forced myself to retain technical information and memorize the internal details of computers—memory maps, ROM locations, hardware switches, and tons more stuff. I did it quickly, which, in turn, expanded my ability to retain and access precise memories of almost everything else.

Of course, there's irony here. I can remember precise details of games I played forty years ago, conversations with high school friends, or long code-crunching nights with my partners at id Software, but I can't remember when, exactly, I first noticed my ability to approximate something like total recall.

At any rate, I thought I'd mention my condition up-front. A lot of ink has been spilled about my life and my projects. A great deal of the reporting on me and the work I've done has been filtered through other people. Some of it has been accurate. Some of it has been way off base. I can't speak to other people's ability to accurately recall events, but I can speak to mine. Several people, including my id Software co-founders John Carmack and Tom Hall, have said they leave their memories with me because I'll remember them and refer journalists to me when they can't remember something. More than once, I've provided gentle corrections to people online because I believe history—accurate history—is important. So when I say that my version of events is "true," it's based on a condition that is rare, strange, and real.

As many before me have noted, we are our memories. They provide us with our background, with our context, our perspective. They cement our most important relationships, and they inform our future. We are also shaped by family, which in turn shapes those memories. Where you come from and who you come from will always be a part of the equation of you.

I'm a true American hybrid—part Mexican, part Yaqui and Cherokee, part European. My father, Al Romero, was a mestizo with Yaqui blood, from Tucson. He was a talented musician, a ladies' man, a high school dropout, and a lover of fast cars. To my mom, Ginny, he was a real catch, and vice versa.

He was also a second-generation miner and fourth-generation badass; his grandmother, my great-grandmother, Elvira Duarte de Morales, was a full-blooded Yaqui and a powerful, successful madam in Nogales, Mexico, a fact I only discovered in the last decade. I met her once, when I was five years old, on a visit to Nogales, which is a town that sprawls across the Mexico-Arizona border. I remember bouncing along a rut-filled dirt road, Calle Galleña, to a house on a hilltop with a small chapel across the street. Inside the sizable house, I was shown a picture of her as a beautiful bride. Decades later, as my wife and I were doing research for her Chicago-gangland strategy game, *Empire of Sin*, we learned about the family brothel.

"Mama Elvira was a businesswoman and did not put up with any weakness from anyone," Aunt Yoly, one of Elvira's grandchildren, told me. "She raised her family during very hard times and did whatever she had to do to make ends meet. She was a very proud woman, hard and strong. I was sort of afraid of her because she was so rigid and tough."

Mama Elvira opened three brothels. Each of these clubs—which included the Wakiki and the B-21—was fronted by a legitimate restaurant and bar. Her sons worked as bartenders. The Wakiki issued bordello tokens stamped with "Your Place in Nogales" and "Open Day and Night." I've seen a number of them for sale on coin-collector websites. These tokens were likely purchased by patrons and redeemed for sex or booze to circumvent money-for-sex laws, and there's little doubt they also functioned as promotional items.

Mama Elvira was a tough, powerful woman, but she was also a madame with—if not a heart of gold—a serious sliver of kindness. Her business had a frequent side effect: Women got pregnant. According to Aunt Yoly, Mama Elvira would support them and even raise their kids if they couldn't afford it. This meant she built additions onto her house with rooms and beds for all the kids. Family lore has it that she raised about forty children this way.

She finally exited the business after winning a quarter of a million pesos in a lottery. She had a little chapel built across the street from her family home, sold the three brothels, and lived out the last third of her life as a law-abiding woman. When her first husband, Duarte, got sick in his old age, Mama Elvira took him in, caring for him until he died.

I don't think she softened up entirely. My favorite story of my gritty great-grandmother might be this: In her old age, when she complained of crippling pain in the back of her neck, one of her friends told her about a local folk remedy—that eating rattlesnake meat would relieve her symptoms. Mama Elvira decided to give it a try. She hired a man to hunt rattlers and bring them to her. Then she would grind up the meat in a blender, cook it, and eat it. She claimed it helped.

My father's mother—my beloved Grandma Suki—exuded a similar unstoppable, deal-with-it, housemother vibe. She was the only one of Mama Elvira's children born in the US. Elvira specifically traveled to Tucson at the end of her pregnancy with Suki to make sure she had an American daughter. Given her own sons' behavior, Grandma Suki also didn't recoil from living on the other side of the law.

Suki remained in Tucson until eighth grade and then rejoined her mom in Nogales. I count her as one of the most instrumental figures in my life: a loving, caring woman who steeped Mexican culture into my bones—the music, the food, the style, the love of family. More importantly, she provided a dose of stability, comfort, and ballast for everyone who crossed her path, including my parents.

My parents needed that ballast. They were high school sweethearts who got married as soon as my mom turned eighteen. They were young, poor, unworldly, and pregnant, with a limited network of support—not the ideal circumstances to start a family—but they were in love, so they really didn't care. My mom wanted away from her family, and who could blame her? Her parents, John and Ann Marshall, were the opposite of my grandma Suki. They weren't badasses, they were hardasses—a judgmental, unsupportive, Depression-era couple, and as I mentioned, my grandfather was also incredibly racist.

More than he hated non-whites on TV, Grandpa John really hated my father, the Mexican who married his daughter. When my mom walked down the aisle in her self-made wedding gown, he wasn't there.

Tired of the racism they experienced as a mixed couple in Tucson, my newly-wed parents relocated to Colorado. My mom was four months pregnant when they pulled into town, and my dad soon got a job selling jewelry at Zales—but the gig ended when he got caught stealing. I was born six weeks early in Colorado Springs on October 28, 1967. My arrival didn't do too much to warm up the Colorado winter for two lifetime desert-dwellers, and a few months later, they packed us up, and we returned to my grandma Suki's house, and my father went to join his dad, Alfredo, in the mines.

One fact eased my mother's transition into the house—the fact that Tucson was a very Mexican place, even if you were white. Unlike 99 percent of America, the Mexican influence was everywhere there. Spanglish was a part of the local language. My dad's best friend at Sunnyside High School, Pat Snyder, and his wife, Judy, my mom's best friend, were both white, but they used tons of Spanish phrases. When I met them decades later, after they relocated to Idaho, I was shocked by how much Spanglish filled the conversation. So my mom, who grew up in a more middle-class neighborhood, wasn't totally behind the curve at her in-laws' house in the Tucson barrio. Grandma Suki welcomed her—and me—with open arms.

"Barrio" means neighborhood (like "borough") in Spanish, but in the US, it has come to mean a lower-income urban area populated by Latinos. My grandparents lived on South Sixth Avenue near East Nebraska, raising a family of eight in a three-bedroom house. There were paved streets, but the alleyways and side streets were dirt. My grandfather had purchased the lot behind the house, which served as a junkyard.

Sometimes I think about my mother, eighteen and from the nicer side of the tracks, coming back to Tucson with her baby to live with her in-laws in a house next to a junkyard filled with rusting cars, discarded kitchen appliances, and tires. Despite her Tucson roots, that still must have been strange for her: Who lives next to a junkyard?

My grandfather, Alfredo, never ran the junkyard as a business. There wasn't even a sign outside the lot. He and his sons amassed car, truck, and camper parts and sold stuff when the opportunity arose. My uncle Tito eventually went into business renovating used RVs, but that was the closest the lot ever came to being an operating business. I assumed it must have done well since Uncle Tito was always flashing lots of cash, walking around with $4,000 in his pocket. (I later learned that another family business was responsible for that.)

Inside Grandma Suki's house, activity was constant, a welcoming refuge filled with food, music, and life. My father was the youngest of six kids. He had two brothers and three sisters, and they were frequently in the house, too. My uncles Ralph (Rafael) and Tito (Alfredo) also worked in the mines at various shifts, and often dropped by with their kids and wives and girlfriends. So there were cousins to look after me and to play with. Grandma Suki cooked continuously, all day, every day, churning out fabulous, spicy food—paper-thin flour tortillas with deliciously shredded machaca, carne asada, carnitas, and pollo, and frijoles, frijoles, and more frijoles. There was plenty of music—traditional mariachi favorites, norteño, and rock.

There was also plenty of drama, even in the early days of my parents' marriage.

They had problems. Or perhaps I should say my father had many problems and my mother had one big one: my father.

My dad was a drinker, a gambler, and prone to explosive violence. His problems turned my mother's life into a daily nightmare. Her violent husband was also her primary provider, and she was almost entirely dependent on him for money, but even when he was working, she couldn't rely on even part of his salary making it home because he sometimes gambled it all away. She was an excellent seamstress and took in whatever sewing and mending work she could find to earn cash.

For years, Suki was her main support network. When our cupboards were bare, when my father went AWOL, when my mother was barely hanging by a thread, my grandma was there to take care of us, feed us, love us.

Adding to the drama and domestic chaos, no doubt, were my uncles' extra-curricular gigs, too—although I was completely unaware of them when I was little. Uncle Tito sold heroin and wound up serving time. Uncle Ralph ran drugs north and south for a cartel and sold weed until the day he died. I remember him trying to gift me a bale of weed when I was visiting my father in Idaho. I turned him down. Sometimes I tell people this, and I think for a moment that my dad was a comparatively law-abiding citizen, as far as I knew. Of course, I then remember the drinking while driving, gambling, and committing armed robbery for diapers, not to mention the many moments of domestic abuse.

Eventually, after a few months of living at Suki's, my parents scraped together money to buy a small two-bedroom house on South Oregon Drive. It cost $10,000 in 1968, about $77,000 in today's dollars. It was a humble abode in a humble part of town, not far from Twelfth Avenue and Nebraska, the big cross streets.

The little house on South Oregon was liberating for my mom—she had her own space. She didn't have to ask Suki or any of her in-laws for permission to do anything. It was also confining, exhausting, and dangerous. I was a toddler when they moved in, and toddlers are a lot of work. They didn't have the money to ship me off to daycare, so my mom and I were together in the little house a lot. Soon, she was pregnant again, and Ralph was born the November shortly after I turned two. It must have been hard, lonely work caring for two boys. At Suki's, there were always other people around. On South Oregon Drive, there weren't any distractions—no uncles and aunts and cousins laughing, and teasing, and Grandma Suki and her daughters weren't around to shield my mom from my dad's ugly drunkenness or pick up the slack from his absences. My dad was a hard worker—he went to the mines every day—but coming home was another matter. He liked going out, shooting pool, and drinking at the bar. Sometimes he didn't come home at all.

My dad could keep a party going for hours. He loved hosting his friends, cooking and talking. He and my mother would bundle us into the car and take us to the home of Pat and Judy, their best friends, where they would drink and smoke and play card games all night, while Ralph and I played with their kids, Alan and Samantha, who were the same ages as we were. We played with Maggie, their dog. I liked going to that house. It was in a new development with '70s interior design and unlike any other house I had seen before. Eventually, all of us kids fell asleep while the partying continued. Hours after midnight, a slumbering Ralph and I were carried to the car by our partied-out parents, and we'd wake up the next morning in our beds.

I don't remember my dad ever being violent with us at social events. It was always at home. He drank from the moment he got home from work: beer, beer, and more beer. When he got older, he drank from the moment he got up. At one point, I thought beer was the only thing adults drank.

The violence was usually sudden and fierce. My dad used heavy equipment in the mines, drilling against the earth, hauling ore, hour after hour, day after day. He was incredibly strong. I remember him hoisting and tossing car tires like they were nothing. That strength meant his eruptions were terrifying in their force and efficiency.

He abused my mother and made life horrible for her. It could be anything. Sometimes, the dinners she fixed weren't good enough, and he'd fling full plates of food across the room. My mother cleaned it up and started over. Unfortunately, she was accustomed to this type of behavior. My mom grew up watching her own father pummeling her brothers. It bothers me to think that must have played into her enduring this brutal treatment from my dad, and because her father had opposed the marriage to begin with, he certainly wasn't going to save her or let her move back in with him. She must have felt stuck between a rock and a hard place. She couldn't protect herself, and she couldn't protect her kids. Escape must have seemed unfathomable.

Even as a little boy, I sensed that she felt this way. I didn't understand that she didn't have a means to support herself or was tragically in love with and dependent on a violent alcoholic. I didn't know that her own dad shut her out and refused to help her. However, even at that young age, I did understand that the world was sometimes unfair, and that was that. There weren't really any easy options, and so you had to play the cards you were dealt. I believed that for both my mother and father, violence was part of the equation of living.

Eventually, we became the target. One day, I was in the backyard throwing darts at the back of the garage. It was a wooden wall, and the darts stuck into it and made a nice sound when they hit. My aim needed work, though. I was a little kid. Eventually, a dart hit the window and broke it. When my mom found out, she went into her standard refrain when I did anything wrong:

"Just wait till your dad gets home."

I knew I was in big trouble. To me, those words meant only one thing: My dad would remove his belt and use it on me. It wasn't a daily or even weekly occurrence, but it happened. Sometimes he would whip me pretty bad. Another time he suddenly grabbed my wrist and stubbed out his burning cigarette on it. He was buzzed—he was always buzzed—and I was playing with his lighter and that upset him. I still have a scar on my wrist and others elsewhere. I processed these events the same way computer engineers look at coding: input in, output out; x triggers y. To my kid brain, the events translated this way: You did something wrong, and this is what happens when you do something wrong. You get whipped, or you get left out in the desert and have to walk home. Mostly, for self-preservation, I accepted what happened and moved on.

In spite of all of this, I never hated my dad. He told me he loved me, and I loved him. He picked me up and hugged me. He brought me things he found in the mines—huge centipedes that seemed to belong in horror movies, shiny crystal rocks. He made us all laugh with jokes and sang to us. To this day, when I meet someone who knew him, they always say how wonderful he was, and I agree. One of my favorite memories is him serenading Grandma Suki with "La Malagueña" on her birthday. He was a passionate, troubled man, and I have far more good memories of him than I do bad. I loved him, and I know that he loved me. At age fifty-seven, he passed away in his childhood bedroom at Grandma Suki's. Among his few possessions was a folder with articles he saved about me.

I was and still am incredibly close to my mother. She kept us alive, kept us sane and safe, and got us through some difficult times, especially when she was having such difficulty herself.

CHAPTER 3

Sonoran Son

As a little kid, my favorite place to visit, besides Grandma Suki's food-filled house, was a place my father never set foot in during his entire life: Grandpa John and Grandma Ann Marshall's house. And who could blame him? As I mentioned, Grandpa John was an unabashed racist who completely opposed my parents getting hitched. Even though his grandmother was Cherokee, he was disgusted that his daughter had married a Mexican who was Yaqui! I'm sure nobody expected him to embrace me, the offspring of the union that he was dead set against, but life is funny that way. I was his favorite. He adored me instantly, according to my mother, and I adored him back.

Our relationship felt completely natural, and it was. Thankfully, blood, even blood he didn't like, was thicker than water where Grandpa John was concerned. As I got older and started talking and interacting with him, his affection for me grew and grew.

My Grandpa John was originally from Henryetta, Oklahoma. He had the chiseled features, short gray hair, and a weathered, rugged face. Every time I was around him, he was the gentlest person. It was only later in life that I learned how violently he treated his own kids. He drank vodka every night, but I had no idea he was an alcoholic. In fact, I never saw him drink during the day. There were few times that my grandpa was out of the house: I recall him attending my eighth grade graduation and going to see *Silverado* in Prescott. He really lived like he was personally quarantined. He watched TV all day and took naps. I rarely saw him eat anything.

Grandma Ann was a petite woman originally from Chicago. She lost her mother when she was ten years old, something that affected her for the rest of her life. Her father sent her to a Catholic boarding school for a couple of years, and when she returned home she found him remarried, to a woman who had kids of her own. So she took a back seat and became more reserved, sometimes even cold. That said, she did have a soft side, but she would not put up with anything that didn't agree with her. She spoke up often. Overall, I heard her speak more negative comments than positive. She never traveled, because my grandpa John didn't want to leave home. Once they settled in Tucson, Arizona, that was it.

My grandpa and I were an odd couple. Grandpa John was a crusty, creative, passionate man. A survivor of the Great Depression, his life had taken him to hell and back. His mother died when he was three, and his father was rarely around—when he was, he wasn't much of a parent. Food was scarce and so was supervision. Grandpa John quit school after fourth grade. When he was eleven, his father threw a pitchfork at him, aiming to injure. The sharp-tined missile missed its target, but the message was received. John Marshall took to the streets, even though the Depression was on, and food, work, and money were hard to come by. He spent his early teens hopping train cars across the country with hobos. Eventually, he decided to join the army at fifteen, lying about his age. According to my mother, he needed food and a secure place to sleep. He also needed shoes. Joining the army was a move that ended nearly four years of hustling, hoboing, and hunger. As promised, his uniform included the first pair of new shoes he'd had since the death of his mother; his army cot was the first bed of his own, and the three daily seatings in the mess hall were the first regular meals he'd had in more than a decade. Grandpa served from 1933 until the end of WWII. After that, he worked as an air conditioning engineer and landed a job at Davis-Monthan Air Force Base in Tucson in 1954, where he worked until he retired in the 1970s.

As for me, I was his funny-looking, faithful sidekick (he was on the outs with Ralph because Ralph slammed a door). I wore thick glasses, and for a time, I had to wear an eye patch to fix an eye that was looking at my nose instead of straight ahead. I inherited my father's strange teeth problems, too. He had a tooth in the roof of his mouth, and although I didn't have that specific problem, my teeth appeared to be procedurally generated without a logical algorithm—overlapping each other and growing at slanting angles. I also bore my father's dark eyes, brown skin, and dark hair, but they didn't unleash Grandpa's toxic prejudices.

Grandpa John was a self-taught oil painter and craftsman. There was an easel in the spare room, and he also liked working with wood, building stools and bookcases. He'd set me up at the kitchen table with paper, pencil, and crayons, and I'd draw, hanging out for hours together while he watched game shows and screamed at the people on TV. Then, after the game show was over, he'd come look at my drawings, which I was always proud of. The act of creating something from nothing is incredibly empowering. I think most kids discover this on some level. Drawing provides instant gratification—especially if you do it well. If grown-ups *ooh* and *aah* over your work, that gratification grows. Of course, creation is often at the heart of play; it doesn't matter if you are playing make-believe with dolls, dress-up games, cops and robbers, or, in my case, drawing sports cars and 18-wheelers.

At the time, I loved drawing cars, probably because my dad loved cars. Our house on South Oregon Drive always had a car or two in front of it, and sometimes, much to my mom's fury, he bought cars on credit, rolling the current loan into the next loan, building up debt. More than once, he raced for pink slips—illegal street races where the winner takes the loser's car. My mother remembers, none too fondly, only the times he lost, and they were left *with* the debt and *without* the car. During those times, he always seemed to get another car for them, whether by playing pool for money, borrowing someone else's car, or making an old junker run. He also took us to drag races at the Tucson Dragway, where he shared his love of hot rods and the raw power of roaring engines. Cars were a big deal in our world.

Once, Grandpa John came to the table and picked up my drawing of a Lamborghini Countach, one of the coolest-looking cars in the '70s, and asked, "Did you trace this?"

"No." It was an honest answer, and I was surprised he asked me.

"Come on, Johnny. You must have traced this."

"I didn't!"

"Let me see you do that again." He sat down and watched me while I drew another Countach, complete with the rear spoiler. "I can't believe it!" he said. "That is really impressive."

No doubt part of his joy came from thinking *He's taking after me*. I even remember him saying stuff like that, comparing my early drawings to his paintings. He clearly thought I was talented and was the first person to express a sense of pride at my skills.

As much as I loved drawing as a kid, I also loved stories. My mother read to Ralph and me every night, and I also listened to stories on my own, putting my beloved 45 RPM single of a performance of "The Legend of Sleepy Hollow" onto my little record player. The story was terrifying to me at the time, but I couldn't resist its lure. I suspect this early interest in horror and the macabre is something I carried with me going forward. I picked up reading quickly and began exploring the books around me. Grandma Ann was a big fan of Charles Schulz's *Peanuts* cartoon strip and had a dozen paperbacks chronicling Charlie Brown, Snoopy, and the gang—kids like me. I devoured those books, and although I didn't realize it at the time, they clearly inspired me a few years later, when, as a teenager, I started writing and drawing my own semi-autobiographical comic strips about a boy named Melvin. Like Charlie Brown, my cartoon creation was a long-suffering kid whose painful reality provided the punchlines.

Of course, TV was as compelling as *Peanuts*. I grew up with *Sesame Street, New Zoo Revue, Mister Rogers' Neighborhood,* and *The Electric Company*. Like most of my generation, I also imbibed a steady diet of Saturday-morning cartoons—with Scooby-Doo, Tarzan, and live-action characters like Electra Woman and Dyna Girl. I also soaked up animation reruns after school—the *Looney Tunes* and *Merrie Melodies* series featuring Bugs Bunny, Daffy Duck, Elmer Fudd, and so many others. These shorts exploded with gags, crazy voices, absurd plots, and soaring music. It was joyful, anarchic entertainment to me. Little did I realize how these elements would shape my creative future.

Grandpa John didn't just love game shows; he loved games in general, and so did Grandma Ann. They played cards—hearts, spades, rummy—at the kitchen table for hours at a time. Grandma Ann was a huge fan of bowling, and so was my mom. They went to the bowling alley practically every week. While I loved games of all stripes, I didn't bowl much. At the lanes, the grown-ups were serious about their fun—little kids got in the way—but bowling, indirectly, was a gateway to games for me. I liked the bowling alley because there were pinball machines, and I loved pinball. The glitzy games offered action, flashing lights, and loud sound effects. To me, they were the definition of fun. Everything about pinball was thrilling: putting a quarter in a slot to initiate this mechanized ritual, the "chunk" sound as five balls were released for your game to start, pulling back the plunger—the spring tension was different on every machine—to launch a ball, and then locking in. My fingers slapped the flipper buttons as I battled to control the game, beat the machine, and top the other scores on the board. The scores themselves were great too! You never had time to see the numbers climbing until a ball went into the gutter, but, man, you could hear the points piling up while you played, which really fed into the excitement.

Grandpa John and Grandma Ann's house was near a strip mall with a small arcade called Spanky's. It was a narrow place with a deli counter at the front and a line of pinball machines on one side. On weekend and summertime visits, my grandmother gave me a dollar, and I walked to the mall where I debated buying a Hot Wheels car, which I collected and played with, or playing four pinball games. It was a tough decision. The acquisition of another beloved toy or the utter excitement of trying to control an uncontrollable pinball machine? Since I already had a lot of Hot Wheels, I chose pinball most of the time. I was barely tall enough to see what I was doing, but the machines called out to me. It's the first example I can recall of seeing a game respond to my actions in such a visceral way, engaging all the senses. Pinball was also competitive. I competed with myself plus everyone else who'd ever played the machine before me for the high score. It taught me the value of mastery—the better I was, the longer that quarter lasted. Though I wasn't aware of it at the time, pinball set me on a path I couldn't have imagined.

At home, I didn't draw or play games. My mom struggled to provide food, and so art supplies and toys were out of the question. When I did find something to occupy myself, I was often on edge, waiting for something to happen. Life on South Oregon Drive was unpredictable. My Dr. Jekyll dad continued to come home late at night, acting more and more like a drunken Mr. Hyde. Nothing had prepared my mother to leave situations like this—she was programmed to endure and to survive by her own family. As children, as horrible and surreal as this sounds, we became accustomed to this, too. It didn't happen every day, but sometimes being scared felt like part of everyday life. We froze in place or were told to run. We steered clear of our dad when he was angry to avoid provoking him further.

In spite of the challenges at home, I was happy most of the time. Everything I needed, I had—a loving mother, enough food to eat, friends to play with, and loads of places to explore. My brother, father, and I spent many nights sleeping under the stars at Madera Canyon, the Pantano Wash, and Patagonia Lake, and I grew to know the Sonoran Desert like the back of my hand. When he wasn't the Mr. Hyde version of a drunk, my father was outgoing and fun. There was so much of my life that felt happy. Perhaps because things in my homelife were often chaotic, I grew to expect bad things to happen, so when they didn't, that was good enough for me.

Even the challenging aspects of my life—the poverty and alcoholic chaos—had an upside: I learned to escape into my imagination as a protective device. Behind my drawings of trucks and cars, I imagined whole stories: what life would be like as a trucker or someone who raced a super sports car. Eventually, that escape turned into fantasy, war, or sci-fi settings. Because we didn't have any games that kids could play, I had to make my own fun and games from things I found in the desert or around the house. These early experiences are foundational to the game designer I would later become.

Around the time I was in third grade, I began to notice that my dad was disappearing for days at a time. This was not new behavior, but the frequency was a new development. Sometimes, during his longer absences, my mom ran out of money. She called Grandma Suki, and we went there to eat and bring home supplies. It was a mixed blessing when my dad was gone. There was no chance of sudden flashes of rage. No whippings. No dish throwing. No attacks on my mom. When my dad reappeared, an alcohol-fueled assault was always a hair-trigger away, but we embraced fun and humor whenever we could, the better to escape the lows we sometimes endured. I am sure that my mother felt differently. She never asked my father where he had been and neither did we. We knew better.

Perhaps hoping to show that things were fine, it was around this time that I got something cool from my mom and dad. A radio wristwatch! Or rather, a radio you wore on your wrist like a watch—it didn't actually tell time. I guess this was the mid-'70s equivalent of a kid getting their first smartphone now. My Aitron Wristo transistor radio was made of white plastic, with a rounded, dappled black speaker cover in place of a watch face. It had three silver control knobs for power, volume, and tuning, and a black wristband so I could attach it.

I thought my Wristo was so great—it played FM and AM stations crystal clear. It was something straight out of the Dick Tracy comic strip I read in the funnies at Grandpa John's. I wore it all the time, but since it was battery-powered and batteries cost money, I learned to be judicious about playing it. At night, in bed, I tuned into *CBS Radio Mystery Theater*. I remember every show started with a creepy, squeaking door opening—I imagined a giant vault, actually—and the sound morphed into ominous, dramatic strings. Then, there came a voice: "Come in. Welcome. I'm E. G. Marshall." It was a classic, old-school horror series hosted by a guy with my grandpa's last name who narrated and commented on these creepy horror stories. When the chilling episode was over, E. G. delivered his cynical sign-off: "Until next time, pleasant . . . dreams," which I thought was both wicked and funny.

The biggest event that occurred during third grade was also a kind of horror story, but it began as a mundane-sounding venture, almost like the beginning of a country song: My dad told my mom he was going to the store for cigarettes.

He got in the car and drove away.

He never came home.

CHAPTER 4

Uprooted

As the days ticked by, my mother became increasingly concerned that my father wasn't coming back. My dad may have stayed away from us, but Grandma Suki knew all. Her wayward son was still in Tucson, but he had moved in with a woman he'd been messing around with for months. They lived in a trailer home. It was not a big secret—Grandma Suki talked to my dad, and she relayed information to my mom. My father regularly cheated on my mother. Moving out, on the other hand, was new and left my mother in a precarious position. She was twenty-six, had two kids, and no job training or work experience. Her extended family support network—the thing most people rely on—was limited to her homemaker, fifty-something mother-in-law. She refused to approach her parents for support, and it's not entirely clear that they would have given it anyway. Both were fans of the "you did this to yourself" line of reasoning.

Learning this information about her cheating husband directly from my grandma helped clarify the situation for my mother. So did the fact he wasn't sending her any cash. That meant confronting two immediate problems: First, she didn't have money to buy food, and second, she didn't have money to pay the mortgage. That meant the house on South Oregon Drive was either going to be sold or repossessed by the bank.

By necessity, my mother reinvented herself. We got food from Grandma Suki, but we didn't live there. Instead, we bounced around, staying at the homes of my mother's friends, whomever would take us in. A couch this week and a spare bedroom the next—we moved when we had to. My mom became self-sustaining with astounding speed. I know necessity is the mother of invention, but I also feel invention had been gestating in my mom. On some level, she was ready to change her life after eight years of struggling to survive with a man who wasn't, on multiple levels, equipped to provide domestic stability. She took a test to become a bank teller and aced it.

Once she landed a job, we moved into an apartment near my maternal grandparents, and I switched schools. The morning of our move, I was pulled out of class by the teacher. "Your mom's waiting for you in the office," she said. My mom grabbed my hand, nodded to the school's secretary, and that was that. I never saw my friends, or that school, again. I missed them and the schoolyard, but I was accustomed to unexpected changes, and I didn't ask questions. More than anything, I welcomed the end of our homelessness.

My mother became friendly with an account holder at the bank, a military man named John Schuneman. They engaged in some casual window flirtation, but the only things my mom knew about him were the things she saw. He was tall and lean, seemed like a polite gentleman, and his savings account contained about $40,000, which was $40,000 more than her ex-husband ever had. This isn't to say that my mother was a gold-digger; far from it. My mother knew what she *didn't* want, and that was anyone with an account at or near $10 and frequently dipping below zero. Instead, she was looking for someone she liked who, ideally, was financially stable and could provide for her and her kids.

They started dating. John Schuneman was a buttoned-up guy. In some ways, he was the opposite of my dad: fiscally responsible, frugal to an almost obsessive level, dedicated to his career, sober, conservative, and willing to be a good provider. He and my dad had things in common, too. Both were drawn to machinery—John specialized in audio and video recording electronics while my dad loved car engines—both were bright in their ways, and both were domineering.

There was another similarity I didn't find out about until a little later: Both men sometimes resorted to violence or threats as a parenting tool.

That first year was a honeymoon period for everyone, while John courted my mom. He took us to the circus and treated us to meals in restaurants, which was a rarity with my dad. He was a serious alley cat who bowled professionally at one point and would frequently take my mother bowling. It was a match made in heaven, and their relationship progressed quickly. My mother got a high-speed divorce, gaining full custody of Ralph and me.

A few months later, John got a job transfer, effective immediately, from Davis-Monthan in Tucson to Beale Air Force Base in Marysville, California. He was a consultant for the Air Force and an expert in electronic data transfer from classified Air Force surveillance systems. They were apart just over a month when he asked my mother to fly up to Reno to meet him. It was her first time on a plane.

Once there, he asked her to marry him with a ten-dollar ring. Of course, she said yes. They got married on July 4, 1976, two hundred years to the day of the signing of the Declaration of Independence. It was both a surefire way to never forget your anniversary and a symbolic date to end a long, troubling saga with my father. My mother returned to Tucson, put in her two weeks' notice, and packed what little we had to move to California to join John.

Over the years, the phone would ring with an assignment, and John would react instantly, like he had when he moved from Tucson to Marysville. Thirty minutes after hanging up, he was off. That's how I remember leaving Tucson. One day I was told we were moving, and the next week we flew northwest from Tucson to Sacramento, California.

I didn't realize it at the time, but leaving Tucson also meant leaving behind much of my culture. Prior to the move, I was surrounded by Mexican and Yaqui people, eating and sharing in the preparation of our incomparable food, singing our traditional songs, participating in our traditions, and loving and fearing our myths (particularly La Llorona). Not a day passed where I didn't hear a grito, a Mexican outburst of joy that heralds the beginning of many a mariachi song, or people speaking Spanish (even though my father refused to teach me Spanish and forbade me from speaking it). On the weekends, I played in the desert and visited San Xavier del Bac, the mission on the reservation. My stepfather hated my father, and I suspect that anything Mexican or Yaqui was nothing more to him than a reflection of the man that had caused his new wife so much pain. He was glad to leave it behind, but for me, its absence left a hole. For Ralph, who had less time in Tucson than I did, the initial impact was smaller, but I could tell he still felt it. These days, whenever I read articles about how important those early years are, I smile, because in spite of the move, in spite of the separation from my culture, I have never felt anything less than what I am—proudly of Mexican and Indigenous heritage. I am grateful to my relatives, particularly my father and my Uncle Ralph, Aunts Yoly and Gracie, and my cousins Trisha and Olga for keeping it alive and sharing so much of it with me.

We arrived in Roseville, California, sort of the midway point between Sacramento and Beale Air Force Base. We lived in the Flamingo Motel for about three months while my parents looked for a house. It was there that I was introduced to the next big influence in my life—horror films, and specifically the horror films of William Castle. I will never forget watching my first William Castle movie.

Castle is not exactly a household name, but among fans of horror movies, he is widely revered. *Back to the Future* director Robert Zemeckis has called him his favorite filmmaker. So has cult-camp auteur John Waters of *Hairspray* fame. The movie I saw, *Mr. Sardonicus*, was a black-and-white film about a cruel, wealthy man who summons a doctor to cure him of a freakish paralytic condition—a hideous, tooth-filled smile that has locked itself on his face. The makeup for Mr. Sardonicus looked like it had been melded from high-tech silly putty and was super creepy. I loved it. Another thing that impressed me came toward the end of the film when the William Castle himself appeared and gave viewers a choice—or the illusion that they had a choice—to influence the ending via a "Punishment Poll." Each audience member was provided a voting card. When it came time for the voting, Castle broke the fourth wall and spoke directly to the audience, asking them for their choice, before announcing the winner of the vote: punishment. It was predetermined, but that illusion of agency made it seem real for many. For Castle, it was a fun, entertaining marketing scheme. However, that scheme made something resonate for me. I spend my life designing games where players (viewers) made choices that determined how their story ends.

My mom and stepdad finally found a house in Rocklin, just north of Sacramento. It was a great awakening for a low-income kid from the desert. Our backyard bordered a lush golf course. There were no scorpions, tarantulas, or rattlesnakes underfoot to worry about, so I could go outside without risking sudden death. Instead of parched earth and cacti, there was a creek that ran behind our house, before you reached the golf course, and I'd play there, surrounded by cattails and leafy trees, looking for tadpoles and frogs. Other kids would come over, and we'd play hide-and-seek. After six o'clock, when the golfing was over, we'd play on the green. It was a little bit of heaven. This isn't to say I didn't love Tucson, too. I did! But this new landscape meant new adventures. Because I was nearly nine, I also had more freedom to explore.

The house in Rocklin was a bastion of stability in many ways. There was always food in the kitchen, my mother didn't want for anything, and John provided us with dental insurance. My mom could finally afford to get the rest of my messed-up teeth fixed. It wasn't exactly fun for me. Rare is the kid who relishes getting full-on braces and headgear to sleep in. I knew it was for the best, though, and that it would pay off—I didn't want a mouth like Mr. Sardonicus.

The only threat to my well-being, ironically, was the guy who made this semi-idyllic new life happen: my stepdad, John Schuneman. He regularly threatened physical violence. He told me he knew karate, told me he'd kick me into tomorrow and other general threats whenever I wasn't behaving as he expected me to. This was his major tool, and it worked, particularly since I'd come from a home where violence was the norm. I did my chores as soon as I was asked or needed to because I didn't want to find out what would happen if I didn't.

As I got older, and increasingly independent, we clashed. John had been a drill sergeant in the Air Force, and in many ways, he was a drill sergeant out of the Air Force, too. It was his way or the highway. His rules and manner often struck me as arbitrary and unreasonable. I was an easygoing, neat, good-natured tween who did whatever was asked of me. Even my mother would say that I "was always a good boy." Of course, like every kid my age, I also embraced being a kid. I was into playing, joking around, expressing myself, and experiencing new things. My even-keeled demeanor was a good thing, because my survival depended on literally rolling with the punches—mental, verbal, and eventually, physical ones. It's easy to see with twenty-twenty hindsight that my being a pleasure-seeking kid named Romero did not bode well in the Schuneman household. John loathed my dad, scornfully referring to him as "the Latin lover." No doubt he detected my dad's genetic traces in my quest for fun, entertainment, and thrills. It probably didn't help that I looked just like him.

One day in 1977, my dad's quest for fun caught up with him. My mother called Ralph and me into her bedroom.

"Your father is in the hospital in Tucson," she told us. "He's going to survive, but he's going to be there a long while."

"What happened?"

"He had an accident."

He left work on his motorcycle, passed a car while going eighty miles per hour, ran directly into an oncoming vehicle also doing eighty, and wound up under it. The impact should have killed him, and it almost did. He flatlined four times on the operating table. My mother communicated with my aunt Gracie daily until she knew what to tell us—if he would live, or if he would die—but she didn't want us suffering, sitting on pins and needles worried. My father was a tough guy. He spent a year in traction, and came out of hospital with one leg noticeably shorter than the other. I was grateful he survived.

Unlike my father, my stepdad was about practicality, consistency, and financial security, but he was also big on fostering independence. (As my cynical teen self would later observe, he promoted independent behavior as long as it didn't conflict with his wishes and opinions.) The former drill sergeant who had transformed recruits into battle-ready soldiers came by his unrelenting, hard-ass work ethic honestly, and he deployed his mania for work on me. When I was about eleven, I wanted a stereo in my room. At the time I don't think I'd ever wanted anything so much in my life. We cut a deal: In return for getting a Symphonic-brand stereo for Christmas, a three-speed turntable with a cassette deck and a radio tuner, I would get a job and pay my parents back.

That's right: *I bought my own Christmas present.*

Somehow this was bestowed to me as a gift, and I suppose it was, since I didn't have any collateral. Still, it's hard not to laugh as I look back now and think my stepdad was engaged in parental loan sharking. In the end, my gift cost him nothing. I suppose maybe there was the greater gift of learning to be self-reliant, and I sure did love having that stereo.

I mowed lawns to earn the money, charging five bucks a lawn. Finding a steady stream of clients was easier said than done for an eleven-year-old kid in the California suburbs, where everybody had a lawnmower. I decided to try my hand at delivering newspapers.

My alarm clock would go off at 3:00 every morning, and I'd drag myself out to the porch in front of the house where two bundles—about one hundred copies—of the *Sacramento Bee* awaited my attention. I undid the bundles and started folding the papers that had just come off the press, which meant the ink was not entirely dry. I couldn't bring the papers inside because the ink would get all over the carpet. I did all my folding outside, even on freezing mornings. If it was raining, or threatening to rain, I'd huddle under the overhang on our porch, folding the papers and shoving them in plastic bags. Then I'd place the folded papers in my delivery bag, stuffing as many papers as I possibly could inside. It became a game of optimization—each time I had to come home to refill my bag translated into tripling the distance I had to bike. If I was a mile away, I'd have to bike a mile home, then bike a mile back to the house where I'd run out of papers.

All of this folding, bagging, and stowing took about ninety minutes. So, it was around 4:30 a.m. when I'd get on my bicycle and begin my rounds through the often-freezing, foggy, dark predawn. I had to be alert. My clients went on vacation, they suspended delivery, they canceled their subscriptions, and I had to keep track of all this in my head. When I ran out of papers, I had to be sure to remember where to restart my route. The details of the paper route gave me one of my earliest insights into how my brain stored and retrieved details. I did not find it hard to remember all these pieces of data, and I enjoyed the logistical challenges that it presented as well as the responsibility of a job.

I tried to be done by 6:30 at the latest. On weekdays I had to get home, take a shower, eat breakfast, and be at the bus stop at 7:15 to get to school. Of course, Sundays were a different story. The papers were usually five times the size of the daily papers, and I could fit only about eight copies into my delivery bag. I rode back to my house constantly to reload. I finished my route a few hours after the sun had come up.

At the end of every month, I spent my afternoons collecting money from subscribers. A month's subscription for the *Bee* cost about $5. That meant once a month, I gathered anywhere from $250 to $500, and I kept half of that. Working about three hours a day, seven days a week adds up to around ninety-three hours a month. For that, I cleared $250—at best. I'm not kidding when I say this was some of the hardest work I've ever done in my entire life, and I'm a guy who has done his fair share of grinding, hundred-hour workweeks. It wasn't all work for me, though. I also had great friends I enjoyed hanging out with.

Christian Divine was oe of my first and best friends in our new neighborhood. He was a great artist, and we both drew comics. Sometimes we drew cartoons with blank dialogue bubbles and let the other person fill in the words. Sometimes we collaborated on stories where I wrote a paragraph, and then he wrote the next paragraph. They were funny scenarios, where we wrote from opposite points of view, with Christian trying to kill the character while I'm trying to keep him alive. Christian introduced me to *Advanced Dungeons & Dragons*, a role-playing game system that was beginning to work its way from the niche wargaming miniature groups to board-game players and fans of the fantasy genre. The magic of creating a character and taking them on adventures felt like an extension of our comics and stories. Instead of just reading the work of other people, we were creating whole adventures and participating in them. The *AD&D* system was rudimentary in 1978, particularly compared to what it is now, but even then, it provided an excellent scaffolding for our active imaginations.

In our early teens, Christian got ahold of a video camera, and we made short films, enacting comic skits. We made films whenever we crossed paths for the next fifteen years, including a live-action short when we were twenty-seven. If you've played the BAFTA award–winning game *Life Is Strange*, for which Christian was the lead writer, you will find many references to our young lives and early films.

Between *AD&D*, school and my paper route, I was busy. I went to bed at 9 p.m. every night to get six hours of sleep before the alarm clock shocked me awake, and I kept up the entire routine for more than two years. Why?

Well, I had to clear my stereo debt, but then there was another payoff—a more enjoyable one: $250 equals one thousand quarters.

That was the other thing I spent my time doing. Playing arcade games.

In October 1978, Taito's *Space Invaders* was released in the United States. Thirteen months later, Atari's *Asteroids* came out. They were cool games—fun, kill-or-be-killed thrillers. *Space Invaders* was the first game to save high scores and let players put their initials next to them. This was a smart marketing move. What kid didn't want bragging rights when they had skills at a kickass game? This was the first baby step in competitive video gaming. I loved both games, but *Asteroids* let players move more freely than *Space Invaders*. Your ship could move both vertically and horizontally, which wasn't the case for the move-left-or-right options of the *Space Invader* canon. Having that control of movement was a liberating sensation.

As much as I loved pinball, these video games were a step up for me. Pinball, as great and nuanced as it is, always felt a little uncontrollable or random. The tools at your disposal weren't highly nuanced. The spring of the plunger varied from game to game. The flippers were your only constant tool, but there were so many elements of the game you couldn't control. Some bumpers were fast, others were softer and slower. The angles and speed always felt variable. With *Asteroids* and *Space Invaders*, the computer-generated experience was consistent machine to machine and game to game; the playing field was level, generally speaking, no matter where you played it. Pinball and arcade games also differed in another key area: Pinball, regardless of the artwork or the name of a game, was locked into the same basic formula. Video games could be anything they wanted to be and could defy the rules of time, space, and gravity.

I spent a lot of time and money playing *Asteroids* when I was eleven, and my stepdad was not happy about it—neither was my mother. Eventually, he banned me from playing after school. I was supposed to come home and stay home. This made no sense to me. I was doing well in school and in my paper route. Why couldn't I spend an hour playing games while using my own money to do it? One time, I chose to disobey my stepdad and went to Round Table Pizza down the street. Most kids parked their bikes in front of the pizzeria, but I knew who I was up against, so I hid my bike in the back of the building, figuring if either my mom or stepdad drove by, they would never spot my bike.

I was having a great time hanging out with my friends, and I was locked into a game of *Asteroids*, racking up points and earning extra lives. Then, out of nowhere, my face was smashed into the screen of the game.

"What the hell?" I cried.

It was my stepdad. He had driven by and decided to conduct a spot check.

"Let's go, John. You are coming home. Now!"

Both sides of my head were throbbing. My stepdad grabbed the back of my head and pushed as hard as he could. It's a miracle the glass didn't crack. My face had borne most of the impact. I was hurt, furious, and humiliated. I didn't say a word. My hands rose to my face to brace for a bloody nose. He grabbed me by my shirt with both hands and pulled me away from the game and threw me ahead of him. I stumbled and then walked out to his pickup truck and got in. He swung the truck around to the back, grabbed my bike, and threw it in the bed. It hit with an impact I knew was sure to damage it.

Two minutes later we were home.

Grandma Ann, who was visiting at the time, was sitting in the dining room.

"I told you not to go to the arcade!" he ranted. "I expressly said it was off-limits. No more video games. You went anyway. You didn't give a shit. Now take off your glasses."

I knew what he meant. My stepdad was a big man, six feet two and muscular. As a kid, I didn't have his muscles, and I definitely didn't have his height. (I'm five feet nine inches.)

"I don't want to take off my glasses," I said to him.

"Take them off now, or I'll take them off."

I didn't say anything. I knew if I said "no" again that I'd provoke him.

"I'm warning you."

He was directly in front of me. Bigger. Stronger. Menacing. I pulled my glasses off.

My stepfather punched me in the face. I went sprawling, knocked on my ass.

I stood up as quickly as I could. My lip was bleeding, and my jaw was sore. I refused to cry. I looked over at my grandmother, who was sitting calmly in a dining room chair. She had seen the entire exchange.

"You got what you deserved," she said.

Sure, I misbehaved, but I don't think a kid ever deserves a punch, especially from a man in his forties. I bolted from the house—the house that I was supposed to come home to straight after school—and went over to my friend Tommy's (not his real name). I couldn't believe what had just happened, or my grandmother's reaction. Then I remembered my mother telling me that her father had beaten her brothers. This was history repeating itself for my grandmother. I never told my mom, but I assumed she heard from my grandmother.

Tommy greeted me at his front door. "What the hell happened to you?"

"My stepdad found me at Round Table. He just punched me in the face."

"Oh man."

We were an unofficial support group. His parents had beaten him far worse—his father once lifted him off the floor by his hair, and his stepmom once woke him up by smashing a frying pan in his face. Later, he'd spend many years of his adult life in mental institutions. We were grateful to have someone who understood, but he wasn't an entirely reliable friend, either. A year later, he came over to my house after I had collected my paper route money for the month—about $500. When he left, I noticed the money was gone. When I told my mom, she accused me of having blown it on arcade games.

I couldn't believe she thought that. I owed that money to the paper route supervisors. It would have been like stealing from myself.

"Mom, I owe this money to the delivery company. If I don't pay them, I don't have a job anymore. Why would I do that?"

She still didn't believe me, and neither did my stepfather. I wasn't surprised that John thought I'd stolen money, but I couldn't believe my mother doubted me. It was a horrible moment; I felt like my stepfather was poisoning my mother against me. It was bad enough that I knew a friend had ripped me off. Not having my mother trust me somehow felt worse. Adding insult to injury, I worked for free that month and had to take money out of my savings account to pay off the route. A lot had changed for me during this time, and looking back, I suppose I felt alone.

This dynamic of distrust and scorn was a big part of my early teens. One of my most painful memories is overhearing a discussion between my parents when they talked about me.

"He's a Romero," my mom sighed. "He's going to be a loser just like his dad."

It felt like a punch to the chest. My heart sank. I know she said this in a moment of anger because she was mad at me. Deep down, I don't think she really believed it.

I often wonder about the events that shape our lives. If my dad hadn't walked out on us, my mom would have never met John Schuneman, and we would never have moved to California, and if that hadn't happened, what was arguably the most important event in my life might never have occurred.

It was a Saturday in the summer before my twelfth birthday. My brother and my other great friend, Rob Lavelock, pulled up on their bikes and came to find me. They were breathless with excitement.

"John, you've got to see this!" Ralph said.

"See what?"

"A place where there are video games, and it doesn't cost any money. You can play for free."

I looked at Rob. We were the same age, although he was a grade behind me at school.

"It's true." He nodded.

"No way!"

"For free," Ralph said again.

Sign. Me. Up.

I immediately hopped on my bike and made the ride with Ralph and Rob to Sierra College. They led me to a big room with CRT computer monitors. I was a little in shock at first. When someone said "video games," I automatically thought "arcade," and I imagined playing game after game of *Galaxian* and *Lunar Lander* for free. As it turned out, that was a little too good to be true. This was the school's computer lab, although it didn't look like a laboratory to me—there were no test tubes or anything like that. Rob explained that his neighbor, Lenny Lipson, had told him about the lab, that it was a place where you could program computers. Lenny gave Rob his password to log into the system.

Rob was a unique kid. He was super-smart, and his family nurtured his interest in video games and computers, unlike mine. They were generous, well-to-do people. His dad was the chief of the Rocklin Fire Department, and his mother was a homemaker. She was happy to drive us to arcades and give Rob money to play games. At the time, *Monaco GP* and *Head On* were new, and he played them a lot, trying to get further with each quarter. She must have spent hundreds of dollars on Rob's arcade game interest. His parents also bought a steady stream of home computers. Since we were great friends, I slept over at Rob's countless times and played hours and hours of games on his various systems over the years—the Magnavox Odyssey 2 and the Atari 800 computer.

So, while it might seem unlikely that an eleven-year-old had wrangled a computer account password at a local college, it was totally in keeping with Rob's personality and connections. Like me, when it came to gaming, his enthusiasm and curiosity were infectious. Fortunately, the college students were happy to share their knowledge about computers and games.

We walked around the lab the way we walked around a new arcade—gazing over people's shoulders at the screens. We watched students typing on keyboards that were connected to a giant computer in the next room. It was all fascinating to me. Eventually, we asked a student what he was doing. We learned the terminals were attached to something called a "mainframe" running "Unix." He told us he was playing a game, but it looked unlike any game I'd seen. He typed his command, and the game posted a response. One of the games, *Hunt the Wumpus*, involved going into caves to look for a monster. A question appeared on the screen, and the player chose the direction of their search. It wasn't a graphical game. Everything was left to the player's imagination.

We sat at a terminal and logged in with Lenny's password, and we figured out how to access *Hunt the Wumpus*. It was challenging in its way—a logic game that forced you to explore a series of caves. It wasn't that scary, I guess, but it was still cool.

Not everyone was playing games in the lab. One student explained to us that he was writing code for a programming assignment.

"What's programming?"

"That's how you tell the computer what to do. Like, how you make these games. You have to speak its language. It's called programming."

"You mean, you can make your own games?"

"Sure. These games are written in a language called BASIC. You have to give each line a number and format commands correctly and in order so that the program understands what you want it to do—what should show up on the screen and what it should do with the user input."

That was all I needed to hear. Not only could I play games, I could make my own. Right in this room.

Now all I needed to do was learn BASIC.

I started writing down commands I saw on people's screens.

PRINT.

INPUT.

GOTO.

Then, I went over to my terminal and wrote the same thing. I was nervous, though. I was scared someone would complain about annoying kids in the lab. Instead, someone took pity on me and gave me a book that had been left in the lab, an HP BASIC book. It was a godsend. I looked up what I needed to know and experimented with new commands.

That day kicked off my self-imposed, two-year crash course in programming as a non-enrolled student at Sierra College. Rob and I were devoted novices, preteen apprentices to the UNIX computing system. Every Saturday, we biked to the campus and spent hours watching students, reading whatever guides and manuals we found. When we discovered that one computer gamer showed up at 7 a.m. on Saturdays to play *Colossal Cave Adventure*, supposedly the coolest game ever, we got there at the same time to sit and watch the "action." Gaming today is light years ahead of *Colossal Cave Adventure*, but to give you an example, here's how this funny, irreverent game introduced itself:

SOMEWHERE NEARBY IS A COLOSSAL CAVE, WHERE OTHERS HAVE FOUND FORTUNES IN TREASURE AND GOLD, THOUGH IT IS RUMORED THAT SOME WHO ENTER ARE NEVER SEEN AGAIN. MAGIC IS SAID TO WORK IN THE CAVE. I WILL BE YOUR EYES AND HANDS. DIRECT ME WITH COMMANDS OF 1 OR 2 WORDS.

After that explanation, the game began:

YOU ARE STANDING AT THE END OF A ROAD BEFORE A SMALL BRICK BUILDING.
    AROUND YOU IS A FOREST. A SMALL STREAM FLOWS OUT OF THE BUILDING AND DOWN A GULLY.

From that point on, you made choices to find the cave and find the treasure, writing "north" or "west" or "left" or "right."

I loved this game and its agency. I made choices, and it reacted and took me places. The game was funny—when you died, the program might say it was out of colored smoke, so you couldn't be reincarnated. I had no idea that *Colossal Cave Adventure* was regarded as the first work of interactive fiction, or that it spearheaded a major genre. I just liked it and savored the new knowledge that it had been created by somebody who was interested in computers, like we were. Before Sierra College, I'd never given much thought to making arcade games. Now the world seemed full of possibilities.

I found my calling then and there. It was all I cared about, all I wanted to learn, and all I wanted to do. I thought about code when I woke up and fell asleep committing commands to memory (GOSUB and RETURN, FOR and NEXT, IF and ELSE, END).

Ralph never expressed much interest in learning to code, but Rob was an instrumental ally. We had knowledge races, competing to see who could learn more about programming faster. When I built my first game in BASIC—a simple game in which you explored a few rooms—I showed it to Rob. He was the only one. I didn't want to bother anybody in the lab or call attention to myself or Rob. That's why getting that HP BASIC book was a huge relief. I needed to keep access to the lab, and going around asking students to look at my games or to teach me could hinder that access.

I think it is likely that my thirst to absorb everything about BASIC propelled the onset of my hyperthymesia, or made me and others aware of it. I was obsessed with retaining everything I learned, and so I compulsively repeated the things in my mind. There was no internet to look things up. There were precious few books, and I didn't have the money to buy them anyway. So, necessity was the mother of retention. I took notes, I read whatever handouts and books people had in the lab, and I tried diligently to remember everything I encountered. Absolutely everything.

CHAPTER 5

AJR

The arcade incident left my stepfather less trusting, and for a brief period, he insisted we accompany him whenever he took my mom bowling. One week, right before I turned thirteen, we went to the Foothills Bowl. This was probably the best alley in the area. It was clean, and it had floor-to-ceiling windows overlooking the pines—a real Northern California touch.

As always, the view that interested me was the alley's arcade area. My stepfather's periodic ban on games didn't apply if I played games when they were bowling, so long as I paid for them myself. There were pinball machines and several arcade games, including *Battlezone*, *Space Invaders*, *Crazy Climber*, and *Asteroids*. On this visit, there was something new at the front of the arcade: a single *Pac-Man* machine. I didn't have any money, but I walked over to see the new game.

It reeled me in and mesmerized me. I was spellbound. First, the game exploded with color and sound. Until *Pac-Man*, all arcade games were black and white (except for *Galaxian*), or they had one color. The non-white color of these games, like the colored rings of *Star Castle* or the multicolor *Breakout*, was nothing more than a tinted film overlay placed on the plastic or glass screen. As for *Pac-Man*'s soundtrack, I thought it was fantastic. I loved the endless "waka-waka" sound of the bright yellow Pac-Man as it devoured dots, and the futuristic synth-fed score was unparalleled.

The second thing that enchanted me was the game itself. It was dazzlingly innovative. *Asteroids* and *Battlezone* were about shooting and blowing stuff up. It was all kill or be killed. It seemed like most new games were derivative of one or the other. This was a different vibe. It was more task-oriented—you had to gather dots—and survival-oriented. You ran away or you died.

I must have watched for thirty minutes. I'd never experienced such arcade rapture—not since my initial little-kid-acting-grown-up thrill of pinball. I had to play it. I had stopped badgering my folks for change by this time, especially since I made money with my paper route, but I didn't have a cent on me. I had to play this game. I begged my mom, and she gave me fifty cents.

I put the first quarter in the slot and began what I can only describe as a joyous, spontaneous mind-meld between me and the game as I entered the blinking, blipping digital maze. If you've played *Pac-Man*, you know this feeling, particularly if you encountered it in the 1980s. It was the thing everyone was talking about. *Pac-Man* is a game of virtual tag where you get three lives as a chomping yellow icon that races around a maze lined with "Pac-Dots," chomping the dots and other goodies (fruits, a bell and a key), while ghosts chase you. Any contact with the ghosts—Blinky (red), Pinky (pink), Inky (blue), and Clyde (orange)—and you lost one of your lives. It was exhilarating. Everything about the *Pac-Man* experience was different and just flat-out better than other arcade games. Its innovation was a revelation to me. Musicians sometimes describe a piece of music that changed them. This was the game that changed me.

Looking back, it was a substantial departure and innovation on the themes, mechanics, audio, and video of games made to date—an explosion of creativity—but that's my older, wiser, student-of-gaming-self talking. It was challenging, it was stressful, but it was fun and funny, too. As you reached new levels, there were comical intermissions—little computer skits that played. Humor was nowhere in sight with previous arcade games. The other enticing thing was that I felt this game was challenging but winnable. I had no idea that the game had 255 stages, but on the surface, it seemed so simple. The player followed a path through a maze, scooped up dots and fruit, and avoided ghosts.

I was breathless and hooked when my fifty cents of fun was over. *Pac-Man* was the greatest arcade game ever. I was smitten. I sought out *Pac-Man* machines wherever and whenever I could. As I played more and more, I figured the game out. I got the sense that the ghosts had different personalities. Blinky seemed to be the most aggressive, while Pinky liked to shadow Pac-Man. Clyde just wandered around, came closer, and then flaked out, like his heart wasn't in it. It didn't take me long to realize that the game followed a distinct pattern. The way the ghosts pursued Pac-Man didn't randomly change at the start of a new game. It was all rigidly pre-programmed. I figured out a way to evade the ghosts in the early stages of the game, and it worked every time.

Another light went on in my head. Beyond its other innovations, *Pac-Man* introduced me to game design patterns, and the knowledge that those patterns could be mastered. Seeing a pattern in *Pac-Man* made me aware of design patterns in other games, and I was as determined to commit them to memory as I had been to commit code.

I spent hundreds of dollars mastering *Pac-Man,* and after a while, I committed the opening moves to memory. Eventually, I had it down so that I didn't have to look at the screen to get through the game's first two stages. I looked at my friends and had conversations while my Pac-Man feasted on dots and evaded the ghosts. It was my impressive party trick. Well, for the first two stages. At my best, one quarter could take me deep into the game, and I reached screen twenty-six. The special item on every stage after thirteen was a key worth 5,000 points. I must have spent hours playing the game to get to that stage. Then, I faltered. I didn't have the full pattern yet. However, after spending hundreds of dollars on the game, my initials were on the top of every *Pac-Man* machine in the Rocklin area: AJR, for Alfonso John Romero.

I wasn't the only one who couldn't get enough of *Pac-Man*. It was a national craze. A pop song called "Pac-Man Fever" documented the obsession. The singer crooned that the game was "driving me crazy." He didn't have a lot of money, but he had a callus on his finger and was determined to "eat up" the dots. The song hit number 9 on the Billboard Hot 100 chart by March 1982.

My stepfather was not impressed by the game. He continued to see all arcade games as a waste of time, and he and my mother tried to restrict my gaming. The negativity was a challenge to counteract. It wasn't just a conflict; it was, I realize now, cognitive dissonance. These games were absorbing, challenging, and fun. I wanted to learn everything about them and to make my own games. In them, I saw my future. Even at age twelve, I was sure there was an upside to arcade games that my parents couldn't see. I realized that *Pac-Man* was a computer game, and the connection between it and the code I was learning at the Sierra College computer lab were evident to me. That isn't to say I knew about graphical interfaces or the languages I'd need to learn to render images on a computer screen, but I knew that computers both allowed you to create games and to play them. I didn't know much about how the world worked—and neither, in a way, did my parents, who were middle-class pragmatists, not dreamers—but I had this idea that you could get work in computers. Just from being at the computer lab in Sierra, I knew you could study computers, teach computers, write books about them, and build programs.

I made a connection—that the games I saw at Sierra College, such as *Colossal Cave* and other text adventures, were stage one, and *Pac-Man* and these other arcade games were many stages beyond. I had no idea what programming wizardry was required to make *Pac-Man*, but I knew that whatever it was could be learned, and I was determined to learn it. My desire to learn became all-consuming.

The home computer market was heating up, but given the cost—an Apple II was around $1,300 in 1981—owning one seemed out of reach. I'd go to the computer store in downtown Roseville and a nearby RadioShack and use their floor models—the Apple II at Capitol Computers and the TRS-80 at RadioShack—grabbing time whenever I could to see how they worked and to practice BASIC on them. Nothing remains of this early work, however. I never saved any of it, because the cost of 5.25" floppies dented my *Pac-Man* budget. The adventure games I created at Sierra College were saved on paper punch cards, but those fell off my bike and landed in a puddle of water. I remember looking down at them, heartbroken. They were wet, scattered, and out of order. I gathered them up and disposed of them at home. That loss coincided with the end of my time going up to Sierra College. I was about to turn fourteen and had entered ninth grade at Roseville High School, where they had two Apple IIs. Between those machines, my friend Rob's Atari 800, and the local stores, I had other ways to access computers.

I was never a kid who hated school, and I was a responsible student, often getting As and Bs. I also liked the social aspect of school. I liked meeting different kids, making friends. I had two skills that helped me connect with other people. One skill involved computers. I was a total evangelist for programming, and I started a computer club. My idea was to share my work with other kids—which had a twofold purpose: I wanted others to play my games so I could get their feedback, but I also figured I might meet some kids who liked to code as well. Anyone who was interested could come by, and we would share knowledge. I was so into programming at the start of tenth grade that I decided to write a book about programming games in BASIC for the Apple II. A student from the school newspaper heard about my project and even wrote an article about it.

My other skill was drawing. In tenth grade, I created a comic strip I thought was hilarious, which also provided me with an outlet for processing the aggression and occasional violence of my stepdad. It was part comedy, part therapy. *Melvin* starred a teenage kid whose over-the-top, sadistic father constantly punished him. Melvin had bright yellow hair and fair skin; he bore no physical resemblance to me. Melvin's dad, however, a chrome-domed baldy who wore glasses, was based 1,000 percent on John Schuneman. Some of my *Melvin* storylines were autobiographical. Melvin's dad catches him playing video games, smashes his head into the video screen, and then pulls back his scalp to reveal Melvin's brains. Unlike the real-life episode, where Schuneman punched me in the face, this strip ends, as all of them do, with Melvin's dad making a smug, snarky quip: "Kids, remember: Video games are bad for your eyes." Meanwhile, off stage, Melvin is dead.

My friends laughed their heads off at *Melvin*. I didn't spend huge amounts of time on these strips. Someone shared an idea, or I had a thought, or something happened between me and my stepdad, and then I'd sketch out fifteen panels and develop a rough idea in my head about how to lay out the action. I didn't do pencil sketches or multiple drafts. I just went for it. Some are better than others, but even now, I think they are strong for an untrained teenager. I understood comic strips' visual techniques—alternating close-ups, faces that squashed and stretched, added sound effects—without knowing that these techniques had names. I learned the glory of comics storytelling purely by osmosis. I never took a class. Scott McCloud had yet to write his classic *Understanding Comics*. I learned everything by reading *Peanuts*, *Mad*, *Cracked*, and *Weird* magazines.*

Ironically, as I was exorcising the demons that came with having an abusive stepdad, he was seeing the light. I talked to him a lot about the things I learned at Sierra College, at Rob's, and at the stores that allowed me to use their computers. His electronics background gave him some degree of insight into what I was doing, even if he didn't understand any of the code. Eventually, my programming progress and unbridled enthusiasm made a dent in his thoughts about computers. He saw that I was onto something. One day in April 1982, I came home to find an Apple II+ still in its delivery box. I was ecstatic. My stepdad had told me he was considering getting one—he thought it would help him manage the house and business finances—so it wasn't a total surprise, but when I saw the box, there was no holding me back. My mom told me to wait, but I couldn't. I set up the Apple II+ in my mom's sewing room. When my stepdad got home, the new machine was ready and waiting. He was mad, but my mother took the fall, telling him that she forgot to tell me not to open it.

My stepfather and I had a difficult relationship, as readers have no doubt gathered. However, he also had a significant positive influence on my life. He took us in, took care of us, gave me lectures that I hated but that also somehow sunk in, and ultimately recognized and enabled a talent he knew I had. There are tens of thousands of kids out there whose parents ignore their desire to code or to make games or insist they pursue fields that are more traditional. Getting that Apple II+ changed my life.

The Apple II+ was a significant purchase in our house—a significant purchase in any house. My stepdad went for a complete setup: the computer, supplemental hardware, a monitor, and a printer. It set him back at least $5,000. If you had asked me months earlier whether I thought we'd have one in our house that year, I would have shaken my head. That amount of money was well beyond

---

* Speaking of magazines that inspired me, about fifteen years later, when I'd become well-known, I sent my *Melvin* comics to *National Lampoon*. I was a big fan of that magazine, and I would have been honored to have *Melvin* grace their pages. Alas, their editors didn't agree.

what we could afford. However, he hoped I would start making business-related programs, things that would be "useful"—like a software program to organize an address book. As he saw it, this would lead me on a path where I would one day land a "real" job. Games were still not part of the equation for him, but they were the endgame for me. Every day after school, I was programming games one after another. I remember thinking, "I want to do this every day for the rest of my life." I was finished going outside.

I still wasn't clear on how, exactly, to make a graphical game on a computer that echoed my arcade favorites. Rob Lavelock opened my eyes to this next step, tipping me off while we were playing *Gorgon*, written by legendary Apple II programmer Nasir Gebelli. He got in early, in 1980, and made a name for himself, quite literally: "BY: NASIR" appeared on the title screen of every one of his games. He made his games quickly, they were technically advanced, and they were fun.*

Beyond his programming genius, Nasir understood how to get the core loop of gameplay feeling good. I really loved how every one of his games was different. From overhead high-speed car racing to a horizontally scrolling spaceship shooting aliens and rescuing humans to an airplane flying over and bombing enemy territory, his games showed he was attempting new technical challenges and keeping himself fresh with different game designs. From his work, I learned to make games around a specific concept or gameplay mechanic, giving the player everything they wanted while avoiding superfluous features that didn't improve the gameplay itself. I could also tell that some of Nasir's games were the result of him learning a new programming technique. The graphics might appear in a unique way, and he used that same technique throughout the game. From Nasir's games, I learned that the best form of learning is project-based. I could use a game to learn and hopefully master new programming techniques. Nasir went on to become the sole programmer for *Final Fantasy I, II*, and *III*. He remains one of the most legendary programmers of all time.

Bill Budge is another legendary programmer whose impact on me was significant. He was a great example of the Apple II spirit in the early '80s. He wrote some engaging, early games like his Space trilogy and Penny Arcade games. His next game was huge—*Raster Blaster*—the first pinball game on the Apple II. It was

---

* Years later, I found out from Nasir himself that he programmed directly into the mini-assembler and used no source code, which is like writing a novel by typing a single sentence at a time and having it disappear directly into your computer. Eventually, the whole novel will be done, but you have no way of looking back on anything you've written previously while you're writing it. Nasir was so skilled that he was the first coder who did things on the Apple II that made other Apple II programmers ask, "How?"

incredible and made everyone want to create a pinball game, but it was difficult to do those physics calculations in 6502 assembly language. While everyone was puzzling that out, Bill released Pinball Construction Set in 1982 and stunned the industry. Making a tool that lets you create a pinball game yourself was unprecedented and represented a substantial technical achievement.

As Rob and I sat in front of the computer looking at *Gorgon*, I said, "Man, that's the kind of game I want to make!"

"You want to see the code—what it's made of?"

"Yeah!"

Rob pressed RESET on the Apple II+. He typed "CALL -151" and typed "800.9FF". Suddenly, the screen filled with a stream of numbers. It looked like numeric gobbledygook, but it was my first look at hexadecimal numbers and letters.

"That's machine language," Rob said. "That's what you need to learn to make video games."

I stared at the screen. It might as well have been ancient Egyptian hieroglyphics. It looked nothing like BASIC, which I knew well at this point. I had read that if you knew one coding language, you can usually figure out others due to linguistic and logic similarities, but figuring out machine language seemed impossible.

"Man, I have no idea what this is," I said, "but if it's what people are doing, I'm going to have to do it, too."

Rob typed "800L". This time, it showed the code in Assembly language format. "This is Assembly language," he said. "This is what the programmer typed in." He explained that a program called an "assembler" took the language and assembled it into machine language.

With Christmas 1982 approaching, I asked my parents for two books. *Assembly Lines: The Book* by Roger Wagner was a how-to bible. The other book, *Apple Graphics and Arcade Game Design* by Jeffrey Stanton, was about making arcade games in Assembly. My parents still didn't "get it," but they had become less damning about my passion and were still hopeful that I'd move on to developing "useful" software. On December 25, the books were under the tree. I was elated.

"Finally, I can learn Assembly," I said.

I already had the Apple II Reference Manual, but I could not understand the advanced Assembly language information in there, because it lacked the critical initial steps. I felt as if I were staring at the twentieth stair on a staircase that was missing steps one through nineteen. Wagner's book, I hoped, would unlock its mysteries for me, while Stanton's book would show me the tricks that commercial game programmers used.

At this point, my self-imposed crash course in programming really went into overdrive. I was hell-bent on cracking Assembly. One of the first things I learned was that the machine language Rob showed me did everything BASIC could do and more, but at super speed. The numeric gobbledygook was hexadecimal, a series of sixteen digits or letters in twenty-four rows. Assembly code is plaintext, but you need an "assembler"—itself a program—to convert Assembly to machine code.

First, I needed to learn the hexadecimal number system, because that's what the Apple II used for assembly language. The decimal system we learn in elementary school consists of ten digits, zero through nine. Hexadecimal uses sixteen digits: zero through nine and A through F. Here's a concrete example: The number 11 (in the decimal system) is rendered as the letter B in the hexadecimal system and the number 94 is rendered 5E in hexadecimal.* I taught myself to make these conversions automatically, just the way a schoolkid might learn by rote that 12 × 12 is 144.

In those early days, Rob was my greatest ally and teacher. When the Apple II+ arrived at our house, I immediately set out to create a version of *Crazy Climber*, a favorite arcade game of ours, but I couldn't get it right. Rob looked at my code and asked why I didn't use variables. The answer was simple: I didn't know what a variable was.

Rob explained that variables held values that could change as the program ran in response to player input or other events in the game. For instance, the variable "Lives" holds the value of 3. If the player got an extra life, the variable "Lives" incremented to 4. I could use variables for things such as X coordinates, Y coordinates, number of bullets, or any other thing I needed to keep track of. It is one of the most basic concepts in programming, and I had been blind to it. Put in the simplest terms, think of any bowl in your kitchen as a variable. It can hold three hundred beans or ten. It's still a bowl, but its contents are variable.

I finished my version of *Crazy Climber*, but I was such a novice that I accidentally deleted it—my first Apple II+ game in history vanished into the ether! I wasn't that upset. I figured my next games would all be better. I set to work on a game called *Dodge 'Em*, in which a player's ship had to avoid lasers shot by an alien spaceship.

Thanks in part to Rob pointing out machine code and variables and the books my parents got me, I learned how to access the inner workings of the Apple II+. The week I got my Assembly book is a blur. My mind was constantly whirling and processing as I explored the Apple II+, the code that drove the machine, and the code I could run on it. The Apple II+ and other early home computers were fully knowable machines. My Apple II+ had 64K of memory—65,536 bytes—and I told myself I needed to learn what every byte did. The top 25 percent of memory

---

* An understanding of the hexadecimal numbering system is useful for programmers now and was essential for programmers in the 1980s. Explaining hex is beyond the scope of this story, but I encourage you to look it up if you're interested.

was devoted to Read-Only Memory (ROM), which contained the programs that defined how the Apple II+ worked. Anyone building a program to run on the Apple II+ needed to know the precise locations of different functions in the machine's ROM. There were even books that broke down the "geographic addressing" for the Apple II+ ROM. To learn faster, I took notes, wrote down these addresses, and referenced posters that listed the most important memory locations (the Beagle Bros. Peeks & Pokes chart). I was determined to memorize everything about the computer—how the 6502 microprocessor worked, how the interlaced hi-res screen was laid out, and everything in ROM and zero page.[*]

There were a couple reasons I was pushing myself so hard. First, I felt like I needed to catch up with other programmers who were so far ahead of me—people I didn't even know but whose games I played regularly, like Nasir Gebelli and Bill Budge. The second reason was much more serious: I was about to lose my computer just as I finally figured out how it really worked.

At the start of tenth grade, my stepdad was offered a military assignment in England at a 50 percent pay increase. He accepted the three-year assignment at the Royal Air Force Base in Alconbury, England. We were going to move at the beginning of the new year, 1983.

The plan was for movers to come and pack up all our belongings and ship them on a slow boat to the UK. The one possession I cared about most, the Apple II+, was due to be placed in a box a mere week after I'd gotten my Assembly books. I plunged into their pages, absorbing everything as fast as I could, coding as I read to get the hang of it. I was in a race against time, and once again, necessity was the mother of retention. About five pages into the first book, I typed some machine code into our Apple II+ and ran it. It worked! I was on my way.

One week later, our computer was gone, headed to England, and so were we.

I didn't let that stop me: I started writing code in notebooks. I'd fill a page with Assembly language in a column on the right and then hand-assemble the code in a column on the left, manually converting the Assembly into machine code. Then, I would find an Apple II+ somewhere to type the hexadecimal machine code in to see if the program ran correctly. It was a laborious process, but I was learning and polishing my skills. I thought only of code. In school, my grades started to dip as I coded or assembled code in class. If we had a test, whatever I happened to remember went on the paper, but what I cared about, the only thing I cared about, was code.

Before we set off for England, we drove to Tucson to say goodbye to family. On the way, we stopped by the San Diego headquarters of Beagle Bros., a company that

---

[*]　Zero page is the first 256 bytes of an 8-bit computer's memory space. It's special because the 6502 CPU had special instructions to use that area of memory at high speed.

sold disks that contained a mix of programmer's utility programs and, sometimes, games. I say "headquarters," but Beagle Bros. existed in a home office in the house of its founder, Bert Kersey. It was a huge thrill for me to meet him; he was a rock star in my eyes. Beagle Bros. programs and manuals always had a sense of humor about them, and it was perfectly in keeping with that when we stepped up to the front door and saw a sign beneath the door buzzer: "Press once for trapdoor, twice for doorbell." The rest of the house had quirks, too, including a table with roller skates on its legs, which I thought was great.

That visit was inspiring, not least because it showed my parents were warming even more to my zest for computers. A year later, I devised a program that claimed to take your pulse when you touched the space bar. It was a prank program, obviously, written in two lines for Uncle Louie's Perpetual Two-Liner Contest. I mailed the game from England as an entry to the contest, and Bert included it on a 1983 release called *Silicon Salad*. It was my first published program.

The Royal Air Force Base in Alconbury, England, is in Cambridgeshire, sixty miles north of London. There was a huge community of American military in the area, and we lived in a house about a thirty-minute drive from the 1,000-acre base. I covered the walls of my bedroom in computer game ads I cut out of magazines.

Since I transferred in the middle of the school year, I met with a guidance counselor at Alconbury Middle High School, which was an all-American school the Department of Defense Education Activity operated. The guidance counselor told me the school offered an introductory BASIC class.

"I know BASIC," I said, "but I'd still love to take the class." It seemed preferable to taking physical education.

"The class is halfway through the year, so you'll have to talk to the teacher and see if it's the right fit. We'll need to convince her you haven't fallen behind."

"Oh, sure," I said, and we headed toward her classroom.

He introduced me to Gail Rachels, my first formal programming teacher.

"I don't think being behind is going to be a problem," I told her. "I know a lot about BASIC. In fact, I've got some disks with my work on it. I'm starting to learn Assembly, too."

She didn't say much while I gave her a quick demo, but I got the sense she was impressed. The next day, my second day of school, I walked into her class. She posted an assignment on the board, telling the class they needed to finish it by the end of the period, and then she said, "Come with me, John."

We walked to her car and drove across the base to the aggressor squadron, which is where fighter pilots train. She introduced me to Captain Spencer. He seemed like a funny, fast-talking guy. In the middle of our conversation, he picked up the phone and jabbered some world-class military speak: "Delta

Eagle, this is Squadron Captain Spencer, please initiate the protocol we discussed earlier."

He stood up and a giant vault-like door opened slowly. He ushered us into a cavernous room with officers seated at terminals and led us to a Cromemco minicomputer.

"Do you think you can program this, John?"

"Can I check it out?"

"Please."

It was a CP/M operating system running HP BASIC.

"Yeah, I can program this, no problem."

"Would you like a job?"

I'd been in England for two days and landed computer work!

"Yeah. That would be awesome."

At the age of fifteen, I started programming for the US Air Force. Captain Spencer was high octane like Tom Cruise in *Top Gun*. He told me that he'd met my teacher at the bar at the Officer's Club, and she told him about this whiz kid who was going to be impossible to teach. My stepfather talked to Captain Spencer and made sure I wasn't working with any classified information—just placeholder data. He was worried that I might be kidnapped and wanted to be sure I didn't access anything "important." That might sound a little over the top, but my stepdad was, in his way, on the front lines of the Cold War, retrieving and monitoring surveillance operations behind the Iron Curtain. Captain Spencer arranged for me to work after school and over the summer.

In 1983, the average adult had no real idea about computers. I was so far ahead of the curve that I wasn't just a novelty, I was an in-demand rarity. At the time, I wasn't really aware of this. My eye was on the coders who were ahead of me. I suppose a university town like Cambridge had its fair share of computer-knowledgeable people, but in Alconbury, I was the only real programmer around. Soon after the family Apple II+ arrived, my stepdad asked me to create report forms. So I made a program for him. I was happy to code, happy to have my Apple II+, and he was happy to have the forms he needed.

I started to make game after game after game. With each completed project, I put the code and a disk in a letter and submitted my work to programming magazines like the Apple-only *Nibble* and *inCider*. The first few months, I was rewarded with nothing but rejections, but I was determined, and eventually *inCider* bought my maze game *Scout Search* for $100. In it, players take the role of a Scoutmaster charged with gathering their lost scouts before a rampaging grizzly bear finds them. I was incredibly proud, and it fed my confidence. I was a professional programmer and game designer. Nobody could take that away from me.

A magazine called *A+* announced a programming competition. Each month, from June to December, they planned to choose and publish a winning program submitted by readers. I got to work and sent them a side-scrolling shooter game called *Cavern Crusader*. I felt so good about it, I actually told them I was going to win the competition. Looking back, I can't believe I did this, but sure enough, *Cavern Crusader* was picked for the December issue, and I got $500 for my work. I'd made money—*real* money—with one of my video games.

Aside from my computer obsession, I was a regular teen. I had always liked music, and I found myself gravitating to loud guitars. Although I looked squeaky clean, I was listening to heavy metal and debating the finer riffs of Mötley Crüe, Dokken, Iron Maiden, Black Sabbath, and Judas Priest. Unlike a lot of music-loving teens, I really wasn't into the rebellious, let's-get-wasted side of the music scene. I experimented with booze exactly once back in Rocklin when I was thirteen. Rob was over, and my stepdad was away in Asia. We were up late watching movies when I decided it would be a great idea to sample every bottle of booze in the liquor cabinet. I passed out and woke up feeling horrible. It was a lesson learned. My mom didn't even have to lecture me. I had zero interest in booze after that. I loved the visceral experience of the sound of metal. It charged me up, and although I looked middle-of-the-road, I liked the theatrical, badass look of metal bands.*

When we moved to England, I realized that I could reinvent myself. In Rocklin, I had been a funny kid who had braces, glasses, and strict parents. Now, the braces were off, and the parents were a little more forgiving. My buddies who might have teased me about liking a girl were thousands of miles away. That first week, riding the bus to school, I figured this all out, and I decided I may as well start dating. At the Christmas dance on base, I met a girl named Jennifer Monroe, and we really connected. She was smart, pretty, and, like me, industrious, and we remain friends to this day.

My senior year of high school was busy. I was writing games and sending them to magazines, and I even created my own company, Capitol Ideas Software, a name inspired by Capitol Computers, the local computer store in Roseville near Rocklin. I didn't actually register the name, but I wanted to sound more official and grown-up when I submitted my work to magazines. Of course, I also undercut that "sophistication" with my sign-off on every submission letter:

John Romero, Ace Programmer.

---

* Growing my hair long had nothing to do with heavy metal. At first, it was time saving. Letting it grow meant I didn't need to make time for haircuts. In my thirties, I embraced it for its Indigenous cultural importance.

I was trying to make an impact and do something memorable with my teenaged query letters. I thought it was both aspirational and funny. Some part of me also hoped it was true. I did not personally know any programmers who knew more than I did, including my teachers or other professionals at the base. I've also never been good at navigating the fine line between being vocally enthusiastic and honestly proud of my work and appearing to be cocky or egotistical. My wife, Brenda, calls this "Programmer Nuance Deficit Disorder." By that, she means programmers don't generally deal in ambiguity. We are binary creatures: Code works or it doesn't; input in, output out. Fortunately, my sign-off didn't work against me in those early days, judging by the acceptance rate on my games.

I was also an ace grocery bagger and inventory stocker my senior year, working every day after school in the on-base commissary—a super-cheap grocery store filled with American products for the enlisted people and their families. I saved each penny of that money hoping to get myself a new computer—an Apple IIe. I also worked mornings in the commissary with my mom and brother. For months, we drove to the base at 12 a.m. and unpacked boxes and stocked the shelves for a few hours before going home. The money was for our big summer plan: going to Disneyland—the most fun, thrilling, and immersive experience I'd had as a kid. My mom and brother loved it, too, and that was what we wanted to do when I graduated—spend an entire week at Disneyland riding the rides.

Graduation was sort of bittersweet, mostly because Jennifer and I were a great pair. Her dad, a senior Air Force officer, liked me. My parents liked her. Our parents liked each other. There was some talk about me going to college in England while she finished her last year of high school, but I told Jennifer I needed to be more focused on the future. The technology in England was far behind the US in the 1980s. I knew everything was happening in California, in Silicon Valley, in the US.*

"I need to be there," I told Jennifer.

I had to make games, and to do that, I had to be in the United States.

I wasn't just going to Disneyland. I was leaving England and my friends and family to follow my dream.

---

* Of course, I found out later in life that the tech industry was also exploding in England and Scotland, but at the time, California was all I knew.

EPISODE TWO
DEVELOPMENT

CHAPTER 6

Programmers' Roundtable

California was calling—not just Disneyland, but Silicon Valley. I knew I had to be back in the US to learn what I needed to make it as a programmer. I strongly believed going to college was a necessity. Despite signing letters with "John Romero, Ace Programmer," I didn't think I could get a full-time job as a programmer, especially straight out of high school. My parents suggested Oxford and Cambridge, but in my head, all I could think was, *I need to make video games, and I need to go to college in the US, closer to where this is happening.* To me, what was happening in Silicon Valley was massive and the center of the universe. So, the logical next step seemed to be to live with my biological dad in Salt Lake City and go to Utah Technical College (now Salt Lake Community College). Sure, it wasn't California, but it was college, and it was closer to Silicon Valley than Alconbury. It was a good next step.

My mother, Ralph and I flew back to Los Angeles in the summer of 1985 and celebrated my graduation in Disneyland as planned. Maria, a family friend, lived in LA, and put us up.* Disneyland was my favorite place in the world. I loved the rides, the junk food, and the illusions that the park created.

I was five years old the first time I went to Disneyland. I especially remember the Matterhorn, the massive alpine roller coaster at the center of the park. We got on the bobsleds, and as I ascended, I looked down and saw nothing but the

---

* Not her real name.

beams holding the Matterhorn together. When we reached the top of the ride, the power went out. This was freak-out-level scary to a five-year-old, but it was also cool to be frozen above the park, looking into the guts of a nonexistent mountain. My five-year-old brain didn't process this moment as one where the curtain had been pulled back and the secrets of the great and all-powerful Oz (or in this case, Walt Disney) were revealed. That was what took place, though, not that it made the Magic Kingdom any less magical.

Looking back at my younger visits, both as a five-year-old and as a teen fresh from high school, I wonder, did the park resonate so powerfully with me because everything about it touched on the same elements as game construction or vice versa? Did Disney influence me as a game designer, or did I like it so much because I was one? Every inch of Disneyland is meticulously designed so that visitors have not just a shared experience, but *the same experience*. Considerable detail and planning go into every aspect of the park to heighten expectations and deliver even bigger payoffs. If the Matterhorn inadvertently opened my eyes to Disneyland's constructed illusions, I saw their mastery when I was older. From the level design of the waiting lines to the colors and shapes of its buildings, the experience design in Disneyland is magnificent. Imagineers—Disney designers—deploy techniques to create illusions. For example, Main Street grows narrower as it nears the castle, making the building seem much bigger than it is. Meanwhile, the humdrum elements of Disneyland, the garbage bins, the transformers, and so on, are painted "no-see-'em green." Why green? The human eye sees more green than any other color, so green is the natural color choice for camouflage. All these elements are important to a game designer trying to design both an illusion *and* an experience.

Decades later, my wife Brenda and I regularly piled the kids into the car and drove eight hours from our home in Santa Cruz to the Magic Kingdom. For me, each visit became a quest to learn something new about the park. I'd ask cast members questions: "What is something about the park or your job that nobody knows?" I'd study the level design of a ride, list elements of environmental storytelling, or consider the parallels between NPCs and cast members who provided both information and quests, if asked. I loved learning new things about the park each time we visited.

Of course, at age seventeen, I wasn't exactly thinking about game design or Disney in these terms, but I was still thinking about game design nonstop. With the money I saved, I ordered my own Apple IIe and waited for it to be delivered to Maria's house so I could get cracking. My plan was to take my new machine to Utah, where my father lived. I would enroll in college and begin my ultimate gaming quest—to land a job as a game programmer.

After Disneyland, Mom and Ralph went to Tucson to visit family for a few weeks. I stayed behind to work with Maria to earn more money before moving to

Utah and starting college, and boy, did I work. If I'd known I was going from living in decent conditions in the UK to state-of-the-art Los Angeles sweatshop hell, I might have looked for other options. I didn't know what I was getting into at her place. Every morning at 6:45, I hopped in the back of her pickup truck, and she drove around collecting her crew of undocumented Mexican immigrants. We'd arrive at her machine shop, located in an industrial complex of many different machine shops, and work until 11 p.m., assembling rivets and clinches. It was brutal work performed in furnace-like conditions; the shop wasn't air-conditioned. I was given a block of metal with twelve poorly drilled holes in it, and my job was to pop rivets into the holes, attach a clinch, and then use a press on every one of them to make them solid. I moved thousands of these pieces every day, nonstop from 8 a.m. to 11 p.m., and when we got home there was little relief—Maria didn't have AC there either.

I baked in 90-plus-degree weather the entire time, trying to communicate in Spanglish with my workmates. The only saving grace of the job was that there was a radio in the shop and the dial was set to KNAC—LA's legendary metal radio station. I couldn't believe bands like Accept, Poison, Mötley Crüe, and so many others were on the air. It was my one, solitary escape. I was so exhausted at the end of the day that I didn't even *think* of coding. It was hard work, and I got paid only in room and board. However, she promised me a few hundred bucks at the end of my time that I could use toward college. All in all, I was happy for the work and glad to be back in the US. When Mom and Ralph returned from Tucson, my Apple IIe arrived, and we drove to my mom's friend Opal's home. I was thrilled to leave the sweatshop behind.

My mom and Ralph returned to England, and my dad eventually drove from Salt Lake to fetch me, my computer, my clothes, and not much else. I hadn't seen him in about three years. He looked a bit older than I remembered, but he was still very much the same guy. Lean, powerful, muscular, well-groomed (even drunk, my father cared deeply about how he looked). It was obvious to both of us that we were on new terrain. We loved each other, but now we didn't really know each other that well. Yes, he was my dad, but I was older, bigger, and smarter. I was no longer just a kid.

Like my mother and John Schuneman, my father didn't really care about computers or gaming. He just loved playing pool. So while I could talk to him about my achievements, the games I'd made and sold, and the jobs I'd gotten, much of it was over his head. This was true of most people in the mid-'80s. Computers were typically the domain of researchers, scientists, and some office workers. Electronic typewriters were still the rage.

He lived outside Salt Lake City in Midvale with his new wife, Kaaryn, and was now a building superintendent for EIMCo, a large mining operation. He was out of the mines and managing the twelve buildings that surrounded them. He was different, too. Being surrounded by scientists day in and day out changed his perspective and educated him. Even though he didn't have a day of college in him, he was a naturally curious man who liked to learn and absorbed whatever was happening around him.

I was given a room in their basement, where I set up my Apple IIe on a computer desk, complete with a kneeling chair—the cutting-edge ergonomic furniture of the day. I programmed and bided my time until I could register for school at Utah Tech.

Strange as all this was, it was a much better setup than the last time I'd seen my dad, which was the summer of 1982, before we moved to England. Summer vacations in my tweens and early teens with my dad were always fraught. At that time, he was dating a Mexican woman named Francis, who had three young kids. They were living in a trailer, and his idea of childcare was to give me a list of chores to do. I was fourteen and bored out of my skull. One day, I found his .22 rifle and started firing it out our window, shooting out windows of neighboring trailers.* The cops came, of course, and I lay low as they went around knocking on doors. I didn't answer when they knocked on ours. This is not my proudest moment.

One day, we drove out to the desert home of Francis's parents. My dad barbecued and drank while I supervised the kids—Johnny, Dina, and Ronnie. By the end of the night, my dad was loaded, but he packed up his now-empty cooler of beer and ordered me and Ralph to get in the car. Francis and her kids planned to stay behind at her parents.

"Are you sure you can drive, Al?" Francis asked.

"Oh, sure. No problem," my dad insisted.

We got in the car and drove off. About a mile down the road, he pulled onto the shoulder.

"Mijo, sit here in front of me and drive."

"What?"

"Come on," he said, pushing himself back into his seat. "On my lap. You can drive."

Fortunately, I knew how to operate the gas pedal and the brakes, because within no time at all, my dad passed out behind me. The tough thing was figuring out how the hell to get back to Tucson on dark roads at 2 a.m. Somehow, I remembered and guessed my way back, surprised that I recognized major streets.

At one point, we came to a big intersection with a Church's fried chicken place on the far-left corner. As a rookie driver, I was in the wrong lane when I

---

*   It never occurred to me that there might be people inside or that doing this could possibly hit them. I shake my head in shock every time I think of this.

realized I needed to make a left. I was waffling in no-man's land, the car pointed toward the fast-food joint.

"I don't know where I'm supposed to turn!" I yelled, panicked.

Suddenly, my dad grabbed the wheel and jerked it to the left, guiding us into the correct lane.

"Oh, man," I said. "That was close!"

"Yeah, we almost had fried chicken," my dad said.

One minute later, he was asleep again.

Here in Utah with his new wife things seemed different—more organized, less chaotic. My dad and Kaaryn drove to work together in his Honda Accord, so my new stepmom said I could use her Toyota 4-wheel-drive truck to get around town. I couldn't believe my luck. That was the kind of gesture I never expected a step-parent to make! The only hitch was I didn't have a driver's license. I got my license almost as fast as I said "thank you" to Kaaryn.

Registration at Utah Tech was a fiasco. The (mis)guidance counselor put me in the wrong program: data processing, not computer science. Data processing had nothing to do with programming a computer. Sure, it involved using computer systems, but using a system is different than creating one, and many of the classes had a business angle that didn't feel relevant.

This could have been a rough time for me. I'd just turned eighteen in a strange town, my ex-girlfriend, who I still cared about, was thousands of miles away in England, and the college experience I hoped would change my life pointed me in the wrong direction. My living situation was so-so. I got along with my dad pretty well. He'd come down to my room and have a look at the games I was working on, but he didn't really connect with them. He was still a major drinker. Spending time with him, I noticed one trait hadn't changed: He'd become ornery and mean if he was sober, and far more sociable and friendly when he had booze in his bloodstream. He still liked to go to bars. Alone. So, on many evenings, I'd be home with Kaaryn. To top things off, I didn't have any money. Everything I had saved from Maria's was going toward my tuition. I had to borrow money just to put gas in Kaaryn's car to get to school. As always with my dad, money was scarce, and after a month of school, he told me I needed to get a job.

Fortunately, Kaaryn's sister had a brother-in-law who owned a computer store. He hired me to work the floor as a salesman. I was in heaven, surrounded by PCs, Commodores, and Apple IIs. Having spent the better part of the last six years reading everything I could about computers, I was the ultimate salesman. Harnessing my undiminished passion and appreciation for the machines and the software, I was an evangelical fanboy, eager to share my knowledge with anyone who wanted it. My fervor resonated with customers. I sold the hell out of our inventory. My secret? Talking my head off. All of my passion was genuine, though. Back then, computer enthusiasts were few and far between, so if I had an audience—a tech ally—I relished the conversation. The combination of sincerity, enthusiasm, and knowledge didn't just help close sales, it also built relationships. Customers became friends as we bonded over the new technology.

Phone calls with two of my old pals in California, Rob and Christian, and my programming work also kept my spirits up. I sent out games as they were finished, and the games I published in computer magazines broadened my universe. Each of my game instructions also listed my address. So, I got mail. Often the letters were from people who claimed my code didn't work, and I wrote back explaining that it did work, and they most likely made a typo when entering the code. This was still a time when "publishing a game" meant getting a listing of your code in the pages of a magazine. I also got fan letters from people who liked my games. One letter, from a guy in New Jersey who owned a machine shop, asked if I was interested in doing some programming for his business. He paid me in games—pirated games on floppies—but that was as good as money to me.

After crawling through the first semester at school, I'd had enough. The courses were a waste of time. I mean that in the literal sense. The computer revolution was moving fast. As I sat there studying data processing and flowcharts, others outside college were mastering Assembly language, making games, creating new ways of interacting with players. Time spent in class was time not spent getting ahead. In other words, every minute I spent in class was time I was falling behind. I told my father I was in the wrong program, and I was quitting to work full-time at the store. My dad asked me to start paying rent. That marked the beginning of the end of my time in Utah. I didn't want to have a career at a computer store, as fun as that was. I wanted to make games for a game company, and if I was going to have to work to pay rent, I'd rather be near my closest friends or in California, the epicenter of America's computer revolution. I just had to figure out where, exactly, to go.

Rob Lavelock rescued me. Over the phone, I told him I was done with Salt Lake and needed to figure out my next move. I wanted to get back to California, but I wasn't sure how to make it happen.

"Why don't you come here? You can stay with us."

"Seriously?"

"Yeah."

"That would be awesome, but I'm not even sure how I would get there."

"We'll come get you. My mom and me. We can put your stuff in the back of our truck."

I couldn't believe it. It was the perfect out. I wouldn't have to pay rent. I could focus on my games, and I would get to hang out with my best friend.

"Oh man. That would be so great. Are you sure your mom is cool with it?"

"Totally."

It was hard to tell my dad this. He was less than thrilled, but he knew things hadn't exactly gone as planned with school. He also understood that I wanted to be closer to the game industry in California. I packed up my things, thanked my dad and Kaaryn for everything, and got chauffeured to the Lavelocks' new home in Yuba City.

Looking back, I am grateful for my time with my dad and Kaaryn, and thankful for Kaaryn's influence in his life. I think Kaaryn was the only woman my father really, deeply loved. He treated her well, and he regularly told her, "I adore you." I know she loves him to this day. Kaaryn was good to me and to my brother, writing us letters, calling, and keeping us connected with our dad. She loved us, and we loved her, too. She told me how proud my father was of me and my games. When his drinking turned to drug use, she gave him an ultimatum, and as is the case with many addicts, the drugs made the choice for him. I'm sure it was one of the hardest choices she ever made, but it was the right one for her. My dad returned home to Tucson.

Years later, in 2013, I was at a conference in Salt Lake City, and Kaaryn arranged to come and meet me, Brenda, and the kids for lunch. As I walked toward her, she smiled, gasped when she saw me, and then started to cry. She brushed the tears away, but they kept coming. We enjoyed the afternoon, sharing memories, looking at old photos, and reminiscing. When we left, Brenda said something that hadn't occurred to me.

"I can't imagine how wonderful and difficult that was for her."

"Difficult? What do you mean?" I asked.

"Imagine loving one man your whole life, but not being with him. Then, here you come, the spitting image of that man, and nearly the same age as when she last saw him, too."

It hadn't occurred to me, and I'm sure Brenda was right. I'm grateful Kaaryn is still in my life.

When I left Salt Lake and bid goodbye to my father and Kaaryn, I was beyond happy to be at the Lavelocks. Rob had just graduated high school, but he was already a budding entrepreneur with a business designing aquariums for rich people. His parents had built their new house in Yuba City, which was about thirty miles from our old stomping ground of Rocklin. It was rural and naturally scenic. The house was roomy and had a great pool in the backyard. Rob and I spent lots of time swimming, lounging, and growing our respective careers.

I worked on my games and got better and better at designing them. In June, I cranked out a new creation in eleven days. Rob, who was deep into his aquarium design business, gave me the idea of a seaworthy game I called *Twilight Treasures*. Players took the role of a diver in scuba gear who moved vertically, hauling treasure from the bottom of the ocean and evading sharks, piranhas, deep-sea mines, and other obstacles. It was a fun game, and the editors of *Nibble* magazine agreed.*

Rob and I decided to get to work in earnest, and we had a plan. We started work on a role-playing game called *Aberration*. Rob's parents would provide funding for the game in the form of housing and feeding me, and in return, we planned to give his parents a percentage of the game's eventual proceeds. There was just one problem: We hadn't cleared this with Rob's parents. Not surprisingly, I didn't get too far with my pitch. Rob's dad didn't know anything about games and wasn't interested in starting now.

In late June, after about three months of living at Rob's house—although I started working at Taco Bell to make some cash—Mr. Lavelock mentioned it might be time for me to move to greener pastures. I totally got it. I'd been living there rent-free, and Mrs. Lavelock was feeding me. I think Rob's father may have also had it with Rob and his live-in business partners. Believe it or not, I was not the first. In another room lived the aquarium business cofounder, Scott. Three teenage boys under a single roof is a bit much for anyone. After all their kindness, I did not want to wear out my welcome with the Lavelocks.

I called my mom to help me develop a plan B. At the time, she was getting ready to leave England and move back to Rocklin with Ralph in the middle of August. My stepdad would follow three months later, after he packed everything up and sold the house and the car. My moving back into the house in Rocklin was not a sure thing, however, because my stepdad considered my decision to live with my biological father an act of betrayal. Mom said she would lobby him, though. Hopeful, I moved in with my mom and Ralph, counting on her to iron things out before he arrived. This seemed like a workable idea.

My mom convinced John to let me move back home on one condition: I attend Sierra College, the same college where I had taught myself to code seven years earlier. I didn't care much about college, but it seemed like the thing to do while I figured out how to land a gig in the game industry. By the time my stepdad returned in November, I was already enrolled and taking classes while working on my games at night.

---

* *Nibble* magazine accepted the game, but they did not release it until December 1989, when they put it on the cover. It was my first game to be accepted for a cover, but not the first printed cover.

The only thing I had to figure out was transportation. Mobility in Northern California was a major issue for any eighteen-year-old who wanted a semblance of independence. My ten-speed bike was nice but didn't cut it. I went to a local Burger King and got a job for $3.50 an hour. I cleared $100 after taxes for a thirty-five-hour week, and that meant I could afford the $121 monthly payments on a Yugo.

The Burger King was owned by former NFL star Jim Otto of the Oakland Raiders, and we were constantly being told it was the top-rated BK franchise in California, and we worked hard to keep it that way. That sense of accomplishment was important to the whole team. Working nights, I had to clean the fryers and broiler, disassembling and washing them in acid at the end of every shift. I was asked to be an assistant manager repeatedly and said no every time. I had no intention of getting deeper into the fast-food business. In my nine months at Burger King, the most interesting thing that happened to me was that a young woman passed me a note at the cash register.

"Hi. My friend likes you. She asked me to give you her number."

I looked up and saw the friend, a beautiful woman around my age. Apparently, I hadn't given her a second look when she'd placed her order a few minutes earlier, and that made her curious about me. Her name was Kelly Mitchell. She was a year younger than me and still in high school. Before long, we started dating. Things progressed quickly for us. I got the sense that Kelly's family was not too happy about the relationship, though. They were devout Mormons, and I was a devout atheist. In my experience living in Utah, most of the Mormons I met were friendly, warm people. They reminded me of model TV families from the '50s: positive, happy, clean cut, and living clean. Kelly's family wasn't mean or nasty to me—and her mother even bought me a bunch of expensive clothing for Christmas—but it was clear to both Kelly and me they hoped we would break up.

One night I got home around midnight and Kelly swung by. Normally, we'd just talk outside, but it was a chilly night. My stepdad had made clear that no extramarital sex was to happen in his house. Ever. It was a message I'd received loud and clear. So when I suggested Kelly come in, there were no ulterior motives in my nineteen-year-old brain. I knew what a strict and sometimes punishing disciplinarian my stepdad could be. We hung out for about an hour, and then I walked her to the door and said goodbye. I turned around and heard his voice calling me to the living room.

"I told you: no girls in the house. You disobeyed me."

"It's freezing out. I just invited her in to talk."

"I'll bet. That's it. That's the end. You are going to find another place to live tomorrow."

"I have nowhere to go," I told him. I was respectful. There was no way talking back to him would make it any better.

"That's *your* problem. You are done here. Tomorrow, go find someplace else to live. You are not welcome here anymore."

Part of me couldn't believe it, but that was life with John Schuneman. The most dependable thing about him, from my point of view, was that he was always the most hard-assed adult in the room. For years, the frustration I dared not express came out in the *Melvin* comics I drew. The stepdad choking Melvin to death, Melvin's head stomped in, Melvin's eyes bulging out of his skull. If my kid had been drawing those comics, I'd be more than just a little concerned.

I spent the next day scrambling, looking for cheap places to live. Surviving on my Burger King salary was not an option. I needed to make more money. My mom appealed to John to give me more time. Otherwise, I'd drop out of school and all that work I'd done would be wasted. I got a temporary reprieve until the end of the spring semester, but the writing was writ large on the wall. I quit Burger King, signed up with a temp agency, and got a series of nine-dollar-an-hour jobs with tech companies around Sacramento and Rancho Cordova.

Two months later, I had my own apartment in Citrus Heights, a few towns away from Rocklin. When Kelly graduated high school, she moved in with me. At that point, I abandoned school. I didn't need someone at the front of a room to tell me how to program in C at a snail's pace. Too often, the lowest common denominator set the pace in our classroom, and the pace didn't feel quick enough for me. Because I knew Assembly and BASIC, C was easy for me. I worked my way through the C programming language textbook in the first week. I learned at a much faster speed on my own, and I was only too aware that there were people out there who had a decade of experience on me and had already graduated college and learned what they needed to learn. I didn't have any time to spare.

I was out on my own and no longer dependent on John Schuneman for anything.

It felt great.

At the same time, nine dollars an hour wasn't living large. In fact, between Kelly and me, and given where we lived, it was definitely living small. I knew I could do more. All around me, the game industry was booming, and although I could code in Assembly language, C, and Pascal, I still wasn't a part of it. That needed to change.

On September 15, I gathered up copies of my games on Apple II discs and went to AppleFest 87 at the Moscone Center in downtown San Francisco. The first thing I saw in the pavilion was the *UpTime* booth. *UpTime*, a magazine that billed itself as "The Disk Monthly," sold floppies loaded with software for various computer platforms. The booth had terminals set up, and as I got closer, I saw a familiar sight on some of the screens—my newly published game *Zippy Zombi*! I couldn't believe it. In a way, I was already in the industry; I just hadn't known it.

Zippy Zombi was in the new *UpTime* release, and many people were playing it. On the screens, a creature named Fuzzy jumped from cube to cube on a pyramid, changing the color of the cube with each touch. An evil snake tried to get Fuzzy. When the entire pyramid has changed color, the player got to a new level.

I introduced myself to Jay Wilbur, who ran *UpTime*'s Apple II products. We had been corresponding for about two years, and Jay, of course, was the guy who bought my games. So we already had an unspoken mutual admiration society going on, and it was great to meet in person. I also met Lane Roathe, who handled Apple IIgs programming for Jay. He was the first hard-core Apple II programmer I'd ever met, and I was one of the first he'd met, so we had a lot to talk about—we spoke a language that few others did. As I left the booth, I made sure to say goodbye to Jay. The publisher of *UpTime*, Bill Kelly, was also there.

"We could use you in Rhode Island, John," Bill said. "How about you come work with us?"

I was floored by the offer, but I played it cool and told him I would think about it. As I walked away, I was thinking, "This is the best thing ever! I got a job offer from the first booth I visited!"

I walked over to the *Softdisk* booth. They were *UpTime*'s competitors, and I told them that not only had I published with *UpTime* but that my game was featured at their booth. That raised some interest.

"We would love for you to send your games to us," the rep said, trading contact information. I was two-for-two!

Eventually, I made my way to the Origin Systems pavilion. If there was one game company I dreamed of working for, it was Origin, the company behind *Ultima*, one of the most important and beloved role-playing games to date. I was a total fan of the franchise, which involved many classic fantasy elements—dungeons, dragons, character creation and development, exploration, quests, and combat. I'd played every *Ultima* game since the series launched in 1981, eagerly waiting for each new release and lining up to purchase it on launch day.

Richard Garriott, the creator of the *Ultima* series and the cofounder of Origin Systems, was a rockstar of the game industry and was, like game developers Bill Budge and Nasir Gebelli, god-level to me. Richard was doing what I wanted to do at a level I had yet to attain. I could do all the same things—design, code, create art, and write—but he was doing it at a huge scale and with a team of developers, turning out gold with every game. At the time, they were developing *Ultima V*, and there were advertisements for it at AppleFest: "Coming October 31st!" Even being in the Origin booth felt magical to me, not unlike going to Disneyland. I had not yet made it into the industry, but I was standing at its front door. I kept my eyes peeled for Richard, or Lord British—the childhood nickname the English-born Texan was widely known by throughout the industry. I knew exactly what he looked like, and to this day, I'm sure he has a long, thin braid reaching to his mid-back and a silver serpent around his neck. I was confident in my abilities, but I knew I had so far to go to get to where Richard already was. He was a huge role model to me—he started out publishing his games in baggies, taking them to his local computer store, and now here he was defining the industry, and one of its true celebrities.

One of the games Origin was promoting at the pavilion was a new edition of *Ultima I* that they converted to Assembly from its original, much slower BASIC programming. I stood in front of the computer displaying this new game and decided this would be an opportune moment for show-and-tell. I removed the *Ultima I* floppy and popped in one of my disks, which contained my newest work: *Lethal Labyrinth*. I used a new graphics mode called "double hi-res." This was a calculated move on my part. Few people had mastered double-res, which rendered graphics in sixteen colors. To anyone who saw it, I hoped it would speak volumes about my programming ability.

However, I needed to make sure someone saw it. Commandeering a computer—a computer that was there expressly to promote another game—seemed like a perfectly good idea. Now? I cringe at the audacity of this maneuver. It was a risky thing to do. The Origin director of marketing immediately walked over, which was the whole point. As soon as the game came up, her attitude switched from "Hey, what's going on over here?" to "Oh wow, that looks really good. What is this?"

I told her it was a game in double hi-res and shared my enthusiasm about what double hi-res meant for games going forward. I said, "It has more colors than most Apple II games you'll see in this building," which led her to ask for my contact info. I gave her my phone number and address.

"By the way," I said, "I'm looking for a job, and I would love to work at Origin if there were a position available."

She explained that she worked in the marketing division but would put me in touch with the right people in the company's New Hampshire office. I took out my disk and put *Ultima I* back in the machine, rebooted it, and got it running again. Then she gave me her business card. I felt like I'd just gotten the golden ticket, Willy Wonka style. I was walking on air. My head was full of the possibility of landing my dream job.

That Monday, I went back to my temp job as technical editor at a company called Jones Futurex that made encrypted communication peripherals for bank PCs to transfer sensitive data between banks. Twice a week, during lunch, I called the Origin marketing director's phone number to find out if there was any opening. This went on for three weeks, until she said that she could get me in touch with someone who could help. My new Origin contact lived up to her word, connecting me with John Fachini, a programmer in New Hampshire who was responsible for porting Origin games onto new platforms—in other words, making a game that was coded for an Apple II work on a Commodore 64. In October, he told me a position was opening up.

"We need a Commodore 64 programmer to convert our role-playing game *2400 A.D.* from the Apple II to the Commodore 64."

I'd never worked on a Commodore 64, but I said, "Awesome, I'm ready to do that."

"Okay. We'll schedule you for a phone interview. Our final candidate will come to the main office in New Hampshire for the final interview."

The next day, I went out and bought a book called *Mapping the Commodore 64*. I consumed the book. In two days, I felt I understood the entire machine—the operating system, its memory capability, the architecture, everything. A few days later, three programmers interviewed me on the phone, and I answered every question instantly and confidently. I studied for the "test" the way lawyers study for the bar. Since I'd just absorbed the Commodore 64 bible, I was hard-selling them on what you can do with a machine I'd never touched, but I was clear about that. At no point did I lie about my own hands-on experience. The next week they called; I beat out four other Commodore 64 programmers. It was time to fly to New Hampshire for the final interview.

I tried to act casual and wise, like I'd seen everything before, but I had never set foot in a game company office, so just being at Origin was a thrill. I was led into a conference room with nine other Apple II programmers. Seeing them didn't intimidate me. If one could be over-prepared for a test, I was as over-prepared as they came. I wanted this job. For me, this was less an interview than a party with members of my tribe. I knew everything about the Apple II the same way some kids know everything about their favorite sports team or band. In that room, I was with people who cared about programming, who loved games the way I did. For years, I had existed as a tribe of one (or two, counting Rob), studying and worshipping computers, games, and Apple IIs. Now, it felt like I was among my people. Gamers. Game developers. My future may have been hanging in the balance, but the interview was a fun, liberating experience.

Until this interview, I had no idea where I stood in comparison to other programmers, especially ones who worked inside the game industry. Working in solitude for eight years, I always felt behind, anxious the technology (and folks like Bill Budge and Nasir Gebelli) was outpacing me. I coded constantly and read everything I could get my hands on. This was the first time I would put my technical knowledge to the test, the first time I would see myself not in isolation, but comparatively. I also had no idea what a programmer interview was supposed to be like. Was I going to write code in front of them? Would they quiz me on 6502 opcodes? Would they give me buggy code and ask me to fix it? I had no idea.

I walked into the room and the nine programmers stared at me. Never before had I seen a group of programmers collected like this. I'd never seen nine programmers, period! My anxiety was being displaced by an overwhelming feeling of excitement. I could not wait for this to happen. *Let's do it. Ask me anything,* I thought. I didn't think there was anything they could ask that I didn't know. "Think," of course, is the operative word here. You never know what you don't know until someone asks it.

"Have a seat," John Fachini said. He was the project manager.

I took a seat. I wanted to start talking, but thought I should wait for the questions.

Steve Meuse went first. "So, you're here to do porting between the Apple II and the Commodore 64. Can you tell us about the similarities between the two computers?"

Where to even start? I didn't want to risk leaving anything out, so I started at the beginning.

"They are 8-bit computers that have 64K of RAM and a ROM bank that controls all the functions of the computer. There are special memory locations that control hardware specific to both computers. The Commodore has a 6510 CPU and the Apple II has a 6502 CPU, which means they both have the same instruction set, but the Commodore has an 8-bit bidirectional I/O port on the back."

No one stopped me, and so I kept going.

"The great news is that you can switch out the ROM and I/O on the Commodore, so you have a full 64K of memory. The Apple II has bank-switched memory that can also get you close to that, but you cannot switch out the $C000 range since that controls hardware. The C64 has a sixteen-color mode that can display even more colors than the Apple II, so I plan on using that. Really, most of the port would be handling input and graphics and sound output to maximize the Commodore hardware."

Nodding, the programmers pivoted: "We'd like to talk to you about your knowledge of 6502 assembly."

This was the moment that I was waiting for. I was so eager, and it showed.

"Ask me anything. Instructions, ROM locations, anything at all about the Apple II. I can answer anything."

Some of the older programmers smiled and looked at one another. *Sure, kid.*

And so they did. They asked me anything and everything. It was the most fun I'd had in weeks, talking with nine experts about a language I loved. I was so grateful for the experience and enjoying the conversation so much that I think I lost sight of it being an interview.

I found I could talk their talk and walk their walk. It was a watershed moment. I felt energized and liberated. Concerns I had about being behind the curve left me and were replaced by a drive to get ahead.

One perfectly timed coincidence helped set the mood for the interview: My new game, *Major Mayhem*, had been accepted by *Nibble* magazine. When they asked me what I'd been doing, it was a timely thing to mention, and it served as a lead-in to all the other games I'd created. Even though I was younger than everyone else in the room, just going through my games and the magazines that published them was a tangible way to communicate that I knew my stuff and let them know I could handle the work.

They offered me the job, and I accepted.

I was now part of the game industry—and that made my existence in the real world easier. Finding a good job was more important than ever because Kelly was pregnant. We decided to get married, at my parents' insistence and much to her parents' dismay, and then drove across the country to my new job.

I was barely twenty and bound for glory, or so I hoped, anyway. My starting salary? $22,000. It was a certainly a livable salary at the time, particularly since I would have done all of it for free. I was exactly where I wanted to be.

CHAPTER 7

An Origin Story

In early November 1987, we drove across America in tandem—Kelly in her Ford EXP and me in my Yugo—but it was not the road trip we'd envisioned. In Nevada, the heater in Kelly's car died, and we wound up switching back and forth between cars so we could both be warm some of the time. In Albany, the Ford's transmission died. We left the car there to get repaired and drove together, in a race against the clock. I was due in Manchester, New Hampshire, to start work the next day, and the truck delivering our stuff was arriving, too.

Nothing was easy back then. We didn't have a lot of support, fiscal or moral. One month earlier, when we'd decided to get married, Kelly's parents were not at all pleased. Mormons, generally speaking, don't believe in unwed couples cohabitating or having sex before marriage, and they were understandably upset about their daughter. On the other hand, we didn't think we were doing anything wrong. My parents liked Kelly, but they were quietly wary about two young, inexperienced, and underfunded kids building a life together. My mom never said as much, but Kelly was following in her footsteps by marrying a Romero straight out of high school, and Kelly, like my mom, got pregnant early on. I'm not sure if these similarities made my mom want to urge caution, or whether the similarities prevented her from saying anything because it might have sounded hypocritical. It wouldn't have mattered much. Once Kelly was pregnant, we wanted to get married. We went to city hall and took our vows and that was that.

I started at Origin in mid-November, the same week *Nibble* magazine splashed my game on the cover of its new issue. "MAJOR MAYHEM," read the featured headline, "Complete Type-in Arcade Action Space Adventure." The accompanying artwork showed our hero inside his rocket blasting out from the screen of an Apple II over the legs of a nasty tarantula. Puffy clouds of smoke—presumably from the rocket lifting off—poured out of the monitor and swirled around the spider and the rocket.

I had mentioned the game in my interview with Origin. Now it was out, and I was here. It was perfect timing, helping me cement a good reputation. My manager, John Fachini, was the lead coder on *Ultima V* for the PC, and he had programmed for PCs and the Apple II, so I was impressed with him. I had no experience coding PCs, but they were becoming a larger segment of the home computer market. Despite my love of Apple IIs, I recognized that Fachini was a programming badass, and I could learn from him. Fachini was happy to share; he was a great boss who explained the industry to me in terms of salaries and expectations, stuff that I had no way of knowing. For instance, he told me that $30,000 was the top pay for someone who did straight coding. He told me he made $45,000 because he was the lead coder and managing a couple projects. "The more responsibility you take on, the more money you'll be paid." He was only six years older than me, and we really clicked. We ate lunch together, discussed games, projects, and programming.

One night in December I was working late at the office and Robert Garriott, brother of Richard Garriott and cofounder of Origin, asked me to help him for a minute. It just so happened that Robert was having a meeting with Sir-Tech Software, publishers of *Wizardry*. The first *Wizardry* game came out the same year as *Ultima* and was just as influential in the role-playing game (RPG) universe. In my personal pantheon, it ranked as one of the most important computer games in history, and now somehow at 9 p.m. I was randomly meeting the company's cofounder, Robert Sirotek. With Robert was a game writer named Brenda Garno. She was just a year old than me, and she'd started at Sir-Tech as a teenager, running the *Wizardry* phone hotline. Like me, she was working her way up. It was nice to meet someone else who'd started in the industry as a teenager and who was into RPGs, too. When the meeting was over, she went back to northern New York, where Sir-Tech was based, but she'd made an impression.

I went back to my work for John, being a department of one, responsible for porting—re-coding a game built for one computer system to work on another. I started to examine *2400 A.D.*'s Assembly code for the Apple II, and my job was to convert it to run on the Commodore 64's hardware. It didn't take long for me to realize there must be a way to move the files from one machine to the other. In 1988, there were no standard interfaces between different computers, no compatible floppy disks, and no cross-platform APIs (application programming interfaces)—the intermediary programs that now allow different systems to share information seamlessly. If I couldn't move files between the two machines, I had to retype the Assembly language for the gameplay code and then write new code for the input/output (I/O) to make it work on the Commodore 64. Retyping all that Assembly wasn't an exciting option because the Commodore 64's keyboard was horrible compared to the Apple IIgs's keyboard.

I asked Fachini if there was a way to connect machines to move a lot of the code.

"We don't have anything like that here," he said. "Why don't you call the tech team in Austin and ask them."

I contacted the person who wrote software development tools in Austin, Alan Gardner, and got the same response: "We don't have anything like that."

"Well, what do you normally do for porting between systems?"

"We just re-create everything from scratch on the new computer."

That makes no sense, I thought. I can figure this out. I went to RadioShack and bought what I thought the job would require: a soldering iron, solder, some four-wire telephone cable, and a nine-pin D connector, which plugged into the Commodore 64's joystick port. For the Apple II, I got a sixteen-pin IC chip with two rows of eight pins that fit inside the computer. Back at the office, I soldered four wires to the IC chip. Then, I soldered the remaining four wires on the other end of the cable into the D pin connector. Once finished, I plugged it into the joystick port and plugged the sixteen-pin IC chip into the Apple IIgs motherboard. Now that the machines were connected—the Apple II I/O port connected to the Commodore joystick port—the Apple could send data to the Commodore. I had to write the code so the Commodore 64 would accept data, but it was a net time win for me. The Apple II was much faster than the Commodore, so I had to figure out what speed to send the data without causing the Commodore to lose any of the transfer.

As I was doing that, I discovered something about the Commodore 64— coding on it was physically painful. Commodore was a calculator company, and the 64 had calculator keys that were not ideal for sustained typing. The Apple IIgs keyboard, in comparison, was a thing of ergonomic beauty, even in 1988. It was low and sleek with shallow keys that didn't feel like I was pressing down on large buttons. I decided the most efficient course of action was to program the Commodore version of the game on the Apple IIgs, and then just use my new interface to send the program over to the Commodore. Years later, I found out Will Wright, creator of *The Sims*, did the same thing for one of his early games.

I finished this project in about four days. I showed it to Fachini and explained how it was programmed on the Apple IIgs and then transferred to the Commodore.

The next week, I got an 18 percent raise. My salary went from $22K to $26K. I had been there less than two months, and I was thrilled.

Kelly, thankfully, had a trouble-free pregnancy, but our timing for the actual birth was a little off, thanks in no small part to an arctic-level snowstorm that gripped the northeast US on February 13. As two kids from Northern California, we'd never seen anything like it. Concord, New Hampshire, just 20 minutes north of Londonderry, where we had settled, reported thirteen inches of snow on the ground. Snow and ice were everywhere when Kelly's contractions started getting faster. I rushed out to the car and found the doors frozen shut and the keyhole iced over. I heated the key to slot it in and turned the lock, but the door itself was still frozen. Finally, I put one foot up against the car and wrenched the door open. I got Kelly inside and poured windshield wiper fluid all over the window to melt the ice. We made it to the hospital, and twenty-four hours later, on Valentine's Day 1988, Michael Alfonso Romero made his entrance into the world.

I was a twenty-year-old father with a new job, but I made it a point to work 9 to 5 and come home and give Kelly some downtime. Unfortunately, Kelly didn't have a lot of other support. She'd barely been in town three months. She wasn't working, hadn't made any real friends, and our families were thousands of miles away.

In April, the project I was hired for at Origin was canceled. The game I was porting hadn't sold well in its Apple II incarnation, and the company figured it wouldn't sell well on other computers either, which seemed logical. I switched projects to a game called *Space Rogue*, a 3D flight-simulation game with RPG elements being developed by Paul Neurath. While I was working on it, John Fachini approached me. He was unhappy about the internal politics at Origin and asked me if I wanted to form a start-up. Whatever politics there were, they were over my head. I loved everything about Origin. He pitched me on forming a game company that would initially code ports and eventually build original games. He wanted me as his cofounder. My response was immediate: *Yeah, that would be awesome.* As much as I loved Origin, I was fresh off the *2400 A.D.* cancellation. What if they canceled *Space Rogue*, too? I couldn't afford to be out of a job now, especially with a new baby boy. Running my own company with another person I trusted would be a great learning experience. As a safeguard, I told John I couldn't leave unless my salary was guaranteed and equal to what I was making at Origin.

I didn't know when another opportunity like this might come along. Finding jobs in the 1980s, particularly in a fledgling industry, wasn't as simple as hopping on the internet. Most jobs were filled via word-of-mouth, advertisements in local papers, or listings in computer magazines. Résumés and cover letters were sent by mail, provided you knew the company and its address. So I took the chance I had, reasoning that it would be in our best long-term interest. I was willing to work hard to make sure we succeeded.

As it turned out, that "next chance" happened just a week later. Paul asked if I was interested in cofounding *his* new start-up after I shipped *Space Rogue*. Paul's studio, Blue Sky Productions, went on to create many seminal titles, most notably *Ultima Underworld*. Sometimes, I do wonder what might have happened if I had been paired with their amazing programmer Doug Church. Why didn't I join Paul? Two reasons. First, I gave John my word, and he had already started talking with potential clients for two ports. Second, I hadn't worked long with Paul and didn't know him as well as John. There was also a third reason, I suppose. Paul used the ORCA/M assembler, and I used Merlin 16, a much faster 6502 assembler. It took hours to assemble *Space Rogue* because it used ORCA/M, and I never understood why he wouldn't switch to the faster assembler. Paul used a lot of macros in his Assembly language, and macros take time for an assembler to interpret. Although its name was macro backward, ORCA/M was far slower at processing macros than Merlin. It's an odd reason not to join a start-up, I suppose, but these little details matter to programmers.

I left Origin without meeting my idol Richard Garriott, who worked out of the company's Austin office, just seven months after landing my dream job there.

The new company, Inside Out Software, began with promise. We got a business loan to buy John a 20Mhz 386DX, a state-of-the-art PC, for $5,000, and John signed a porting contract to translate the Apple II version of New World Computing's *Might & Magic II* to the PC and Commodore 64. I started working in John's apartment on his Apple IIgs and, after a couple months, we rented space down the street from Origin's offices.* Things were going great, and not just for the business, either. My wife was again pregnant, and we looked forward to expanding our little family. She missed her family back in California, though, and the pregnancy only increased that longing. She supported this New Hampshire journey of ours, and our new company, and we hoped for the best.

Before long, Inside Out Software had a relationship with Infocom to finish developing Brian Moriarty's *Timesync* (and move the Mac game to the PC), and to create an original game based on the 1979 movie *Alien*. We also got a conversion contract to move a great Mac game called *Dark Castle* to the Apple IIgs. With more conversion work coming in, we decided to hire more staff, a couple of coders to finish my *Might & Magic II* port, and I started on a new port called *Tower Toppler* (Commodore 64 to Apple II). For *Timesync* and *Alien*, we hired two artists. As

---

* We heard that Robert Garriott blocked us from renting next to Origin so we wouldn't hire its employees.

luck would have it, one of my friends at *UpTime*, Apple programmer Lane Roathe, told me he was looking for a new gig. Both Lane and my old editor at *UpTime*, Jay Wilbur, said that *UpTime* was hitting the skids. Lane immediately accepted our job offer and moved to Londonderry.

Lane and I had a real bond. We both loved programming, games, and Apple IIs. Lane, though, was much more of a purist than I was. He hated PCs with a vengeance, and his contempt rubbed John the wrong way. John was agnostic on the PC versus Apple question. It didn't help that John was coping with business growth issues at the time and didn't want Lane's negativity in the office. In less than a month, the relationship between my partner and my pal became toxic. Eventually, Lane had had enough and quit, which was a fatal blow for the *Dark Castle* port. We needed an Apple IIgs programmer, and Lane was a total pro. Adding fuel to the fire: John delayed paying Lane's final check, and Lane filed a complaint with the Better Business Bureau, something no start-up company wants. Then Lane placed a call to Three-Sixty Pacific, the company that hired us to port *Dark Castle*.

"I'm the guy who was handling your game, and I just quit," Lane told them. "How about you guys transfer the contract to me?"

This sent John over the edge.

"You brought this fucking guy into the company, and he's screwed us!" he yelled at me.

"Don't get mad at me because you drove him away, and we don't have the person to do the contract."

"He just stole our client!"

"John, if you think about it, Lane actually just did us a favor. We don't *have anyone to do that work*. If he didn't take it, we would have blown our deadline, for sure."

Things were tense in the office after that, and in February, they got grimmer when the *Tower Toppler* client canceled their porting contract. I had been in the industry for fifteen months, and this was now the second canceled project I'd worked on. *Was this normal for the industry?* I wondered. The answer was no. I realized that the computer industry was undergoing a shift. An entire generation of computers that limited a unit of data to eight bits was about to go the way of the dinosaurs. Computers like the Apple II had lasted longer than they should have—most likely because they were the first generation of a new technology. The PC, introduced in 1981 by IBM, had a 16-bit processor. The additional power and lower cost of these machines translated into growing sales. The market for the computer Lane and I loved was shrinking and destined to become obsolete.

I knew I needed to bite the bullet and become fluent in PC programming as quickly as possible. That old feeling and fear of falling behind returned. John was

stressed by financial pressures and his own personal issues. I decided to seize
the initiative.

"John, my project is canceled," I said. "That was money we needed to pay me
and run the business. I know we're partners, but I think this is going to be easier for
both of us if I sign over all my shares of the company to you, and I'll just move on."

That marked the end of my first "real" start-up. I had tried to make my own
luck and failed within nine months, largely due to factors beyond my control: the
computer industry's evolution—which I probably should have seen coming—and
the personality clash between John and Lane. Both these things were valuable
learning experiences, as all failures are. *In the future*, I told myself, *I need to think
about game development from a broader perspective, one that factored in technology trends like increased processing power and the new computers that really drove
the industry*. I also needed to safeguard any companies I founded by making
sure our revenue stream was diverse and not able to be so easily wiped out (this
desire to grow the business—to have multiple streams of income—influenced
me heavily during the later id Software years). I also needed to remember that
not everyone had grown up with an Alfonso Romero or John Schuneman in their
life. I survived by trying to avoid creating friction with others and steering clear
of disagreements that didn't involve me. That was one of my survival strategies.
I needed to either pick better partners or be a bit more proactive in helping iron
out workplace differences.

Tower Toppler's toppling created a cascade of issues at home, too. Kelly was
eight months pregnant now, and more than anything, we needed stability. Life in
Londonderry was lonely for her without her mother and father, and she wanted
them around when she gave birth. So she moved back to her parents' house in
Folsom, California, to have the baby while I figured out our next steps. Michael,
of course, went with her.

Just fifteen months earlier, I'd been on top of the world, living out my dreams
and planning for our future. Everything seemed possible. Fortunately, I didn't bottom out into despair. I just needed to make something happen. My other survival
strategy—solving problems to eliminate friction—needed to kick in.

CHAPTER 8

PC Conversion

I was out of a job, away from my family, and also out of an apartment, so I moved into Lane's place. We were good friends, and I didn't have any hard feelings over him leaving Inside Out Software. After all, we didn't know he and John would clash. I worked on the graphics for *Dark Castle*, taking the black-and-white art and converting it to sixteen-color SuperRes to help him finish the porting job. We named our impromptu company Ideas from the Deep. Our lives revolved around game development and metal, and so, from morning to night, we made games while listening to Skid Row, Dokken, and Mötley Crüe. In the meantime, I was searching for my next gig.

As it turned out, Jay Wilbur had left *UpTime* and told me he was interviewing for a gig at a software subscription company in Shreveport, Louisiana, called *Softdisk* that shipped monthly disks full of software to subscribers. I had seen them at AppleFest in 1987. It sounded interesting, and I needed a job. At the time, I was naive enough to think anyone could just call up a company and ask to speak to its top brass about a job. So that's exactly what I did: called *Softdisk* and asked to speak to the president of the company. Unbelievably, I got through.

"This is Al Vekovius."

"Hi, my name is John Romero."

"Oh yeah, I've heard about you."

Wow, I thought. *That's good news*. Turns out Al had hired *UpTime*'s editor in chief, Mike Amarello. He had sung the praises of Jay and his old crew. Jay mentioned me to Al, because I was his primary game provider at *UpTime*, sending him stuff every month.

I plowed ahead. "I'm calling because I'm interested in working at *Softdisk*. I really want to learn the PC and write games for it."

"Our PC disk is our biggest moneymaker."

"If you need someone to program, especially games, I think I'd be a good fit. I used to work for Origin, and I sold a lot of games to *UpTime* and *inCider* and other magazines."

"Oh, Origin? Wow. Great. That's impressive. How about I send you a plane ticket for this weekend? You can see the company, check out Shreveport, and we can meet."

"That would be awesome. By the way, I don't know if you need anyone else, but I'm living with a great programmer. His name's Lane Roathe, and he used to work at *UpTime*, too."

"Okay, I'll send two tickets."

Lane called Jay to tell him that we were heading down to Shreveport, the same weekend Jay was heading there for his interview. While some deep grooves of talent and companies existed in the tech hubs around Boston and San Francisco, in the early days of the game industry there were smaller tech companies scattered everywhere, so finding one in Louisiana didn't seem odd to me. I was excited to meet the *Softdisk* team and to sell them on what we could do.

Lane and I flew down to Shreveport and met with Al. Or "Big Al," as the six-foot-plus boss was often affectionately called. A mathematician who was the former head of the computing department at LSU's medical school in Shreveport, Big Al was an impressive character with an open, warm demeanor. He still taught at the school as an adjunct while he ran *Softdisk*.

Big Al and his cofounders hit on a compelling model to distribute computer disks with preinstalled software tailored to specific computer systems via subscription. Previously, computer magazines like *Nibble* contained code for random programs in each issue. Subscribers got an issue and typed in the code for each program they were interested in. Now, they popped in a *Softdisk* floppy, started browsing, and used the content immediately. Like those early programming mags, there was little rhyme or reason to the content in any given *Softdisk* release—a mortgage calculator, a biorhythm calculator, clip art, a puzzle, a daily planner. Games were a rarity, as they had been for the early magazines. If I had any say in the matter, I would make sure *Softdisk* had games in as many issues as possible.

The company's biggest title was *Big Blue Disk*—a pointed reference to IBM's nickname, Big Blue, that telegraphed the content: all the programs were for PCs. With 50,000 subscribers, each putting down $87 a year, *Softdisk*'s model was good from my perspective. I can't imagine it cost more than $2 to manufacture and mail each disk. Most of the software on the disks was submissions from external "authors," the title *Softdisk* used to refer to software developers. The internal authors took the external submissions, made them professional, fixed bugs, and got them fit for public release. *Softdisk* didn't want to talk to me about that, though. They brought me down to Louisiana to lead a newly created Special Projects Division with the sole purpose of making games, and not just small games for their monthly disks, either. The Special Projects Division was all about big games like the ones that Origin made.

Al understood the appeal of gaming. He made clear he was interested in adding that to *Softdisk*'s arsenal of releases during our talk. I explained that I needed to get up to speed on PCs to develop games, and he was okay with that. He took us on a tour of Shreveport, too. I think he worried that we wouldn't like it, but after two winters in New Hampshire, I loved the town's steamy climate and Cross Lake on the west side of town. Al also threw a big party at his house during our visit, and we got to meet a lot of the staff. Everyone was friendly and welcoming. Afterward, Jay and Lane remarked how cool everyone seemed. Months later, we learned it was all an act; the programmers were terrified that these three East Coast gunslingers were going to come in and take everyone's job, but the fact was, nobody's job was at risk at the time. Al offered each of us $27,000; we accepted; nobody got fired.

Jay, Lane, and I flew back East. We had two weeks before we were due in Shreveport, so we decided to take advantage of that time. Lane and I got to work on *ZAPPA ROIDZ*, an *Asteroids*-like game. I made the Apple II version while Lane got busy with the Apple IIgs. We finished within the week, and promptly sold them to *Softdisk* under our company name, Ideas from the Deep.

With a job secured, I was excited to get my family under one roof, and it was not a minute too soon—Kelly was going into labor. I hopped a flight to California and welcomed my second son, Steven Patrick. Like Michael, he was a beautiful baby, and I felt an incredible mix of pride and pressure to make sure that my family was secure and cared for. While there, I shared the exciting news about *Softdisk* and tried to sell Kelly on moving to Shreveport. She agreed to give it a try. It was a different world then without text or video calls or email. Home computers were a relative rarity still and long-distance calls were expensive and reserved for important things like "I'm going into labor." Prior to my visit home, we exchanged only letters. There was so much to tell her, and it was a lot for Kelly to take in. I spent some wonderful time with Kelly, Steven, and Michael before heading back to New Hampshire to pack up my stuff at Lane's while Kelly recuperated from the delivery.

There wasn't much to pack in New Hampshire: a bed, a stereo, and a TV, as well as my computer, its manuals, and some clothing. I also had amassed a few boxes of personal papers that contained everything from source code to drawings to acceptance or rejection letters for every game I had created to date. Movers came to collect our stuff, and Lane, Jay, and I hit the road. I faced an enormous learning curve when I arrived in Shreveport. I was determined to learn every byte of the PC, just like I did with the Apple II, in a matter of months. I'd been programming for about ten years at this point, which gave me confidence, but the architecture of the PC was completely different than the Apple II. The biggest challenges were grasping the ins and outs of the 8086 16-bit processor. The PC had more sophisticated hardware than the Apple II and could address 640K of RAM, which meant I could write bigger games. While it used Assembly language, it was a different Assembly language written specifically to the computer's processor. Conceptually, there were similarities, but the instruction sets, or the words used to tell the CPU what to do, were completely different. It was like learning a new coding language, though easier for me since I already knew several.

I dug in to face the challenge of learning a brand-new computer with its new hardware and instruction set, and I was excited to do it. A pattern became apparent to me then, a pattern that continues to this day: Technology reinvents itself. As critical as it was to get ahead, the best one could ever do was to get there first and excel at the new technology.

That first month in Shreveport, Jay took over as editor of *Softdisk Apple II* and *Softdisk G-S* while Lane and I got to work as the sole members of the new Special Projects Division. Lane got to work on a new, small game for *Softdisk G-S* while I started a deep dive into PC programming that rivaled my days of manic focus converting my main programming language from BASIC into Assembly as a fifteen-year-old. The PC market was growing, and I needed to be part of it to succeed. When it came to programming, I was competitive. The drive to be an exceptional programmer was still all-consuming for me, but at this stage, my thirst was, in part, fueled by a combination of my unflagging passion for games and the pressure I felt to develop a career so I could support my growing family.

I spent every minute poring over magazines, books, and manuals to embed PC programming knowledge in my brain. You can only learn so much from books, though. As I picked up the fundamentals, I realized learning is always better when it's project based. My hands wanted to code, not turn pages. So I took an Apple II game the company had published already and ported it to the PC using Pascal, which I had learned at Sierra College. Pascal was not the optimal language for games, but it worked and was quick and easy. In porting the game, I didn't want to be creative and consider its design. I wanted to devote all of my brain to learning the tech as fast as I could. Sometimes, the different sides of my brain work independently like that. When I showed it to Bob Napp, the *Big Blue Disk* editor, he said, "Oh my god, a game! Our users love games." So I ported games during my learning process and gave them to *Big Blue Disk*.

I kept at it. The next month, I dug up *Twilight Treasures*, the game I'd sold to *Nibble* magazine in 1986, and used Assembly language and Pascal to convert it to PC. I wrote all the game logic in Pascal and the graphics drawing code in 8086 assembly language to speed up the game's graphics drawing. That went into the next *Big Blue Disk* release. In addition to games, I was also writing tools for *Big Blue Disk*, again to increase my knowledge. The more I programmed, the faster I learned. My goal was to write a game fully in Assembly. I'd be as close to the machine as possible then, and ready to code a big game for the Special Projects Division. Of course, the *Big Blue Disk* editor loved all the content. Surprisingly, another editor suggested I curtail my submissions a bit, saying, "I know you're eager, but they're going to continue to expect this." I blasted heavy metal and spent some of my time writing stuff other than games, like game reviews and articles that were also included on each disk.

One of the key players on the *Big Blue Disk* production team was a forty-five-year-old programmer named George Leritte, who had mastered 8086 Assembly language. After a month there, I had learned Assembly, too, but obviously I still had gaps in my knowledge of PC hardware. One day, I hit a wall on a tool program; it lacked a critical piece of technical information about the PC, and I couldn't figure out how to solve the issue. Naturally, I asked George.

"I don't know."

"Come on, George. This seems like something you would know."

"Yeah, no. Sorry."

"Where can I find the information? I'm trying to get this program done to get published on *your* disk. It's going to be great."

"I don't know what to tell you."

I thought he was lying. I couldn't understand why he clammed up at first. Then I realized I was less than half his age, and I was infringing on his territory. Maybe he felt threatened, which is ironic because I had zero interest in coding for *Big Blue Disk*. All my interest in programming was so I could make games. Maybe he was just pulling my leg.

Two days later, George came by my desk and said, "I found this program that does what I think you need."

"Great," I said. "Where's the source code for it?"

"I don't know."

"I need to know exactly what it's doing."

"I just found it."

Of course, I found out later he'd written the program. He knew exactly what I needed to know, but he wasn't going to tell me. I finally dug up the solution myself, locating the technical information in a PC magazine, and finished the program. Then I stomped over to Bob Napp and told him what had happened.

"This is ridiculous," I said. "I'm doing this stuff for you."

Instead of advocating for me, Napp came back and said: "New rule: Don't ask George any questions."

"*What?*"

"You are not allowed to ask George any questions."

I was dumbfounded.

But I wasn't deterred. In fact, I was ready. The previous month while quarreling with George, I had finished *Pyramids of Egypt* for *Big Blue Disk*. It was written fully in Assembly language, and I felt that I had an expert-level understanding of the PC and its architecture.

Lane and I got together to kick off the Special Projects Division's first big game: *Eskimo Jo*, a *Bomberman*-type game, but on ice. After two weeks of work, however, we got a message: The Special Projects Division was killed. I was needed full time on *Big Blue Disk* to fill the lull in content that I had inadvertently created. Lane, meanwhile, went back to the *Softdisk G-S* division. We were crushed.

At the end of my first year, I was finished learning the PC, and I was finished trying to help a department that had a grumpy lead programmer who wouldn't allow me to ask him questions to help the product he was supporting. It was precisely the opposite of the excitement I felt when I considered the opportunities before us. I was also not making the kind of games I wanted to make—bigger games than my old Apple II games, games that took a year to make and would be displayed on store shelves. Although I'd mastered the PC, I wasn't doing what I wanted to do or what Al originally hired me to do: Make big games.

"Al," I said, "thanks for having me here. It's been amazing. I've been here for a year, learned the PC and cranked tons of stuff out, but I need to leave. I want to make games."

"Wait wait wait, John. Hold on!" Al stammered. "We can solve this. I don't think you have to go anywhere."

"I'd love to stay. I really appreciate you hiring me, but if I'm not making games here, I'm going to LucasArts." I hadn't contacted anyone at George Lucas's gaming division, but it was the first choice on my list of plan Bs.

"Let me see what I can do. I'll get back to you within the week."

A few days later, Al came back to talk.

"How about we start a subscription disk where you're making a game every month?"

"One game a month is impossible. Unless you want really shitty games," I said.

"All the other titles are monthly. I guess we could try every other month."

"Two months would be amazing, and if I could actually have a team—an artist and another programmer—that would be perfect." It was a big ask to go from one to four (including a managing editor, *Softdisk*'s title for a producer), but I knew that I could make much better games if I had help.

It took Al a few months to make it happen, but he did it. He walked by, and with a big smile on his face said, "Get ready to hire your team for *PCRcade*!"*

He believed in me and had the vision to see how important games were. I was completely stoked. I asked Lane if he'd be interested in being the editor/manager, and he thought that would be cool (he still wasn't interested in learning the PC). Then I asked Jay if he had any suggestions for a game programmer, and he told me about a kickass whiz kid who provided Apple II games and had even begun porting them to PC. There was only one problem: *Softdisk* had already tried to recruit him twice, and he had turned down those offers. The elusive programmer was named John Carmack.

I'd played Carmack's game *Tennis*, which I liked, and I also knew he'd made an RPG called *Dark Designs*. The perspective view of the gameplay in *Tennis* was of particular interest to me, as it offered a tilted side view, showing that he had physics working on an Apple II, which was a rare thing in games at that time. Further, it featured fluid animation. I knew that this was the work of a great programmer.

"Jay, can you call him again?"

"He's not interested," he told me. "Like I said, we've tried."

If he was a game programmer like me—and everything pointed in that direction—I could see why he might not be interested. After all, I had just threatened to leave.

"I think he would be interested in working with another game programmer," I said, remembering about how I felt working with the Origin coders for the first time.

"We'll try it, but he said he wasn't interested, and was happy to keep doing what he was doing."

"Tell him that he'll be coming here to make games and to join another experienced game programmer. I think that will make a difference." I hoped so, anyway.

It turns out that I was right. At the time, meeting another game programmer was like finding a needle in a haystack. I couldn't imagine why he wouldn't want to do it, because I had been in his shoes. And, as luck would have it, Carmack was looking for something more stable than the sporadic pay his freelance game developer lifestyle gave him.

We invited him down to Shreveport for an interview. Carmack liked to drive and had spent money fixing up his clunky MGB, so a road trip from his home in Kansas City to Shreveport didn't seem like a bad idea. He told me later that he fully expected to turn *Softdisk* down again, that this "other experienced game programmer" would turn out to be a myth, but it couldn't hurt to listen.

---

* PCRcade was the working title for what would become Gamer's Edge.

Big Al took us all out to dinner at the Italian Garden—Jay, Lane, Carmack, and me. When Carmack and I met, it was an absolute meeting of like minds. He was a fresh-faced nineteen-year-old who looked like he had yet to shave. I was all of twenty-two. I eventually discovered that we came from different sides of the tracks—his family was far more affluent than mine—but as we talked that evening, it was almost as if we had inhabited parallel lives when it came to games and programming, having both spent thousands of hours mastering our three obsessions: games, computers, programming. When I say "thousands of hours," I mean that literally.

Over the course of my life, I have bonded with programmers, including some of the most legendary figures in games and computer design, from Steve Wozniak to Bill Budge to Nasir Gebelli and others. However, on that first meeting, Carmack and I instantly connected on multiple levels because we shared a deep knowledge base and passion that creates instant bonds; we understood each other and the significance of our respective work, and we admired each other's abilities. We spoke a language that, while rooted in normal, everyday English, was unique. We saw a world of possibility in games, and we knew we had the knowledge and drive to master it. We saw that in each other. It's hard to describe how it felt. Imagine caring deeply about something, so deeply that you feel compelled to master it. Imagine no one around you gets it—not your family, not your partner, not your friends. Not really. Imagine meeting someone else just like you for the first time. That's what it felt like when we met each other.

Jay and Al spent the whole night listening to a nonstop stream of programmer-speak that was all game programming techniques at a totally granular level. Which assembler did you use on the Apple II? Did you use the TASM assembler for the 8086 on the PC? Do you know C? Have you written double hi-res code on the Apple II? How much do you know about DOS 3.3 or ProDOS? Have you memorized the memory map of the Apple II? Have you done any BIOS programming on the PC? Have you written any TSRs? And on and on. Carmack, Lane, and I were kings of the Apple II, but from today's perspective, we were kings of the computer stone age. Our machines were unbelievably primitive compared to the modern computer—they had minimal memory and limited processing power, so everything, as a rule, ran slow. A good game requires speed, and that meant we had to optimize the hell out of our games. Today, you can run code on a modern computer that is capable of running at a speed of 5 billion cycles *per second*. You can make a lightning-fast game without knowing a line of assembly code. In 1988, programmers were working with 32-bit microprocessors that ran 33 million cycles per second, not multiple billions, and we still had to write code that put each and every pixel on the screen as fast as possible. To get that speed required Assembly language. That block of code did all the graphics work, and when we constructed it, we needed to use maximum efficiency and logic, every coding trick, to build the fastest, most reactive games. The CPU executed the code, the graphics card on your machine displayed it, and let the gameplay start. Today, the majority of graphics processing is handled by a graphics card, not by game programmers trying to directly put dots on the screen.

We were members of an unofficial secret society that studied the same sacred texts, knew the best hacks, and enjoyed the same rituals. Our chatter started with a discussion of Apple IIs and moved on to processors and PCs, which Lane couldn't contribute to, because he stopped learning with the Apple IIgs. We riffed on video games that had impressed and inspired us, detoured to *Dungeons & Dragons*, and shared our mutual love of tricks to speed up our code.

Eventually, other parallels between us surfaced. Like me, Carmack was a huge comics fan as a kid. He went to college for a year and hated it. He had parents who derided his passion for games. I had more experience on PCs than Carmack, but he told me something that impressed the hell out of me during our first chat. He realized that if he took an Apple II game that he'd sold to *Softdisk* and converted it to PC, he'd more than double his money since *Big Blue Disk* paid more for PC games than *Softdisk* did for Apple II games. One month, he was low on cash, having moved out on his own, so he rented a PC for a week, learned how to program it, converted his game, and then returned the rental.

"Dude, that is genius!" I said. That innovation totally appealed to my roots as a freelance game developer, and the fact that he had learned the PC in one week was seriously impressive.

I spun my idea for *Gamer's Edge*, which was the name that had replaced *PCRcade.*[*] I wanted to crank out top-shelf computer games that were better than anything on the market. I'd spent a year broadening my PC knowledge base, and now, with another top coder, I could finally start to fulfill my life's mission: making the most fun and engaging, best-looking games possible.

Games I wanted to play.

Although Jay had warned us that Carmack was a lone wolf, I didn't get that feeling at all. It felt like two of us—Carmack and me—were in total alignment. He was an animated, extremely knowledgeable programmer who would be an asset on any team. He later told people that my thorough understanding of the PC and graphic design and art skills were what swayed him to join us. I knew things he didn't. Given his all-consuming mania for game programming, that was the deciding factor.

He took the job, and I was beyond excited. I was even more excited when I saw Carmack in action. He could and would sit for hours and hours studying and coding.

---

[*] A trademark search revealed that PCRcade was already in use.

Like me, he didn't smoke, drink, or do drugs. Unlike me, he didn't have a family or even a girlfriend. He lived alone, which meant he could spend every minute of every day poring over the PC. And that's what he did. The only time he wasn't programming was when he slept or walked to our office refrigerator to get another Coke. He was in boot camp, working 24/7, trying to learn as much as possible about PCs.

It was incredible to watch someone else besides me run a programming ultramarathon. The three of us set up our office for serious work: In addition to Intel 386 PCs provided by Big Al, we invested in a fridge, a microwave, and a Nintendo Entertainment System (NES). We liked metal, so we cranked our favorite tunes. Our eyes were locked on code, on books, on magazines, downloading it all into our heads. Carmack and I shared information with each other, teaching techniques picked up along our solo paths. We didn't do this because we had to. We did this because we wanted to. If you've ever stayed up far too late because you were playing a game, bingeing a series, or reading a book, code had the exact same effect on us. Learning more was its own reward.

If I was fast, together we were super-fast. Carmack's ability to understand and retain knowledge of systems, programming patterns, algorithms, and computer languages equaled mine. I had never worked with anyone like me before, and he had never worked with anyone like him. It was amazing. Educators have called me a child prodigy with code—and I suppose I was. It also helped that I had hyperthymesia. Carmack was unquestionably gifted, too, but in a different, deeply analytical way, synthesizing information and using it to innovate technically. His solution to problem-solving was lodged in his unique ability to upload programming systems knowledge into his brain and allow it to gestate and cross-pollinate at high speed. Like me, he was also competitive with code. He wanted to be the best. Whatever I knew, he was going to learn it, and learn even more. I also thought critically about design; what gameplay patterns, not just technical algorithms, could we make with code? I was fascinated and sometimes awestruck by evolutions in game design, always thinking what a new play pattern or technology might be capable of, not just when it first appeared, but for the future. What could we do with it? We had zero regard for its known horizons. Our strengths were perfectly paired. We were eager to make games do things they had never done before.

Looking back, I believe these traits were the essential keys to our future collaborations: his desire to push game tech and my desire to push game design through tech. But the magic, I think, was rooted in our joint understanding of code and trust of each other. Because I was a coder, I knew what was theoretically possible with code and was therefore able to push the horizons of game design. I trusted Carmack implicitly; if he said it was possible, it happened. Carmack trusted my design vision. If I said it would be fun, he trusted that, and knew I would make it happen. Great tech without great design is just an interesting exercise.

Great design without great tech (or at least the right tech) fails. I'm getting ahead of myself here, but the point I want to make now was that Carmack's growth as a game programmer was breathtaking.

It was a lucky thing to have Carmack around in July 1990, because Big Al came in one day and announced that we would need to launch two games on the *Gamer's Edge* sampler disk, insisting it would lure subscribers. "And I need them in one month," he added.

The sampler disk would be sent to all 50,000 of *Big Blue Disk*'s subscribers. We planned to develop two games in *two* months for the sampler as soon as we got the green light to start work. The office had yet to be set up for our team, and we didn't even have the computers we needed to create the games.

"A month? I thought we had two months once you guys were ready?"

"It took them longer to get the publishing works set up, but we'd like to keep that launch date since we have already advertised it to our customers," he said.

We absorbed the impact of what this announcement meant. This was not ideal. As far as I was concerned, the company's future was also my *only* future, at least in the short term. Kelly and I were getting divorced. I knew she was getting increasingly homesick. Shreveport was not for her, and she wanted the support system of her family in California. I could have moved back to California, but even that wouldn't have saved the marriage. During our early separation, we had grown apart. She had become accustomed to a life without me. I had become accustomed to pouring myself into my games and focusing on my career. It was a difficult time for us, but I was determined to care and to provide for them.

Fortunately, I knew how to harness my abilities to do that, and kept my mind busy trying to accommodate Big Al's request. The plan—I dubbed it "the death schedule"—was to work from 10 a.m. to 2 a.m. We realized the quickest solution was for us to repurpose previous work. In 1988, I'd made an Apple II game that *UpTime* had published called *Dangerous Dave in the Deserted Pirate's Hideout!* And I decided to rewrite it for the PC. Meanwhile, Carmack decided to rewrite his Apple II game *Catacomb*. As for Lane, he was going to interface with the production team and work on specific assignments that needed to be executed in parallel.

There was a kind of competitive aspect to tackling an impossible task, one that, in a sense, defined my work with Carmack. Amped on cans of Coke and fueled by pizza, we did the impossible. We launched ourselves into the unknown, driven by the knowledge that no one had done what we were about to do, confident we would come out successful on the other side. With Big Al, we were also driven by inhumanly tight deadlines. In hindsight, we certainly could have said, "No way, Al," but we never considered it. Our competitive natures caused us to think of it as work-intensive adventure, akin to the greatest adventures in our future *D&D* campaigns, which required endurance, risk, and suffering, but ultimately ended in triumph. The death schedule had all that and more. Carmack and I didn't look at this as an unreasonable imposition by Big Al. We looked at it as a challenge.

With those early grinds, living on the death schedule, we learned a lot about each other. Where we had come from and things we'd endured. About how games and coding fit into our lives. Our successes and the interesting places our respective obsessions had taken us as well, like accepting every job that came my way in high school and then working in a sweatshop so I could buy my own Apple IIe after graduation.

Carmack had taken his obsession with tech a few steps further than I had—and synthesized information he might have been better off ignoring. When he was fourteen, he learned that thermite paste could burn through glass. Using this information, he hatched a plan for an Apple II heist. He applied the paste to a window at his high school, removed part of a pane, and crawled into the room. His larger accomplice, however, was unable to fit through the burned-out hole. He snaked his arm through the gap to unlock and open the window, setting off a silent alarm. They were caught red-handed, and Carmack was sentenced to reformatory school.

I had done exceedingly risky, dangerous stuff as a kid, too, including shooting out windows of neighboring homes. "What the hell was I thinking," I told him, "shooting out the windows of our neighbors' trailers?" As far as I could tell, Carmack was reliable. He took on assignments and delivered. We were both proud of each other's work. I had zero reservations about my new friend. In fact, we had nothing but high hopes for what we could do together.

I did, however, have questions about my pal Lane. It seemed to me that his head was not in the game. A lot of the disconnect probably had to do with his loathing of the PC, but he was also working as a roadie for a local metal band. Whatever the reason, he just couldn't muster the drive and do what needed to be done. At the start of this project, I assigned Lane a task to write a program to compress some of our files. It wasn't a huge job, but it was a necessary one. I checked in with him on day ten, and he said he hadn't done it. I checked five days later and got the same answer. Finally, Carmack and I had both finished our games and Lane still hadn't written the code.

I was steamed.

"I'll just do it now," Carmack said.

Thirty minutes later, Carmack was finished.

I wanted to get Lane off the *Gamer's Edge* team and replace him with Tom Hall, who worked on the Apple II team. I hadn't really worked closely with Tom before, but I had seen him around the office and took an instant liking to him. He was just an incredibly funny, friendly guy, offering up hilarious turns of phrase and game titles. It was also apparent that he was smart. He understood every game reference, was happy to have in-depth discussions on game mechanics, and knew how to code in Assembly. As I got to know him, I realized he was probably the most creative person I had ever met. He was a gamer who had finished college and put his programming degree to use by writing tons of games. He understood game design and the elements of games—from character names to sound effects to narrative flow—and had an overactive imagination. My first attempt to draft Tom was nixed by Big Al, but Tom became a regular presence in the *Gamer's Edge* office anyway.

After Carmack and I finished the death schedule—with a day or two to spare—we had two months to design the next game. We also had a new member, a guy with an easy-to-remember last name: Adrian Carmack. Adrian and John were not related. Adrian, a Shreveport native, was interning in the *Softdisk* art department and earning about $5 an hour. All I knew about him at first was that he had really long hair and seemed about our age. One day, I approached him.

"Hey, you listen to metal, right?"

"Oh, yeah. Metal." He was soft spoken and seemed reserved.

"Metallica?"

"Yeah, Metallica, Pantera, Slayer."

"Cool. Do you want to do some art for computer games?"

"Huh? Sure. If my boss says it's okay, then sure."

I went to Adrian's boss and told him that Al said I could pick someone from the art department for *Gamer's Edge*, and Adrian would be joining my department in a month. As it turned out, that turned into a surprising accusation about poaching staff, which I thought was ridiculous because he was *an intern*, not a full-time staffer. Giving people opportunities to grow is the whole point of an intern program. Thankfully, it got worked out, and I'm glad it did. Adrian had excellent fine arts skills, an affection for horror and gore that outstripped my own, and a work ethic that matched ours. He worked his ass off to learn how to create graphics for computers.

On the weekends or when we needed a break, we bonded over *Dungeons & Dragons*. When Carmack moved from Kansas City, he brought his most prized possession: a huge wooden table. It sat ten people, and its exclusive purpose was for programming and playing *D&D*. Right after finishing the sampler disk, Carmack introduced us to his campaign, which he had been running for several years. Carmack was the dungeon master, and Tom, Jay, and I rolled new level-one characters.

Carmack led us through his eerie, dark fantasy world full of demons, mysterious places, ultrapowered beings, political intrigue, and much more. He was an excellent dungeon master and loved crafting campaigns. I admired his abilities to design gameplay for us within the *D&D* system, which was, at the time, a shadow of what it would eventually become. This was the beginning of a pattern for us that would continue in the future as we grew closer and more united: Make games during the week and play games on the weekend.

The new game we decided to build was called *Slordax*, a fun space-shooter game in the spirit of *Xevious*. Before we got started, Carmack and I discussed how we could divide up the work. Time was always an issue, and we wanted to work as efficiently as possible. At that point, I was the more experienced game programmer, and *Gamer's Edge* was my operation. So, knowing projects always go better when people are working on what's most interesting to them, I asked him what he was most interested in working on. Carmack said he was really into the architecture of the code and wanted to handle that. He also said he was interested in graphics and wanted to learn more about that.

"Fine," I said. "You do that stuff, and I'll handle everything else."

"Everything else," as it turned out, was a lot more work. It's designing the game, which means envisioning the overview of the game. What's the object? What happens? What are the rules? What do players see? What do they do? It's the art direction, planning the levels, writing the tools to make levels, then making the levels. It's producing the game itself: taking all the pieces of the game—text files, image files, sound files, data files, and more—so they can be put on a disk that players can pop into their computer. I was too excited about *Slordax* to care about the uneven workload. I wanted Carmack to write kickass code that pulled all the elements together to make *Slordax* the fastest, best game around.

We wanted players to have a feeling of traveling through space. To do that, we needed the backgrounds to move, smoothly scrolling down the screen as our spaceship flew ahead to give the illusion of flying forward. Creating this effect meant the background images on the screen all had to update and refresh continually, basically sixty times a second. We had to find a way of doing this smoothly the way the NES did it. Considering our options, Carmack and I discussed methods of scrolling vertical backgrounds. One of the most important things I did after that discussion was give Carmack a book I'd bought. It was called *Power Graphics Programming*, written by Michael Abrash and published that year. I'd only browsed through half of it, but I thought it might be fuel for his knowledge quest.

I didn't realize I was putting him directly on the path to game development heaven, but I'd done exactly that. *Power Graphics Programming* provided the keys to the computer graphics kingdom. Abrash was the first author to unlock the mysteries of something called Cathode Ray Tube Control (CRTC) registration. His book described how programmers altered the location in graphics memory where the CRT started displaying graphics.[*] Changing that value allowed us to simulate scrolling. Beyond the information in Abrash's book, Carmack added his own techniques to make the scrolling even smoother by reducing the amount of

---

[*] A deeper explanation is beyond the scope of this book. However, Abrash's book goes into extensive detail, for those interested.

drawing he needed to do. He did this by remembering only the areas that needed to be updated, and drawing only in those areas instead of the entire screen.

Building *Slordax* and nearing the final stages, Carmack showed me his CRTC experiments. They were extraordinary. I had never seen a computer game with smoother vertical scrolling. This wasn't just moving one line of graphics down the screen to the next line—it was smoothly scrolling at a hardware level like NES. *Gamer's Edge* was going to shock the industry with this. I told John this was terrific, but I knew the real win wasn't a smooth vertical scroll but instead a smooth, limitless horizontal scroll.

The world loved *Super Mario Bros.* I loved *Super Mario Bros.* Action games depended on smooth movement, and gaming systems like the one Nintendo created to run *Super Mario Bros.* had the computing power to shed the static screen. New backgrounds unspooled seamlessly behind a character as they moved, or in Mario's case, bounced, to the left or the right. I believed that horizontal scrolling was a key to visual storytelling, expanding the player's world around them. I knew matching the smooth scrolling of dedicated gaming systems would revolutionize PC games. I didn't explain my thinking to Carmack then. I just tossed off the comment. As he worked on vertical scrolling, I just wanted him to keep horizontal scrolling in mind. Both of us liked to work toward challenges.

Slordax was a total team effort. Tom Hall came up with the name, wrote the story, created half the levels, and had suggestions for what some of the enemies might look like. Adrian did a great job creating all the art for the game, except for the title screen (which, as you will soon see, was a big oversight). I designed the game, programmed and designed the level editor, created the other half of the levels, created the audio for the game, handled the production of everything that shipped with the game, and made sure it was going to fit on a 1.44 MB disk. It was our first game as a team, and everyone felt we worked well together.

At the last stage of development, Carmack contacted the art department, which always created the title screen that appeared at the beginning of every *Softdisk* game—in this case a purple planet and futuristic green lettering announcing:

SLORDAX: The Unknown Enemy
By John Carmack
©1991
Softdisk Inc.

When the disk arrived in November 1990, we were all shocked to see Carmack with the solo credit. Since Carmack had made the request, the art department designers just assumed he was the only author. We were all so busy getting it ready to go out the door that none of us noticed. I created the final master disk, which was locked and loaded in 1990, not 1991, contrary to the date on the title screen. That's when it got into subscribers' hands, but it was finished the previous year.

Shipping *Slordax*, our first game as a team, was a monumental occasion, but it was not the most monumental thing to happen during this time, not by a long shot. During the development of *Slordax*, John Carmack took my challenge to heart. He dove deeper into *Power Graphics Programming* and his own genius.

Then we made gaming history.

CHAPTER 9

Lightning Strikes

I was speechless.

I know that may be hard to believe. I talk passionately about games to anyone who listens whether it is about programming techniques, upcoming games and consoles, or the latest game I am into. *Softdisk* even had a conversational atmosphere.

Still, on September 20, 1990, I was at a total loss for words. But my silence wasn't the real story. The reason for my silence—that was the real story.

In the space of about one second, at the age of almost twenty-three, I had glimpsed my future, my colleagues' future, and the future of PC gaming, and that future was phenomenal.

Moments before losing my capacity to utter a single word, I had arrived early to an empty *Gamer's Edge* office to find a 3.5" floppy disk on my keyboard with a note from Tom instructing me to run the program on the disk. I inserted the floppy.

I was greeted with a brown title screen announcing, *Dangerous Dave in "Copyright Infringement."* One side of the screen had a circular portrait of Dangerous Dave, a character I had created a couple years earlier, in his signature red baseball cap. The other side had a portrait of a judge bedecked in a powdered wig holding up a gavel. I took in the image and wondered how Dave was going to interact with the halls of justice. I had no clue where this was going.

I hit the spacebar and got the shock of my life.

A familiar video game lit up my PC screen. I was looking at a replica of *Super Mario Bros. 3*: the billowing white cloud characters, the green shrubs, the construction blocks, and rotating gold coins. But *Super Mario* didn't exist on the PC, because the technology that powered it didn't exist on the PC. It existed only on the Nintendo Entertainment System and a couple of the '80s' best computers, the Atari 800 and the Commodore 64. These systems had the custom chips to handle two-dimensional side-scrolling. PC games, due to a dearth of graphics support and processing power, had been restricted to static screen games and chunky scrolling—until Carmack created smooth vertical scrolling just a few days earlier with *Slordax*.

Now I looked at *Super Mario Bros.*'s Mushroom Kingdom and wondered what it was doing on my PC screen. I also noticed Dangerous Dave standing at the bottom of the screen. The character I created two years earlier who was inspired by *Super Mario Bros.* was now inhabiting the Mushroom Kingdom. I laughed. That was the copyright violation of the title, but how far did this parody go?

I hit the arrow key to move Dangerous Dave and find out.

What I saw destroyed me.

The scenery on screen was changing, moving. As Dave walked and bounced his way into the game, moving right, new scenery and new challenges emerged. Everything scrolled smoothly, seamlessly, continually to the left. I hit the direction keys, moving him back and forth and up and down. As much as it looked like I was playing, I wasn't. I was processing the enormity of what I saw.

You know how in *Star Wars* when the *Millennium Falcon* goes into warp speed and the stars start whizzing by?

That's how I felt.

Teleported into the future.

I had to stop and process what I had just witnessed, what Carmack had done. I was sure Tom had done the nuts-and-bolts re-creation of *Super Mario Bros. 3*'s gamescape, which was funny and cool, but the horizontal scrolling that knocked me out? That was clearly all Carmack. The two of them had created this little program as a joke. As a fun way to tell me that Carmack had figured out a cool programming trick, that he took on my challenge and delivered.

Only this wasn't just a cool trick. This was a revolution.

For me, the implications of horizontal scrolling were so vast it was hard to fathom. I saw the entire universe of PC gaming expand in that split second. Horizons were no longer finite, no longer limited to the fixed dimensions of a computer screen. I had been immersed in the PC game market for a good two years now. My goal had been to understand every game, all the technology, all the programming tools. I had immersed myself in the PC because I needed to know where the leading edge was. When I saw Dangerous Dave moving effortlessly to the right, I knew the leading edge was right before my eyes. I mean this quite literally. I knew what I witnessed, and I knew this was our future. Ironically, Carmack and Tom didn't.

I knew what part of the video hardware Carmack had to use to create the side-scrolling effect, but he had figured out another optimization that reused background graphics so that the PC could read, render, and react with maximum efficiency. Remember that processing power and available memory were a fraction of what's standard today. Carmack had created a rendering engine that rewrote the rules of the game, of all games, and yet he didn't realize it. In fairness, nobody else did either.

After about thirty minutes of sitting there in silence, I finally got my act together and decided to show a few people this revolutionary breakthrough.

I took the floppy disk down the hall to my friends at *Big Blue Disk*, booted it up, and waited for people to freak out.

"That's really neat."

"Nice! How funny!"

"That's cool."

I couldn't believe it. I was waving a paradigm-shifting demo before their eyes, and they couldn't see it. In the world of programming, *Dangerous Dave in "Copyright Infringement"* was like a coding version of the Rosetta Stone. It was like E=mc2. It was like nuclear fusion. Instead, they told me it was "neat." This surprised me even more.

"Are you serious? *Neat?* This is incredible!" I said. It was all I could do not to go on a rant. These were people who lived and breathed computer programming, who understood and were invested in the PC revolution. They should have been saying: *That is fucking amazing.*

The ability to program games that move so smoothly on the horizontal axis within the game world was earth-shattering technology. It meant we could write games for the PC that rivaled the games created for gaming systems like Nintendo, Sega, and Atari without the need for their specialized hardware. Players didn't need to invest in a new console! All they needed was a PC and the game files. Nowadays, this is what venture capitalists mean when they talk about "disruption."

When Dangerous Dave moved, he wasn't just moving right in pursuit of the gold coins of Mario's kingdom—he was stepping into a completely new future for PC computer gaming, and we were going to step with him. Not just into a new technological and gameplay standard, but into entirely new lives. I knew right then that we were going to make groundbreaking games. We were going to be the team to follow. Like Wozniak. Like Nasir. Like Budge. Like my game dev heroes. We were going to build our own game company!

I walked around with that disk—the actual leading edge—thinking about all the new dimensions this programming capability would open up. I saw untapped possibilities on the horizon. There was the obvious universe of porting the offerings of Nintendo, Atari, and Sega to the PC. We also wanted to make new games. That was always the goal—to create games that we loved playing, that challenged us. Carmack knew he had broken the fourth wall of gaming on PCs. He had defied programming gravity. But he didn't care about the business implications of his triumph. The programming achievement was all that mattered.

Giving Carmack the runway and opportunity to laser focus on code and nothing but code, specifically the EGA adaptor, paid off, and we were just beginning to discover how our individual sets of unique traits worked with, challenged and celebrated each other. If I stated an achievable design or technical goal as a challenge—like smooth horizontal scrolling—he enjoyed and happily took on the challenge of solving it. I was the design/code yin to his engineering yang, and I had the programming knowledge to know what I was suggesting was certainly possible. As a team, we didn't just work well together, we propelled each other. I was obsessed with pushing the boundaries of design. He was called to push the boundaries of code. We had the vision and the goals to see beyond the current industry horizons. Achieving those goals meant solving tricky game design, computing and graphics problems.

Despite his gaming genius, Carmack wasn't that interested in advancing game design—the mechanics, the player progression, the narratives, the environment design, the sound, the surprises and Easter eggs—and quite often he didn't think about the limitations that needed to be conquered until we presented them to him. That's not to say that he didn't care about design at all. He cared *deeply* about the design and the architecture of code, and games were at the frontier. Because of the kind of programming that goes into games, they were (and still are) the most taxing form of programming. You can use a computer to crunch a bunch of numbers, sure, but spreadsheets don't generally need sound cards and GPUs (graphics processing units). Games require the whole of a computer to immerse a player in an experience, and game developers push computers to do interesting, fun, and innovative tasks, and it drives hardware innovation.

I thought Tom Hall would see it. Unlike Carmack, Tom loved games *and* game design. He loved the narrative, the journey. He didn't really give a damn about computer languages or rendering issues, although he had good programming skills. He was about flights of fancy and having fun. If I had to bet, I would have wagered that he understood the importance of side-scrolling beyond the amusing "copyright infringement" demo he had meticulously created, but I would have lost that bet.

They had stayed up late into the night to create the demo, and when Tom finally showed up for work that afternoon, he was eager to see my reaction. I was equally eager to see if he knew what they had done. "Cool, right?" Tom said with a laugh.

As for Carmack, I found out he called part of his innovation "adaptive tile refresh." He didn't see it as anything to shout "Eureka" about. I suspect he viewed the inability to side-scroll on PCs as a functional, programming and graphics conundrum.

It seemed to me that they had missed the forest for the trees, both of them. I was still in awe.

"This is massive," I told them. "Revolutionary. This is it. We are gone!"

I was elated and nervous at the same time. I never doubted my analysis, or my vision, of what side-scrolling meant, not for one second, but the implications, the opportunities that loomed as a result of that conclusion, were non-trivial. A tremendous, unique opportunity can also a daunting opportunity. I wanted to make no missteps. Everything had to be exactly right.

Now, I regretted sharing it with a few people in the office. Even giving them a glimpse of the golden ticket was stupid. I didn't want the enormity of this discovery to get out. I realized I needed to be clear with Carmack, Tom, Adrian, Lane, and Jay. We now had the opportunity to do something that was too big for *Softdisk*. It wasn't even a part of *Softdisk*'s business model.

I put the disk back into the drive and let it fly, lifting my voice over the beeps and blurts of the soundscape Tom had assembled. "This is the coolest fucking thing ever. We need to get out of here. This is our ticket."

Jay Wilbur, the guy who had known me longer than anyone at the company, walked by our office door as I was talking.

"Hey, what's up guys?" he said.

"Jay, you saw the demo, right?" I said.

"Yeah. It's really cool."

"Dude, it's beyond cool. It's 'we're out of here cool' is what it is."

Jay snorted at this as if he thought I was just spouting off, hyping something up, which he'd seen me do dozens of times in the four years we'd known each other.

"I'm dead serious, Jay."

He must have heard the commitment in my voice and concluded I was not blowing smoke, because he closed the door.

I laid out my vision: "We have to get out of here. That's the plan. We're going to keep working together, and we can totally make some unbelievable games, but we need to get out of here. Side-scrolling means we can create PC games that rival the games of the biggest-selling videogame companies in the world. We have the perfect team right here in this room. We need to refine this and develop our own games for PC. If we do, they will be superior to every single PC game out there. Think about it. There is not a single game on PC that lets you move like this, and the market for PCs is exploding! We can do this. We *have* to do this."

Everyone heard me loud and clear. It made sense. Jay believed something big was happening, too.

"This is what I think," he said. "We need to take this to Nintendo right now. Straight to the guys at the top and get a deal to port it to PC. Then we are talking serious money that can fund other development."

It was the obvious play, the one I'd thought of instantly when my head was exploding with ideas. Now Jay had expressed it and confirmed my thoughts. Everyone was on board. We just had to figure out how and when to do what needed to be done. Continuing to work for *Softdisk*, we went into heavy stealth mode with our new tech. We were all work all the time, with only sporadic breaks to play *Super Mario Bros. 3*, *Lifeforce*, or *The Legend of Zelda*.

Carmack, Jay, and Lane found a perfect house on the shores of Cross Lake, Shreveport's massive man-made lake that serves as a water-sports hub for the area. This meant we had a workspace away from *Softdisk* where we could jam 24/7 if need be and focus on our work. We had only one problem: We didn't own PCs. At the time, we were still living on modest salaries, and since I had to send money to Kelly and the kids, I really had to live on the cheap. Our solution? We "borrowed" PCs from *Softdisk*. When our workday ended at 6 p.m., we stayed in the office, changed directories, and started on our other project. We spent an entire week of after-hours work churning out a two-level PC demo of *Super Mario Bros. 3*. We even videotaped the original game so we could be sure our demo captured every single pixel. On Friday evenings, we pulled our cars up to the *Softdisk* office and quickly and quietly removed our PCs, packing them into our cars. With Jay grilling food and feeding us, Carmack and I programmed in the living room while Tom and Lane handled graphics and enemy AI (how enemies made decisions and acted upon those decisions) on other PCs we'd eventually bought. Adrian, who worked with us on *Gamer's Edge*, wasn't a part of this initial stealth mode[*] team; we had yet to get to know Adrian well, he was relatively new, and Tom planned to handle the art for the demo.

The sense of urgency and excitement among the team was palpable. We had the ability to execute the right idea at the right time. For years to come, this was our strength. There is nothing more fun than making games when you have a solid direction, an experienced team, and the knowledge that you are ahead of the competition.

With our mission complete, Jay sent our demo to Nintendo with a request to let us develop the game for PC. Three weeks later, Nintendo turned us down. They wanted to keep their intellectual property exclusive to their proprietary system. This, of course, made perfect sense, even if it didn't initially work in our favor. Fortunately, I stumbled onto a terrific plan B while making the *Super*

---

[*] Our stealth mode was not due to any noncompete or other contractual agreements. We just knew we had something innovative and wanted to be as silent about it as possible.

Mario Bros. 3 demo. I had gotten plenty of mail from gamers over the years, especially when I was publishing games in *inCider* and *Nibble*. Some of them were people having difficulty typing in the source code of my games from magazines, and some were complimentary. Since I'd arrived at *Softdisk*, though, my work wasn't exactly front and center. The disks we mailed out every month didn't have my address on them. So I was surprised when I started getting fan letters sent to me via *Softdisk*.

When the first one came, from somebody named Scott Mulliere, I pretended to make a big deal of it, showing it off like I was somebody's idol, but, obviously, I was honored. Scott "loved" my game and pronounced me "very talented" and himself "a big fan." As a game developer, particularly in the 1980s and early 1990s, it was rare to have any kind of fan interaction, and so I was grateful that people played my games and liked them enough to write me. Behind the barricades at *Softdisk*, mail was exceedingly rare. In fact, some companies, wary of talent being poached, made it hard to reach programmers. A few more "fan mails" followed Scott's letter. Some of them asked me to write back or even call collect. I taped them on the wall near my PC, but I didn't give them too much thought. Since I was so busy, I didn't feel the urge to write back.

Right around this time, I read a story in *PC Games* magazine about a new game distribution model that was paying off for a guy in Texas named Scott Miller. The article mentioned his address on Mayflower Drive in Garland, Texas. That rang some bells. Who did I know in Garland, Texas? I racked my brain and then glanced at the letters on my wall. Every one of them was from Garland. Every one of them had the exact same address. Every one of them was from an allegedly different guy.

What the hell was going on? Who was sending me these letters? How the hell had I not noticed this before?

I didn't understand what his problem was. Was he a freak? A stalker? A practical joker? Was he trolling me? I immediately wrote him a long, nasty response, but I cooled off and reread the letters on the wall, noting the invite to call collect and make contact. Bizarre, for sure, but he must have had a motive behind his madness. So, I enclosed another letter along with my more reactionary first letter, telling him that I was mildly intrigued by his strange method of making an approach. I included a phone number at *Softdisk* where he could reach me.

Soon after that, he got in touch.

"Oh my god. FINALLY! John Romero!" he said when I picked up the phone.

"Who is this?"

"Scott Miller. We so need to work together."

I thought of saying some of the nastier things I wrote in my first letter, but settled on something less confrontational. "Dude, what was with those letters you wrote me? All those different names? It's unbelievable. Can you—"

"Never mind the letters. I *had* to write that way to make sure they got to you. It's hard to make contact with programmers, but forget all that. What I really want to do is talk about you making games for me."

After that, he backed up, and we got on track.

He told me his story, focusing primarily on the new company he'd created, Apogee, and how he had solved the computer gaming distribution puzzle—a challenge for any independent game start-up—with a disk- and BBS-based[*] grassroots solution.

He didn't exactly put it in those terms, but that is what it amounted to. In the fall of 1990, there was no Steam, Epic Games Store, or online App Store. If you wanted the latest games, you ordered them via mail order, or you went to smaller retailers like Electronics Boutique, ComputerLand, Egghead, or Software Etc., if you were lucky enough to have any one of those in your town. In bigger cities, everyone who wanted games went to large computer stores like CompUSA or Babbage's, found the game section, and bought what are now called big box games off the shelf. The managers of these outlets organized the games by genre, and in doing so, organized the industry by genre, too. The world of downloading games online was in its infancy on BBSs but was gaining popularity.

Scott had adapted the shareware model—where developers made applications or games available for free download and hoped users would appreciate their work and send them money in return. Scott had been writing games since he was a teenager, mostly text-based quiz and adventure games. Instead of giving the whole game away, Scott decided to post a sample version of a game on bulletin boards and Usenet groups. The idea was to hook users and then make them pay for the complete version. When they finished the free sample, a screen popped up with Scott's address and instructions to buy the rest of the game from him.

He said he was making a fortune—thousands of dollars a week on a *rogue*like game called *Kroz,* a game mentioned in the *PC Games* article. He gave away the first episode of the game, "Kingdom of Kroz," and the thousands were coming from people who wanted to complete the trilogy with "Caverns of Kroz" and "Dungeons of Kroz." He'd even given the first episode away on *Big Blue Disk* #20, but that was before I got to *Softdisk.*

The reason he wrote me those letters, he told me, was that he wanted me to make a clone of *Pyramids of Egypt* for Apogee. "It's a perfect shareware game and will sell like crazy."

"We can't do that. *Softdisk* owns *Pyramids,* Scott."

But I saw an opening for our stealth plans and went for it.

---

[*] A BBS, short for bulletin board system, was a common means for people to exchange or download files.

"You wouldn't want *Pyramids* anyway. We've got something way better. You have no idea how cool our current game is," I told him. "It is light years cooler than *Pyramids*. I'll send you a sample. You've never seen anything like it on the PC."

"Then I want to sell it."

I loved what I was hearing. Even if Nintendo rejected our PC port of *Super Mario Bros. 3*, this was a potential solution for taking our breakthrough to the next level. If Scott was making money hand over fist, so could we. At *Softdisk*, we were all salaried employees. No matter how well our games did, we got paid our set amount, and there's one thing for sure, it wasn't thousands of dollars a week. I'd told Carmack about Scott Miller the previous week after piecing together his multiple letters, and he knew I had given Scott our number. After the call, I came back into our *Gamer's Edge* office and shared the details with Carmack, who seemed slightly interested but skeptical. I was stoked, though, and sent Scott the demo straight away. He was impressed when he saw our work. He got it, understood its potential, and called me immediately.

"I need you guys to make a new game with this tech."

Making an additional game for Scott was exactly the opportunity we had been looking for. I felt like Carmack's breakthrough—which had come long after business hours in the *Softdisk* office—and the plans to capitalize on it were ours, collectively, to use. Carmack and Tom worked on their own time—nearly to dawn—to make their extraordinary *Dangerous Dave* demo, and I knew side scrolling was a game changer before I started *Gamer's Edge*. Though all the ingredients had come together here, they had come together on our own time. Yet, excited as we were to charge ahead, we had our day jobs and were currently developing *Slordax* for *Gamer's Edge*. In my opinion, using groundbreaking horizontal scrolling for a *Gamer's Edge* release was a waste of an opportunity. The entire company's business model was not suited to capitalize and promote the kind of hot-selling and groundbreaking games we could now build.

At this point, we had to make a big decision: Do we stay, or do we go? In the end, we decided to do both. We worked at *Softdisk* by day and created our future at night. Eager to get going, we needed a name for our new company. We had named our little *D&D* team "In Demand" as a joke—we were level-3 peons and no one ever needed us, but IDF (Ideas from the Deep) and the moniker "ID" for In Demand seemed destined to stick to us, so Tom suggested we go with "id." It was a Freudian term and described the primitive, instinctual part of the mind—a way that we hoped our games would connect with players. We decided to add "Software" to it. Looking back, we could have used "Entertainment," "Studios," "Games," or something else more interesting than "Software," but that's what most companies did back then. I often hear people pronounce "id" as "eye dee," but that's not correct. It's "id" and rhymes with "did."

After the *Super Mario Bros. 3* demo, we decided to part ways with Lane. It seemed to us that the PC was not for him, which doesn't work in a PC game company. We decided to leave him out. Also, Lane didn't play in our *D&D* group.

Eventually, Scott laid out the terms of a deal: Our team would make a 45 percent royalty on every copy sold. To cement the deal, I asked Scott for a $2,000 advance.

When the check came in the mail, it proved to me and the team that this was a real deal. The $2,000 worked out to $666 per person. We would have started making the game for Scott without it, but getting this advance showed us Scott was serious and believed in us. We did some rough math to determine what kind of money we might bring in if our game did well. As long as we made enough to pay rent two times per person, we knew it was enough to do this full-time on our own. For the time being, though, we continued our day jobs working on *Slordax* for *Softdisk*.

The three-game component of the Apogee model (first game goes out for free and if players like it, they buy the other two) was critical, and we held a quick meeting to figure out a plan. "Okay. Does anyone have an idea for a trilogy?" I asked.

Carmack said, "How about a genius kid who saves the world, and his parents are oblivious to it?"

Tom Hall loved it and said he'd be back in ten minutes. He ran to his Apple IIgs, fired up AppleWorks, and banged out a three-paragraph overview about Billy Blaze, an eight-year-old genius who builds a rocket, dons a football helmet, and jets off to Mars. Fifteen minutes later, he returned to read the initial "defender of justice" paragraph aloud to us in a Walter Winchell voice. Carmack applauded. I loved it, too. It was an amalgam of Tom's passions: punny, subtle, often kitcshy humor; a love of science fiction; an awareness of being a kid; and his vast game knowledge. As he got deeper into developing the idea, he came up with a design for a secret level and other Easter egg–type treats, like having signs written in the Standard Galactic Alphabet, Tom's futuristic cipher for the English alphabet, all over the place. Curious gamers could even decipher the alphabet and translate the signs.*

The game was called *Commander Keen in Invasion of the Vorticons*. The name and the idea itself had just come out of thin air, on demand. Tom was like that, and he still is. I have never known anyone as intensely creative as Tom Hall. Give him an idea, go get a coffee, and when you come back, he has your universe created. Tom later told me that the name was inspired by old movie serial names, like *Buck Rogers in the 25th Century* and *Flash Gordon and the Planet of Death*.

---

* SGA is now part of the Unicode, the generally accepted standard for digitally rendered writing systems and it is also used in *Minecraft*.

The drive to build it before Christmas was epic. Carmack and I spent sixteen hours a day together, pushing each other, inspiring each other. The first eight hours were on *Slordax*, the second eight were on *Commander Keen*. Tom wasn't far behind. Adrian still wasn't part of id Software at this time, so his focus was solely on *Slordax*. Tom did all the graphics for the first *Keen* trilogy, and we brought Adrian in at the end to create some graphic tiles and the Vortininja enemy that players would encounter in episodes 2 and 3.

When Adrian left the office for the day, Tom came in, and we began to work on *Keen*. I continued coding tools and other parts of the game such as the world map, menu system, secret Loch Ness Monster transport, and other touches like that. John spent his time coding enemy AI, and Tom and I made the game's levels. Tom created an entire universe, and these first three games were just a glimpse into it. There were alien races and tons of creatures with their own backstories.

Each of the *Keen* games had sixteen levels, so we made forty-eight levels in total. These levels were exciting to make—they were the first levels we made that felt like we were crafting an adventure that was meant to excite, to surprise, and to provoke curiosity in the player. We hid secrets everywhere, and we made sure the game was challenging but not too difficult.

As we worked, Scott Miller would send us $100 checks just before the weekends with "Pizza Money" noted on them. Once again, we were on a 10-to-2 death schedule. In hindsight, I know this schedule sounds nuts, and the fact that we did this to ourselves may seem even nuttier, but at the time this didn't at all feel like work. We were chasing greatness, and we ran as fast as we could. We knew someone would get to the finish line, and we wanted to get there first.

We finished *Slordax* for *Gamer's Edge* on October 31 and started on our next game for them the day after. We decided to make a ninja action game and called it *Shadow Knights*. We used the *Keen* scrolling tech for this game, making it the first *Gamer's Edge* game to horizontally scroll. Working with this code during the day made our evening work on *Keen* that much easier.

Though we were challenging ourselves and working around the clock, I still stopped now and again to talk with Beth McCall, a woman who worked on the production line putting disks in mailers to send out to *Softdisk*'s many subscribers. She had a calm and easygoing demeanor, a thick southern accent, and a pleasant laugh. When we'd bump into one another, she'd ask about what we were working on. Like a person who had spent a good portion of their life behind a monitor, I launched into answers with technical details, and seeing I was speaking only to myself, followed up with gameplay details.

"I don't play games," she told me. She rolled her eyes in mock anticipation of my response.

"Everyone plays games," I said. "There just might not be a game for them yet."

I believed what I said. I had been in the industry long enough to see the incredible breadth of games that developers had created, and I knew that there was still so much ground to cover.

"Maybe so," she told me, but I knew that she was speaking more from politeness than hope of finding that perfect game for her.

I enjoyed our conversations and decided to ask her if she'd like to go on a date with me. Since she knew how committed I was to my job and to my growth as a game creator—she saw firsthand how hard our group worked—I wasn't worried that it would become an issue and kept on with our development schedule.

On December 12, we finished the *Commander Keen Trilogy*. While the rest of the team got some sleep, I brought the disk to the post office and sent it off in the mail. Scott got it two days later, and Apogee released the free first episode of the game "Marooned on Mars," that day. Scott uploaded episode one to Dan Linton's popular gaming BBS, Software Creations in Clinton, Massachusetts. Dan created a big text banner with the name *Commander Keen* crafted from a block of ASCII art symbols, which everyone saw as soon as they logged in. Players could buy the remaining two episodes, "The Earth Explodes" and "Keen Must Die!" for $30.

The response was immediate and remarkable. The first month, Apogee generated about $25,000 in sales; the vast majority of it from *Keen* purchases—all with zero advertising. Just as gratifying was the feedback from gamers. When journalists pen obituaries about id Software team members, *DOOM* and *Quake* will be name-checked in the first paragraph, along with first-person shooter games. *Commander Keen* may be just a footnote, a passing paragraph in the inventory of our work, but if you look back at the reviews of *Commander Keen: Invasion of the Vorticons,* the critical acclaim was every bit as breathless and loving as the response was to *DOOM*. Accolades abounded: *PC Magazine* said it "has a Nintendo feel" and was a "tremendous success," while *PC Computing* wrote, "*Commander Keen's* standard-setting quality has made addiction all too easy!" *Commander Keen* was a revolutionary game and design that took advantage of never-before-seen PC programming techniques. We'd set out to astonish everyone, and we did.

On January 15, 1991, our first check arrived in the amount of $10,500. We had more than hit our team budget requirement of two times our rent per person. None of us had ever held a check for an amount that large. We passed it around in wonder. We had made it, partially anyway. I went to see Al Vekovius to tell him Carmack, Tom and I were leaving, and Adrian was coming with us.

"I know this is not an ideal situation," I said. "And I'm totally grateful for everything you've done, but the *Softdisk* model isn't going to work for us."

Once again, Al surprised me, insisting "we can work something out." I have to say, part of me was relieved. Tom was worried about getting sued by *Softdisk*.

I had downplayed that concern with logic: "What can they sue us for? We don't have any money! What's he going to take from you, Tom? Your couch with a spring popping out of it?!"

Instead, Al had collaboration, not legal action, on his mind.

"How about I work with you guys to make your own company? I'll own a piece of it, but you'll own the rest. We'll be partners, and I can manage all the business aspects of it. You can be wherever you want to be."

On the surface, this sounded good. No potential legal hassles, we wouldn't have to deal with business issues, and we could make games that used the shareware model—which seemed far more profitable and liberating than *Softdisk*'s subscription model.

As we hashed this out, Al was thinking on his feet. His plan was to move some of the programmers who handled his cash cow, *Big Blue Disk*, to take over *Gamer's Edge*, as they *were the only other PC programmers in the company*. We would help train them and then spend all our time making games for this new Al-and-Us company. This sounded like a great plan, and we were seriously considering it, but Al had concerns, saying, "I have to have a meeting with the other editors about this. Everyone's going to find out about it."

The next day the deal was off. His staff had threatened to quit. From their perspective, Al was rewarding us for screwing over the company, for using *Softdisk* to build our careers. Meanwhile, they were going to get shafted with more work.

"I can't do it. They said they will all quit, and then I'm really screwed."

Eventually, after some civil negotiation, we agreed that in return for *Softdisk* not suing us or making claims to our intellectual property, we would spend the next year making a game every two months for *Softdisk*, while their new *Gamer's Edge* team trained themselves to use our code and tools. He offered to pay us $5,000 for each game.

We took that deal quickly. Living in Shreveport, our living expenses were about $400 a month each. So with the money coming in from *Keen*, we'd have no cash flow issues at all. We would still have to code like maniacs, but in the end, we would be beholden to nobody. Apogee was ready and waiting for our next project.

Before I leave the *Softdisk* era behind, I want to address a few things. A great deal has been written about this period—our time at *Softdisk*, John Carmack's horizontal scrolling breakthrough, and the creation of *Commander Keen*. Most of it jibes with my version of events. I have, however, seen some reporting that overstates the group's creative tensions and personality clashes. I realize this was a dramatic device that obviously added tension to our story, but at the outset, we were unified and in sync. Suggestions that John Carmack was reclusive and antisocial were not at all evident in the first few years. Yes, he had a superhuman work ethic and was brilliant, but he was a regular guy like me, and nobody spent more time with him than I did. As for tensions that existed among the rest of the team, I can't speak for the inner feelings of everyone, but we were as high-functioning and collaborative and positive as it gets. It was a dream team of motivated, talented game developers. Once, I read a report that Adrian Carmack truly loathed Tom Hall. He absolutely didn't.

As I've said, none of us smoked, drank regularly, or did drugs, and I think this speaks to just how in sync and focused we were, but there was one night, New Year's Eve 1990, where some of us got drunk and Carmack famously stated, "I am losing control of my faculties." He normally did not talk like a computer, but apparently the drinking caused him to. I think we would have been turned off if someone lit up a joint or started doing shots. We got high on games and programming. That was it.

I've also read similar reports that I didn't like Al Vekovius. On the contrary, I thought Al was a great guy and so did the others. We were happy to have jobs at *Softdisk*. The statement itself was attributed to John Carmack, a statement Carmack disputes as untrue and out of character. Why would I dislike the guy who gave me a chance to learn the PC? Everything he did for us was always positive. There was zero negativity from me, or any of us, toward Al, as far as I knew. I consider Al Vekovius a major and helpful figure in my life and the history of video games.

EPISODE THREE

LAUNCH

CHAPTER 10

The Bootstrap Start-up

On February 1, 1991, id Software was officially founded. After gathering our CDs and boombox from *Softdisk*, John, Adrian and I set up shop at the lake house at 7450 South Lakeshore Drive. The house itself was large, more than 2,700 square feet, and was set on a half-acre lot that backed up to Cross Lake. In addition to the regular rooms, it had two large rooms that were, presumably, for entertaining. We took one for our office. Jay, who was still primarily working at *Softdisk*, already had a desk on one wall of the large room, and so Carmack, Adrian, and I decided to set ourselves up on the wall opposite him, but next to one another, so we could communicate and exchange disks quickly. At the time, proximity mattered. We didn't have any source control in the cloud or on a server because there *was* no cloud or server. Everything was handled by 3.5" floppy disks handed back and forth.

After dropping off our measly office furnishings, we set off for Sam's Club, where we got three $40 brown folding tables for our desks. Getting computers was next on our list. Thankfully, we had the commitment check from Apogee because we were going to need a good chunk of it. We purchased the same kind of computers we had at *Softdisk*, three 386 DX/33s, and five monitors. Carmack and I got two monitors each, a color 14-inch VGA monitor for the game and a 12-inch amber monochrome monitor for debugging, and Adrian got a 14-inch VGA as well. Tom was still at *Softdisk*, with plans to join us in a few months. We could worry about his computer and setup later.

Our *Softdisk* schedule had worked well for us, so we decided to keep our hours what they were: 10 a.m. until we were done. Every morning, Jay headed off to work at *Softdisk* while Adrian and I headed to the lake house. We felt great. The sense that we were working for ourselves and that we didn't have to go to *Softdisk* was energizing, even if we were still satisfying our contract for them. At least we were working toward our future. Our initial goal was to satisfy the *Softdisk* agreement, creating one game every two months for *Gamer's Edge*. In the second half of the year, we planned to pivot to a second *Commander Keen* trilogy.

We weren't really corporate types, but the setup of a company forced us to become those types real quick. We talked about who should take what role. In reality, the titles didn't mean anything to us, but they were a necessary part of our company formation. We decided Carmack would be president, Tom would be secretary, Adrian would be VP, and I'd be treasurer. Internally, we didn't give ourselves any titles like CEO, CCO, or lead this or that. We just started making stuff.

Shortly after forming id Software, I had my first real disagreement with Carmack. It was about equity in the company. The original id team had 25 percent shares allotted to me, Carmack, and Tom Hall. Adrian got 15 percent, and Jay, who was working evenings balancing the checkbook, payroll, and bill-paying while still at *Softdisk*, got 10 percent. Despite what has been reported elsewhere, Adrian was totally engaged in what we were trying to do, and if he was miserable about working on *Commander Keen* or any of our early games, he sure didn't show it. In fact, he worked his ass off, even though we'd brought him in with a smaller share of id ownership. I was so impressed with his talent and professionalism that I told Carmack I thought we should make him a full partner. Carmack immediately said no. I kept pushing. We were both adamant about sharing knowledge and not patenting technology, but when it came to sharing the fruits of our collective labor, he became proprietary. Looking back, I think part of his reluctance may have been inexperience; he didn't realize that equity terms often get overhauled as start-ups evolve. I kept pushing him. We would never have made all the *Gamer's Edge* games we were working on as quickly as we did without Adrian delivering stellar work in a fast and efficient manner. I finally wore him down. The four of us would each get 22.5 percent of the company. It was the right thing to do.

Our first year was going to be a busy one as we hustled to fulfill our obligations to both *Softdisk* and to Apogee. First up was *Dangerous Dave in the Haunted Mansion* in January and February, followed by *Rescue Rover*, a puzzle game in which dognapping robots capture a mutt named Rover, and players navigate a maze to get Rover and then help him escape. These games fulfilled our *Softdisk* obligations up to April 30. *Dangerous Dave* was a sequel to my 1988 design, and the other came from Tom Hall. We were flying, working as hard as we could to get these games finished and out the door. Not only were we responsible for the design and development of our games, but we were also responsible for finding errors, glitches, or bugs in the game as well as assessing its ability to run on a variety of machines and hardware. Today, most game companies have their own QA department. At id, we tested our own stuff before we checked it in. Carmack and I were competitive about it, too. Finding a bug in one another's code was something of a sport, and so we worked hard to bulletproof our work. If we found a bug, we immediately fixed it—we did not believe in building new code on top of a shaky foundation. Gameplay-wise, we didn't really know how our *Softdisk* games were hitting with players, so we relied on our own opinions. *Softdisk* was a vacuum and, at the time, the game press wasn't interested in covering smaller releases.

Outside of the *Gamer's Edge* obligations, we made four other games that we sold to *Softdisk*: *Catacomb 2, Double Catacomb, Double Dangerous Dave,* and *Dark Designs III.* Carmack and I had a coding competition to see who could convert our hi-res Apple II games, *Catacomb* and *Dangerous Dave,* to double hi-res the fastest—Carmack won.

In April 1991, we made our first real exploration into the design and development of 3D games. It was a significant turning point for us and for the industry.[*] At the time, there were a number of 3D games out there—notably 1987's *Deep Space: Operation Copernicus* by Paul Neurath and Ned Lerner and 1989's *Archipelagos* by Astral Software—and while they were interesting, they were also slow or sacrificed detail for the sake of speed and therefore looked incredibly sparse. *Archipelagos* lacked graphic details, while *Deep Space* restricted the view of the player to a small window. No one had cracked it yet. The limitations—either the sparseness or slowness or both—made immersion difficult. Theoretically, these games had the ability to envelop the player, and critics seemed to love them, but they lacked speed. Fast 3D, we knew, was the next frontier beyond horizontal smooth scrolling.

Up to this point, we had been mostly poking around the edges of 3D. Earlier in the year, Carmack wrote a 3D demo of a rotating cube, and he followed up with a 2D scaling *Gamer's Edge* logo for *Dangerous Dave in the Haunted Mansion.* Carmack and I wanted more of a challenge from technical point of view, and 3D provided that challenge, but it wasn't just the technical challenge that spurred us. Devising more realistic perspectives and depth of field wouldn't just look better; coupled with good design, we hoped it would create the immersive experience gamers had been waiting for.

With those goals in mind, development on *Hovertank One,* a pre-apocalypse rescue mission where players drive the titular hovertank and blast away enemies while rescuing survivors, began in April. *Hovertank One* was our first foray into a

---

[*] Every few years, the game industry leaps forward spurred on by either a hardware innovation, a programming innovation, or a design innovation. The transition to 3D was one of its bigger leaps because it forced innovation across the board in hardware, programming, and design.

new dimension—literally—of graphics programming and game design. Carmack's approach to 3D graphics started here, rendering objects with a depth of field that required an entirely new type of math calculated at high speed on a PC in 1991 without a math processor (or floating point) chip.* His high school education left him without the skills he needed to approach the problem, though. So, before we programmed *Hovertank One*, he bought some books and decided to teach himself trigonometry and the higher-level math necessary to understand the problem before him. There was no room for failure; if the new math and screen drawing slowed our frame rate, the game would be forgotten, because nobody wants to play a slow action game. Carmack devised some rendering optimizations and a wall-line projection algorithm to determine how to draw the screen in vertical strips intermingled with 2D images for the characters—key to creating the illusion of 3D on the two-dimensional computer screen.

While Carmack focused on the engine, I got to work on all the tools the team required to interface with the engine to put the game together. While tools will always be the least sexy form of tech and game dev, tools make game development easier, and well-designed and -developed tools make it not just easier but fun and enjoyable.

First, I focused on updating TED, our Tile EDitor. The idea for TED came from a tile editor I made when I was developing *Dangerous Dave* in 1988. Rather than having to do the time-intensive work of creating levels by hand or putting text on the screen as a replacement for graphics as we did on the Apple II, I used the *Dangerous Dave* level editor to create the levels. When Carmack and I first met, he was impressed by the editor in *Dangerous Dave*, and we knew we wanted something similar for our upcoming games. So I improved TED steadily over six months, starting with our game *Slordax*, moving from TED 1.0 to 5.0. Each version of TED had more features added—tileblock† copying, more planes of information, game launching, map printing, and more. TED ended up being used for thirty-three shipped games—not just our own products, but games at *Gamer's Edge* as well as *Corridor 7: Alien Invasion, Rise of the Triad*, and lots more. It was even used to create the *Dangerous Dave in "Copyright Infringement"* demo. TED was designed and coded to be as useful for 2D games as it was for simple 3D games. It even worked in multiple graphics modes: CGA (4 colors), EGA (16 colors) and VGA (256 colors). At the time, it was an innovative tool, and Tom and I loved using it. In addition to TED, I developed MUSE, our MUsic Sound Editor and IGRAB, a tool that took everything that was required to play the game and put it into a

---

*   "Floating point" is a term used by programmers and mathematicians to describe numbers that may include a decimal in them (1.666, for instance). Calculating numbers with floating points required a floating-point processor.

†   A "tileblock" was a 16-pixel by 16-pixel image used to tile a level much like one might tile a floor.

single data file. Great tools make great games. I think it's important to spend as much time on tools as possible.

Design-wise, just like Carmack, Tom and I were operating in a new dimension. It's something we take for granted now, but 3D required us to rethink the possibility space* of gameplay. Everything from movement to AI to the player's tactics and strategy was affected. It's a design we learned by jumping into it— putting ourselves in the game and walking around, wondering what could happen and asking ourselves questions like every game designer does. *What does the player want to do? How can we challenge and surprise the player? How can we do this without ruining Carmack's rendering optimizations?* Throwing ourselves into this new space, we learned on the job to design the levels for *Hovertank One*.

Hovertank One only made its May 31, 1991, deadline due to Carmack's heroic programming hours. In comparison, the levels were easy. He knew he could do it, and basically didn't let up his focus until it happened. It was an incredibly tight two months writing our first 3D engine and game. We were creating this game for *Softdisk*, but we always had tremendous pride in our work. No matter who it was for, we wanted to do our best.

Hovertank One pushed the PC envelope hard at the time and marked our first steps into first-person shooter games. It also introduced the first comically sinister elements that came to define id sensibilities—you could run over or shoot the people you were supposed to rescue. Despite all this innovation, the game is largely regarded as a footnote and a sign of greater things to come.

In retrospect, I see plenty of good reasons for *Hovertank One*'s lower status in the id pantheon. First, it was released by *Softdisk* on *Gamer's Edge*, so it didn't have the viral potential of our shareware games or any retail distribution. Second, the game itself was inferior to Atari's 1980 tank classic *Battlezone*. Speaking critically, the game also just didn't feel great. The tank's gun never felt as immediate, or as immersive, as other weapons we eventually created. Any amazing tech is only as good as the design that uses it. Carmack's tech would get better. So would my design.

Financially, however, the newly minted id Software was doing great. In addition to the $5K that we received from *Softdisk* for each game, we also received money every month from Apogee. We took out only what we each needed to live and not a penny more; everything else was saved. The money increased at a steady monthly rate, and by January 1992, we were up to $50,000 per month. Two of us grew up below the poverty line. Two of us grew up in middle-class homes. It was

---

* Possibility space refers to everything that could potentially happen within a game. Usually, this is a conceptual design consideration in which designers explore everything that play could potentially do.

a shocking amount of money no matter how we looked at it, and we held on to all of it because we didn't know when it might end.

After *Hovertank One*, it was time to start working on a new *Keen* release. Tom Hall's plan for *Keen* was to follow George Lucas's vision for *Star Wars*—to create a trilogy of trilogies. The goal was to hammer out three more episodes of *Commander Keen* in time for Apogee to release for Christmas 1991. We also wanted to introduce some next-generation enhancements with new technology, including showing *Keen* from a tilted perspective instead of straight-on from the side. This would require a lot more complex tile work and level design skill. In the new *Keen* engine itself, there would be a major improvement in the way the EGA memory was used to draw the screen so we could gain more speed. Discussing our strategy, Carmack and I began talking about the most efficient way to complete the next set of *Keen* releases—episodes four, five and six. Collectively, the three would make up the next trilogy—*Commander Keen in Goodbye, Galaxy*.

We were really excited to start work on them. At this point, Carmack knew most everything there was to know about video graphics cards—the removable circuit board used to display images on a monitor. This more advanced *Keen* engine would be faster because it would slide the monitor-viewable display area throughout the entire EGA screen memory space, only drawing new tiles at the scrolling edge. It was vastly more sophisticated than the graphics code we used in the original Keen game.

We had all this new technology and ambition, but we needed to fine-tune it, and fast (we wanted to take advantage of holiday gift giving). So we decided to kill two birds with one stone: We'd make a single episode as a game—*Commander Keen in Keen Dreams*—for *Softdisk*, which would allow us to experiment and to prepare for building out our full three-episode *Commander Keen* trilogy.

The one-off game, *Keen Dreams*, was filled with good-natured gags, puns, and references to the evils of television, as our eight-year-old hero turns enemies into flowers and battles the ever-sinister potato king Boobus Tuber, who has a Dream Machine that enslaves children. As we got deeper and deeper into making *Keen Dreams* and prepping for *Goodbye, Galaxy*, Carmack and I created and shared code that we began calling the *Keen* engine. At the time, I don't recall ever having heard someone refer to a game engine. That was partly because, for so many years, game development was a solitary pursuit with programmers making games single-handedly. Carmack, Tom, and I had all worked solo, writing code for all aspects of a game. So each game had code that made everything work, but there was never a specific name for it. Now that we were collaborating, the idea of a game-creation system and management tool made a lot of sense. We wanted something with some extensibility, something we could reuse so we didn't have to invent the wheel again and again. I suppose we could have called it the Keen Brain or the Keen Heart or the Keen Processor, but we both loved cars, and engines are what give vehicles the power to make everything run. That is how we visualized the *Keen* engine—a multilayered program that was the central core with which we could make any 2D game.

The *Keen* engine was conceived of as a reusable device to power different *Keen* episodes, each with new rules, images, soundtracks, and characters while reusing the central core engine tech like drawing graphics on the screen and playing sounds. There was no reason to limit it to *Keen*, however. As the de facto business strategy guy at id, and mindful of my experience at Origin Systems and Inside Out Software, I was always thinking about finding new revenue sources. When we were done making *Keen Dreams* and the engine was in place, I thought, *What else can we do with this thing?* What if we showed other game companies our engine? They might license it to save development time. They could, theoretically, make games as cool as ours.

If it was useful to us, it had to be useful to others. We just needed to show it off. I thought we could have a summer seminar of sorts at the lake house where we demonstrated how the engine works, and we could help some developers, plus prove the concept. I called Scott Miller at Apogee because we really valued his input. He was also an ideal partner since, as a game publisher, he knew a ton of authors. We put the word out and made plans to show off our new *Keen* game, the existing engine, and talk about what it could do.

A battalion of great programmers and game developers descended upon the lake house. Scott was there, of course, as was George Broussard, who later helped found 3D Realms and made *Duke Nukem 3D*. Developers who worked with Apogee also came, including Frank Maddin, Todd Replogle, and Jim Norwood. Ken Rogoway and Dave Farquharson also showed—they were authors who had worked at Epyx, a prominent game company that published a lot of games in the '80s. We started to go through the engine and answered questions, but I knew the best thing we could do was to create a game right in front of them.

We built a *Pac-Man* knockoff called—what else?—*Wac-man*. Over the course of a couple of hours, Adrian drew ghosts and dots and other design assets on his computer. Meanwhile, Tom made the level and sounds, and Carmack coded like a madman. I was the proverbial master of ceremonies, the only one comfortable and technically able to discuss anything from the engine through to the gameplay. I discussed how all the elements fit together and talked about how our engine might work on a case-by-case basis. All told, it took between 90 and 120 minutes, but we did it. *Wac-man* was chomping on dots and our guests were impressed.

Today, game engines are a massive business. Millions are spent on building engines, and billions more are made by licensing them. In 1991, we were ahead of our time. Engines save time and money, and they mitigate risk. In the early 1990s, a team might save mere months with our engine; now engines save development teams years. Factoring in a 1991 team size as compared to a modern-day team, the cost-benefit analysis is even stronger today. In 1991, a large team might have ten programmers. Today, a large team has hundreds, even thousands. That's a lot of time and money saved. It's possible our marketing outreach was flawed, but for whatever reason, our id Summer Seminar resulted in only a single offer: Jim Norwood licensed it, cutting a revenue share deal that gave us a percentage of his earnings. With it, Jim built a game called *Bio Menace*. But we weren't disappointed; one license was one more than we had, and we were growing.

When *Bio Menace* was done, though, Norwood didn't license the engine again, and we discovered a flaw in our plan. Giving out our engine also required giving out the source code so that the game could run. Once developers had that code, they didn't need to renew anything. They had the keys to the kingdom and could potentially use it or refer to it to write their own engine. We didn't really have a huge problem with this, per se. Carmack and I were both programming evangelists, and we believed in sharing information to make better games. My attitude was shaped as a young teenager by my hero Bert Kersey, the founder of Beagle Bros. He ran a company that created software tools and regularly shared them. In fact, when you bought a utility, he included a manual, and the first thirty pages were filled with cool programmer knowledge. He was just giving stuff away. In doing that, he took a stand against software copy protection. If people copied it, then they copied it, but it was more important to him that people who needed information got it. We took that idea and were very open with our technical information. Jim Norwood and Apogee had the source code so they could create and sell *Bio Menace*. We heard rumors—we don't know if they were true—that they then allegedly gave our engine to a programmer who adapted our work slightly. We heard even more unfounded rumors, and we also didn't know if they were true, that it was shared with other Apogee developers to build other games—without paying us a dime.

Carmack and I thought, if these rumors were true, that it was uncool of Apogee. We had no problem with anyone using our work, but in the spirit of shareware, if a company was using our engine to make money, they should have shared the wealth. Surprisingly, we didn't think to check with Apogee. We had learned a lesson, regardless. If we pursued the engine licensing deal as a real moneymaker, we needed to figure out how to retain the source code to make engine licensing a scalable, proprietary business.[*]

The rumors around the *Keen* engine's use at Apogee caused me to question whether the company was the right fit for id. Scott had certainly helped us build

---

[*] Interestingly, that is just what modern game engine giants like Epic and Unity have done. They charge a lot of money to provide companies with their full, all-access package.

our company, but I thought we could do it ourselves, too—sell the games and keep all the profits. Shareware made distribution easy; all we needed to do was produce the disks and packaging, take orders, and fulfill them. If Scott's outfit could do it, we could, too. I mentioned this to Carmack, but he didn't want anything to distract the team from our core mission of making the best games around. It was a valid point. Our first diversion into engine licensing hadn't exactly convinced him otherwise.

By this time, we were averaging $35,000 per month between *Gamer's Edge* checks and royalties from *Commander Keen*. I was multitasking in unexpected ways, almost by default. I started to think about the fiscal future of id Software and its business prospects. We were doing fine, but that didn't mean that planning wasn't necessary. Just as I got us a game publishing deal with Apogee, then the bimonthly *Gamer's Edge* yearlong deal, I thought about how we were all working full-on every day, but no future planning was happening other than what the next game was going to be. I wanted more time spent on company strategy. I didn't want id to become another Inside Out Software.

Carmack, Tom, and Adrian had no business experience, whereas id Software was my fourth game company. I had created and sold twenty-three games and had the most experience, so handling of business deals and business development fell to me. Fortunately, it was something I enjoyed. Finding a way to distribute games and connect with an audience to buy them was easily just as important as creating the kickass games themselves, since sales paid for game development. Despite my aptitude on this side of things, though, I wanted someone else to handle it so I could continue making games.

Enter Mark Rein, a Canadian gamer and businessman from Toronto who contacted me in March 1991 about a bug he found in *Commander Keen 2*. Mark was a upbeat guy, something I related to. Initially, I asked Mark if he wanted to be a beta tester, but he had another idea: handling business for us. He had business experience and even offered to fly down to Shreveport to discuss things further. In the end, we signed him up for a six-month unpaid probationary stint. During that time, we let him represent himself as the company president. Since Mark was making $100,000 a year at his day job, and we were still at $2,500 per month each, we told him it had to be pro bono (id was pulling in good income at this time, and we kept as much money in the bank as possible). He accepted, and Mark got to thinking about what he could do for us. Knowing that the end of 1991 was going to be challenging development-wise (we had to make *Commander Keen* games and *Gamer's Edge* games at the same time), I told Scott Miller that Mark was going to represent our business so we could focus fully on development. Scott agreed he'd communicate with Mark from then on.

To solidify our break with *Softdisk*, we decided to leave Shreveport. That led to another recalibration of ownership, because we told Jay he needed to be all in or give up his 10 percent. He wanted to stay at *Softdisk*, and he said he understood. So, now the four of us—Carmack, Adrian, Tom, and me—each owned a quarter of the company.

The world was our oyster. We could have moved anywhere, but in the end, we chose Madison, Wisconsin. It wasn't exactly a software mecca, but then again, few places were at that time. Madison was Tom Hall's hometown. He went to college there, too, and loved it. It was a great college town, he promised, which sounded appealing. The other reason we moved there was that, well, we were game programmers. All we cared about was having a place to sleep and code. I remember when Al Vekovius was wooing Jay, Lane, and me to come to *Softdisk* and he drove us around Shreveport. The oil industry had left years earlier, and downtown Shreveport was a grim sight, with empty and boarded-up buildings, but Al was playing tour guide. He tried to show us the best of the town. I remember thinking, "I don't care about the town. I care about *Softdisk*'s offices. That's where I'm going to be all the time." So I had a similar attitude about Madison. Affordable rent, electricity, and pizza deliveries were my three main criteria. Carmack felt the same.

Tom and I flew up in August to survey the scene and find a place for id Software. In August, Madison was amazing and full of big leafy trees, boulevards bustling with small shops, and lots of restaurants. The University of Wisconsin dominated the city's landscape. Its prosperity stood in stark contrast to Shreveport. We looked for four apartments in close proximity, one of which needed to also double as our office. We didn't have any time to waste since we were still working on *Commander Keen 4: Secret of the Oracle* and had more games to make to fulfill our contract with *Softdisk*.

We found the apartments and office we were looking for in nearby Fitchburg in The Pines apartment complex on High Ridge Trail just off Fish Hatchery Road. There was nothing particularly outstanding about the apartments, but they fit the bill—four units together in an area that was safe and wouldn't leave us worrying that our computers were going to get ripped off. Our office was walking distance away, at 2622 High Ridge Trail; Carmack lived upstairs. It was an efficient setup, which was lucky because we had a mountain of work to do.

Flying back to Louisiana with the news, we were eager to pack up our stuff and leave Shreveport behind. We hired a single moving truck, threw most of our belongings into it, and prepared for our journey north. Carmack and his cat Mitzi rode with Tom, as his MG had died recently. Our computers and monitors traveled with us. Each night, we carried them from the trunk or back seat of our cars and into our motel rooms for safekeeping. Nothing else mattered except what was on those computers. We had no backups except the data replicated on our four machines. If the whole moving truck had caught fire and then fallen into an alligator-infested bayou, we would have cared far less than if even one of our computers had gone missing. Looking back on this time, and other even earlier times, I remain amazed that a single machine and a whole lot of work can so dramatically change the trajectory of one's life. We knew what those machines meant to us and to our livelihood.

On September 1, 1991, we agreed to meet for our first day of work in the new location. It was a two-story brick building that had a kitchen and workspace on the ground floor and a bathroom, washer and dryer, and game room for *D&D* and our Super Nintendo Entertainment System (SNES) upstairs. Carmack's bedroom was also upstairs. I never paid any attention to his bedroom, but one day I peeked my head in. There was a pillow, a lamp, and a stack of computer books on the floor next to a blanket. He had no bed. I felt sorry for him. How could you sleep on the floor and still work long hours and not be fatigued? I went out to the local mattress store and got him a single mattress so he could at least sleep well. The rest of the bedroom setup was up to him.

We settled in, hooked our machines up, and got back to work on *Commander Keen 4*. Our goal was to get the second *Keen* trilogy done by Christmas. We also had two more games due for *Gamer's Edge*, but we could worry about them later.

At this point, and like many PC games, our audioscape consisted of whatever the PC speaker was capable of, which wasn't much. While consoles had evolved and featured fantastic soundtracks, the PC market lagged well behind. PCs required a special sound card to produce music of any quality. The AdLib was the first sound card to hit the market in 1987, followed by the Soundblaster in 1989. More and more gamers were adopting this hardware, and in reading magazines, I could see that the bigger companies were developing for it. *The Secret of Monkey Island* and *Ultima VI* were the first games I played that featured FM Synth MIDI. It transformed the play experience.

Everyone on the id team had spent years designing games, but out of all of us, only I really cared about the sound. Maybe this was all an extension of my obsessive interest in music and the sound quality of my own games in the '80s, but I embraced the responsibility of handling id's audio performance. We were going to be able to play MIDI music starting with the engine for *Keen 4*, so I asked Scott Miller if he knew anyone that made MIDI music. He told me about a guy named Bobby Prince, a lawyer turned musician who had just gotten into computer MIDI music. Bobby is an interesting guy. He started his career as an original member of The Jesters, a soul band that shared bills with top R&B acts in the mid-sixties. He led a platoon in Vietnam. He got a law degree in 1980, but also pursued his interest in jazz, eventually leaving law altogether and making music full time when Apogee had several games in development.

I contacted Bobby and told him we were just starting to get music playing in our new game, and I asked if he could send us a short song so we could test it out. By that point, we had a modem, so Bobby sent a short MIDI tune titled "Too

Hot." I converted the music file to our own proprietary IMF format or ID Music Format, and showed the game off to Carmack, Adrian, and Tom with Bobby's music in place. The song was great, and we felt that its inclusion took our games, if not to the next level, then to a higher standard of quality. Bobby was hired as a contractor. Adding music to *Keen 4* put it on the same level as games produced by bigger developers.

While we were working on *Keen 4*, we got a surprise. Mark Rein called to tell me that he signed a retail game publishing deal with a Toronto-based publisher named FormGen. We had never heard of them. The surprising news was that Mark had promised them a new *Keen* game in time for Christmas. It was early September 1991, we had just moved to Madison, we were almost finished making *Keen 4*, and we were ready to start on *Keen 5*. We had two more games to deliver to *Gamer's Edge* in 1991, too. Five games in fewer than four months! Even if *Keen 4* was almost done, it was still a monumental task. And now he wanted to add another game? To top it off, he had already signed a deal. This was a challenge that even a death schedule could not solve.

We had to talk it over and decide what to do. It was a good problem to have, but a problem nonetheless. The only answer that made sense was to shorten the second *Keen* trilogy, *Goodbye, Galaxy*, to two games, and the third game would be for FormGen. We knew this would disappoint Scott Miller at Apogee, but there was no way we could get four *Keen* games made by Christmas on top of the two games we had to deliver to *Gamer's Edge*. We'd be lucky to finish the five we planned to make during the last six months of 1991 as it was. I called Scott to tell him the bad news, and he explained exactly what we knew already.

"You cannot split up the trilogy," Scott said. "It's a proven marketing win, and anything less means fewer sales."

"Mark already signed us up," I explained. "Plus we still have to do those *Gamer's Edge* games."

Scott doubled down, reiterating his concerns.

"We can't squeeze any more time into the day," I told Scott. "It's already an impossible task."

There was genuinely no way we could do it all, and we didn't want to cancel the FormGen deal. Getting onto store shelves was an important next step for us, and it wasn't just one game, either. After we delivered a *Keen* to them this year, they wanted another game in 1992.

Seeing no other alternative, Scott decided to go with our plan and see what kind of sales a two-game *Keen* set might bring. With the benefit of hindsight, I can answer that question: not as many. The second *Keen* set had one-third the sales of the original trilogy. It's a pity, because *Keen 5* was the best game of the bunch.

At least we had our plan for the rest of 1991. For a game to hit retail game stores, we needed to finish the retail *Keen 6* immediately after *Keen 4* shipped. Retail games required a much longer lead time than mail-order games. First, the games were boxed, then sent to a distribution outlet, and last, sent off to retail stores where they are available for purchase. We could start on *Keen 5* when *Keen 6* was done.

On September 14, 1991, we finished work on *Keen 4*. Beginning to end, it took us two and a half months. The following day, we started working on *Commander Keen 6: Aliens Ate My Baby Sitter!* We needed to shorten *Keen 6*'s dev time to just two months so we could finish by the middle of November. To do so required that we scope it way the hell down. By now, we knew we went overboard with *Keen 4*'s design. There were forest levels, deserts, ice levels, and underwater levels. It was way too much art and way more code.

Tom kept his design laser-focused on *Keen 6*. He only invented an entirely new planet, Fribbulus Xax, where Keen's babysitter, Molly, was kidnapped by Bloogs and guarded by Blooguards, Grabbiters, Fleex, and Bobbas. Of course, we had to make eighteen levels with an entirely new set of graphics. This was going to be a retail version of *Keen*, after all.

We became exceedingly efficient. We worked on multiple games at a time, moving from one game to another, in an attempt to get everything done. It was a frantic pace that required expert-level focus and real-world optimization. We decided to cut down any travel outside of going to the office, not only because of the workload but also because it was miserable outside, with ice and snow starting to appear. We may have known how to code in Assembly language, but it had never occurred to Carmack or me to ask the critical question: "What is it like here in the winter?"

Not going outside meant no trips to State Street to get Cellar Subs and the elimination of time spent reading *The Onion*. We ordered pizza for delivery instead. We knew we needed to start on another *Gamer's Edge* game soon, so we hit *Keen 6* hard at the start, quantifying every asset that needed to be created and powering through the creation of the characters and levels as fast as the art was made by Adrian. Code-wise, the *Keen 4* engine already had so much functionality in it that Carmack instead focused on new enemy AI for the first couple weeks; it was the only new code the game needed.

For short breaks, we continued our tradition of playing *Dungeons & Dragons* on Saturday nights. Carmack's *D&D* campaign took place in a large, cohesive world with many characters playing politics for power. We stumbled upon vampire castles with crystal coffins on an underground shore, traveled with the Silver Shadow Band on the back of a silver dragon to a forbidden land, watched a superbeing named Quake as he destroyed parts of huge buildings with his hammer and attempted a smash-and-grab in a fortress. We were along for the ride. It was so nonstop and ruthless, and it was the most fun we ever had in *Dungeons & Dragons.*

On October 1, once *Keen 6* was rolling and Carmack had finished his work, he switched gears and moved over to work on the next game for *Gamer's Edge.* In total, we had three games left for them, two of which needed to be finished before Christmas. We decided to make another 3D game based on the *Hovertank One* tech. *Catacomb 3D* was to be the third game in the *Catacomb* series, which started with Carmack's Apple II original game, his first game at *Softdisk. Catacomb 3D* was a medieval dungeon crawler where the player takes the role of a sorcerer named Petton Everhail, who fireballs demons and orcs to get to the lair of Grelminar the Lich to save Nemesis. Since *Keen 6* was also in the works, Adrian had to deal with both games at once, as did Tom and I. We made levels for *Catacomb 3D* in addition to the *Keen* games.

Like *Hovertank One, Catacomb 3D* doesn't get much credit for its role at the vanguard of gaming. Again, this probably had to do with the fact that it was a *Gamer's Edge* release, and it was only our second 3D game[*]: design- and tech-wise, we had yet to really find our groove. It was, however, the first action game to use texture maps.

I'd heard about texture maps from my friend and former coworker Paul Neurath back in November 1990, when Carmack, Tom, Adrian, and I were just starting work on *Shadow Knights.* We were catching up, and I talked for a bit about my current job at *Gamer's Edge.* Paul was at his new start-up, Blue Sky Productions. He said, "My team is working on a game with a popular IP, you can probably guess it. We're using a technique called texture mapping."

I suspected his team at Blue Sky was working on something related to *Ultima* since he had left Origin, but since he didn't offer that information, I didn't ask. By this time, I had gotten used to the necessarily vague ways game developers talked about games still in development and not yet announced.

"Texture mapping? What's that?" I asked.

"It's where you take a graphic and map it onto a rectangle that's at an angle, like looking down a hallway. It looks great," Paul said.

"Awesome, I can't wait to see it."

---

[*] It was also our second first-person shooter, but that name had yet to be invented.

Once I was off the phone, I told Carmack about texture mapping. He thought about it for a few seconds and said, "I think I can do that."

Just under a year later, he did. As it turned out, *Catacomb 3D* even came out before Blue Sky Productions' *Ultima Underworld*, the game Paul had been referring to.*

Prior to *Catacomb 3D*, texture mapping for games was used once in 1985 with a game called *Alternate Reality: The City*, but that was a much more primitive game that used a lot of text. *Catacomb 3D* had great-looking animated walls and gargoyles that melted into a puddle that really made the gameplay visceral. To track the character's health, we displayed his face on the right side of the screen, and as he took damage, he slowly turned into a skeleton—first you see your neck bones and then your skull, something that would become a mainstay of early FPS games. *Catacomb 3D* truly heralded the future of 3D: smooth movement in any direction, and fast-drawing, texture-mapped walls, something no one else had done in a game before. Drawing a texture on a wall is the digital equivalent of wallpaper. However, it was extremely time-consuming and processor intensive and slowed everything down. Carmack found a way to draw pixels four times faster.† As it turns out, *Catacomb 3D* was the last id Software game for *Gamer's Edge*. While we still had two more games to satisfy our contract, things were getting too busy for us. Our time was better spent creating the future than unraveling ourselves from the past. We outsourced both *Gamer's Edge* games to other programmers and delivered them to *Softdisk*. One of those games, *ScubaVenture*, was completed by none other than George Broussard, the future architect of *Duke Nukem 3D*.

Meanwhile, we were all barrels blazing on the development of *Keen 6* while Mark Rein was getting things primed for its retail release. He had an agency ready

---

* An important piece of information I'd like to clear up is the erroneous story that John Carmack was at the Consumer Electronics Show (CES) in the summer of 1990 where there was an alleged demo of *Ultima Underworld*. The story goes that Carmack saw the demo and declared he could write a faster texture mapper. While I don't doubt that Carmack could indeed do that, this story suggests that Carmack saw and appropriated the tech, and he did no such thing. It's true the idea to add texture mapping into 1991's *Catacomb 3D* came from Paul Neurath during my 1990 phone call with him, but that's all the contact we had with anyone involved with that game during its development. Time-wise, it's also impossible. *Ultima Underworld*'s development started just a couple months prior. That game took two years to make and was released six weeks before *Wolfenstein 3-D*. I know John never saw *Ultima Underworld* because he was working at Softdisk every single day with me. Neither of us had been to any shows in 1990—we worked constantly. Carmack had not been to a show until KansasFest 1991 in July. He had not even heard of texture mapping until I mentioned it to him after talking with Paul in November 1990.

† If you're interested in how he did this, it has to do with how memory is laid out and how Michael Abrash's book described a mode called CHAIN-4 that allowed Carmack to write four pixels at once instead of the usual single pixel.

to make the *Keen 6* box and asked if we could send over art they could use for the front and back.

"Wow," was all I could think to say to him. "Adrian already has a lot going on at the moment."

We were growing with the industry, learning the new requirements as it evolved. While boxed games had been around since the late 1970s, it hadn't occurred to us that we needed to create the art for our own box. We later learned that most game companies outsourced that work to artists who specialized in big box art. Adrian spent a few hours taking his game art and mocked up the front and back covers in Deluxe Paint II.

In early November, the box arrived for us to approve. As our first boxed game, we were eager to see it, and we had high expectations. After all, the company that designed Lipton tea boxes was handling our account. When it arrived at the office, we gathered around for an unboxing, and everyone was speechless. Adrian broke the silence.

"What the fuck?"

The box was horrible. Even though Adrian made great art, it just didn't cut it for a box—it was too low-resolution and set inside a square that made it look far more like a cereal box than a computer game. The color scheme was hard to get your head around: yellow, blue, and red stripes on a white box with weird ruler lines on the side. It featured five different fonts. The *Keen* name was in red on blocked 3D letters while "Aliens Ate My Baby Sitter!" was instead shadowed in red and blue. To top it off, there was even an error with an inverted letter B in the title. We told Mark they needed to get an artist to redo the box—we had no time left.

FormGen found an artist named Ken Rieger, who created an excellent box cover for *Keen 6*, and we approved it immediately. It was so nice seeing a professionally designed box for a game of ours. All Apogee games were just disks mailed out to customers—no boxes. We were in the big leagues now!

We finished development on *Keen 6* on November 10, 1991, and it shipped to stores in December. Making a complex game like *Keen 6* in such a short time—especially a game we were proud of from a design, technical, and, thanks to Bobby Prince, musical perspective—felt like a tremendous achievement. Holding the finished box in our hands, it was another moment where we felt we had arrived.

Years later, a game collector showed me his *Keen 6* box: It was the terrible one with the ruler marks on the side and the five fonts. It was only then that I realized that FormGen shipped the approved box in the US and the ugly box in Canada, outright ignoring our feedback. It's possible they had gone to production in Canada and didn't want to put the brakes on it. Maybe they reasoned that we'd never see it since we lived in the US. In spite of its ugliness, its rarity makes it one of the more sought-after Keen boxes.

Now we were down to the last month or so of our hardest year, a year in which we shipped thirteen games. It's challenging to explain to people why we were doing this and just how much we were also enjoying it. We were running the equivalent of a programming marathon, and as a team, we were at peak performance and always hitting new peaks. We were doing precisely what we wanted to do and loved working together.

We wasted no time celebrating *Keen 6*'s delivery and immediately started making *Keen 5: The Armageddon Machine*. With the scope of *Keen 6* taking two months, we figured we could get *Keen 5* done in one month because *Catacomb 3D* needed just a couple more weeks.

For a year now, we had been using what we called SneakerNet to transfer files between our PCs—we copied the files we had been editing onto a 3.5" floppy and walked it over to each other—typically among me, Tom, and Carmack. Adrian didn't run the game; he just made the art. Every once in a while, Tom got new art from Adrian, and he'd integrate it using my IGRAB tool, then pass that disk to me and Carmack.

We needed a better way to do this. We decided to get a file server PC with a huge hard drive, network cards, and cables so we could connect all our computers together. Then we could save our work for easy retrieval in one place. It also served as a necessary backup. At conferences, I am regularly asked what we used for backups and source control. Programmers are both surprised and horrified to find out that we didn't use anything. That said, we were exceedingly careful, and source control and backup systems weren't common at the time.

As we developed the game, I knew we had to fit everything on a 3.5" disk for distribution. One more disk would double the cost of goods and return less profit, so cramming it all on one disk was important. To ensure the maps could fit, Carmack came up with a clever way to compress them—a modified version of a Huffman algorithm. I called it Carmacizing the maps and programmed that compression into TED5. It worked well, helped us fit on 3.5" disks, and kept our costs down.

To get *Keen 5* done on time, we shaved off five levels for a total of thirteen, including a secret level. If you look closely at the title screen, you can see the secret level in the window next to Keen as he's running from Robo Red. It's a little red and blue metal building. We loved putting in Easter eggs like this, hoping players might discover them, and thus rewarding them for that discovery.

We could tell Adrian was getting into the swing of things with *Keen 5* because he did some outstanding art. He created all the graphic tiles to populate the levels using our new tilted perspective, all the animated items and enemies. In addition,

Adrian created all the tile art for the world map, the Armageddon Machine, plus the title screen and menus. With one month to finish the game, he plowed through. By the end of November, *Catacomb 3D* was off to *Gamer's Edge*, and Carmack focused on *Keen 5* with the rest of us.

In early December, I saw an advertisement in the local paper from a company called Raven Software that was looking for a programmer. I thought Raven sounded like a game company name, so I gave them a call, and Brian Raffel answered the phone.

"Hi, I was wondering if you're a game company? Do you develop games?" I asked.

"Yeah, that's what we do. RPGs," Brian answered.

"I'm with a game developer in town named id Software. Mind if we come over and say hi?"

Brian enthusiastically agreed and gave me their address.

Tom, Carmack, and I drove over. It was a fun time talking to other game developers, something we hadn't done in months. We met company owners Ben Gokey, the programmer, and the Raffel brothers, Brian and Steve, who were graphic artists. They showed us *Black Crypt*, a graphically impressive RPG for the Amiga, and we shared what we were up to.

The next day, I had a plan. Could we interest Raven in licensing our engine to make a platformer? To do this, we needed to find a way to fund the game and cover Raven's burn rate.[*] Once the game was done, we would recoup that investment and earn a license fee and royalties, a traditional business arrangement in games between publisher and developer. I asked the guys if they would agree to cover half of Raven's $10K per month burn rate if Apogee covered the other half. Once they agreed, I called Scott Miller and told him about Raven, said that we wanted to offer them a license for *Keen 4*'s tech, and asked if Scott would fund the other half of their burn rate. Excited about another *Keen* engine game trilogy, Scott was in.

I called Raven and talked to Brian. I offered him development funding of $10,000 per month to create a game for the PC using our *Keen 4* engine. Brian sounded excited and said he'd discuss it with his two partners. As it turned out, the Raffel brothers weren't interested. They just couldn't limit themselves to sixteen-color graphics. It didn't matter that the Amiga market was waning. For the time being, they stuck to their guns, but we agreed to keep in touch.

By the middle of December, we were putting the finishing touches on *Keen 5*, inspired by our love of sci-fi to get *Keen's* space setting just right. We drew from our shared knowledge base, having all read Isaac Asimov's Foundation series,

---

[*]   A burn rate is the amount of money it takes to keep a company afloat for a period of time. Weekly, monthly, or annual burn are common terms in business.

Frederick Pohl's *Gateway* (The Heechee Saga), Arthur C. Clarke's *Rama* series, Dan Simmons's Hyperion Cantos series, and much more. We knew it had to be a good game because, as a part of a set, it was the only game that players paid for. When we finished, the setting, the levels, the enemies, and the music were better than *Keen 4*. To me, it's the best of the series. We finished a year and a day after our first *Keen* trilogy went live. On December 15, 1991, I uploaded the zip file to Scott.*

Having shipped thirteen games without a break, we were as ready as people could be for vacations.

I spent that winter break in California with Beth, who I'd now been seeing for a few months. We stayed at my parents' house, and I visited with my sons Michael and Steven, who were still young, just two and three, but I was amazed at how much they had grown since I last saw them. Each month at such a young age is leaps and bounds, and I traveled home as often as I could during the year. Even though I was holding them in my arms, I longed for us to be together and see each other more often. Both were smiley, happy boys. As they opened their gifts on Christmas, I got down onto the floor, too, playing with them and their toys, putting them on my lap, treasuring the time we had together. I couldn't get enough of them, really. Kelly was doing a great job with them. I was also happy to see that Kelly, back with her family and support network in California, was back to being the happy person that I'd known.

---

* Astute readers will note that *Keen 6* came out first. However, players didn't know what the game numbers were. They only saw the game titles. *Goodbye, Galaxy* contained *Keen 4* and *5*. *Aliens Ate My Baby Sitter* was *Keen 6*.

CHAPTER 11

Foundation

Over the Christmas break, while the rest of us headed home to visit our families, Carmack stayed in Wisconsin. He was expecting a package, cash-on-delivery: an impressive workstation, the NeXTstation by Steve Jobs's new company, NeXT Computer. The machine used the incredible NeXTSTEP operating system, which was light-years ahead of MS-DOS. It was the future. Carmack ordered one and needed to get an $11,000 cashier's check for the delivery guy, but with his MG left for dead in Shreveport and all of us out of town, he trudged to the bank on foot, cursing the snow, ice, and freezing temperatures the whole way.

When we got back from vacation, we saw the NeXTstation in action. It was incredible, mind-boggling even. John told us about the research he had completed, running tests on vector quantization compression of VGA screens to see what kind of gains he could get over JPEG. I happened to have a copy of *King's Quest V* by Sierra Online, which I'd picked up over Christmas, and the screens provided some good compression benchmarking data for him. Carmack and I discussed its technical prowess and what it might mean for our fledgling company. For now, though, it was just research, and the NeXT was a tool and an expensive toy. It was time for us to get back to work.

Recharged, we started on the next *Commander Keen* trilogy: *The Universe Is Toast*. We decided to test out a couple of new features to make *Keen* even closer to a console game. We added parallaxing layers to give the illusion of depth. With parallaxing, we draw multiple layers of background and foreground art and move them at varying speeds so that the entire scene appears to be 3D. We also decided to go with 256-color VGA graphics instead of Keen's current sixteen-color EGA. These features were expensive memory-wise and speed-wise, however. VGA data was double the size of EGA data, and parallaxing layers drew over layers below, which could slow down the frame rate. To do some speed benchmarking, Adrian took some of *Keen 4*'s EGA graphics assets, turned them into VGA graphics and Carmack made a demo. It both looked good and ran fast enough. With more optimization, it could run even faster, but the initial results gave us the confidence to start developing.

Tom put together the demo map for Carmack to use. Luckily, TED5 already had the ability to edit a map's background layer and foreground layer. It needed more than just that to get parallaxing working, though. I started updating the editor, but for now, background and foreground was all we needed.

With that, we had our quick plan, and we began work on *Keen 7*'s tech demo. Quick plans were normal for us. We jumped into everything headfirst. As a streamlined team, our workflow was efficient. We charged on for a week, but somehow, instead of picking up steam, we seemed to be running out of gas. It was 11 p.m. on Friday night. We should have been full of excitement after a week's work on a new game.

"I am just not getting excited about making another *Keen* trilogy," I said to the room.

"Same here," Adrian added.

After seven episodes, we had just had enough of *Commander Keen*, shiny VGA parallax scrolling or not.

"The parallaxing looks great, but I just can't get excited about another sidescroller," I said. I knew that 3D was the way to go, and I felt like with each new 3D game, we were getting further ahead. *Keen* felt like a step backward. "*Catacomb 3D* was cool. I think we should be making 3D games instead."

Carmack swung around in his chair, nodding in agreement.

Tom was left as the lone *Keen* holdout. To him, Keen was more than just a character in a video game. Tom *was* Keen. With *Keen 7*, we started a new trilogy, and if we finished this game and two additional games, *Keen* entered a pantheon of rare creative efforts, a trilogy of trilogies! Plus, there were the two weeks we'd invested in creating the demo.

Looking again at *Keen* and our new demo on the screen, none of us saw the future. Parallaxing already existed on consoles, and *Keen* existed in seven other games. Besides, after doing so much *Keen* in 1991, we needed to try something new. It was time to make a big decision again—what was our next game going to be? Beyond that, there was another question looming, a bigger one: What were *we* going to be as a company?

The previous year was a challenging and exciting year for id Software and for the four of us as individuals. We formed our own company, shipped thirteen games, signed our first international distribution deal, and moved from a bayou to a blizzard.

We were excited about the potential the new year held, particularly working on a brand-new game. We had all the work we wanted, and every month $50,000 was going straight into our bank account. Our success was staggering to us, but it was not something we dwelled on. Making the next game was more interesting to us than whatever we might do with the money. That said, financial security meant we could take a step back and design a better way of working.

Throughout 1991, we had been beholden to the calendar, slicing our time this way and that to get all the games done and delivered. We were focused on *completing* games to our standard of quality, and each provided an innovation in some way. What we had done in that year was impressive, particularly when I compared our output against any other small group of developers. However, we fought the clock the whole way and exhausted ourselves. Money was great, but money wasn't all it took to make a great game. For that, we needed time. So in designing the next phase of id Software, we decided that our games were done when they were done. We put the focus on quality, on making something great, instead of making something as good as we could in the time allowed. It was a pivotal change that allowed us to focus on both tech and design innovations to create games we really wanted to play. We were in a fortunate position—as hard-core gamers, we knew great gameplay.[*] As game developers, we knew how to make it happen.

We kept things in place that were working for us. Carmack and I liked how we had divided the code responsibilities. Having Carmack focused exclusively on developing the game's engine and AI gave us a technical edge. As a game designer and a programmer, I focused on all the design-side code, programming the gameplay that we separated out from the core engine and AI code. Also on my plate were level design, music and sound effect integration, intermissions, and menus, as well as the production-side details such as the creation of the final master disks for distribution. Tom focused exclusively on creative direction, game design, sound effect creation, and level design, while Adrian, of course, handled all art.

The question remained: If not *Keen 7*, then what? We agreed that 3D was the future.

We brainstormed to come up with a new game that improved on *Catacomb 3D*'s engine. A few ideas were kicked around, including Tom's suggestion for a game about a lethal lab with mutants running amok called *It's Green and*

---

[*] We were so busy trying to define the cutting edge and making a ton of games that we didn't do a lot of competitive analysis. During 1991, we played a lot of the new NEO-GEO console games, and each one cost us more than $100. We played SNES and Sega Genesis games, and also bought a handheld Atari Lynx. We played everything new on the consoles because PC games had nothing like that. To us, they felt dated, and we were trying to change that.

Pissed. It was a funny title, but as I told him, it was the oldest idea this side of *Frankenstein*.

I started thinking along retro lines, too, but my idea was to make a totally new game out of a classic video game.

"Why not just make *Wolfenstein* in 3D," I suggested.

Castle Wolfenstein, was a fun and revolutionary Apple II game that came out in 1981. Silas Warner, the developer, was ahead of his time in many ways. His game had an overhead view of each room in a huge, multistory castle. Stealth was an important gameplay mechanic—that is, your survival required cunning and avoidance as much as a killer instinct. It was also one of the earliest video games to have characters that spoke via audio and not just text. The game centered on a soldier, the player, who had been captured by Nazis and imprisoned in the dungeon of a castle. He obtained a gun, ten rounds of ammo, and three hand grenades and used them as he attempted to steal Nazi plans and escape. I played that game so often that I learned how to escape every one of the castle's randomized floorplans (the exits were always at the same places). Like me, Carmack and Tom had also spent hours running from digital Nazis. Only Adrian, who grew up a non-gamer, had missed out on the masterpiece and its sequel, *Beyond Castle Wolfenstein*.

The response to my suggestion was immediate.

"Ah, yes! Of course!"

"That would be awesome."

Their reaction was one of the reasons I loved working with these guys. It's like we had lived parallel gaming lives.

Tom gave us a pitch in short order. Captured American operative William "B.J." Blazkowicz single-handedly attacks the Nazi regime in three different episodes: "Escape from Castle Wolfenstein," "Operation: Eisenfaust," and "Die, Führer, Die!," the last of which ends in battle below the Reichstag with Adolf Hitler in an armored suit—we dubbed him Mecha-Hitler—complete with chain guns. The name of the third episode mirrored *Commander Keen*'s third episode, "Die, Keen, Die!"

Of course, there was one sticky problem with remaking *Castle Wolfenstein*: the name of the game. Assuming MUSE Software owned the trademark, Tom and I started brainstorming alternative names, but nothing stuck.* So we put the name on the back burner, which we had the luxury to do since the game didn't have a ship date. For the time being, we were content calling it *Wolfenstein*.

We started going over all the features we wanted in the game, starting at the beginning. We wanted a graphical loading screen, something new for our games,

---

* The similarity in names between our MUSE tool and MUSE software are coincidental.

and one that was tech aware. Like the *Keen* games, we wanted it to show how much memory you had, which graphics modes you had available, and tell the player the game detected your gamepad, joystick, sound card, and other info. Since we were building upon *Catacomb 3D*'s source code, we started making *Wolfenstein* with sixteen-color EGA graphics as we had always done. Tom came up with the roster of enemies for the game, and it looked like we would need some help with character animation. Each character was more involved than a *Commander Keen* character, because we wanted these enemies to appear 3D even though they were sprites (2D images). We planned to draw them at every angle so you could even see their backs—something *Catacomb 3D* didn't do. *Wolfenstein* would know which sprite to draw depending on the angle from which you viewed them. To help us, we contacted Jim Norwood, who made *Bio Menace* with our *Keen* engine. He agreed to start drawing sixteen-color Nazi rotations.

We were only a couple weeks in when Scott Miller called me to hear about the new game, eager to publish it. I gave him the rundown *Wolfenstein*'s cool features, and he loved the concept. However, he had one suggestion.

"Make it in VGA," Scott said. "Forget EGA. It's the past."

I had to admit he had a good point. We planned to make *Keen 7* in VGA, but we didn't think about it for *Wolfenstein 3-D* because we were using *Catacomb 3D*'s EGA engine.

I shared Miller's comment with Carmack. He thought about it for a few minutes. Then he said, "It would be cleaner code-wise."

Art-wise, it wasn't so clean. With the switch to 256-color VGA from sixteen-color EGA, all the art made up to that point had to be scrapped, including the art we outsourced to Jim. Adrian spent some time considering the change and assessing Jim's style. He decided he could do better on his own, and was even feeling excited about it: His color palette just multiplied by sixteen.

Scott wasn't the only one looking for a game. We still had one more to make to fulfill our two-game contract with FormGen. It made the most sense to use the *Wolfenstein* tech and make a new game with our existing *Wolfenstein* IP. I rang FormGen and talked to Randy MacLean, one of the owners.

"We're developing a game called *Wolfenstein*," I said. I barely got the name out before he jumped in, excited.

"That's great! What's it about?"

"It's a 3D World War II Nazi blast-fest," I answered. The enthusiasm of the whole team was in my voice.

The line went silent.

"Ah, guys, don't go digging up that World War II stuff," Randy said. It was a funny comment, considering the success Indiana Jones had at that point, not to mention numerous other books and movies.

"Sorry, Randy, but that's what we're making!" I answered.

To create the levels for *Wolfenstein*, we decided to use TED5 once again, since the levels were going to be based on a 2D grid like *Hovertank One* and *Catacomb 3D*. Tom got to work making the icons we'd need that represented characters, items, and features such as Nazi patrol paths, level start, and exit.

Meanwhile, Carmack got the project established and running quickly. It was able to run levels within a day or two, and a couple of weeks later, every asset was quantified. We just needed to make them and put them in the game. Carmack didn't take long to convert the renderer to VGA and optimize it. I worked on the menu system and made levels with Tom. Adrian cranked out art constantly.

I wanted *Wolfenstein*'s audio to stand out as well. To date, none of our games had digitized audio. We'd previously used the PC speaker, which was primitive, and FM synth audio (the sound of the 1980s). Digitized audio, on the other hand, is like listening to an MP3. I saw it as another opportunity for us to innovate and pull ahead of our competition. The Soundblaster was capable of supporting digitized audio, and we figured we could replicate the original *Castle Wolfenstein*'s digital audio but go over the top. Once that feature was added to the game, for players without a Sound Blaster, we still needed to support only the PC speaker and AdLib FM Synth sound effects. So, in effect, we needed to support three different sound systems. I modified MUSE to handle digital audio files so everything could be packaged cleanly.

The most important thing, of course, was the gameplay. At first, we started by reproducing several of the gameplay features of the two previous *Wolfenstein* games made by Silas Warner. It wasn't a clone, but rather a reimagining of features we knew game players would expect, except this time, all in a 3D space. Players searched dead bodies, dragged bodies around to hide them from guards, and unlocked chests for loot. Our game even allowed you to wear a Nazi uniform to sneak past guards and hold up others to take their guns and ammo. They were some great features, sure, but when we played, something else was happening. We were having more fun running and gunning Nazis than using the slower-paced game features like looting. "Speed" became our operative word, the core around which the game was to be built.

As a game designer, playing the game is essential, not just to test out the features you've created, but to find the fun. Sometimes, that fun isn't in the things you thought were features, as was the case with the early *Wolfenstein*, or worse, the features are getting in the way of the fun. This is why completing an early "first playable" of a game is so important. "First playable" is an industry term and defines the point at which the core loop of the game is completely playable. For a first-person shooter, that core loop is often something like this: Players and enemies can move, shoot at one another, take damage, and die.

The drive for speed ended up simplifying our game design. Anything that slowed the game down got cut. Goodbye, loot chests, dead guard dragging, and holding up guards. The fun of the game was in destroying screaming Nazis as fast as possible. To that, we added high production values.

Our core was this: Kill everything in sight. By the middle of February 1992, we had our template down.

Although Mark Rein was assisting us, I was still involved in the business strategy for id Software.* I had read that Sierra was thinking about entering the kids' game market, and I thought we would be a good fit, especially since our newest game, *Commander Keen in Goodbye, Galaxy*, was a great all-ages title. So I wrote to one of my heroes, game designer and entrepreneur Roberta Williams. She and her husband, Ken, built Sierra Online, a gaming empire, and scored multiple hits with a series of *Quest* adventure games. Their company was a true industry behemoth. My letter was part fanboy, part business. As always, I was interested in making contact with such an influential game designer. More than that, though, I thought we might be able to work on a new IP for kids and publish it through them. I sent my letter off with a copy of *Commander Keen in Goodbye, Galaxy*.

Roberta liked the game and showed it to Ken. He liked it, too. She wrote back and requested a meeting. I was completely stoked that my initiative had paid off. I was going to meet two of my idols and convince them to fund development and publishing of more *Keen* games. It certainly felt possible. We were already making $50,000 a month from *Keen* and *Gamer's Edge*. We had the team and the talent, plus we had the early levels of *Wolfenstein* in our back pocket. It was worth a try.

In mid-February, we flew out to California and drove to Sierra's offices in Oakhurst, about twenty minutes from Yosemite National Park. Mark Rein flew from Toronto, too. It was a great getaway for all of us. We'd been grinding in frozen Madison, Wisconsin, for months. Now we'd been transported to beautiful, warm California. Meeting Roberta and Ken was an honor. They were warm, kind people and game developers who walked the walk. Their offices were in a huge metal building with at least two hundred people working there. We saw an adventure game in development, and Ken showed us how the hand-painted art was scanned in for each scene. He introduced us to Warren Schwader, an Apple II legend, and Tom and I went into Warren's office, got on our knees, and bowed, saying, "We're not worthy!" He also introduced us to the AGI (Adventure Game Interpreter) team. We got together in a meeting room to talk. They could tell Carmack was, let's say, a more advanced programmer.

At one point, Ken wanted to talk business.

---

* Mark was still in his voluntary six-month probationary period.

"I'm curious how the shareware model is working for you," he said. By this time, Sierra Online sold full versions of their games exclusively at retail outlets.

"Great," I told him.

"How much are you making?"

"A little over $50,000 a month in sales."

He got deadly serious. "No way," he said. "That's not possible."

Because we were independent and geographically isolated, we had no idea whether it was possible or not. We just knew what we had.

I showed him our earnings statements. He was stunned. His reaction made us all proud. If he was impressed, we must be doing well indeed.

Later, we went out to dinner at Erna's Elderberry House, the fanciest restaurant in town, where Ken and Roberta were royalty. The management gave us our own dining room with a fireplace and a long banquet table. It might have been the most posh, fancy experience I'd ever had in my twenty-four years on the planet. It felt like I was in a dream. The Williamses ran a great company and made great games. It was like we were commoners dining with the king and queen.

That night, back at the hotel, Mark wanted to talk to us in my room. He was trying to make the case for getting company stock because a major deal might be happening the next day.

"C'mon man. You're not serious," I said. "We've been working incredible hours for a year." His probationary period was meant to get him a job, not ownership. The discussion of stock ended, and we returned to talk about the experience we had at dinner with the Williamses.

The next day, Ken and Roberta took us to their house in the mountains, situated on a lake. The views were breathtaking. After putting them on a pedestal for so long, we couldn't believe they brought us to their house! We were in shock for the next hour. Tom got a peek at Roberta's *King's Quest VI* design guide while I installed our current work in progress on Ken's home PC. We'd only been building *Wolfenstein* for about a month and a half, but it was already head and shoulders above any other PC game, including *Keen*, which had gotten us in the front door. Plus, I knew that he and Roberta were part of the generation that worshipped the original *Castle Wolfenstein*, so I thought this would knock his socks off.

I finished the demo, eager for his response.

"That's cool," he said. "Let me show you *Red Baron*."

I was stunned. I had just demoed a groundbreaking 3D game that represented a whole new paradigm, a VGA texture-mapped, first-person shooter with more depth and detail than any other game out there—and his response was to show me a flight simulation game in a genre that had been around since the 1970s. It felt like a replay of everyone's initial reaction to *Dangerous Dave in "Copyright Infringement,"* but worse. An industry giant, a guy I considered a legend, seemed to miss the revolutionary game design and concept that was right in front of him. Or did he?

Ken may have been more impressed by our shareware earnings than *Wolfenstein,* but he was definitely interested in what we had to offer. The next day, when we sat down in his office to talk, he offered us a $2.5 million stock deal to buy id Software. It was a major opportunity for us—we stood to make half-a-million bucks each. I told him that I would get back to him once we were back in Madison and had a chance to talk about it.

We left Sierra feeling good about our visit. Adrian even created an image with the question, "Part of the Sierra Family?" because acquisition looked like a likely result.

When we were back in the office, I wanted to talk about the Sierra offer to get everyone's pulse.

"Do you know how long it will take us to make that kind of money?" I told the team. "If we do this, we will make it all in one day."

Despite my enthusiasm, I followed the script I'd used with Scott Miller. I called Ken and made a modification to the proposal by asking for $100,000 in cash up front. I had a number of reasons for doing this. First, I'd realized that we wouldn't, in fact, all make half-a-million bucks in a single day; there are always vesting timelines for stock deals. By asking for this advance, we would get some cash immediately, but we had to wait for the rest. Second, I wanted Sierra to put some real skin in the game and $100,000 seemed like a modest amount to me for a company like Sierra Online.

Modest amounts, however, are in the eye of the beholder. Our request for a down payment was too much for Ken and Roberta Williams. He nixed the up-front cash, and we walked away. I felt a strange combination of disappointment and defiance. Doing the deal would have been gratifying, but I knew we were better coders and game developers than anyone at Sierra, so once Ken refused to add cash to the deal, my attitude was: "Too bad for them. We don't need them." I knew that with a few more releases, we'd be in even better financial shape, making money on new and old games and our game engine. Stacking income was a valuable lesson to learn. The more games we made, the more money we made. That could only happen if we continued owning our own company, not by selling it to someone else.

We had a game to make, so we got back to work, and I forgot about doing deals and focused on finishing *Wolfenstein.* At this stage of development, the engine was pretty solid. We had several Nazis in the game, like the Guard, SS, Officer, and the German shepherd. The AI was working well, and they would walk on paths that we set up in TED5. We were mostly excited about a new engine feature we could use in devious ways: sound zones.

Alerting guards is a bad idea in *Wolfenstein*, so you want to kill Nazis when the doors are closed. When you open a door, the sound zone you're in will connect to the sound zone outside the open door, making a much bigger sound zone. Our sound zones were color coordinated, and we had thirty-four different sound zones at our disposal. We filled a room with one color, then made sure the halls outside were a different color, but we'd then use that same color in another room far away, thus alerting those guards anytime a sound was made in a sound zone of that color. It was a basic idea, but it allowed for some scary surprises. Sound zones increased realism because it made sure if you shot someone in a room, someone would hear, whether in that room or in a similarly colored sound zone.

We realized that there was a lot of art to make, and it would be smart to get some help for Adrian. We threw some names around for a minute, then someone mentioned Kevin Cloud. Kevin was a Shreveport native who was a calm, competent workhorse. He was *Softdisk*'s editorial director and had become id's primary contact while fulfilling our obligations to the company, but he had also worked as a computer artist at *Softdisk* doing art for the Apple II department. Everything we saw of his we liked, and moreover, we liked him. We decided to invite him up to our office for an interview a week later. It was March and still snowing, so we warned him to be careful.

Madison's snow was heavy and wet and prone to send those not used to it off the road and into a ditch. Tom, Carmack, Adrian, and I stayed inside and spent our weekends playing *Dungeons & Dragons* instead. I always enjoyed our *D&D* sessions in Shreveport, but that winter in Madison, as the storyline grew darker and more gripping, I found them even more exciting. Once, when I was hiding out in a pocket dimension with a semi-powerful figure, Carmack presented me with an option to give a demon *The Demonicron*, the book that controlled the demons' ability to enter the prime material plane, where we lived. I took the chance. I made a deal with the demon hoping to get a magical sword, the Daikatana, along with a couple other powerful artifacts. It was a disastrous decision. I got the sword, but it didn't matter because ALL the demons wound up teleporting onto the material plane and destroying every last thing in it, and thus the game over the next several sessions. The human race was obliterated, and it was all my fault—although a roll of the dice shares some of the blame.

I was crushed when our *D&D* world ended. We'd spent dozens, if not hundreds, of hours exploring this alternative universe, and Carmack spent years building it up. Now it was gone. I still have no idea why he allowed his world to end like that; maybe he was tired of playing with us or was an absolute stickler for the rules. To play again, we had to start over, and that meant waiting for our Dungeon Master to devise another world. Sadly, we never played *D&D* together again, but in the obliteration of our game was hidden an odd circle of life: Not too far in the future, the storyline of our *D&D* saga inspired both a gaming revolution and my most troubled project.

A lot of id's biggest decisions happened late at night. Our unofficial motto was "We are the wind," meaning we could blow out of wherever we were or change direction at any time. We worked superhuman schedules. We developed games faster than anyone. To do that, we quickly absorbed information, analyzed it, and made decisions. We also were id-driven. We wanted whatever it was we wanted—to make the best, coolest, most fun games—and we wanted it now. We called our decisions bit flips—when a computer value changes from on to off, or vice versa.

Our decision to move out of Madison, Wisconsin, happened late one night. It was instigated in part by the impending arrival of Kevin Cloud from *Softdisk*. He drove nineteen hours straight up to Madison with his wife, Lacey. When he arrived at the office at 8 a.m., way too early, he knocked on the door and Carmack answered in his underwear.

Carmack said, "Come back later" and closed the door on them.

Kevin came back later, interviewed with us, and we decided he would be a great addition to the team. He was hired.

It just so happened that our leases were about to be up at The Pines, and we wanted to move to better apartments down the highway near the West Towne Mall. Our apartment complex was becoming riddled with drug dealers and police visits. Kevin and Lacey came along with us to hunt for something in that area. We spent a full day looking at apartments, and finally settled on a complex that we could all move into. It was much nicer than where we were, not that The Pines set a high bar. We had dinner on State Street and decided to go and sign our leases in the morning. Kevin and Lacey went back to their hotel and planned to do the same. As usual, Carmack and I went back and started coding again, Tom worked on levels, and Adrian picked up where he left off.

Around 1 a.m., I just blurted it out: "I hate the winters here. I hate the snow and ice and shit."

"Yeah. I hate it, too!" Adrian blasted.

"I really don't want to stay here anymore," I added. "We should just leave the state. Fuck this. And fuck those new apartments."

"I agree," Adrian said.

I went on a brief rant about not being able to walk outside all winter long. I grew up in the desert and Northern California. I knew there were other, warmer options almost everywhere.

"Remember how cool it was by the lake?" I said to Carmack, reminding him of his waterfront house in Shreveport. "I don't want to go back there, but there must be somewhere else that's warm."

We started throwing around destinations like Jamaica and the Bahamas, but eventually, we decided we needed to be in the US. I offered Salt Lake City, where I had lived with my dad.

"But it has snow, so fuck that place, too."

I mentioned Arizona, but there was no water, and it was hotter than we wanted. New Hampshire? Snow. No.

Then Adrian said, "How about Dallas?"

I grabbed a map from Tom's desk. He had a bunch of maps from our earlier travels.

"Look! There's a lake there," I said and pointed to Lake Ray Hubbard. "We can just get a place on the water!"

Tom was silent. He loved Madison, and he didn't want to go. He started making a list of pros and cons on his computer. There weren't many pros that outweighed the snow.

We started checking off the selling points for Dallas: Scott Miller was there, and so was Apogee. It was warm. Texas had no state income tax, so we would make more money. Origin Systems was headquartered in Austin, so there was already something of a development community. That was it. At 3 a.m. our fate was decided. It was three to one. We were moving to Dallas.

Then someone remembered: "Oh, shit, Kevin's signing a lease in the morning."

We made frantic calls to his hotel room and left messages: "Don't sign the lease!" and "Call us before you go anywhere!"

All we were trying to do was stop Kevin from putting down a deposit. We never considered how he might interpret the messages. When he received them, he immediately thought he was fired. Why else would we tell him not to sign a lease? He even told his wife something must have fallen through. When he showed up at our office at 10 a.m., we told him that id Software was moving to Texas. Though he was surprised at our overnight decision, he was also relieved. Dallas was a lot closer to his hometown of Shreveport, so he and Lacey loved the idea.

The wheels were in motion. We didn't even mind when we discovered that Lake Ray Hubbard was run by the Army Corps of Engineers, so there was no lakefront property.

"Maybe we'll just have to settle for a swimming pool," I said.

Tom and I flew down to Dallas to scope out real estate. Scott drove us to several apartment complexes in Garland and Mesquite, walking through the model units.

It took about eight hours, and we were talking about games the entire time. We settled on La Prada Club Apartments in Mesquite, just south of Apogee's offices in Garland. It was better than all the places we looked at—two-story black-tinted windows, amazing air conditioning, and all the luxury amenities, including a big swimming pool. We rented four apartments plus a one-bedroom loft that would serve as our office. Scott loved the idea that we were closer to Apogee—he loved it so much he increased our royalty to 50 percent.

Hanging out with Scott Miller and his business partner, George Broussard, opened my eyes to living large in Texas. Scott was driving a Nissan 300 Turbo ZX. George had a red Acura NSX, which Honda had just unveiled a year earlier. They bought these cars with the money earned from all the *Commander Keen* games, plus their other titles. We just saved all our money. Our last night in town, we went out to dinner and then headed over to SpeedZone, a local arcade and amusement park, to play video games and race go-carts. Afterward, I got to race around in George's NSX. Finally, Scott drove me and Tom back to our motel.

It was during this time that we decided to part ways with Mark Rein. I'm happy to report that, despite this, Mark has gone on to do great things at Epic Games, helping to turn it into an industry behemoth. In 2021, it was revealed that he was a billionaire, at least on paper.

With Mark's departure, we were once again in need of a biz guy. Our old friend Jay Wilbur called us and said he heard we were moving to Dallas. He was ready to leave *Softdisk* if we'd have him, and it was a unanimous "Yes" on our side. We set April 1, 1992, as his official first day on the job. Jay became id's biz guy on the same day Kevin Cloud started work.

Set up in new offices, making *Wolfenstein* was some of the most fun we'd ever had making a game. A lot of that had to do with our liberation from Madison and our new life in Texas. It was warm. It was sunny. We had apartments at the La Prada Club Apartments and a separate apartment that served as the id office with a swimming pool right behind it. You could open the door and take a dip and lie in the sun. We'd had fun in Shreveport, too, going kneeboarding on the lake, but we were consistently working seven days a week back then and had all been in survival mode.

The truth is that we relished the enormous pressure. You know that moment in a game where you're on your last life? Sometimes that's what it felt like. We had to keep going, keep playing, or the dream would be over. Now, in Texas, we had a financial cushion from *Keen's* success, and *Wolfenstein* was bound to make far more money. If we wanted to hang out and play games, we could. *Street Fighter II* and *Fatal Fury* were our two favorites at the time. There was pressure and a lot of work, but life felt a lot more balanced now that we were focused on delivering just one game.

The hardest thing about making *Wolfenstein* was finishing the levels. The level design was not visually sophisticated, but that is because we made a trade-off, sacrificing visual nuance—textures, colors, angles—in favor of rapid-fire speed, which was part of the thrill of our FPS killfest. Adding those features would have slowed the game down and required more work on the engine. We felt that the slimmed-down feature set was exactly the type of gameplay we wanted. That kept the core loop clean and easy to understand, which was important since it would be the first fast 3D game that anyone had seen.

Earlier in March, Tom and I noticed *Wolfenstein* was missing something, something fun that we were used to, but that this engine didn't support: secret areas. They were a staple of exploration and of our games. We lobbied Carmack to add some way of pushing a wall to reveal a hidden area, but he didn't want to violate the purity of his engine to hack in a secrets-revealing "pushwall." The next couple of months, we pressed him on it until he finally agreed in April to hack it in. It was a trying situation for Tom because, as the creative director, his design was expected to be supported by tech, and now there was pushback that affected the gameplay. The functionality of the engine should support fun gameplay, provided it was possible, not be constrained by it.

Wolfenstein was filled with more artwork than any game we had made. The walls featured great-looking textures, more detailed than those in previous games, while the floors and ceiling were solid colors to maximize engine speed. Room after room, level after level, the walls were a variety of brick, turquoise-blue metal, and wood paneling. Yes, Adrian and Kevin did a great job adding warning signs, swastikas, iron crosses, and Hitler portraits, but from a level design perspective, this creativity was limited. Tom and I found the 3D space exciting, but the levels themselves somewhat tedious to create. Fortunately, the gameplay was fun. The blood-and-guts details made it the most violent game around, and the premise—blowing away Nazis to save yourself and steal their plans—was hilarious.

As our new biz guy, Jay Wilbur's first order of business was trying to hunt down the owner of the *Wolfenstein* trademark. This was before the internet, so it was not easy. Eventually, after many, many phone calls, Jay discovered that a woman in Baltimore had bought all of MUSE Software's intellectual property. Jay offered her $5,000 for the *Wolfenstein* trademark, and she accepted. No more trying out alternate names, none of which stuck—our game would be an official *Wolfenstein* sequel! We decided to call it *Wolfenstein 3-D*. It was the third in the series and 3D.

We felt like we were getting close to the end of the shareware episode's development, but we didn't have all the music and sound effects we needed. Jay called up Bobby Prince, with whom we'd collaborated before, to see if he would fly down to Texas with his equipment and do the work on site. Bobby brought what seemed like a whole studio with him: a huge sampling keyboard, professional monitor speakers with mounts, a studio microphone setup, and a rack of audio processors. Bobby was the real deal.

We let Bobby use the entire bottom living room area in our La Prada office, and he made the music right there. For the voice over (VO), Tom wrote down all the German phrases that needed to be said by the Nazis. We had a German-to-English translation book, and Tom and I spent an afternoon yelling, *"Spion!," "Achtung!," "Mein Leben!," "Mein Gott in Himmel!,"* and all the other lines except *"Schutzstaffel!"** We cajoled Adrian into saying that one. The death screams were the funniest ones to voice. We got good at using Bobby's setup to record stuff.

By the end of April, we knew we were in the home stretch with *Wolfenstein 3-D*. It was getting close. Part of the final polish was making sure all the title screens, end screens, and help screens were in the game with the correct text. One of the extra screens we added just before we showed the title screen was a light-blue screen that said:

This program has been voluntarily rated
PC-13: PROFOUND CARNAGE
By id Software

We designed the screen to look like the 1970s rating screen shown at the beginning of a movie. We added it as a joke, but little did we know it was the first instance of a game being voluntarily rated.

One last detail remained. We had no size limitations on *Wolfenstein 3-D*, so we just made the game and decided to figure it out later. Well, later was now, and the game was bigger than a single disk. We had never made a game bigger than one disk, so I needed to figure out how players were going to get the game off two disks and onto their hard drives. There were several games that were distributed on multiple floppies by 1992, but they had their own proprietary install systems. Today, it's even a business that makes decent money. There was no market for this in 1992, however, and so I had to write it myself. My idea was to create an install system and give it away, to get rid of the proprietary nature of this tool that, to me, should be free for everyone to use. First, I needed to write a tool to take a single ZIP file and split it into 1.44 MB–size chunks that could be copied onto 3.5" disks. Next, I needed to write the installer program that took all the chunks, put them together, and decompressed the game to the destination folder.

---

*   "Spy!," "Danger!," "My life!," "Oh my god!," and "Protection squad!"

The program became known as ICE, the Installation Creation Editor, and took about six hours. Then I started writing DEICE, which would copy files off floppies, put them together, and UNZIP the files at a destination the player specified. I wanted it to be bulletproof, just in case a player pulled the floppy out of the drive mid-copy. I got it all working by the end of the next day. It wasn't long before I gave that system to Apogee so they could use it for all their games.

Everything was ready to go on May 5. The master disk was made, and all of us were testing the game on our PCs. No errors, no crashes, no bugs—the game was solid. After testing every kind of weird scenario we could think of, we knew it was time to upload. It was nearly 3 a.m. We called Scott and George and invited them over.

At 4 a.m., we dialed into Software Creations to upload the 2 MB shareware version. Scott had been talking to Software Creation's owner Dan Linton that day to prepare him for the game's imminent release. For Dan, it was 5 a.m., but he was ready, knowing he was getting the hottest game around. The upload finished, we high-fived, and left the office to sleep until whenever. We knew everything was going to change from that day onward. We felt it.

Wolfenstein 3-D's shareware release was ten times bigger than both *Keen* releases. The first month, we sold 4,000 preorder copies of the *Wolfenstein 3-D* bundle at $60 each, which included two disks with three episodes each, plus a hint book we still had to write. Some players bought just the disks and came back to order the hint book later. *Wolfenstein 3-D* generated $240,000 in sales in May, and our first royalty check for the game was $120,000. Even Randy MacLean at FormGen got behind *Wolfenstein 3-D* when he saw the reviews of the shareware version. Seems digging up that World War II stuff was a good idea after all. We felt it was going to be big, but not *this* big. We didn't change much, but we did decide it was time for raises.

At this point, we had only uploaded the shareware version and still needed to finish the other five episodes. Apogee was accepting orders for all six episodes and the hint book, so we needed to get moving. Even so, it was great to see the reaction from players and reviews in the press from our free shareware release. Four years later, Scott replicated this marketing tactic with *Duke Nukem 3D*.

Based on the promise of the shareware version, *Wolfenstein 3-D* was selling like hotcakes, and it wasn't even done. We had to finish five more episodes, each one containing ten levels. New episodes meant new bosses and new secret levels, and we had to write a hint book. All as fast as possible!

Fortunately, we were good at this. Unfortunately, it was difficult to get the levels done quickly because they were so boring to make. Creatively, Tom and I were used to more visually interesting design spaces with *Commander Keen 4* through *6*'s lush visuals, EGA graphics notwithstanding. Tom was easily distracted, and to get him pumped up again, I would chant, "NSX! NSX! NSX!"—a promise that he could get a car like George Broussard's if only we could finish these damn maps!

We buckled down and tore through them. Bobby Prince wanted to make a level, too, and so we let him. It was one fewer for us to create. After the maps were done and tested, we jumped onto the creation of the hint book. Kevin had already started on the hint guide using the NeXTstation to create it. The NeXT was the perfect machine for it since, in addition to its superior tech, it also had superior graphic design programs. It was made for desktop publishing, and even used Display PostScript, so what you saw on the screen was exactly what you saw printed on the paper. Compared to MS-DOS, it was significantly more advanced. Kevin also created a *Commander Keen* brochure on it.

Tom and I started having fun again. The hint book was more fulfilling creatively because it was our job to inject it with some humor. How many ways can you describe filling a Nazi full of lead to go get a key?

"Get the key, after the SS find themselves more horizontal than normal" was one instruction. Others included:

"The key is hidden behind a wall of uniforms. Lay the uniforms on the floor and you can easily grab the key."

"Here we are at the fabled Elevator of Floor Six. I see no white-bearded magi, golden unicorns and majestic crystalline gate. I guess the ancient description was somewhat . . . embellished."

Not your typical hint book instructions, but they made us laugh.

Kevin wrote the intro text describing the characters in the game, showing Tom's sketches and hints, and then it was on to the maps themselves. At the top of each level's description, we put my fastest time through the level—the first printed instance of FPS speedrunning. Page 25 describes my fastest speed through the first episode: five minutes, twenty seconds.

On June 15, after testing, I made the master disks using ICE and drove them to Scott at Apogee, the first time we had handed over a game in person. Previously, the disks were sent through the mail, and so we were removed from the final process. Scott had his disk duplication people ready to start copying. Soon, they were sending customers an envelope with disks and a manual in it. It would be a year before we sold the game in a retail box through GT Interactive.

We were finally done. The shareware episode took us four months from start to ship, and the other five episodes of *Wolfenstein 3-D* were done in one-and-a-half months. In total, just shy of six months for a six-episode game.

It was time for a short rest. Tom and I spent time in the pool, Carmack bought some nice leather furniture for his place (having had enough of highly optimized but minimal furniture), and Bobby bid us adieu and went back home after a job well done.

Now that customers were getting their orders, we started paying attention to the reviews. None may have been more laudatory than Chris Lombardi's write-up in issue 98 of *Computer Gaming World*. It ended this way:

> Castle Wolfenstein 3-D* is, with Ultima Underworld, the first game technologically capable of creating a sufficient element of disbelief-suspension to emotionally immerse the player in a threatening environment, even when viewing it on a flat screen. I can't remember a game making such effective use of perspective and sound and thereby evoking such intense physiological responses from its players. I recommend gamers take a look at this one, if only for a cheap peek at part of interactive entertainment's potential for a sensory immersed virtual future.

Lombardi also praised the sound and music, even name-checking Bobby Prince's spy-thriller soundtrack and his fantastic stylized, minimalist versions of fight-song favorites, like the "The Marines' Hymn" and "Anchors Aweigh." *Wolfenstein 3-D* also won many awards, including being inducted into the Computer Gaming World Hall of Fame. Many positive reviews cautioned readers about the graphic violence, and in Germany, where Nazi imagery and paraphernalia were illegal, the ratings board refused to give it a rating, which meant it was banned.

While readers may have heard that there was an outcry over the violence in *Wolfenstein 3-D*, it wasn't actually the case, at least not that I saw. On the contrary, most reviews sounded like this one from Peter Olafson in *Electronic Entertainment*: "*Wolfenstein 3-D* is drop-dead gorgeous, outrageous to the ear, stay-up-all-night addictive, and easily the best action game available for the IBM." If they wrote about the violence, it was simply as a disclaimer—"if you find blood and shooting offensive, don't get the game." I don't recall any articles bemoaning the decline of video games, or how horrible *Wolfenstein 3-D* was. That said, I am sure there were some. We were still in the height of the Satanic Panic, and any new media, particularly successful new media, was viewed with suspicion.

---

* *Computer Gaming World* incorrectly identified the name of the game.

The first true FPS was, in its way, the perfect shooter game. Players were escaping a Nazi dungeon as an American war hero blowing Nazis away. Who is going to complain about a game where you're killing Nazis, the universally accepted symbol of evil? The people who complained about shooting the dogs surprised me. They chose to ignore the fact that you're mostly shooting people.

One of the positive messages we received came from an unlikely source: a former Vietman POW who noted that he hesitated to play, fearing flashbacks. He and his friend had dared an escape of their own, making maps and hoarding food in preparation. He made it out, but his friend did not. He said *Wolfenstein 3-D* allowed him to "face the past" and cured him of endless nightmares.

Another unlikely effect of Wolfenstein was finding out that Jewish kids loved playing it because they felt they were getting revenge for their ancestors' suffering at the hands of the Nazi regime.

In retrospect, the id founders should probably thank Ken Williams for rejecting our counteroffer—id's $100,000 in-cash demand—just nine months earlier. We made a lot more money by remaining an independent company. Instead of thanking him, we razzed him just a few months later when we met at the 1993 CODiE Awards, the black-tie gala that was the game industry's equivalent of the Oscars, run by the Software Publishers Association. The four of us were decked out in tuxedos to attend the festivities, and we strutted away with the Best Action/Arcade Game of the year for *Wolfenstein 3-D*. It was an historic victory—*Wolfenstein 3-D* was the first shareware title to nab a CODiE, and id Software was the smallest company to win the honor. If we had joined Sierra Online, the trophy would have been theirs. We saw Ken afterward and I couldn't resist teasing him. "This could have been yours, Ken!" I said, waving the trophy at him. It was a good-natured ribbing.

"I know, I know. I've made mistakes like that before, believe me! It wasn't the first, and it won't be the last."

We laughed, although maybe Ken wasn't laughing quite as hard as we were.

The success of *Wolfenstein 3-D* provided a lot of great moments. We now had three best-selling shareware games all earning money and accolades. The amount of cash pouring in was both gratifying and liberating. As a kid who grew up with his mother using food stamps and clipping coupons, it was an enormous, unfathomable shift. Financial pressures ceased to exist. So did the normal rules of work: The kid who used to wake up at 3 a.m. to deliver newspapers to earn *Pac-Man* money could now sleep until noon, and when he woke up, there was a *Pac-Man* machine in his office. Rest assured, though, if I got in at noon, it was because I had been there until 5 a.m.

However, one of the sweetest moments tied to *Wolfenstein 3-D*'s release occurred during the July 1992 KansasFest. This was the annual computer jamboree held at Avila College in Kansas City, Missouri. It evolved out of AppleFest—the short-lived Apple II series of conferences, the one that landed me a job with Origin Systems. Tom, Carmack, and I had attended previous KansasFests and loved them, because they were filled with Apple II programmers. To us, this was the best thing ever; we'd stay up all night in the dorms just talking with members of our unofficial Apple II–loving tribe. In '92, we showed up and learned that Silas Warner, the creator of *Castle Wolfenstein*, was the guest of honor and was going to give a talk about his former company, MUSE Software. This was a great coincidence. In preparation for the festival, we bought the world's first color laptop—a $5,000 Toshiba—and installed *Wolfenstein 3-D* on it. Now we would get to show it to the man who inspired the game.

It was a great experience. Silas's talk was about the history of MUSE Software and all the different tools and games he wrote. Afterward, he was swarmed with coders who had questions. We waited until the crowd died down and showed him *Wolfenstein 3-D*. He was impressed and happy that the game lived on, even though we left out the stealth aspects and accentuated the violence. Later that evening, a group of us were sitting on the floor in the hallway hanging out. Silas came over and sat on the floor with me, Tom, Lane,* and Carmack. It was an incredible moment: The visionary who inspired us, who we idolized, had literally lowered himself to our level, ready to just hang out and talk about anything and everything. At the end of our long talk, Silas signed the *Wolfenstein 3-D* manual that accompanied the game. That manual is still at id Software's office. I hope someone framed it.

---

* Lane was still at *Softdisk* but regularly attended KansasFest.

CHAPTER 12

Destined to *DOOM*

In 1991, Wolfenstein 3-D assumed the #1 spot on the Usenet list of the Top 100 Games in the World and planted itself there for an entire year. A journalist at a local radio station called us up, and suddenly we were on the airwaves with our first radio interview. Channel 8 in Dallas drove to our office, shot a short clip of our space, and then went over to Apogee. id Software became news, not just in the gaming universe but in the world at large.

Flush with cash, we gave our annual salaries a raise to $45,000 each. I remembered that just four years earlier, my friend, partner, and mentor John Fachini at Origin Systems had told me that no programmer made more than $30,000 and most left the industry before they were thirty years old. That July, we also treated ourselves and our significant others to a week at Disney World on a mega package deal called the Grand Plan. We just had to flash a "Grand Plan" card anywhere in the park, and whatever we were buying—four-course dinners with champagne, cotton candy, or sweatshirts—was paid for. Magic Kingdom indeed!

During our stay at the Grand Floridian hotel, some of us were lounging in one of the hot tubs. There was a bunch of chatter about games and gaming, and a group in the next tub overheard us. As they were leaving, they asked, "Are you the guys who made *Wolfenstein 3-D?*"

"Yeah, that's us," we said.

"Dudes, that game is awesome!"

We thanked them and enjoyed our first buzz of celebrity. Complete strangers knew about us as a result of our work, our games. It was a little unexpected; being recognized and becoming almost famous wasn't something we thought about. That was for rock stars and Hollywood celebrities.

Returning from vacation, we began work on our next game, a prequel episode of *Wolfenstein 3-D* to satisfy the FormGen contract. The original trilogy of *Wolfenstein 3-D* resulted in the player killing Hitler, and its three additional episodes took place on the same timeline and sent players on missions that led up to that pivotal moment. For a prequel, Tom wanted to explore that time in history with a storyline that had Hitler searching for powerful artifacts that he believed would help him win the war. One of these was the spear that pierced the side of Christ, the Spear of Destiny. We thought it was a good idea and a great name. To make it quickly, we planned to reuse the *Wolfenstein* engine, add new bosses, and make it twenty-one levels in a row instead of dividing the levels into multiple episodes. With only a single episode, we didn't have to concern ourselves with unique bosses and the other trappings that came with those divisions.

Since we were using the same engine to make *Spear of Destiny*, Carmack decided to work on a more advanced version of the *Wolfenstein 3-D* engine and see where he could take it for our next big game. He was happy going back into R&D (research & development) mode. Meanwhile, I thought it would be a great idea to see if Raven Software was interested in licensing our existing *Wolfenstein* tech for a new game. For us, this was the beginning of what would become a familiar pattern: Carmack improved the tech while I explored and pushed its potential from a game design and gameplay perspective. At the same time, I worked on licensing the tech. When it came to licensing or gameplay, a thorough understanding of the code base and its strengths and weaknesses was necessary.

We last talked with Raven when we were still in Madison. As I mentioned, we hoped that they would license the *Keen 4* engine and build a new series of platformers. Brian Raffel sounded excited about the PC market, but in the end, Raven decided to stick with the Amiga, and so we went our separate ways. As it turned out, shortly after our call, not only had they given up on the Amiga for monetary reasons, they were already working on game concept demos for a couple of big publishers. Their company was a little bigger than before, too. I asked if they had interest in the *Wolfenstein 3-D* tech, but they said it was a little too simple for the kind of environments they wanted in an RPG. I wasn't dissuaded.

"John's working on improvements to the engine to make it look better," I said to them.

That got them interested. I remembered that their reluctance to leave the Amiga behind was primarily down to its graphics ability over the PC.

"John's new engine will deliver several graphics features beyond *Wolfenstein*," I continued. "The new version of the engine has more sophisticated lighting and fog, improved texture mapping so you'll get greater image detail, and the ability to vary the height of walls and ceilings."

The last point was critical to making levels feel less repetitive. Hearing about the new tech, Raven was in. We signed a deal, and I let Carmack know that his R&D was going to be used for a game by Raven.

With the new licensed tech, Raven crafted *ShadowCaster*, a shooter/role-playing game about a long-running war between shapeshifters.* They decided to use a control scheme similar to *Ultima Underworld* where you click to move rather than using the arrow keys. They were fine with the engine speed being a little slower due to the graphical advancements, since it wasn't a fast-action game. Their successful pivot to PC development put them squarely on my radar, though. I wanted to work with them again, thinking that they might develop a PC game for us.

It was important to keep in touch with people in business and a useful skill to grow. It helped us make connections that led to opportunities and, sometimes, useful information.

I developed a good working relationship with Shawn Green, Apogee's head of tech support, and he was sharing a few stories that bothered me. The one I liked the least concerned Apogee's order-taking "process," or lack thereof. Shawn talked me through it: Fans of the game called Apogee's 800 number to reach sales representatives, who sat in a room completely unsupervised. Since they employed a bunch of college students, that meant that chaos sometimes reigned with rubberband wars breaking out.

When they answered the phone, they wrote down the customer's credit card number, shipping address, and the game they wanted on a piece of paper. Then the rep spiked this ragtag order form on a metal rod on their desk like a waiter in a restaurant. At the end of the day, they took their bundle of pierced papers to Scott Miller's mother, who typed the info into a word processor, and the fulfillment process officially began.

I couldn't believe what I was hearing. When I relayed the tale to Kevin Cloud, he immediately dialed the 800 number. It was the middle of the day, and the reps left him on hold for thirty minutes.† There was no excuse for this and no way to calculate the impact of a negative customer experience on lost sales and future sales. A bad experience buying an id Software game was a reflection on id Software,

---

* We hadn't figured out how to license engines in perpetuity, and we didn't copy protect our source. If anyone used our engine without a license, we would be able to tell because the tech was unique.

† Discussing the matter with Scott Miller recently, he was upset and frustrated to hear about the thirty-minute hold time because that was clearly not the experience he wanted anyone to have. He felt it was a rare case and that Apogee was otherwise effective and efficient at taking orders, processing them overnight, and shipping them the following day.

and that was infuriating. We worked incredibly hard on every one of our games, seeking to make each a visceral, fun, bug-proof experience. Apogee's sales team was the first real bug in our system.

I told Scott he had three months, until November, to fix his fulfillment issues, which I'm sure he didn't appreciate. No CEO wants a lecture about how to run their company, but this was absurd. He needed a computer network, templated order forms, and a fulfillment workflow. He also needed a customer database. This wasn't just Business School 101, it was common sense, and since Apogee was making 50 percent on every sale, it's not like the company didn't have the money to upgrade its business. Even if they did have cash flow woes, I didn't care. Any normal business would seek out a loan and get it done.

I talked to Carmack about all this and brought up distributing our next game independently. This time, he agreed with me. If Scott and Apogee didn't upgrade, we would cut the cord. As much as I was grateful to Scott, their current process left too much at risk and made us question everything. The clock was now ticking.

In August, we got a surprise call from Atari. They loved *Wolfenstein 3-D* and wanted it on the Lynx, their handheld color game system, a system we were more than familiar with. In fact, Commander Keen (in *Keen 4* through *6*) has a stylized version of one on his wrist. As an additional request, they told us they needed a mascot to match Nintendo's Mario and Sega's Sonic and wondered if we were interested in that creative conundrum. It took Tom Hall just a few minutes to design Pounce the Lynx, a cat that jumps like Mario and runs fast like Sonic. He told our contact at Atari about his design, but curiously, nothing came of it. Adrian filtered a bunch of his *Wolfenstein* art to the more limited color format of the Lynx system, and Carmack started writing code to get the Lynx version working. Working on a new technology, even if it was not a superior technology, was always interesting to us. For programmers, learning new tech is a thing unto itself. However, only a few weeks passed before things changed. Jay got off a call with our Atari rep and told the team to stop working on Lynx stuff—Atari was troubled, and their issues would probably end up with them not paying us or worse, Atari going bankrupt. So Carmack went back to work on the *ShadowCaster* engine, and we got back to work on *Spear of Destiny*.

Meanwhile, *Wolfenstein 3-D*'s reach kept growing. We discovered the PC version's popularity in Japan when Imagineer, a Super Nintendo publisher, contacted us and asked if we could make a Super Nintendo version for them. Jay fielded the call.

"They're offering $100K up-front," he told us afterward.

Carmack spun around in his chair. I did, too.

"No way. You're kidding."

"Are you serious?"

"I am totally serious."

We were stunned. That was a lot of money for an advance, the biggest in our history. At times, our business success and our lifestyle almost seemed unfathomable, like a dream. It was hard for me to square my early life with the amounts of money that we now discussed, not to mention the respectable salaries we made.

We said yes immediately and had a meeting about what we should do next. Obviously, we had to finish *Spear of Destiny* and then start concepting our next game. At the same time, we had these other opportunities. We wanted to say yes to everything, but it just wasn't possible. Which direction to go? We didn't want to turn into a porting company when there were only six of us. I brought up the idea of asking Robin,* a technically competent person we met at KansasFest, to do the port. They were using the Sluggo III, an unauthorized device used to develop Super Nintendo games to avoid going through the long process of becoming a Nintendo-authorized developer. Games developed on the Sluggo III were okay to publish on the SNES, though. We knew Robin knew far more about it than we did. Jay called Robin up and they agreed to do the port. All the source code was zipped up and sent, and all we asked for were periodic updates. id Software was growing again as we learned how to outsource our growing amount of work. I suppose that we could have just turned it down, but a $100K up-front payment is hard to say no to, particularly if we had a way to make it work.

As *Spear of Destiny* neared completion, we looked forward to seeing a preview of its box art. After all, the last time we worked with FormGen was on *Aliens Ate My Baby Sitter*, and its final box art was great, even when compared against all the other big boxes out there at the time. For *Spear of Destiny*, FormGen got the same artist, Ken Rieger, and, true to form, he did an amazing job. The box art is an interesting collage of B.J. swinging his rifle into the glass case holding the Spear of Destiny, with the outer walls of the castle above him. The FormGen guys were clearly excited at this point, as *Wolfenstein 3-D*'s blitz of reviews hadn't stopped. Randy made sure the front of the box had "Wolfenstein" on it twice for that reason. Even better, the title was printed in holographic foil, which really made it more impactful and, yes, intrinsically cool. To top it off, we got our names printed on the sides of the box—you can see them when the lid is lifted. I always smile reading Adrian's credit: Master of the Pixel.

We finalized and shipped *Spear of Destiny* to FormGen on August 31, 1992. We spent almost two months creating it, starting just after our Disney World vacation ended. While we were busy working away on *Spear of Destiny*, Carmack was a couple of buildings away in his apartment refining the *ShadowCaster* engine. For him, it was a much quieter working environment than our *Spear of Destiny*

---

* Robin is not their real name. I'd rather not say who this is, and you'll find out why later.

workday punctuated with sound effects and jokes. In silence, he focused on solving the problems that come with implementing advanced features like slopes, fog, and diminished lighting with a limited 256-color palette.

Carmack came back to the office, done with his *ShadowCaster* engine, and showed it to us. It was impressive: The entire view could recede into fog or darkness, the floors and ceilings had slopes and variable heights, and he added a sky for outdoor sections. Even to a non-technically trained eye, it simply looked better than *Wolfenstein 3-D*. It was slower, sure, but we could see some features we would like in our next game. We wondered, *Could this engine get us there?* Carmack knew he'd taken the architecture of the engine as far as it could go, but we knew it was not good enough for our next game. For that, he had to architect a new engine to render more complex scenes. He headed back into R&D mode, thinking about that.

We soon found out that some rather enterprising hackers had figured out how to extract and decompress the levels from *Wolfenstein 3-D* and modify them. This was a big surprise to us—not only was it a lot of work, but it required a high degree of technical expertise to hack the *Wolfenstein 3-D* executable and get the maps decompressed. Soon after, several map editors appeared on the internet, and people were busy making levels and expanding the base game. We left in the ability for the engine to load decompressed levels, so it was easy for players to load a new home-brewed level into *Wolfenstein 3-D*. The era of modding our games had begun.

On September 18, *Spear of Destiny* arrived in stores. For the second time, we could walk into a store, point to our box, and say, "We wrote that." It was beyond cool. As kids, all of us spent time staring at shelves in software stores picking up boxes, looking them over, and in most cases, wishing we had the money to purchase them. To see our own games on the shelves was the equivalent of a Dallas kid saying, "The Cowboys? Sure, I play for that team." We couldn't get over it.

We had T-shirts made with the *Wolfenstein 3-D* logo on the front, and B.J. blasting a chain gun while stepping through a destroyed stone wall. On the back was our id Software logo. Walking around in any game store, id shirt or not, we were recognized, and I realized it was a rare occurrence to meet a game developer out in the wild—they don't normally advertise themselves.

Soon after the *Spear of Destiny* launch, we gave ourselves a raise to $60,000. With money he had saved, Carmack decided to buy a red Ferrari 328. To him, his Miata wasn't a real sports car. I bought the Miata from him, and soon he and his Ferrari were the talk of the apartment complex. That car had a distinctive growl to it, like none other. However, it wasn't enough growl for him. He decided to get it turbo-charged at Norwood Autocraft. Carmack's car progression went from MG to Miata to Ferrari. Not bad for your third car.

Carmack also had some news for us. His cat, Mitzi, was angry that he'd come back to the office and was spending so much less time with her. She retaliated by pissing all over his new leather furniture.

"I took her to a new home," he told us.

"Mitzi? What!? Why?" we asked. A lot of our collective history somehow involved Mitzi. She was always around, and we had memories of her sitting on top of monitors, enjoying their warmth, until she was eventually shooed away when the screen started to overheat and change color.

John's answer was nearly robotic. "She was having a net negative impact on my life." We missed her being around, but she was John's cat.

When November rolled around, Apogee had yet to upgrade its infrastructure. Orders were still taken as if the fulfillment team were short-order cooks. They had blown our deadline and, with it, our relationship. Jay called Scott and told him we would be publishing our next game.

There was one other big change that November. We had only signed a six-month lease on our apartment/office headquarters at the La Prada apartment complex, and for the first time, we decided to get a real office. The official name of the building that housed our new space was Town East Tower. Unofficially, we called it the Black Cube, which was fitting because it wasn't actually a tower; it was a seven-story building made of black glass, and each side was as wide as it was high: a cube.

We moved into the sixth floor, office 615, the only office available at that time, and hired an office manager/secretary, Donna Jackson, a big-haired Southerner whose nurturing "feed the boys" instincts earned her a nickname, the id mom. We had a reception area where we showed off the awards we'd won. There was even a designated meeting room outfitted with sleek, custom-made black furniture. From the front reception area, there was a hallway to all the development offices. That area was prebuilt with two offices and a large developers' room. Carmack and I grabbed the two separate offices, the artists took one room for the both of them, and Tom set up shop in the big room along with his workstation and a full-size pool table. He marked off the area surrounding his desk with masking tape, which showed "where the walls to my office would be—if I had an office." Everyone had a ton of space. In the kitchen, we parked our foosball table and our *Pac-Man* machine. There was also a large closet that we turned into a dedicated game room with consoles and a table that we regularly kicked apart out of anger at a game, or rather our failure to progress in a game.

The most important additions to the new offices were our brand-new, state-of-the-art NeXTSTEP workstations to join Carmack's NeXTstation. As far as I know, the only other game dev to use them besides us was Graeme Devine for *The*

7th Guest and its sequel, *The 11th Hour*. They were three times the cost of PCs. The dazzling thing about NeXT computers wasn't the hardware, it was the operating system. It's hard to explain the glory and, at the time, incomparable power of the NeXTSTEP operating system to non-programmers, but it was much more robust and useful than a PC running MS-DOS. NeXTSTEP's operating system had the power and flexibility to let us code more complex apps faster, and those apps were better looking. In the age of the internet and the rise of application programming interfaces (more commonly known as APIs), it is normal for computers to be able to communicate with each other in a more standardized way—APIs essentially provide the interface to talk to an app—but in 1992, when MS-DOS only ran code written for Intel's chips, and Apple's Macintosh only ran code written for Motorola's chips, the NeXTSTEP operating system was the only OS that took care of compatibility on the fly, supporting four different types of chips—PowerPC, Intel, Motorola, and PA-RISC. NeXTSTEP included the code for all these CPUs in one app. It was nothing short of amazing. You just copied your file from one machine to the other, and it automatically ran the correct code for that hardware.

So we had new offices, new technology, and new levels of financial freedom. Now we needed to decide what our next project would be. We gathered in the meeting room to discuss game ideas. Everyone liked the direction we were going with our last few games, and we believed 3D was the future. So we decided we were going to make another first-person shooter. Although at this point, the term and its popular acronym, FPS, didn't yet exist. We didn't know what to call our games other than 3D. We knew we were making technical and design progress with each iteration, though, and this new game was to be our fifth (*Hovertank One*, *Catacomb 3D*, *Wolfenstein 3-D*, and *Spear of Destiny* were the previous four).

Carmack began talking about borrowing the narrative he'd crafted for our epic *D&D* game. Instead of battling Nazis, what if a portal to hell was accidentally opened and demons poured out into the base and killed everyone? That sounded great! Then Tom suggested plots that explained how demons arose from the underworld, and a story began evolving that offered an alternative from the typical sci-fi narrative of space-travel-and-aliens drama that fueled nearly a century of fantastic stories. A demonic invasion was cool, but we decided to base it in the future, where we could have some really powerful weapons. Four characters in the game, all stationed on the planet Tei Tenga Darkside, would journey to hell to do battle. We ended the meeting stoked about the hellscape concept. Unlike so many of our other games, however, there was no plan to rush ahead.

Instead, we had a series of meetings. This was an unheard of, never-before-contemplated luxury. For three years, we'd rushed from one game to the next, rarely stopping to reflect on high concepts beyond vertical and side-scrolling and the evolution of 3D. *Hovertank One* and *Catacomb 3D* got two months each and introduced the world to EGA texture-mapped walls at a decent speed. *Wolfenstein 3-D* got four months and featured VGA texture-mapped walls at high speed. *Spear of Destiny* was another two-month effort. I don't want to shortchange these games or their contributions. They revolutionized the industry, but our breakthroughs in game design and tech had been executed on the fly, with tight deadlines looming over us, in the middle of death schedules, fueled by our passion and smarts and a few tons of Diet Coke, Dr Pepper, and pizza.

Now we had time and resources to breathe, think, and dream. At one of the first meetings, someone asked about a possible title for the game. Carmack said he had the perfect name.

"I was watching the movie *The Color of Money*," he told us.

We were all familiar with it. It's the one starring Tom Cruise as a pool hustler.

"There's a scene where Cruise walks into a pool hall with his cue case and hands over some money to challenge another guy. So, the guy looks at Cruise and says, 'What you got in there?' "

The camera then pans up to Cruise, who has a confident, ear-to-ear smile; Carmack had the same smile on his face. "And Cruise looks at him, smiles, and says, 'In here? Doom.' "

We cracked up. It was the perfect name for the ominous hellscape game we wanted to make.

With a title and concept, Tom Hall set about writing the *DOOM* bible. He worked at a feverish pace, first writing up thirty pages of handwritten notes and then producing a seventy-eight-page document by the end of November. In Tom's vision, *DOOM* opened at a military base where scientific experiments backfired and opened a portal to hell, paving the way for an onslaught of demons. The *DOOM* bible was filled with details: character sketches (complete with backstories), lists of weapons, lists of sounds that would need to be created, lists of graphics. But it was too much detail—or maybe I should say too much narrative and character detail, from my perspective. I wanted to extend the horror, tension, gore, and violence of *Wolfenstein 3-D*, to make a faster, more brutal, kill-or-be-killed game. This was the essence of all my favorite arcade games: survival. Tom wrote characters and tried to create and convey drama in more sophisticated ways, but that missed the point. At a basic level, the fun of a shooter game is the visceral thrill of blasting your enemies at high speed.

Other details in Tom's document were fueled by our meeting room discussions, which served as a sort of programming fantasyland. We talked about doing the impossible—creating gaming innovations that no one had ever done before.

In the land of id, John Carmack's brilliant engines dictated the look and feel of the games we made. That isn't to denigrate anyone's contributions. As I hope

I've made clear, *Keen* benefited enormously from Tom's sense of humor just as *Wolfenstein 3-D* showcased Adrian's entertainingly savage visual sensibilities. I shared both Tom and Adrian's interests, loving laughs and gore in almost equal measure, and was passionate about game design and playability—making sure our work was fun and fast—but now we actually had the time to influence Carmack's engine work, which was how, in a perfect world, every game should be built.

Technology should enable, serve, and inspire design, and vice versa. So ideally, when a game designer talks about their vision, the technical architecture should begin to formulate in the brain of the engine architect. Technical specs must be mapped not only to optimize the look, speed, and efficiency of the engine but to deliver the best gameplay, too. When there is planning, discussion and dialogue, engine architecture evolves with the demands of a game, but development can work the other way, too, as *Commander Keen* did, because an engine creates new gameplay opportunities.

My point here is that while the *DOOM* engine was unquestionably a phenomenal achievement, Carmack didn't just say, "Here, use this." *DOOM* was a collaborative effort. As the possibility space for gameplay began to take shape after the first few meetings, I wanted to make sure everyone realized the opportunity we had. We had all seen Carmack do the undoable multiple times, so it was time to think big. Really big. I wanted each one of us to do the undoable. I delivered an impromptu mission statement for the project:

"We need to make this game the best thing we can imagine playing. We have to think of all the amazing things we've never been able to do and put them in this game."

At that point, the floodgates opened. We talked about our frustration with the level of graphic detail and variation in *Wolfenstein 3-D*. We wanted more textures and lighting. As a horror movie fan, I knew that shadows and light were tools to increase tension, to boost the fear factor, and to introduce elements of surprise. I wanted these tools in our games.

We also discussed gameplay. What if Tom and I could play against each other, head-to-head in real time, with each of us trying to kill the other the most times? Is two the right number of competitors? What about three or four? And would it be fun for multiple players to team up to defeat the enemies together? Nothing like that existed, but faster modem speeds and local network connections in an office or university made interactivity in real time seem possible.

Other push-the-envelope concepts we kicked around included abandoning the traditional level-based gameplay and devising a streaming game that never stopped. Instead of reaching the end of a stage and loading in a new level, the program just streamed new content continually. Adding cinematics—an element where the game plays a short movie—was another enhancement on our wish list.

The idea was that the game perspective would shift so that the camera pulled away, changing from the dominant FPS view to a long shot that includes the player. This cinematic feature would briefly create a whole new point of view that might reveal unknown vistas, hidden demons, and new weapons before returning to the standard perspective. Needless to say, we were enthusiastic about these ideas.

In the original *Dangerous Dave in "Copyright Infringement"* side-scrolling demo, John had inserted the ability to capture every keystroke made during a game. Now we discussed sharing that ability with gamers, so they could watch the game they just played and save it as a file that could be shared with others. We liked this idea, although we had no idea how important it would be to the development of gaming and speedrunning, in particular. It went on the list.

Above all I wanted *DOOM* to be visceral and scary, and for everything in the tech to support that. Diminished lighting was an important engine feature that made normally lit areas eerie and darker areas terrifying. I wanted to hear the demons moving around before you saw them, because suspense is a huge driver of fear. I wanted the ability to put in as many secret areas as I desired, and a wide variety of ways to implement that. Since the demons were going to be coming in through portals, I thought it would be amazing to look at a portal and see hell through it, and possibly go there, even if it was just a small area. I wanted far better weapons than *Wolfenstein 3-D*—and more of them. I wanted the violence to feel more visceral, and to keep the player moving fast, so fast that movement control became a necessary skill like it was in driving games. *Wolfenstein 3-D* was full of mostly gun-based enemies, and I wanted a more interesting mix of gun and projectile-throwing enemies.

On November 28, 1992, Tom finished his draft of the *DOOM* bible, and in our meetings we fleshed out all the goals for the game. It was going to be the fastest, most violent, most immersive computer game in history. Our initial planning mission accomplished, we took two weeks off for Christmas vacation, and then, on January 1, Tom banged out a press release. It was informative, it was funny, and it was brazen. Given the state of game technology, it also must have seemed implausible to everyone *but* us. From a quality control perspective, it was exceedingly risky: We were declaring we would do the impossible before we had actually done it! We were setting ourselves up to overpromise and under-deliver. Here's the entire thing:

For Immediate Release:
Id Software to Unleash DOOM on the PC
Revolutionary Programming and Advanced Design Make For Great Gameplay

DALLAS, Texas, January 1, 1993—Heralding another technical revolution in PC programming, Id Software's DOOM promises to push back the boundaries of what was thought possible on a 386sx or better computer. The company plans to release DOOM in the third quarter of 1993, with versions for the PC in DOS, Windows, Windows NT, and a version for the NeXT.

In DOOM, you play one of four off-duty soldiers suddenly thrown into the middle of an interdimensional war! Stationed at a scientific research facility, your days are filled with tedium and paperwork. Today is a bit different. Wave after wave of demonic creatures are spreading through the base, killing or possessing everyone in sight. As you stand knee-deep in the dead, your duty seems clear: you must eradicate the enemy and find out where they're coming from. When you find out the truth, your sense of reality may be shattered!

The first episode of DOOM will be shareware. When you register, you'll receive the next two episodes, which feature a journey into another dimension, filled to its hellish horizon with fire and flesh. Wage war against the infernal onslaught with machine guns, missile launchers, and mysterious supernatural weapons. Decide the fate of two universes as you battle to survive! Succeed and you will be humanity's heroes; fail and you will spell its doom.

The game takes up to four players through a futuristic world, where they may cooperate or compete to beat the invading creatures. It boasts a much more active environment than Id's previous effort, Wolfenstein 3-D, while retaining the pulse-pounding action and excitement. DOOM features a fantastic fully texture-mapped environment, a host of technical tour de forces to surprise the eyes, multiple player option, and smooth gameplay on any 386 or better.

John Carmack, Id's Technical Director, is very excited about DOOM: "Wolfenstein is primitive compared to DOOM. We're doing DOOM the right way this time. I've had some very good insights and optimizations that will make the DOOM engine perform at a great frame rate. The game runs fine on a 386sx, and on a 486/33, we're talking 35 frames per second, fully texture-mapped at normal detail, for a large area of the screen. That's the fastest texture mapping around—period."

Texture mapping, for those not following the game magazines, is a technique that allows the program to place fully drawn art on the walls of a 3-D maze. Combined with other techniques, texture mapping looked realistic enough in Wolfenstein 3-D that people wrote Id complaining of motion sickness. In DOOM, the environment is going to look even more realistic. Please make the necessary preparations.

The release went on to detail the key features of the game, providing a paragraph on each feature: a texture-mapped environment, non-orthogonal walls, light diminishing and light sourcing, variable-height floors and ceilings, environmental animation and morphing, palette translation, multiple players, smooth seamless gameplay, and an open game. What looks like a long list of never-before-seen technical enhancements also telegraphed a new form of gameplay and a new way of designing game environments. The thing is, implausible as it was, we knew we could do it. We felt like we commanded computers and game design and not the other way around. We were not limited by any constraints. And now, thanks to the success of *Wolfenstein 3-D*, even time and money couldn't hold us back. Our imagination was our only limitation. *DOOM*'s features also introduced a new means of interacting with our community. Of all these, an "open game" was the most important. *Wolfenstein 3-D* taught us a lesson. People *will* mod our games to share them with each other. With *DOOM*, we wanted to make that easy.

DOOM's development started in January 1993. This was to be our first game developed fully on NeXTSTEP machines. Carmack began work on its engine in earnest while I started on DoomEd, the level editor. DoomEd defined the visual presentation of the game and essentially allowed us to construct a map of the physical layout of each level and all the objects that appeared there—walls, windows, buildings, enemies, ammo, weapons, candelabras, whatever. The objects themselves were defined, and their functionality was designed and codified. For instance, let's take *DOOM*'s keycard. First, we needed to have the concept of keycards that open doors. Then, we came up with the specifics of how they work (the design), and then we coded them into the game. So, to open a colored locked door, the player needed the matching-color keycard in their inventory. Red keycards open red doors. I am oversimplifying things here, because at its core, DoomEd was doing some sophisticated data management for a tool in 1993. DoomEd also allowed for fast design iteration—I could create and quickly test any object in the game within minutes. This capability was essential to my design process. Every time I added any functionality to a level or extended or altered its architecture, no matter how small these changes were, I played the level to see how it worked and felt. To this day, every level I design is the result of thousands of playthroughs. Doing the same thing on a PC instead of NeXTSTEP would have taken far longer and would have been less elegant.

By the end of January, I had the basics of DoomEd in place and Carmack had the beginnings of the *DOOM* engine running. Tom was following along, getting new builds of the MS-DOS game, NeXTSTEP updates of DoomEd, and working on building the opening level. As the author of the *DOOM* bible, Tom was understandably focused on the vision he'd laid out, a vision that nobody else had critiqued or edited. The problem was that Tom had some serious designer block happening. He just couldn't come up with interesting-looking places for gameplay.

"Maybe take a look at some military buildings and that style of construction," Carmack offered.

It seemed like a good enough idea. Tom followed Carmack's suggestion and got some books on military bases and buildings. The military installations he built looked clean and realistic, with straightforward, antiseptic lighting. However, when we reviewed his first level, "Hangar," we were less than inspired. The level started with you and three other marines playing cards and standing around a crate emblazoned with UAC logos—for Union Aerospace Corporation. Though it had not yet been implemented, the *DOOM* bible revealed what Tom envisioned would happen next:

> There is a flash of horrible light and energy and two gates open at equidistant points on the moon's surface, the larger of the two at the lightside.[*] Every[one] awake is quickly killed. One reaching for the alarm button has his hand chopped off. Briefly your friend is grabbed, his hat falling off in the lab. Then they[†] spread out through the air ducts and possessing [sic] sleeping people with magic.

It was enough to deal with enemy AI. We didn't want to deal with non-player characters and magic as well. The look of the level also didn't fit with what we were hoping to achieve. Except for the computers in the background, it looked like a conference room in a Marriott hotel, with plush blue carpet, fluorescent lights, and gray drapes. It didn't have the dark, suspenseful feeling that both Carmack and I imagined. We wanted a shadowy, grim, foreboding ambiance, a look and feel to foment Stephen King–level horror suspense. We wanted nothing but blood, fear, and fast action. We wanted *Aliens*. We wanted *Evil Dead*. The design laid out in Tom's game bible was intent on fostering relationships with the character and injecting humor and nuance into the narrative. It was on-brand Tom Hall, but it was also the opposite of the blood and guts, murky shadows, and endless tension that Carmack and I were looking for.

We told this to Tom, who was understandably frustrated—he liked characters and humor much more than horror. He had poured himself into the project, but it seemed like he had hit a wall.

---

[*] "Lightside" refers to the light side of the moon.
[†] In this instance, "they" refers to demons.

Or maybe he had just run smack into a competing vision that Carmack and I shared.

By February, while Tom wrestled with level and game vision issues, I started to design levels of my own, splitting my time between designing levels and programming DoomEd. Adrian and Kevin were working on monster and weapon designs. After sketching out characters, Adrian went out and bought a ton of modeling clay. His plan was to sculpt his characters, which we scanned into the game using a video camera connected to the NeXTstation. The camera was pointed at a lazy Susan that rotated, allowing Adrian to take photos of a model at eight different angles. Instead of creating characters pixel by pixel the way he had been doing for years, this process saved him a lot of time. Rotoscoping, as the process was called, was used for *Prince of Persia* in 1989, and in films before that. We thought might improve our process, and so we decided to try it.

Adrian created the marine main character, the Cyberdemon, and the Baron of Hell in clay. As soon as he was done with the first set of rotations and started animating the walk cycle, however, the clay began tearing. This was a problem Adrian hadn't foreseen. After animating and repairing the model for each frame of animation, Adrian knew he needed to figure out a better way of creating physical models of these characters. Better yet, having someone else make them would save him even more time. Jay contacted Hollywood monster-maker Gregor Punchatz, who had made models for *RoboCop* and other movies, and contracted him to build the Spider Mastermind, a gross, menacing creation with four metal legs, bug eyes, and spindly arms on a brain. It even sported a chain gun in front. Gregor made the model out of a steel-frame skeleton covered in foam latex.

We also thought about how we would deal with the game's weapons. These needed to be modeled and scanned, too. We were all fans of Sam Raimi's *Evil Dead* movie franchise, and we wanted to use a shotgun and a chainsaw as demon destroyers. Rather than go to a gun shop to look for the real thing, we hit the local Toys"R"Us and purchased an American West Dakota Shotgun Rifle Cap Gun, a single-shot weapon from the charmingly named TootsieToy company. As for a chainsaw, Tom Hall borrowed one from his girlfriend. It had an amusing name, too: Eager Beaver. Less entertaining was the oil leak it had; the engine end of the chainsaw sat in a big plastic popcorn bowl in our office until we were done with it.

By March 1993, just as we were entering our third month of development, something rather surprising happened: Executives from 20th Century Fox contacted us.

Jay walked into the main area and said, "Hey guys, I got some interesting news." The tone of his voice told us he was serious, and whatever it was, was something big.

"20th Century Fox is offering us the license to *Aliens*."

Our jaws dropped. The James Cameron sci-fi classic was one of our favorites. It was one of the inspirations for *DOOM*.

"That's awesome!" I said, and I meant it. In fact, it was better than awesome. It felt like winning the geek lottery. *DOOM* wasn't going to be *inspired* by *Aliens*. It was going to *be Aliens*.

It was a tempting offer and fitting aesthetically. We wanted gamers playing *DOOM* to feel as desperate and on edge as Sigourney Weaver's heroic character, Ripley, does during her life-or-death encounters with the lurking, almost invisible killer. We also loved the *Alien* xenomorph, one of the most amazing creatures in film history. Who wouldn't want to make an *Aliens* game? We discussed it, but after a thirty-minute deep-dive into the concept, we couldn't think our way around one major stumbling block: There weren't any demons in *Aliens*—just alien monsters— and that wouldn't be a *new* idea. Aliens in space had been done to death. Plus, we would lose full creative control, and we'd be making someone else's franchise more valuable instead of creating our own new intellectual property. After a breathless roller coaster of a half hour, we scrapped the concept of using the license.

We didn't have long to dwell on it because a sudden, unexpected curveball upended our development schedule: a long-forgotten and still outstanding contract. As I mentioned, seven months earlier, we signed a deal with Imagineer, a Japanese Nintendo game publisher, to port *Wolfenstein 3-D* to the Super Nintendo. Within a matter of days, we'd also hired Robin (a pseudonym), a contractor we met at a retro computer conference, to start working on the Super Nintendo version.

We cashed Imagineer's check, paid our contractor, and promptly forgot about it—until Imagineer called up and asked us where their game was. Good question! The answer, we quickly discovered, was not good. Our esteemed contractor completely flaked on the job, so we needed the entire team to stop working on *DOOM* to get the SNES version made as soon as possible. We had never programmed a Super Nintendo, so we needed to consult all the hardware notes we could find. The cartridge start-up process was particularly complex and hard to find documentation for. We turned to some early 65816 Assembly language code that the contractor had shared with us early on in the project. It wasn't much, but it did show how to set up the hardware switches to the right graphics mode. It was enough to get us going in the right direction.

Not only did we need to figure out the memory layout of the graphic mode, we also had to translate all the graphics to this new type of hardware, get the music in a format that could play on the SNES, and lots of other technical details. Imagineer also had more requests. They wanted us to change the dogs into rats, the red blood to green, and remove all Third Reich imagery. Of course, in addition to those requirements, they wanted it to be done as fast as possible. Before starting development, we needed to ask Robin a question. However, we couldn't reach them. We knew their boss, Brian Fargo, the CEO of Interplay, so Jay asked Brian where the contractor was. Brian wanted to know why. In spite of Brian's question, Jay knew it was all on the up-and-up. After all, we were told by the contractor that doing work on the SNES version was cleared in their contract. There was no harm telling Brian that Robin was porting *Wolfenstein 3-D* to SNES for us.

As it turns out, Brian didn't see it that way. "Oh really? Because that is not allowed. They work here, and everything they do is owned by Interplay. Did you use any of their code?" Brian asked.

"Yes, we used a small bit of start-up code, but that's all," Jay said.

To Brian, that was a problem. He mentioned to Jay that he certainly wanted to avoid any kind of lawsuit and suggested a deal: We pay them $10,000, they get the rights to publish *Wolfenstein 3-D* on the Mac, and we port it.

Seeing no other option and hoping to head off a lawsuit, Jay agreed.

We were furious. Instead of making easy money, we were saddled with a giant headache—one that could have been sorted out months earlier with a simple "I screwed up" phone call from the contractor—but the thing that really made me mad was that we suspended work on *DOOM* while we worked on the Super Nintendo port.

We spent three weeks hammering out our frustration and anger in code. We wanted this thing behind us and worked constantly to get it done so we could get back to making *DOOM*. From having never worked on a SNES before to finishing the port in three weeks was an impressive effort. Although we were clearly irritated for having been put in this situation, we took a moment to recognize our achievement: This was id Software at peak performance.

Having cleared the decks, I went back to working on levels in earnest and finalizing DoomEd while the others picked up where they left off.

By the end of March, we got a shot of adrenaline when legendary illustrator Don Ivan Punchatz, the father of our model maker, finished creating the *DOOM* logo. Over decades, he had provided book covers for some of the most important science-fiction writers in history: Harlan Ellison, Isaac Asimov, and Ray Bradbury. Kevin Cloud was familiar with his work and thought he would be a perfect choice as an artist for *DOOM*'s logo design. So we called him in and discussed the game.

"It's a 3D game called *DOOM*," I told Don. I wasn't sure that this particularly mattered to him. What he needed most was the setting and the overall aesthetic of the game. "The story line is a futuristic sci-fi space marine who meets hell and all its demons. It's an ancient, timeless thing, good versus evil, but good is a space marine with guns."

With that description, Don was good to go.

Fittingly, his *DOOM* logo was a multi-dimensional masterpiece: geometrically complex, visually striking, symbolically appropriate, and, most importantly, instantly readable. I loved that Don combined hell and technology together with a two-toned treatment. The top half of the logo incorporates the circuit boards we used as textures in the game, colored blue to indicate the coldness of technology; the bottom half, colored yellow through orange, implying fire and heat, used textures that were made of metal. So you had cutting-edge motifs set against complex materials. I also admired the logo's layered dimensions, not just because they looked cool but because the execution echoed so much about the 3D world of the game, one in which new dimensions would surface as the game progressed.

With the logo done, Don moved on to illustrate *DOOM*'s box cover. He came to Suite 615 with an expensive-looking camera and a male body model. The model's job was to strike various poses for the marine who would be on the cover of the box.

We set up Don and the model in the same room where Adrian and Kevin spent their days creating new textures and modeling clay characters and digitizing them with the NeXTstation workstation. Adrian, who worked at a hospital prior to joining *Softdisk*, had a collection of hospital photo slides that he was in the process of scanning for *DOOM*'s bloody walls. Adding to the ambience were the periodic sounds of a drill and patient screams through the walls from the dentist's office next door.

The model took his shirt off and started posing with our plasma gun toy. Don asked us for suggestions, so I started telling him that the marine was going to be attacked by an infinite number of demons. It would be cool if he was on a hill and firing down into them. The model was holding the gun in various positions while Don snapped photographs. I watched, but none of the stances were interesting to me. I couldn't see them conveying the "hero-under-siege" aesthetic.

I kept trying to tell the model the scene I wanted to capture. He just wasn't getting it. Frustrated, I took off my shirt and told him to give me the gun.

"Now kneel on the floor, and pose as a demon grabbing my arm," I said. I aimed the gun in a slightly different direction and told Don, "This is what I'm talking about!"

Don took several pictures. I moved the gun to a different angle, the model/ demon grabbed my other leg, then we switched to him grabbing arms. At the end of the session, we decided the arm-grabbing pose was going to be the most dramatic. I had inadvertently become Doomguy.

On April 2, 1993, we were ready to give a select group of people a small taste of what we'd created. The title screen featured Don's *DOOM* logo along with fuchsia "Alpha" below it, and a readme.txt file told them what to expect.

"Dear id Beta-Tester," it began. "Yes, it's the DOOM ALPHA! (Actually we're just trying to release these every two weeks or so. This WAS going to be a pre-beta, but a certain person let us down Super-Nintendo-cart programming-wise, so it's just an alpha. Nonetheless, here 'tis."

We also included what sounded like a personal diary in list form. Among the items we listed: the id crew taking partners to see *The Phantom of the Opera*, Carmack going to Kansas City, the birth of Jay's son Nicholas, and Kevin's softball game scheduled for that very night. After three months of development, *DOOM* featured animating floors, functional doors, flickering lights, and strobe lights—all features I coded into DoomEd and the game itself. Items were visible, and Kevin and Adrian had added a lot of new art. At that point, thirteen distinct levels existed in various stages of completion. We had two guys periodically playing builds for us, Charlie Davis and Doug Howell, both of whom had been beta testers with us since 1991, on *Keen 4* through *6*, *Wolfenstein 3-D*, and *Spear of Destiny*.* They both loved the game and couldn't believe how great it looked even at this early stage. Having outside eyes validate our early direction was reassuring.

In May, I finished DoomEd and decided to turn my attention to the levels themselves. Tom's clean, lean, military bunker style just wasn't cutting it, and Tom knew it, too. He was still struggling with a creative block. I ran through a bunch of his levels and the lighting, ceiling height, and overall shape of the spaces looked like they came from *Wolfenstein*, but with nicer textures. There weren't dark areas—walls were at 90 degrees to each other, and there wasn't much variation in room size. This engine could do so much more: We could even have windows and outdoor areas! I took a stab at a solution, creating an abstract 3D level design style, something new that could not have existed in any of our previous engines. My first attempt was an empty room with a lofty ceiling, dark lighting, and a couple of brightly lit, inset areas up high where imps could be placed to shoot fireballs down at the player. The corners of the room became angles so the place had eight sides. A switch in the far wall, when flipped, raised two doors simultaneously, revealing even darker hallways. Nothing was realistic—abstraction was the point—but it all looked cool. I called Tom and the artists into my office and I said, "This is what I'm talking about." The space felt decidedly new and innovative, unlike anything in our previous games.†

Everyone, including Tom, agreed this was the direction we needed. No doubt this increased Tom's frustration. Because he had designer's block, he had listened to Carmack and made these military block–style mazes, but it led to something neither he nor anyone else found interesting. Hearing our feedback about the state of the game was difficult for Tom, and I'm sure my rejection hurt the most;

---

*   Beta testers were disctinctly different from in-house QA, and mostly used to provide periodic feedback on the overall feel of the game.
†   This room ended up being in E1M2 (Episode 1, Map 2). The long elevator ride near the end of the level brings players into it.

we were best friends, and as I've said, Tom is the most creative talent I've ever worked with. His range is staggering—visual, linguistic, comic, narrative—and his work ethic, up until the end, was always faultless. He was a veteran game developer, though, and a consummate professional. As much as it stung, he saw the same things as we did.

DOOM doomed him.

The team opted to steer toward my designs, abandoning the four-marines-playing-cards scenario from Tom's bible, and the bible itself, and opting for a more simplified, visceral shooter. As we moved deeper into development, Tom lost interest and focus. At one point, examining the levels and characters, we realized we had too many bipedal monsters in the game and needed more flying ones. It was an oversight and another indicator of how out of sync he'd become with the whole *DOOM* project.

Since the abstract-level design style breakthrough, I continued designing episode one's maps. I started with E1M2 (Episode 1, Map 2), the level where I'd had the breakthrough, but halfway through I left it to start working on E1M6. I had an idea for an interesting starting area that had several choices, so I finished that one first. Then, I moved onto E1M7, crafting more ways to hide secret areas. In E1M7, I also started to explore the concept of backtracking—making the player backtrack through the map to finish it. I hadn't played levels in a 3D game that required the player return to places they'd conquered, and so it felt fresh and new. This also meant I needed to make their return more interesting, so when the player came back to get the blue keycard, for instance, I opened up new monster closets (secret areas with enemies in them that open up and release the enemies into the path of the player) so they'd be surprised when they turned around and went back to use the keycard. I also hid a huge secret area inside one of these monster closets, so you couldn't reach it until the player got to the blue keycard.

Around the start of June, we decided to answer a press inquiry about doing a preview. We figured it was time to show off some of our work. Chris Lombardi of *Computer Gaming World*, the biggest publication for games at the time, came to the Black Cube for a sneak peek. He had written about *Wolfenstein 3-D* before and really liked it. To say he was impressed is an understatement. His preview of *DOOM* ran under the headline: "They're Going to Hell for This One", and he was effusive in his praise: "*Doom* is not a typical next-generation jump. It's a high-altitude, wind-aided Carl Lewis of a leap ahead."

Lombardi's reaction was gratifying. Having seen the potential of some of our previous work go over people's heads, it was nice to see a savvy critic instantly understand we were breaking new ground. As it turned out, Chris's preview would be the only preview of *DOOM*.

In July, the biggest breakthrough for me was personal. Throughout the development of *Wolfenstein 3-D* and *DOOM,* Beth and I had been on-again-off-again. Fortunately, things had really turned around with Beth, and our relationship was going so well that we decided to get married. She was always understanding about my relationship with my sons, which was important to me. We honeymooned in Aruba in the middle of July.

When I returned, Carmack approached me. He wanted to fire Tom. He'd had a talk with Kevin and Adrian, and they agreed that he wasn't aligned or bringing the creative superpowers we knew he had to *DOOM*. They both asked to have lunch with me, where they laid out all their concerns and said that they wanted him out of the company. My inclination was to protect my friend. He'd been a key member of id. It didn't feel right to me.

One of the things that influenced my thinking was id Software's termination policy. When we formed the company, we decided that founders could only be fired by unanimous decision and that departing founders would sell their shares back to the company. If we fired Tom, he would never see another penny from *Keen, Wolfenstein 3-D* or *DOOM*, but he'd be paid for the value of his shares as the company took them back. Since we were not a public company, we determined the value of our shares by the last 365 days' profits multiplied by the shareholder's ownership percentage.

I stalled for a short time, but eventually, I had to give in. It was a tortuous decision. Tom was struggling with the subject matter. We were starting to get further into development; he was making uninspired levels and spending more time out of the office. Eventually, I felt I couldn't protect him, and the friction was jeopardizing the company as well as what we hoped would be the greatest computer game in history. So the one truly negative chapter of *DOOM* unfolded.

I was hoping I could soften the impact of the upcoming meeting. The night before, I had Tom over for dinner and planned to give him the bad news, or at least a heads-up that there was serious trouble coming, but I froze. Maybe it was my respect and admiration for his ability. Maybe it was our close friendship. Maybe it was a reaction to growing up in families that believed in nothing but tough love and knowing the incredible hurt that comes with rejection. Whatever it was, I just couldn't do it. Part of me feels like I let Tom down, but as it turned out, I think it might have been the best decision for him. He was struggling at id and unhappy.

The next day, we called Tom into the conference room for a meeting with Carmack, Adrian, Jay, Kevin, and me, but it was really a funeral, and that is exactly what the mood was like. Nobody was talking or even looking at each other. Finally, Carmack delivered the news.

"Tom," he said. "This isn't working out. We're asking for your resignation."

It was a horrible moment. "I tried to tell you last night, Tom," I said, but as soon as the words were out of my mouth, I realized they did nobody any good.

Tom had just been somewhat blindsided by the people—friends—he'd spent years collaborating with. There were multiple points along the *DOOM* development timeline where Tom realized his work wasn't what the game needed. He even apologized for some suboptimal decisions and for not being inspired. Though he was trying on a daily basis to get into some kind of groove, ultimately, *DOOM* was just not Tom's aesthetic. He started talking about his value to the company, defending his work, but when no one responded, he knew it was a done deal. The meeting was an inevitable and painful endpoint, and he realized it.

We talked about how we had noticed that Tom was not having a good time working on *DOOM*, that we felt it didn't match his style, and it was at odds with his personality.

Tom agreed and talked about how the transition to *Wolfenstein 3-D* from *Keen* was a major blow. He had found himself in a creative abyss while making levels for *Wolfenstein 3-D* and fighting over pushwalls. To him, *DOOM* was even darker than *Wolfenstein 3-D*, and it didn't match his spirit. In the end, Tom agreed to resign.

Carmack asked him to leave the room so we could figure out next steps, which included going over the company policy of buying back Tom's shares.

Tom departed, but within five minutes he was back with the look of a changed man. The shock and horror that filled his face moments earlier was gone.

"Guys," he said, "I think this is really the right thing to do."

He spent the rest of the day packing his stuff and saying goodbye. It was a major blow losing someone so talented and a friend with whom I enjoyed working. Anyone who knows Tom knows what an incredibly funny, light, and positive person he is. *DOOM* was not for him. Still, it hurt, and I missed working with him.

Now, with deadlines looming, the id team was concentrated on *DOOM*. With Tom's departure, there was work to be done and shoes to fill. In mid-August, we hired a new programmer to join the team. Dave Taylor was a young electrical engineer from the University of Texas. We assigned him the task of creating several systems: the intermission screen, all the menus, and the automap. The automap was a navigation tool that let players quickly see all the areas they had traversed from a top-down view, and then get back into gameplay.

Our other potential hire was a game designer named Sandy Petersen. Kevin found out about him and wanted to bring him over for an interview. I must admit that I was apprehensive about hiring Sandy. His design background seemed great. The problem, as I saw it, was that except for our id mom Donna Jackson, we were sometimes a foul-mouthed, dark-humored bunch. In contrast, Sandy listed his Mormon religion on his résumé—something I'd never seen done before. Given my experiences with my ex-wife Kelly's family and with friends in Utah, I didn't think our gruesome, demonic games or our curse-filled culture would be a good fit for a Latter-day Saint, but Sandy told me I was wrong. He didn't care about the carnage of our cartoon world, or the obscenities that filled the air at the id Software office. We decided to give him a shot. When he came in for his interview, I sat him at Tom's old desk, fired up DoomEd, and told him what I wanted.

"This is a level editor. I want to see what you can do with it to build levels."

Sandy seemed excited and eager to get going. "Sure, this sounds like fun!"

I showed him the way DoomEd worked, how to compile a level, and how to run it. After a few hours, he had done some good work. Sure, it was slightly *Wolfenstein*-like, with same-height ceilings, but he had slime you had to get through, and he used lighting in ways to heighten tension and change the mood of the space.* I felt he was going to work out well. We hired him, and his task was to make as many levels as possible using Tom's levels as a starting point.

"Change whatever is needed," we told him, "but get levels done."

By this point, my own level design style had become codified. What started as an experiment in April was now a philosophy, and one I shared with Sandy. I believed in these design rules:

- Design Rule 1: The start of the level should present interesting choices or look impressive.
- Design Rule 2: The start of the level should fit its purpose. Do I want to teach the player or make them feel scared? If the former, there are no enemies. If the later, watch out.
- Design Rule 3: Reuse areas in the level as much as possible, as it reinforces the understanding of the space every time the player goes through an area again. For example, if players come back to a central hub before going out to a spoke, they will remember the hub the most.
- Design Rule 4: Provide contrast in every element of the design: light, sound, and action. This keeps a level fun and interesting and prevents it from falling into a monotonous loop of gameplay. We want the player to feel like they are on an exciting roller-coaster ride.
- Design Rule 5: Changes in wall or floor texture should be accompanied by a height change or border texture.
- Design Rule 6: Include at least four secrets in your level.
- Design Rule 7: When the player solves a piece of a puzzle, they should already know where to go next. An example would be that you have already

---

* The level Sandy started making during his interview became E2M6 and has my favorite Bobby Prince song of the original trilogy in it, "Sinister."

tried to open the red door before you found the red keycard. A bad design would be to flip a switch, then see and hear nothing that shows you what you just did.

- Design Rule 8: If an area in your level looks like it could be made in an earlier tech, you have failed. Make the area more interesting and use more of the engine's features to ensure that.

In September, we had to solve our sound issues. The DOOM engine had been in development all year, and so the sound code took a back seat. Our new engine wasn't compatible with the previous sound code written for *Wolfenstein 3-D*. We needed a solution. We learned about a digital sound library—DMX—owned by Illinois-based software engineer Paul Radek, and Jay promptly called him up to license it.

At the end of the month, there was a minor shift in the gaming cosmos. An adventure game titled *Myst* unseated *Wolfenstein 3-D* on the Top 100 Games list. We immediately went out and purchased a copy of the game. When I looked at its static images, I was stunned.

"Why the hell is this game popular?" I wondered aloud.

I couldn't figure it out. The images were beautiful, certainly, but so were some photographs. The future of games was not static images. The future of games, I thought, was dynamic and real-time. That's where we were headed.

"This game is prehistoric," I mused. "It just looks nice because it's using high-resolution SVGA graphics, and it's an excuse to buy a new CD-ROM drive, but it's a boring, static, old-school adventure game!"

Everyone agreed. Obviously, it looked good, but technically? We couldn't believe people were falling for it. To us, what mattered was the *player's* story, the narrative arc they created ripping and tearing their way through game worlds, whether those worlds were *D&D* or *Wolfenstein 3-D*.

The public, obviously, didn't agree with my analysis, because *Myst* sold millions of copies. I came to realize the importance of game narrative to players. It was for the masses. It looked great on a computer monitor, there was no pressure for players to rush and make a move, and it provided challenges that players could solve at their own pace. At id, we were so focused on innovating in real-time fast 3D that any game that wasn't was a joke to us.

In early October, we were getting close to wrapping up the game, so progress quickened. On October 4, 1993, we issued the *DOOM* beta press release version, a build of the game we distributed externally to journalists and video game reviewers to allow them to try the game before its release. Concerned about security and leaks, we coded the beta to stop running on DOS systems after October 31, 1993. We still had useless pickups in the game, like the demonic daggers, demon chests, and other unholy items. I decided to get rid of those things because they made no sense to the core of the game and they rewarded the player with a score, which was a holdover from *Wolfenstein 3-D*. I removed the concept of having lives for the same reason. It was enough to have to start the level over after dying.

There was still one missing piece from the game, and it was a substantial one. We hadn't done anything about the multiplayer aspect. In modern game development, multiplayer would be a feature factored in from day one, and architected accordingly, in an integrated fashion. Not with *DOOM*. It was November, and we were releasing in a month.

I brought it up to Carmack. "So when are we going to make multiplayer mode?"

The short answer was that Carmack was ready to take it on. Looking from the outside in, I suspect some might wonder if I wasn't just more than a bit concerned since we were hoping to ship in 1993. After all, John had never programmed a multiplayer game before. The truth is that I never had a doubt, not for a second. Back in March, Carmack had already done some innovative network programming in DoomEd. He wanted to play around with the distributed objects system in NeXT-STEP, so he added the ability to allow multiple people who were running DoomEd to edit the same level. I could see him drawing lines and placing objects on my screen from his computer. Then, I'd add to his room by making a hallway, and so on.

For multiplayer, Carmack's plan was to explore peer-to-peer networking. It was the "quick and dirty" solution instead of a client-server model. Instead of one central computer controlling and monitoring all the action between two to four players, each computer would run the game and sync up with the others. Basically, the computers send each other updates at high speed over the local network. The speed of Carmack's network programming progress was remarkable. He had some excellent books on networking, and fortunately, those books were clearly written and explained the process of using IPX[*] well. In a few hours, he was communicating between two computers, getting the IPX protocol running so he could send information packets to each computer. I'd worked with him for three years and was used to seeing incredible things on his screen, but this was awe inspiring, even for him. In a matter of hours, he got two PCs talking to each other through a command-line-based tool, which proved he could send information across the network. It was the foundation needed to make the game network-capable. It was great for two players, and good for four, so we capped it at that. We were still on track to deliver on our promise of the most revolutionary game in history before the end of the year.

Carmack called me into his office to tell me he had it working. Both PCs in his office had the game open, and they were syncing up with two characters facing one another. On one PC, Carmack veered his character to the right. On the

---

[*] IPX is an acronym for Internetwork Packet Exchange. In sum, it is a way in which computers can talk to one another.

other monitor, that same character, appearing in third person, moved to the left. It was working!

"Oh my God!" I yelled, throwing in some other choice words to convey my amazement. "That is fucking incredible."

When I'd first truly visualized the multiplayer experience, I was building E1M7. I was playing the game and imagined seeing two other players firing rockets at each other. At the time, I thought, "This is going to be astonishing. There is nothing like this. This is going to be the most amazing game planet Earth has ever seen." Now, the moment had finally arrived.

I rushed to my computer and opened the game, connecting to Carmack's computer.

When his character appeared on screen, I blasted him out of existence, screaming with delight as I knocked "John" out of the game with a loud, booming, bloody rocket blast. It was beyond anything I had ever experienced before and even better than I imagined it could be.

It was the future, and it was on my screen.

"This is fucking awesome!" I yelled. "This is the greatest thing ever!"

I wasn't kidding. This was the realization of everything we put into the design months earlier. I knew *DOOM* would be the most revolutionary game in history, but now, it was also *the most fun, all-consuming game in history*. Now that all the key elements of our original design were in place, it was obvious. *DOOM* blew away every other game I'd ever played. From that moment on, if I wasn't playing *DOOM* or working on *DOOM*, I was thinking about *DOOM*.

Kevin, Adrian, and Jay began running the game in multiplayer mode, too, competing to blow away monsters and each other. They were yelling just as much as I did, cheering every execution, groaning when they were killed and had to respawn. I watched them play. I saw the tension in their bodies as they navigated the dark, detailed world we'd created. They were hunters and targets, engaged in a kill-or-be-killed battle, not just with monsters, but with other, real people. Players were competing in real time with other people in a battle to survive. I thought of boxing or an extreme wrestling match, where you go in a cage to fight. This was much more violent, more deadly. It was all simulated, of course, but in the moment, it felt immediate. It was a new gaming experience, and I searched for a way to describe it.

"This is deathmatch," I said. The team latched onto the name. It instantly articulated the sinister, survival vibe at the heart of *DOOM*.

In mid-November, we buckled down, getting in the "closing zone," where you begin finalizing all areas of the game one by one. Now that Carmack had multiplayer networking figured out, we needed to fine-tune the gameplay and functionality, delivering two multiplayer modes—one in which players work together to kill monsters and demons, and the other where players try to kill each other (usually without monsters around). The first mode was called co-op, short for cooperative. The second, of course, was deathmatch.

Another important word needed to be coined. Deathmatch was all about getting the highest kill count in a game to be judged the winner. What would we call each kill? Well, we could call it a kill, but that felt like a less creative solution to me. Why don't we have our own word? I went to the art room to discuss this with Kevin and Adrian.

"Hey guys, for each kill in a deathmatch we need a word for it that is not 'kill,' " I said.

Kevin said, "Well, maybe we could use the word 'frag.' "

"That sounds like a cool word, but what does it mean?" I asked.

"In the Vietnam War," Kevin explained, "if a sergeant told his fire team to do something horrifically dangerous, instead of agreeing to it, they would throw a fragmentation grenade at the sergeant and call it friendly fire. The explanation was 'Someone fragged the sarge!' "

"So, in a deathmatch we're all fragging each other!" I said.

"Exactly."

And that is how "frag" entered the *DOOM* lexicon.

The introduction of deathmatch and co-op play profoundly affected the possibility space of gameplay in the levels. Crafting an enjoyable level for single-player mode with lots of tricks and traps was complex enough, but with the addition of multiplayer we had to be aware of other players in the level at the same time, and we had to make sure the single-player-designed level was fun to play in these new modes. Our levels were doing triple duty, and we had little time to test every possible situation, so we needed some simple rules to ensure quality. Since multiplayer gameplay was coming in quickly near the end of development, I had to define all the gameplay rules for co-op and deathmatch. We then had to modify every game map so that all modes worked in all difficulty levels. These are the rules I came up with quickly to help guide level quality:

- Multiplayer Rule 1: A player should not be able to get stuck in an area without the possibility of respawning.
- Multiplayer Rule 2: Multiple players (deathmatch or co-op mode) require more items; place extra health, ammo, and powerups.
- Multiplayer Rule 3: Try to evenly balance weapon locations in deathmatch.
- Multiplayer Rule 4: In deathmatch mode, try to place all the weapons in the level regardless of which level you're in.

Additionally, we had to make all the final elements for the game: the intermissions and various menus had to be designed, drawn, and coded; the installation files needed to be created, along with the text instruction files, too. We also had to write code to allow gamers to play these multiplayer modes over their modems, since that was the hardware many people had in 1993. Compared to our previous games, the development pace on *DOOM* had been relatively relaxed, but in November our to-do list was crowded. Fortunately, everything fell into place. The last job for everyone was to stress-test *DOOM*.

Preparing for release, we knew we needed someone to handle our customer support, so earlier in the year, we'd hired Shawn Green, who quit his job at Apogee to join us. Throughout development, at every new twist and turn, we kept Shawn up to date. He had to know the game inside out to assist gamers should any issues arise. Shawn also helped us by testing the game as it went through production.

I noted earlier that id Software never had a Quality Assurance team to test our releases. For three years, John, Tom, and I doubled as the id QA team. We played our games on our PCs, pounding multiple keys, literally banging on keyboards to see if our assaults could affect the game. On the verge of release, and with more people than ever before in the office, we spent thirty hours playing *DOOM* in every way we could think of—switching modes, hitting commands—running the game on every level in every game mode we had, using every option we added to the game to see if there were any glitches.

Things were looking good. We decided to run one last "burn-in" test, a classic test for games where the developers turn the game on and let it run overnight. We ran *DOOM* on every machine in the office. The plan was to let it run for hours to see if anything bad happened. After about two hours of being idle, the game froze on a couple screens. The computers seemed to be okay—if you hit "escape" the menu came up—but the game stopped running.

We hadn't seen a bug like this during development, but Carmack was on the case. He was thinking and not saying a word, evidently poring over the invisible engine map in his head. Ten minutes passed before he figured it out. He concluded that we were using the timing chip in the PC to track the refresh of the screen and process sound, but we weren't clearing the timing chip counter when the game started, which was causing the glitch. Ironically, this logic had been part of the engine from day one, so it was surprising we hadn't noticed it before.

He sat down at his computer, fixed the bug, and made a new build of the game. We put the update on all the machines and held our breath for the next two hours.

Problem solved.

That was the last hurdle. We were ready to launch. That day, December 10, would be DOOM Day.

• • •

Our timing was ironic.

The day before, December 9, 1993, Senator Joe Leiberman, an advocate of writing federal laws to censor game content, was cochairing a Senate hearing on video games. He opened the session describing and decrying scenes in *Mortal Kombat* when "blood splatters from contestants' heads" and for offering a choice of murder methods ranging "from ripping the heart out to pulling a head off an opponent." He also mis-described the object of *Night Trap*, a game set in a sorority house, as keeping "hooded men from hanging the young women from a hook or drilling their necks with a tool designed to drain their blood." Players were actually meant to save the women. The hearings were a big deal. Howard Lincoln, then vice president of Nintendo of America was there, as was Bill White, vice president of Sega of America.

For the members of the Senate committee, video games had hit bottom in terms of depicting graphic violence. They hadn't seen anything yet. The timing could not have been better. Or worse, depending on your viewpoint.

As news of the hearings broke across the United States, we were too busy finalizing *DOOM* to even notice.

CHAPTER 13

The World Is *DOOM*ed

On December 10, 1993, *DOOM* was on the verge of release and everything in the world of games was about to change. It had been an intense eleven months, and we had achieved everything we set out to accomplish in our initial press release. We were completely exhausted, and Sandy was sleeping under his desk. We had been up and working for thirty straight hours to get *DOOM* to this point.

We planned to upload the shareware version of *DOOM* in the afternoon to the University of Wisconsin-Madison's FTP site. We wanted it out on the internet first, and then on smaller BBSes second. Unfortunately, there was a glitch.

We probably should have thought about it ahead of time, but this was all new territory for us. Interest in *DOOM* had been building, but none of us grokked that *DOOM* was set to become "a pop-culture phenomenon." One hint was that fans found our unlisted number and called the office to ask questions:

"When are you going to upload the game?"

"Where's *DOOM*?"

"Release it already, man!"

Another indicator was that we started seeing posts on bulletin boards talking about *DOOM* in anticipation of its release. On Usenet, someone created the alt.games.doom newsgroup. It was the birth of the *DOOM* community, a community that is still going strong to this day. In the upload directory at University of Wisconsin-Madison, people even created joke files to send us a message with file names like "when.is.doom.coming.out" and "we.want.doom.now."

Back in our office, Jay Wilbur had the shareware "doom1_0.zip" file ready to go. Around 2 p.m., he signed on to the University of Wisconsin-Madison FTP, issued the FTP upload command, and waited for the file to upload. Cheers came from Jay's office! We were done! *DOOM* was unleashed!

And then nothing happened.

The expectant fans had created a logjam on the university's site, which had a capacity of 250 people. He only *thought* he uploaded the file, but the server was locked up. Imagine a massive, snarled traffic jam around a concert venue that is so congested, it keeps the headline band from reaching the arena. That was what was happening online. id Software's *DOOM* was the headliner, but its file couldn't get through.

Jay called his contact at the university, the perfectly named computer whiz David Datta, and explained the issue. David said he would increase the capacity of users and told Jay to stay on the phone so that he could start his upload at the precise moment the new user spots opened up.

David did what he needed to do behind the scenes. "Now!" he told Jay.

But that didn't work, either. Eager fans filled the queue in the literal second between David yelling "Now!" and Jay issuing the upload command. We'd just added to the logjam. People waiting for the download were preventing the upload!

Eventually, Jay went on the site's chat channel and posted to the fans who were hanging out. He explained that unless everyone left the FTP site, *DOOM* couldn't be uploaded. "Either I kick you off, and I get this done, or it doesn't get done at all." The fans took the hint, and Jay initiated the upload.

Once the *DOOM* file was successfully uploaded, there was still trouble. The site crashed twice from all the traffic as thousands swarmed to download *DOOM*.

But the launch was on.

And *then*, for real, everything changed.

We felt *DOOM* was the best game we had ever played. We put everything we had into it, and we hoped fans would feel the same way. Even with those expectations, the success of *DOOM* surprised us. *DOOM* was an unqualified smash. Critics and reviewers loved it, and so did gamers. Our new distribution arm received $50,000 in orders every single day. That was an inconceivable amount of cash. We unseated *Myst*, the game that had ended *Wolfenstein 3-D*'s year-long run, on the Usenet list of Top 100 Games in the World. id Software ruled the gaming world. I was on cloud nine.

A few days after the release, I came back to earth. Jay had hired a Dallas fulfillment company called Digital Magnetics to ship our game to customers with the clear understanding they would do so in time for Christmas. With the surge of orders, we figured it wise to check on this new business wing. When Jay, Shawn, and I arrived at their offices around 5 p.m. Friday, December 14, most everyone was gone, but all three of us noticed there were stacks of newly duplicated *DOOM* disks and paper inserts waiting to be placed inside stacks of *DOOM* boxes. We expected to see those boxes finished and shrink wrapped, or at least in that process, which was the whole point of hiring Digital Magnetics in the first place.

"Where is everybody?" I said to the manager who let us in. He could sense the concern in my voice. We had counted on them to handle the surge and to get extra help if necessary.

"They worked their shift and went home."

"This stuff needs to be shipped tomorrow so people can have them in time for Christmas. That's why we hired you."

The manager shrugged.

"We need to get this shit done right now," I said to Jay.

We started packing the boxes at a furious pace for their staff to mail the next morning. I was pissed, but what choice did I have? I was the one who had been banging the drum for distributing the games ourselves. I got my wish and then some, not that moving inventory was new to me; I'd spent months of my life unpacking boxes and shelving groceries at the commissary in Alconbury, England, during my last two years of high school, and, of course, anything was easier than working in Maria's sweatshop.

That evening, after having packed hundreds of boxes, Jay, Shawn, and I left for our holiday break along with the rest of the id crew. Meanwhile, tens of thousands of people downloaded *DOOM*'s shareware version and the registered *DOOM* boxes made their way around the world. Players started to post on alt.games.doom and share copies of the first episode with their friends. Game distributors, free to copy the shareware episode at will, did so and sold those copies with our blessing at software stores big and small for $5 or $10 a pop. Since they got to keep all the money, hundreds of distributors and resellers got in on the act. It was big business, too. Even though players could get it free online, in 1993, people were used to purchasing their games at software stores. Modems with good connections were not the norm. With the distributors' help, *DOOM* was getting around in a big way.

Due to *DOOM*, massive changes were in store for the industry and games as a whole. I've been asked a thousand times if we anticipated its profound effect. The answer is no, unquestionably no. We couldn't have, not the full reach of it.

The multiplayer aspect of *DOOM* transformed games, opening a path that has led to competitive gaming as we know it today. That's why id is often credited with spawning competitive gaming. However, competitive gaming had been around for a while. The 1980s were incredibly active with arcade tournaments all over the nation. Even I competed in a tournament in 1981 at a local arcade, Video Bob's, and it was packed full of kids and excitement.

That said, our games did drastically change gameplay and unquestionably influenced competitive gaming. *DOOM* was used for the first modern computer-based tournaments, giving rise to a fledgling eSports community. With arcade games, the object was always to make your quarter last as long as possible. With *Wolfenstein 3-D,* I created "par times"—the amount of time we thought it would take players to complete a level. We added the same feature to *DOOM,* but as I mentioned in the previous chapter, we combined par times with functionality for players to capture keystrokes, which would let them see the game they just played. I thought it would be a cool feature; gamers could relive great moments, like blowing away a rival in a deathmatch, or it might help them learn from previous mistakes, but it never occurred to me that the combination of par times and the ability to save keystrokes and replay gameplay demos would radically reshape gaming by leading to the invention of speedrunning.

Speedrunning, completing a game or level in the fastest amount of time possible, is now a fundamental tenet of gameplay. We take it for granted, but before par times and *DOOM*'s replay functionality, there was no way to prove that you completed a speedrun in record time. Our replay functionality allowed players that proof by capturing not only the time but replaying the exact means by which they did it. It was a critical tool for speedrunning and competitive gaming. Within two months of *DOOM*'s launch, a gamer created a speedrunning site for players to upload their demos. As I write in 2022, a Google search result on the query "Speedrun YouTube" reveals more than 10 million results, and Twitch, the live-streaming site for games, averaged 2.93 million concurrent viewers throughout the first quarter of the year, according to Statista. Live-streaming a video game is, in a sense, the opposite of speedrun demos, but I believe there is a connection. The *DOOM* speedrun demos were an evolutionary forerunner of Twitch; both allowed players to share their gameplay with others for the purposes of showing off, challenging them, or demonstrating how something challenging might be done, whether live or in replay mode. The idea of gaming as a spectator sport still strikes some as bizarre, but as someone who grew up watching other kids play games for hours in arcades, I have the opposite reaction. I see Twitch as a modern-day arcade, a digital re-creation of the experience of watching someone play at a bar, pizzeria, or game room. Like arcades, people gather online for that purpose, whether to play or to watch, and to find new games.

Modding, the ability to edit existing levels or create new ones, transformed players' ability to interact with and extend their favorite games. One year earlier, our press release had declared *DOOM* an open game and noted our intent to share information about how modders could take advantage of that. Within two weeks of releasing *DOOM,* we put the data structure used to build the game's levels on the internet. Sharing that data made good on our promise. The decision to open our game up to the public was something that John Carmack and I felt strongly about. It was part of our core as programmers; we believed in sharing technology so that players could build their own creations and, ideally, lead to new improvements. We wanted and expected people to build editors, create new levels, make new sound effects, add new wall textures, and design new monsters. In fact, we looked forward to it!

Remember, though, we built the game using NeXTSTEP computers, so sharing our Objective-C–based level editor was useless to 99.9 percent of gamers who played on PCs running DOS.* By sharing the data structure, on the other hand, programmers could figure out how to make their own tools to edit the levels, and that's just what happened. Within two months, utilities and level editors were being traded in the *DOOM* community.

The first level editor to be released was called DEU—Doom Editing Utilities. It wasn't just a level editor, though. DEU also integrated a WAD editor, which allowed players to add custom graphics to their levels. New community-created BSP (binary space partition) programs were next; they compiled maps for *DOOM* so it could run them.† More utilities to edit WAD files were released, and one, DeHackEd, allowed players to modify the hard-coded values in the engine for everything from bullet damage to rocket firing rate to Cyberdemon health points. Players had the tools in their hands to create their own versions of *DOOM*.

With the release of so many editors, a flood of player-created levels soon appeared. One of the most impressive early efforts was STARDOOM, a *Star Wars*–style level with stormtroopers and laser sounds. It was impressive and showed everyone what could be done with WADs. Another impressive level was UACDEAD, which featured some tricky use of the sector format and line segment data to create invisible stairs with candles on them. The level was eerie and darkly atmospheric. These levels surprised and delighted us, and also showed off the potential and extensibility of *DOOM*.

Our decision to encourage modding created an entirely new paradigm. Fans were able to create *DOOM* mashups, like inserting famous images and sounds into our game. I thought it was hilarious—we had set the stage for fans to make *DOOM in "Copyright Infringement."* Although some of the id team objected to our sharing of our information, there was another selling point to the move: It was a marketing tool on several levels. First, players shared their work, which built awareness

---

* Objective-C is a language unique to NeXTSTEP computers.

† The binary space partition, or BSP, was created by Bruce Naylor at AT&T Labs. It breaks a level into logical pieces that allows for the level to be drawn quickly from wherever the player's viewpoint is. This is a simplified explanation. Programmers can find a much more detailed analysis as well as Naylor's original white paper online.

(nobody said "viral" back then). Also, no other game did this, so the move showed us as we really were—hard-core gamers and technologists who cared about game creation and the sharing of technology more than we cared about nickel and diming gamers to death. Today, lots of major games allow modding; it's a cheap way to provide added value to fans, extends the life of the game, and it's a viral marketing tool for any game brand.

What really set *DOOM* apart, however, was deathmatch. I imagined players all over the world reacting as I had initially reacted. That incredible moment—that first jaw-dropping second where I witnessed someone else controlling a character on a screen, and I blew them away—has never left me. It was such a monumental leap forward. Playing a game against a computer is challenging, provided the AI is good. Playing a game against another human is the apex, and the world was seeing it for the first time. It was an addictive, visceral thrill. No wonder sales were through the roof. Deathmatch added an X factor that made competition spellbinding in a way that other games couldn't rival.

Deathmatch was also the ingredient that created a perfect storm that the media couldn't resist. A revolutionary game was making millions and turning the entire industry upside down, and the tiny company behind the game was filled with long-haired guys obsessed with *D&D*, heavy metal and fast cars. What could be better? When the media came calling—and they called every day—we weren't exactly prepared for it. We had no PR or marketing agency. So I became the talking head of id Software by process of elimination. It wasn't a role I jumped into. Carmack had no interest in talking to the media and wasn't comfortable with that role. Adrian and Kevin were art guys, so they couldn't really speak about the engine or the game design, both of which required a degree of expertise. Jay was comfortable with the media and could talk about business and numbers, but not the engine and game design. So, many of the interviews fell to me—the only person on the team who could discuss all of it.

That said, thanks to "Programmer Nuance Deficit Disorder," when an interviewer asked me if I expected *DOOM* to be a smash, I answered directly, "Yes, of course."

I never stopped to think how that might sound or how a writer might hear my words. I was just stating facts. I mean, it was true. We intended to create the greatest game we had ever played and released a press release eleven months before stating exactly that. We expected *DOOM* to be huge because our previous games were popular and we knew this was a much more awesome game. It never occurred to me to say something more measured, like, "Well, we hoped this would be the case, and we're glad it has resonated with gamers." All of this, plus my long black hair, my unabashed passion for gaming, and my well-known love of metal and fast cars rolled into one and resulted in some magazines calling me gaming's first rock star. I still laugh when I think about this—the notion of a programmer being called a rock star. I unintentionally fueled this image by playing *DOOM* deathmatches with an unreserved intensity.

Prior to launch, we played a lot because, as any game designer will tell you, play is essential. We refer to it as "eating our own dog food." Deathmatch was one of the last things we added before launching the game. We didn't have much time to refine play and explore multiplayer, so we played by necessity, and that play resulted in better levels, better co-op, better deathmatch, and, ultimately, the game players held in their hands. The quality of that experience didn't happen by accident. It happened because we put a lot of hours into making sure it felt *great*. This process isn't just true of *DOOM*, it's true of all great games. After release? I played for the same reasons the rest of the world did. It was thrilling, challenging, and addictive. Far from being mindless self-indulgence, though, all that play factored into the design of our future games.

There were plenty of other "firsts" and breakthroughs for *DOOM*. Its use of 3D set a new standard for games that everyone had to match. Most games became 3D post-*DOOM*. It spearheaded a tidal wave of similar games, which the industry referred to as simply "DOOM clones." At that point, the genre didn't even have a name. Within a short amount of time, however, the first-person shooter, or FPS, became the dominant genre in the industry. Thirty years later, the biggest selling, most highly regarded games are still FPSs, including the *Call of Duty*, *Halo*, *Half-Life*, *Battlefield*, *Titanfall*, *Borderlands*, *Destiny*, and *Far Cry* series as well as titles like *Overwatch*, *Valorant*, and *PUBG* *(PlayerUnknown's Battlegrounds)*. Of course, the *Wolfenstein*, *DOOM*, and *Quake* (more on that later) series continue, as well. Surprisingly, first-person shooters still use most of the original keyboard control scheme I designed for *Wolfenstein 3-D*.

Carmack's implementation of Bruce Naylor's BSP algorithm to speed up culling and rendering affected the programming of 3D games for decades. It was such an elegant solution to the problem of determining what should be drawn on the screen that it was the best choice for most games for many years. The use of diminished lighting gave the *DOOM* engine an automatic spookiness, turning light into darkness as it recedes into the distance. As a level designer, it made my job easier, made the game look more realistic, and made the player nervous.

DOOM's distribution model—free to play (F2P)—has become the most popular video game business and marketing model of our times. We can't claim to have invented F2P, which evolved out of shareware, but *DOOM* showed just how powerful a tool it was for video games, particularly when integrated with our innovative physical distribution approach. The predominant distribution model was rooted in selling completed boxed games in stores. The id Software model relied on making an ass-kicking, fun game and providing two ways for players to get it: online or at a software store. Remember, in 1993 most people did not have the internet, and if they did, it was often slow and costly. They were used to going to the local computer store for software. By giving any software distributor the ability to sell the physical shareware version of the game, physical copies were distributed worldwide at no cost to us. If they were willing to pay for the packaging and the disks, they got to keep all the profit. The upside for us was free physical distribution for our shareware, and of course some percentage of those people ended up ordering the full registered version from us.

Because *DOOM* was one of the best games around, and the shareware version was free and legal to copy, all retail-only game publishers felt the pressure—they now needed to create demo versions of their games to entice players, too. Even game magazines got in on the act, distributing cover disks in the mid-1990s. *DOOM* has also become the de facto litmus test for all new tech. "Does it run *DOOM*?" has its own website, and as of this writing, *DOOM* does indeed run on everything from a pregnancy test to a piano.

Of course, *DOOM* was also a target for others immediately after its release. We found that out when a lawyer from Data East in Japan contacted us and told us that we were infringing on their trademark. As any dutiful company would, they filed trademarks for every game they created, and during the time *Gamer's Edge* was starting up, they released an arcade game named *Gate of Doom*. They claimed that *DOOM* infringed on their trademark.

Jay immediately flew to Japan to try to work out a deal. He said the negotiations took about five minutes. They all sat down around the Data East conference table and their lawyer demanded $1 million. Jay countered with $250,000. They countered with $500,000, and Jay said, "It's a deal." Case closed. Jay flew back, happy we didn't have to pay more. We felt like he might have been able to lower the price a little more, but the game was making so much money that we didn't press the issue. We avoided the risks and costs associated with a protracted trademark battle.

As much as *DOOM* changed the industry, it changed our fortunes, too. Jay told us that id was on track to easily make a million dollars in *DOOM* sales in the first month, so we immediately met and gave ourselves another raise, boosting our salaries to $100,000 a year. We also began discussing awarding ourselves bonuses. A collective car-buying binge ensued. Adrian scored a Dodge Viper, Kevin got a Corvette, and Carmack told me he was eyeing a new purchase, too.

"You should come with me to the Ferrari dealership. There's a red Testarossa I'm thinking of buying."

I didn't need to be asked twice.

"Oh my god," I said, arriving at the lot. My eyes were fixed on the Ferrari, a red, low-slung masterpiece, barely three-and-half feet high, with side strakes, and embedded headlights that literally rose out of the car. It was stunning.

"That is beautiful."

"I'm going to get it."

"I want one, too—but in yellow."

Unfortunately, the dealership didn't have a yellow Ferrari in stock. So we left with John's used $100,000 purchase and took it straight to Bob Norwood's automotive shop. Bob had become a trusted associate, souping up John's previous wheels, and John wanted him to outfit the new engine with twin turbos. I asked Bob to keep an eye out for a yellow version of the car. Within two weeks, he had one, a 1991 with 5,000 miles on it. It was in perfect shape, and the owner, who was asking $107,500, had installed stealth radar and laser detectors to help make it speeding-ticket-proof.

I *needed* to buy this car. There was, however, one slight hitch. I might have been making a hundred grand a year, but I couldn't get a loan if my life depended on it. I'd declared bankruptcy after cluelessly rolling up debts during my first marriage. Renting furniture, maxing out my credit card, leaving a car in storage—you name it, young, eternal optimist and credit risk John Romero did it. In 1989, with collection agencies tying up the *Softdisk* office phone trying to shake me down for money I didn't have, I decided to surrender and declare bankruptcy. At the time, there was no way for me to dig my way out of that debt, and I certainly didn't foresee my fortunes changing to the degree that they later did.

All of which meant that I needed a big cash infusion to buy my dream Ferrari. I went back to the office, where everyone knew about my credit woes, and said, "That's it. I want this car. Let's give ourselves $110,000 bonuses."

That motion carried immediately. id Software was making more than $50,000 a day.

When it came time to drive the Testarossa away, I was terrified. I had spent my entire life driving used cars with 75,000 miles on them. I sat in the Ferrari, closed the door, and the seat belt whirled into action, traveling on a rail and encircling my body so all I had to do was snap the buckle into place. It was as if I had stepped into the future. Putting the key in the ignition and driving it off the lot was scary. I was absolutely petrified that I would wreck my new machine.

Of course, I got over it, and years later, on an empty Texas highway, I decided to see how fast the car could go. It reached 175 miles per hour on the speedometer. That was scary, too, but in a different way. At that speed, I was worried about ruining me, not the car. If the car hit anything, it would be destroyed—and I'd be dead.

The Testarossa didn't change me. At least, I don't think it did, but it changed how the id team rewarded itself. Beth and I moved into a rental house in a suburban neighborhood in Plano. I felt proud to park a $100,000 car in my driveway. As the revenue from *DOOM* poured in—not to mention *Wolfenstein 3-D* and *Keen*—more bonuses followed, and for me, so did more cars. I got Beth a Chevy Tahoe and told her she could get whatever else she wanted. Looking back, there were smarter ways to spend cash than on fast cars, but I only knew what I knew. The concept of investing money for the future wasn't something I'd encountered before. In my family, having enough money to get to the next payday was the measure of success. I was having fun. We all were.

As far as my family was concerned, my constantly improving financial situation allowed me to do things that once seemed impossible. I bought houses for Kelly, the mother of my boys, and got rehab help and a house for my dad and paid off all his many debts. I got my mother a new car and whatever else she wanted. Various relatives needed help covering college tuition, and I wrote frequent checks. I funded business start-ups for my brother, Ralph, and my aunt Fay. I gave away cars or got them for friends in need. It felt great to provide for the people I loved. That is one of the most wonderful benefits of financial success.

My family was thrilled for me. Interestingly, neither my mom, my stepdad, nor my father had any interest in playing my games. As far as I know, they never played a single one. I give them points for consistency; some generational divides are impossible to bridge. Many years later, though, my mother traveled to Ireland and attended Dublin Comic Con with me and Brenda. There was a *DOOM* exhibition deathmatch area set up, and I finally got my mom playing *DOOM*. Against me.

"Stand still so I can shoot you," she yelled.

And I did. I walked around and let her shoot me until I died. She was delighted, and truth be told, so was I.

CHAPTER 14

The Icon of Sin

Returning from vacation in January 1994, many things about our world changed, but one thing remained the same: We were ready to make another game, and there was no doubt what game it would be: *DOOM II*. Since the days of *Keen*, we alternated shareware games with full retail versions, and it was obviously working well.

But id was now more than just a game development company. We were growing—not just in terms of who worked at the company but also in terms of new ownership, partnerships, and licensing. Recognizing their significant contributions, we offered Jay and Kevin part ownership of the company, which would be finalized in March 1994. A fledgling community grew, too—and I say fledgling only because the *DOOM* community is easily one hundred times that size today—but even back then, it required and deserved attention, and this was in the days before the concept of community management or eSports even existed. Game developers and gamers lived in different bubbles mediated only by industry press and occasional fan mail. *DOOM*, the advent of LAN* parties, and our consistent presence on the internet blew that all open. I was wearing multiple hats, and it was exciting. I was not only the de facto communications officer/PR talking head and community/eSports guy, I was the quality control officer for all our licensing deals. And offers flooded in! People wanted to write *DOOM* novels and *DOOM* hint books. Companies wanted to license the *DOOM* logo to put on their

---

* LANs, or local area networks, allowed players to connect up to four of computers together to play co-op or deathmatch.

shareware retail versions. Other companies hoped to partner with us to develop their IP and still others wanted to use our engine. Even though Jay negotiated these business deals, he couldn't vet some of the opportunities or final products. He didn't know everything about *DOOM*'s development, technical possibilities, or level design. Besides, he was now biz guy of a small developer that was rocketing upward at an incredible rate. He had a million things keeping him busy, too. For an entire year following *DOOM*'s release, I spent a nontrivial portion of my time vetting all these side projects, giving Jay my opinions, and then monitoring the deals we made. It's not like we could take on *all* these opportunities—we were too few people—so we had to pick and choose. If I have one regret from this time, it is not jumping into the deep end of merch. A couple decades later, games like *Minecraft* and *Angry Birds* were all over merch in a big way, and their efforts not only gave their fans what they were asking for but provided additional revenue that allowed the company to grow.

On top of the licensing opportunities, I worked on a new business venture. As *DOOM* was locking down in November, I had an idea: commissioning Raven Software, the Madison-based company that licensed our tech for *ShadowCaster*, to use our engine and quickly develop a new title to publish ourselves. I envisioned it as a *DOOM*-like knockoff, but instead of basing the game in a futuristic world, I wanted to go back in time and make a medieval game with a different aesthetic. I saw it as id optimizing our engine, retaining control, and expanding our business and bottom line. We already knew that Raven was great at making medieval art.

Presenting the idea to the team, I noted that it was a significant investment for us and assured them I would manage it and take the role of executive producer. We'd have to buy Raven several NeXTSTEP workstations, so their crew could use our engine, and pay for the team to make the game, but I thought it was worth it. Everyone agreed. Raven signed on the dotted line, the NeXTSTEP computers were ordered, and I started to lay out the development plan for *Heretic*.

In January, I visited Raven to discuss the game, install the workstations, and show everyone how to use our tools. With the deal signed and the machines installed, I flew back to Dallas eager for Raven to get to work. As it turns out, they didn't get too far. Raven delayed the start of development because of a new co-owner they brought on, their old *ShadowCaster* producer from EA, and he wanted to renegotiate our agreement. We had a fair 50/50 deal and would not budge. id was about to terminate the agreement, but instead we had them fly down to Dallas to negotiate with us and fix this issue. We ironed out the problems, and they finally got to work.

Even though *Heretic* was a new game, I needed Raven to keep the same amount of weapons and weapon balance as *DOOM*. It was a formula we knew worked. They could make the weapons look different, but messing with the formula was off the table. A change to game balance was a change to the core of the game.

It was difficult enough learning the NeXTSTEP development process. We didn't want them making risky gameplay changes, too. The Raven team and I worked out a great workflow—they sent builds of the game on regular milestones, I played them, and gave them feedback. It was most important to us that it felt like an id software game. It was a year of back and forth and took up a significant amount of my time, but we all felt *Heretic* was worth it in the end.

Outside of id, however, no one knew or cared about the licensing or external projects. Our fans and the press only cared about one thing: *DOOM II*. The calls, emails, and letters started in January, when *DOOM* was less than a month old. Since *DOOM* hadn't received much attention prior to its launch, our phone rang off the hook with requests for interviews, and of those we granted, "What's next?" was the obvious question on everyone's lips. I certainly didn't care much about the publicity; if anything, it ate away at my already limited time, but it was a necessary evil to get the word out there about our upcoming game. We wanted to keep the momentum going.

Even with *DOOM*'s success, the work on *DOOM II* was going to be a challenge. We had everything going in our favor, but one beast of a question kept raising its head: How do you follow up and even top something like *DOOM*? We were determined to try. During an early design meeting, we agreed that the formula for *DOOM* was perfect, and that the new game should just build on what we started without breaking the underlying game feel players loved. We analyzed the experience, system by system and bit by bit. New levels were a given. Because we'd sell *DOOM II* in stores, we didn't have to worry about making multiple shareware episodes, with one to give away and two others to sell. But the player experience in those levels? That needed to set *DOOM II* apart from its predecessor. We got to work considering our options.

As our early design meetings got underway in January 1994, Ron Chaimowitz came to visit us at the Black Cube. Ron was an aggressive, super-smart, multimillionaire hustler. He discovered and managed Gloria Estefan. He turned Spanish pop idol Julio Iglesias into a household name in the US. His company, GoodTimes Home Video, orchestrated Jane Fonda's mega-selling workout videotapes. Most importantly for us, he became Walmart's go-to provider and gatekeeper for any software sold in their stores. He wanted to sign us to their new game division, GT Interactive, to sell retail versions of our games in Walmart. For game developers in the 1990s, getting into Walmart was a huge windfall. They placed orders for tens of thousands of units instead of the tens or hundreds of units like other big box stores. Because they had such a massive footprint, whatever they purchased always sold through. Few people had dial-up in 1994, and it would be another nine years before Steam and regular digital distribution of games was the norm. At the time, though, we didn't fully understand the selling power of Walmart.

We listened to his pitch.

"How can I prove myself?" he asked us.

Jay replied, "Sell 30,000 copies of *Commander Keen*." We expected him to roll his eyes.

"Done," said Ron.

Sure enough, he cut a purchase order. The 30,000 copies of *Commander Keen* were gone in the space of a month. We were all blown away. Our attitude was, "Whoa! These guys can do anything. Let's sign a deal." Negotiations with Ron were easy. We got creative control, kept our copyrights, and GT Interactive committed to a $2 million marketing budget for *DOOM II*—an almost inconceivable amount of money for a company that previously promoted its games by posting them on the internet for free. Behind the scenes, and unbeknownst to us, GT Interactive was quietly trying to acquire the rights to and subsequently publish every single game that we'd made for *Gamer's Edge*, and I'd go so far as to wager that they made far more money from those games than we ever did. They were the biggest distributors of *DOOM* shareware. They also contacted *Softdisk*, got the rights to publish *Catacomb 3D*, and named it *Catacomb 3*. They published *Keen Dreams* in a retail box. Through us, at least, they got the rights to publish *Wolfenstein 3-D* in a retail box.

Meanwhile, and buoyed by our new GT Interactive deal, our design plans for *DOOM II* continued. As before, I took on the role of game director, level designer, and handled game audio while Carmack handled engine improvements and code for the new enemies. Adrian and Kevin created the look and feel of the world and its enemies. Among our biggest challenges was the weapon balance, the same balance I insisted Raven stick with for *Heretic*. It was the soul of the player experience. We needed to make sure that we didn't ruin anything that made the original *DOOM* great. Every implement of destruction was useful in the game.

Could we add anything?

That was a problem. In *DOOM*, each weapon was assigned a number key, one through seven, in order of its lethal power. We didn't want to tie a new weapon to eight, because the seven key already controlled our most brutal weapon, the BFG, which of course was short for "Big Fucking Gun," and we knew players would rebel at remapping their brains to a new number order.

"What about a double-barrel shotgun?" I asked.

After all, we loved the shotgun. It did great damage, even at a distance. It was straight out of *Evil Dead*.

"A double-barrel shotgun would be fucking amazing," I continued. "We're already switching between your fists and the chainsaw on 1, so we could switch between the shotgun and the double-barrel shotgun on 3."

We hadn't even put it into the game, and I was already figuring out the audio for it in my head. I heard a bassy, bigger sound. The reload ended up being a little crisper. Damage wise, it was double the shotgun but had a widespread shot. All these years later, it remains my favorite weapon.

Level-wise, we decided on thirty levels plus two secret levels, with a few intermission breaks. It was a lot of work, and with everything else I had going on between evaluating external licensing partners and dealing with a never-ending barrage of incoming *DOOM*-related stuff, I knew that Sandy and I needed some help. I considered where we might get a level designer—the specialization was still relatively new at the time—and recalled a conversation I had with a new recruit to our tech support department, American McGee. Months before, Carmack met and hired American, then a cool, young auto mechanic and computer geek, to work in tech support with Shawn Green. A few months into *DOOM II* development, American said he wanted to become a level designer, so we promoted him from tech support to level design. He knew my levels and design patterns well and needed little mentoring. Among the three of us, I knew we could create a cohesive feel across the game's level design. I put American to work, and we hired a tech support replacement.

I knew that what players encountered in these levels needed to be different, new, and a step up from *DOOM*. To surprise and challenge players, we focused on lots of new interactive level effects like super-fast doors, super-fast stairs, and other gameplay additions. I also wanted more outdoor maps and more verticality. New textures were important to make the new levels look like they belonged on Earth rather than in hell, too. The real differentiators, however, were new monsters with new abilities. Adrian and Kevin outdid themselves when it came to horrific bad guys from the underworld, like the grotesque humanoid Arch-vile or the Mancubus, a horrific ogre with flamethrowers instead of hands. Gregor Punchatz brought them to life with another round of modeling, and our audio designer, Bobby Prince, outfitted them with macabre monster sounds.

During its design, I remember talking with Kevin about one of *DOOM II*'s new enemies, the Revenant. He was a tall, menacing skeleton who had one rocket launcher on each shoulder with heat-seeking capabilities. The design problem was this: What happened if the player got too close to it?

"It would be dumb if he shot rockets and suffered collateral damage," I said, and then it hit me. "I want him to punch you straight down on the head. That would make a hilarious sound." I was laughing even as I considered the possibilities.

All these changes—the new level effects, new enemies, and new items—also required new code and data for DoomEd, which I added as we went along.

Sandy and American got busy on the first ten levels, and their design and play styles kept the player experience fresh as they moved from level to level. As it turned out, American was an exceptional and natural level designer. From playing my levels in *DOOM*, he totally understood the abstract level design style. He picked up how the player should flow through a level, how the designer gates the player and makes it easy for them to find the key to the next door. He also had a command of throwing in special events like crushing ceilings and surprise reveals of enemies. As the game director, I felt his levels, even from the first iteration, were always really fun to play and fit the id aesthetic. It was apparent that American developed his own style, too. MAP14 is an excellent example of a sprawling level with a lot of surprises that also works well in deathmatch, while MAP04 is the ideal for a small, tightly designed map that is both challenging and aesthetically pleasing. It has its own feel with the dark hallway in which the player flips a switch and sees shadows and lights. Interestingly, American decided to teach the player how to "jump" right away in MAP02—the player has to run from a walkway into a building over a gap. If they couldn't do that, they were stuck.

My first hands-on level as a designer was MAP11. I felt like a kid in a candy shop. It's amazing how the possibility space of a game expands with just a few new tools, effects, and enemies, not to mention the double-barrel shotgun. In addition to the new toys, the year of making *DOOM* and establishing the abstract level design style taught me many things. My understanding of what one could do within an abstract space to guide and surprise a player had grown exponentially. When I established the style, I was learning as I was creating, and I'm fortunate in that it came to me naturally. In brief, I don't see a level as a path or a process, but as an entity in itself—the biggest character in the game. The level has a beginning and an end, sure, but many ways through, and it's not so much a linear experience as a continuous one, where players come to know the space as they might know a person and decide to explore and challenge it as it reveals itself to them. Sometimes, my levels surprise me with possibilities I hadn't considered. Players can always go forward or back, and so what is a beginning and an end becomes murky when the end might just be a new way to approach a beginning. This understanding of space built *DOOM*, and I was building on that to create *DOOM II*. In particular, MAP11 was so different from my *DOOM* levels, and it became one of my favorite maps to play deathmatch on.

MAP11, the Circle of Death (with the alternate name: 'O' of Destruction), was built around a central circle that connected to four main areas. In single-player mode you travel from one area to the next in order until you finish the level. But in deathmatch mode, all areas are open, and each contains a significant powerup or weapon that all players want to get, so much so that it becomes a hectic battle royale, and the player with the best knowledge of the level has the advantage.

While the tools and tricks have evolved, my actual process for designing levels has changed little from *DOOM*'s E1M1. It begins with a conceptual exercise. First I determine a unique play style for the level. *Outdoors, indoors—where does the player start, where does the level end? What are the different ways one might move through the space? What is the character of this level?* Lots of questions to answer, and I find that if you ask questions of a space, the space answers. *What's the unique thing I'm trying to do on this level? How can I lock access to the next area and unlock it in a fun way?* I start by making a room that looks interesting. The more choices, the better. The path forward is clear before long, and then I start to plan each room and what happens there. I figure out where to put locked doors, where the keys should go, and then determine the secrets. When I have a level built, I consider how it might play as players come back through the spaces, so that it's never a purely linear experience.

Using DoomEd, I place enemies quickly, then weapons, ammo, and health. If I have to add new elements, I need to edit DoomEd's code and the game's code before using DoomEd again. With every change, no matter how small, I play through the level again. I balance play for ultraviolent (UV) first so that while I'm playing, I feel pressure.[*] I keep designing room after room, connecting them, changing the shape of the level, releasing enemies to surprise the player, and try-ing to make every new section unique. As I go, the character of the level changes, and this sometimes causes me to revisit earlier areas. Every level has to have a unique feel and identity. I go over the level constantly, searching for a way to reveal its character and make it more interesting. By the time a level is finished, I've played it a thousand times. What the player sees in a completed level of mine isn't so much a perfectly planned design as an artifact of my play experience. To this day, I design levels the same way.

I play the level as a player as opposed to its designer, trying to break the rules. As a designer, I use rules in ways the player isn't expecting. As an example, when I got to MAP20, I trapped the player in a massive room with the Cyberdemon and Spider Mastermind, and both were alerted the second the player was in their sights. The only way out was a door switch right next to the Cyberdemon. The trick is to make the Cyberdemon shoot rockets into the Spider Mastermind so they start killing each other and ignore the player. Then the player can run up to the switch, but they are terrified because they are *right next to* the Cyberdemon, a place no one wants to be. If they get that far, they flip the switch and run out before either the Spider Mastermind or the Cyberdemon dies. I personally called the map Clash of the Titans, but its official name is GOTCHA!

Of all my levels in *DOOM II*, it's difficult for me to choose my favorite. I feel like it's a tie between MAP29, The Living End, and MAP26, The Abandoned Mines.

---

[*] To "balance play" refers to game balance, meaning to provide an experience for the player that feels challenging but not too difficult. The better the player, the more challenge required. Because I have been playing *DOOM* since day 1, the game is not challenging for me unless I am playing it on UV. So, I balance toward that, giving myself a challenging game, and then make it progressively easier for lower difficulty levels.

MAP29 feels like an epically long adventure with the end in plain sight the entire time, if only you could figure out how to get there. MAP26 is where I really played around with the concept of verticality in DOOM II maps—there's quite a bit of switch-flipping to move elevator floors up and down a long way. It's a smaller map, and so perfect for two players. More players turn it into a MAP01-style bloodfest.

While working on my own maps, I played and reviewed Sandy's and American's maps, too. Our collective designs felt like they fit into a cohesive whole, and working with Bobby on the audio direction, I believed the audio design of *DOOM II* supported the spaces and creatures we were building. When something didn't fit, each of us felt comfortable addressing it.

"Have you played map seven?" American asked me.

MAP07, Dead Simple, was Sandy's map, a level he had just finished. It was the first mini-boss level, and it needed to show that, telegraphing that something dreaded was ahead while giving the mini-boss and the player time and space to confront one another. The Mancubus, the mini-boss, was a flesh tank with flame-throwers for arms. He dealt a shocking amount of damage and with his high hit points, he was able to withstand many attacks.

I got the map from the server and started to play.

"I don't think it fits," American said. "It's not up to the quality of the other levels, particularly for the Mancubus."

I finished playing the level and agreed with him.

"You want to make a new one?" I asked him. "It can't be huge, though, otherwise we'll get off track."

American nodded and walked back to his desk, eager to take on the task. As a testament to his ability, he did the level in a day, and that's what you see in the final game. It was a mini-boss map, and so it needed to be compact to force a quick encounter with the Mancubus. The player started in a small room with a double-barreled shotgun, flipped a switch, and caused the walls to come down. Four Mancubi were revealed on top of four pedestals, all firing at the player from within an inner square area. Around that, there is an outer square path. Although it wasn't made specifically for deathmatch, MAP07 has ended up as one of the most popular deathmatch levels.

Sandy had no problem with American redoing his level. As a team, we all wanted the game to be as good as possible. In the end, I created six levels, Shawn made one level, American made eight levels, and Sandy made seventeen levels. Every one of those early maps ended up playing well in deathmatch, as we found out over and over during development.

At work, things were going great. In my personal life, things were challenging. It's fair to say that I was consumed by my job; we all were. I didn't feel stuck or pressured to work. Quite the contrary, it's what I wanted to do more than I wanted to do anything else. I think it's why Carmack and I were so perfectly paired. If given an infinite choice of possibilities, he wanted to solve complex problems with code, and I wanted to code and create something with that code. So, when I left work, I went home to code, create, or research games. It never occurred to me that this was abnormal, because it was normal for me. Games are my work, my hobby, and my passion. Beth didn't seem to mind too much. Though we met at *Softdisk*, she had no interest in computers or games, and what started out as a love affair turned into a pseudo-roommate situation. She did her thing, and I did mine. My aunt Fay, having lost her home, moved in with us, and she and Beth became fast friends. During this time, my father was struggling, too. He had moved from alcohol to hard drugs, and his behavior and demeanor were unpredictable.

By now, we were midway through development and started to consider the cover art for *DOOM II*. Kevin wanted to see if Boris Vallejo, an incredible artist whose work was well known in the fantasy and sci-fi community, might be interested. As it turns out, Boris was out of our price range. Sure, we were making a lot of money, but we tried to set reasonable budgets. Julie Bell, likewise a well-regarded artist, offered to do the job for less. She got to work and created a box cover with the Cyberdemon attacking the player. When we got the finished painting, it was great. Julie's artwork was moody and well rendered, but the Cyberdemon looked more like a massive bull, particularly its horns, instead of a demon with enmeshed machine parts. We paid her but decided to try again with someone else.

This time, Kevin contacted Gerald Brom, a fantasy illustrator whose work we knew from *Dungeons & Dragons*. He created the iconic cover art you see on the shipped box. Brom did such an incredible job we immediately commissioned him to create the box cover for *Heretic*, which we planned on releasing in a few months.

Keeping Don Punchatz's original *DOOM* logo was a given. We couldn't imagine changing it. However, we needed to add a "II" underneath. Kevin had an idea to make a nicely lit, high-resolution piece of art using a tool that was starting to make some waves in the game industry. Over at Cygnus Studios, Steve Maines was learning this program, 3D Studio R4, the predecessor of 3D Studio Max. After talking with Kevin, Steve used it to create the "II" with detailed texturing and lighting. It looked great, so Kevin incorporated it into the box art.

DOOM II was getting close to being finished and coming together like a tornado, all the bits and pieces flying in. The end-of-a-game velocity is an incredible thing to experience. Remaining tech issues are solved, gameplay feels good level to level, art and audio assets are all in place, and, if everything is going as planned, it's just polish from there on out. We did a lot of single-player and deathmatch testing, and altered the levels as necessary. Shawn and his helper learned every level to answer any customer questions. Adrian and Kevin created the remaining screens we needed. Jay gathered all the files that were needed on the disk for legal reasons. We played the hell out of the game to make sure it was bulletproof. It had to be a worthy follow-up to *DOOM*, and we knew it.

One of my last remaining tasks for *DOOM II* was to program the sound effects for the final boss, the Icon of Sin, a massive, frightening, Baphomet-style horned head that launched demon-spawning cubes out of its partially visible brain. What the player shot at, however, was actually a blue ball sprite floating in the air behind its head, and that's where I needed to place the sound effect. So I opened the final level of the game and no-clipped* behind the wall that the Icon was attached to and saw something strange: For a brief second, I thought I glimpsed my own face flash on the screen.

What the hell?

I did a double take.

There was always a hall-of-mirrors effect when a player no-clips outside of a level, causing them to see a bunch of images overlapping one another on the screen. Instead of seeing the blue ball like I expected, however, I saw my head repeating again and again.

Was that a bug? Have I been staring at the screen too long? Am I losing my shit?

I decided the answer was no.

What the fuck is going on?

I kept no-clipping, heading to the blue circle sprite that stood in for the Icon of Sin. When I arrived, I saw it: In a hidden room behind the wall, my head was speared on a stick, oozing blood!

"Holy shit!" I said, laughing out loud as reality set in.

The artists, Adrian and Kevin, had planted a hilarious Easter egg. They didn't think I'd discover it while programming the audio.

I was the Icon of Sin!

This was too cool. I shot my head. My shotgun blast smashed into my head on a stick and sent me to my final, agonizing death.

I couldn't let Kevin and Adrian have the last word. I needed to add an Easter egg of my own.

It was 11 p.m. and Bobby was still in the office making music. I ran into the conference room where he set up his studio.

"Dude, you won't believe what I just found!" I told him.

"What's that?"

"You know the Icon of Sin, the final boss? Well, either Adrian or Kevin changed that blue sprite into my head on a stake! They thought the game was going

---

* To no-clip is to use a cheat code that lets you walk through all the walls in a game. This allows the player to travel anywhere in a level.

to ship, and I wouldn't find out in time. I need to make an Easter egg that shows them I found out what they did."

"What are you going to do?" Bobby asked.

"Well, I figured you could record me saying 'To win the game you must kill me, John Romero.' You can pitch-shift it down low and reverse it so it sounds demonic. I'll make the Icon of Sin play it when it sees you for the first time."

Bobby nodded and smiled. We were in business.

After about fifteen minutes of recording and adjusting the sound, it was perfect. I programmed it into the game and made a new build available.

The next morning, American noticed the new build of the level and grabbed it to test the Icon of Sin. As soon as he picked up all the weapons and went through the teleporter, the Icon of Sin saw him and played the eerie audio Bobby and I put in just hours before. He was stunned, but also realized it was awesome and was a manipulated sound effect.

"Ooo, scary backward message!" American called out, laughing.

American reversed the sound and played it, then promptly told everyone in the office. The Easter egg had stayed a secret for five minutes! We all got a big laugh out of it, and there was no question the two Easter eggs were staying in the game.

DOOM II launched and was available for sale on September 30, 1994. GT Interactive's initial shipment of *DOOM II* was a staggering 600,000 copies. It was such a fast-selling item, the biggest game retailers like CompUSA and Walmart didn't bother putting the game on their shelves because it was a waste of their time. When a giant pallet of games was delivered by truck, they just brought it into the front of the store, took the wrapping off, and let customers take a copy as they entered.

Our new partners were elated. They had planned a "Doomsday" press event following the launch on October 10 at the Limelight, a converted church that was one of New York City's trendiest nightclubs. They flew us from Dallas for the event, and I walked around like a complete nerd wearing a *DOOM* T-shirt that said "Wrote It" on the back. GT pulled out all the stops, hiring a big PR firm to generate mainstream buzz. A machine projected holographic images of *DOOM II* monsters, and the game's soundtrack sounded awesome pumping through the club's first-class sound system. At the back of the club, a bunch of computers were networked together and connected to the giant video screen, so viewers could watch top players deathmatch.

It was spectacular and more than a little surreal—making games is such a solitary activity, and so being in a nightclub, in a party atmosphere with loads of people to celebrate the release of our game, was a massive change of pace for us. Game launch parties are common now, especially for big-name games. Back in 1994, though, they were largely unheard of.

The press event was a wild circus of activity. Access to any of us was both limited and quite controlled. There were dozens of reporters in attendance, and they had lots of questions about *DOOM II* and *DOOM*.

"Did it turn out like you hoped it would?"

Yes, otherwise, we would not have released it.

"What are you most proud of?"

The overall direction of the game—it feels like a worthy successor to DOOM.

"What were the sales of *DOOM*?"

A lot.

In the middle of the group of reporters, one man began ranting over our answers, condemning *DOOM* and *DOOM II* for their violence. It's true that the games were violent—comically violent—with pretend digital guns shooting pretend digital rockets at pretend digital demons. The games were not intended for kids, of course, and we felt that games had the same ability and right to create an experience for adults as other forms of media. We heard what he had to say, but not content with being heard, the man continued to interrupt and was escorted out.

We were answering questions from many people and being pulled in multiple directions with sit-down interviews on camera, quick quotes for an article with someone else, or photos to use alongside the articles. In this swirling mass of people was Bob Huntley, a businessman from Houston who had flown all the way to New York just to meet us and try to sell us on his new product.

Jay introduced us. Looking toward Bob, he said, "You have two minutes."

Bob and Kee Kimbrell, his lead engineer, gave me a quick spiel about DWANGO, which stood for Dial-up Wide-Area Network Games Operation.

"It's early," Bob told me, "but it lets you use our program to connect to our server and launch *DOOM* deathmatches with other people that are on our server."

I nodded.

Bob kept talking, cramming everything he could say into those two minutes. Finally, he gave me a disk and said, "Please, just run this. You won't be sorry!"

I was pulled away to a meeting.

When I got back home, I ran the DWANGO.EXE program on the disk. The UI was rough—sandpaper rough—but it connected to their Houston server, as promised. Once online, I saw all the activity just stream by. Kee, Bob's partner, was in the server lobby, so I messaged him.

"How do I start a game?"

In its early state, I had to type out each of the commands manually as opposed to selecting them in a menu, but it worked. I was surprised that the gameplay felt good, almost as if we were connected to a LAN. The best part, of course, was that I no longer had to wait for a friend or a coworker to play deathmatch. I logged on, chatted with a stranger, and started playing.

This is the future, I thought. There was always someone who wanted to play. Mind you, this was before everyone had the internet and games were connected by default. I thought about my time in Utah, living in my dad's basement, not knowing a soul. I wouldn't have been able to deathmatch. There were thousands of computer and gamer geeks out there, eager to connect and play.

The next day when I got to work, I went to Jay's office.

"So, did you check out that DWANGO program?"

He looked at me in a knowing way.

"Yeah, I checked it out," he said, smiling. "What did you think?"

"It was awesome. I loved it! I mean, it's really early, but I *want* this thing to happen. It means that people always have someone to deathmatch with, no matter where they are or who they know."

Jay nodded. He got it.

"I'm going to contact Bob and get the ball rolling," I told him. "I'll need to rewrite their client, and Kee will need to do a lot of work on the server, but I think we can get this working well by the launch of *Heretic*."

I thought about when this work might slot into my schedule. Even though *DOOM II* was launched, there wasn't time to work on DWANGO. Post-launch is always a busy time, and I was still getting *Heretic* out the door. "I'll do it at home after work. You can figure out the biz details with Bob," I said. I believed DWANGO would be nothing but a win-win for *DOOM* and *DOOM II*, and by extension, id Software.

Jay cut a deal for 20 percent of DWANGO's profits. They charged $8.95 for monthly dial-up service, and it was an instant hit. Bob and Kee started offering franchises for $35,000. Even providing the equipment, a computer, modems, and cables, they must have cleared $30,000 on every deal. Better than that, gamers were connected and playing with people all over the world. From my perspective, meeting Bob and Kee was the best thing about Doomsday. I've always wondered why they didn't just drive the four hours from Houston to Mesquite instead of flying all the way to New York City, but I'm glad he and Kee did.

Within a month, the initial 600,000 copy run of *DOOM II* sold out. It was the top-selling computer game of 1994, moving well over a million copies and generating more than $30 million in retail sales. The critical reception was overwhelmingly positive, with a consensus that we had refined a great game.

By this time, the remaining id founders were fortunate to be millionaires, but success hadn't really changed any of us at the core. I still woke up every day and thought about games and the possibilities before us. I wanted to keep up our momentum, capitalize on our success, and expand on our technological and gameplay lead. With both *DOOM II* out the door and *Heretic* soon to follow, it was time to talk about what was next.

CHAPTER 15

Fault Lines

Back in the early days of id Software, in December 1990, Tom, Carmack, Adrian, and I hatched a plan for the ultimate RPG. We were inspired by our *D&D* adventures, all of us gathered around John Carmack's expansive gaming table with snacks, Coke, Dr Pepper, and plenty of pizza. In our campaign, there was a powerful group known as the ominous Silver Shadow Band. Its members rode on the back of a giant silver dragon, and if anyone saw its shadow, they knew the Band was either high above or nearby. Each character in the Silver Shadow Band was the ultimate expression of one of *D&D*'s stats, from the most intelligent character to one capable of nearly splitting our universe in half with his strength. That strongest character was Quake. To us, Quake was legendary, and he may as well have been *only* that. As a bunch of low-level peons, we rarely saw him or other high-level characters. However, we were lucky to go on an awesome adventure with him once or twice. The Silver Shadow Band did contract work for Justice, an even more powerful group. To us, Quake became more than just a character, and our adventures with him were the highlights of hundreds of hours of dungeon crawling. He was the embodiment of a superhero in a world of our own making.

We thought it would be incredible to play as Quake in a computer game—to wield that kind of superhuman strength, to fly on the back of a dragon. And who wouldn't want to use his two extraordinary superpowers? First was his hammer, capable of destroying most everything in his path, which we imagined players using as Quake used it—to flatten enemies to paste. Second was the omnipotent Hellgate Cube, which floated above Quake and delivered devilish damage to enemies that dared challenge him. Sizzling Quake's foes with lightning bolts seemed to be the Hellgate Cube's favorite action.

As we were finishing up our first *Keen* trilogy in December 1990, we were enthusiastic about making *Quake* our next game and introducing him to our growing fanbase. *Quake* was going to be our next game. We even inserted this promo text into the first, official id Software release, *Commander Keen in Invasion of the Vorticons*:

COMING SOON FROM ID SOFTWARE

As our follow-up to the *Commander Keen* trilogy, id Software is working on "The Fight for Justice": a completely new approach to fantasy gaming. You start not as a weakling with no food—you start as Quake, the strongest, most dangerous person on the continent. You start off with a Hammer of Thunderbolts, a Ring of Regeneration, and a transdimensional artifact. Here the fun begins. You fight for Justice, a secret organization devoted to vanquishing evil from the land! This is role-playing excitement.

Hyped by that premise, when *Commander Keen* shipped on December 14, 1990, we headed off for our Christmas vacations, but our imaginations exploded with ideas. We imagined Quake as a proto-*God of War*-like character battling huge enemies; our *D&D* adventures made real! However, we had just shipped our first 2D side-scroller, which in itself was a huge innovation. The distance between what we just shipped and what we envisioned? Light years. We wanted to put more on the screen and to give the player substantial agency in their gameplay, but CPUs were still slow, and the technology available couldn't match the game in our heads.

Moments like this one, what I call the "possibility bridge," are common in game development. As game developers, we have to see beyond the current horizon to imagine the possibilities that others either didn't see or saw but overlooked. Thinking *What if?* and coming up with functional answers to that question leads to innovation. However, it's not always possible to bridge the gap between imagination and what one can actually do with the available technology or resources. With *Dangerous Dave in "Copyright Infringement,"* Carmack believed he could cross the smooth-scrolling bridge, and he did. With *DOOM,* I believed I could create new dimensions in gameplay and game space by inventing the abstract level design style, and I did. There was no way we were crossing this "Quake" bridge in early 1991, though, and on that we were unanimous. We didn't want to deliver a version of *Quake* that was anything less than what we envisioned Quake to be—supremely powerful, badass, and without parallel. We decided to put it on ice, but the dream of *Quake* never went away.

And so, in late 1994, with *DOOM II* out the door, *Heretic* about to launch, and the continued avalanche of *DOOM*-themed product opportunities, our development team had a meeting to discuss our next original game. Everyone who shipped *DOOM II* was there: Carmack, Adrian, Kevin, Dave, Sandy, American, and me. We knew what we were there for, and the sense of excitement was palpable. While it seems like a no-brainer that another FPS was in the cards, that wasn't a given. When we entered the room, all we knew was that we were making something *new*.

Once everyone was seated, Carmack kicked things off. He had been doing research into a new engine for quite some time while we were cranking out *DOOM II's* levels.

"Okay, we're here to talk about our next big game," Carmack began. "I've been thinking about the next technological improvements we could make, going beyond *DOOM II*."

"That's what I like to hear!" I said. Carmack and I agreed that the *DOOM II* engine was only going to take us so far, especially since the modding community had embraced it and was producing a continuous stream of content. We had to do something new. That, and we liked chasing new tech. Since *Commander Keen*, we had become tech-authoritative, because technology was what enabled our game design to have a leading edge.

American chimed in to agree. "This'll be great," he said, smiling.

"Our next game engine is going to be fully 3D with better gradient lighting,[*] and play over the internet using a client-server model,"[†] Carmack continued. He was eager and excited, and listening to him talk, so was I.

"Awesome, we can finally make *Quake*!" I exclaimed.

Hearing him say "fully 3D" was all it took. The possibilities for enhanced play and game design were obvious to me. *Any* design ideas I had were possible, because in full 3D, *anything* is possible. It gave players a full six degrees of freedom: right and left, forward and back, and, critically, up and down. We were reaching a technological tipping point, where constraints of the past were disappearing. With *DOOM* and *DOOM II*, most players believed that they were playing in a true 3D world, but it was a carefully crafted illusion. The levels were rendered in 3D, but everything else—enemies, walls, floors, stairs, you name it—happened on a 2D plane. Textures were projected onto X and Y coordinates in such a way that it created the illusion of perspective. Enemies were made smaller if they were farther away, and environment textures were stretched accordingly. With the exception of programmers and artists, many people probably didn't notice the illusion, and we

---

[*]　Gradient lighting allows for smooth blending of color from one shade to another. Instead of blue direct to black, for instance, the blue progressively gets darker.

[†]　A client-server model is a network architecture that allows clients to access a server to request and receive data. *DOOM* and *DOOM II* were peer-to-peer.

took that illusion as far as we could with elevators and elevation changes. It wasn't 3D, though. We called it 2.5D, and while it was genuinely amazing, it limited the design potential. With a 3D engine, that was no longer the case. With true 3D, we could have one area directly over another, truly vary elevation, and allow all game entities and objects to exist in 3D space. This innovation dramatically changed the potential of level design, strategy of movement, and gameplay.

As a game designer, with each iteration of Carmack's tech, I pushed the hell out of it, suggesting things I suspected the engine could do and creating the best gameplay from each iteration of the engine provided. Being a programmer myself allowed me to connect with Carmack and understand his intent in a way I suspect few others could. It also gave me a window into the possibility and potential of his engine because I understood it and respected it from a technical perspective. We were a great match and enjoyed working together. While this was a significant technical challenge, I felt confident he could do it. With Carmack, when he says he's going to do something, it's not a wish or a possibility. It's done.

When I said we could make *Quake*, though, most people in the room had no idea what I was talking about.

"*Quake*?" American asked.

"Yes, *Quake*!" I said again.

Sandy echoed American: "What's that?"

"*Quake* is a game idea we had in 1990 that we abandoned because we didn't have the tech to make it. I mean, nobody had the tech. This new engine—a fully 3D engine—could do it," I said.

Sandy was curious. "What's it about?"

"So, back four years ago or so, we wanted to make this game about a badass named Quake," I said. I filled them in on the adventures of the Silver Shadow Band, Justice, Quake's hammer, and Hellgate Cube. As *D&D* players themselves, they got it, and like I said before, who wouldn't want to play as a superpowered character like Quake?

"It was going to be an RPG, but we can make it into anything," I said. At one time, we imagined being kings of every genre.

Adrian remembered *Quake* and our 1991 hopes for the game.

"Sounds good to me!" he said. I knew that Adrian's imagination was already considering new ways to scare the hell out of players in full 3D with the better lighting possibilities offering even more options to him.

"Then it's settled! *Quake* it is!" Carmack declared.

This was usually how our big game decisions went—some quick thinking, some agreement, and our destiny was set for the next year or so. Of course, there were many more meetings to be had, but the big picture, the "where are we going" part of the journey, was decided. Carmack was just beginning his tech R&D, so it would be a while before the rest of the team could jump in, and as much as *Quake* tried to overtake my conscious thought, I decided to wait until January to dig into the possibilities for *Quake*'s design. For me, December was going to be a busy month.

For starters, I was writing the DWANGO client in preparation for shipping it on the *Heretic* disk. There was a lot of activity between me and Kee to get the DWANGO.EXE program working as intended: downloading DWANGO server phone numbers from their master list, allowing connection to any DWANGO server over the modem, authenticating the player logging in, handling a busy lobby full of players talking to one another (and sending messages from the lobby into active games, too), launching deathmatches, and handling credit cards. It was nothing short of revolutionary to have a pre-internet service where players dialed in and just started chatting and playing with other people. Players used to have to call one another on a landline and agree to connect modems to play. DWANGO was the bridge between the dark ages of modems and the shiny new internet. DWANGO supported *DOOM*, *DOOM II*, and *Heretic* at release.

Heretic was also in the closing stages, and I flew to Wisconsin near the middle of December to oversee the final state of the game and to make sure all the features were in. The excitement and energy of the Raven team was unmistakable. Examining the build, I was so impressed. Their skills expanded with their exposure to NeXTSTEP and the DOS cross-development environment.[*] Design wise, creating abstract level designs was an altogether new thing for anyone outside of id, but they had embraced the style and delivered. Beyond that? There are so many things big and small that go into shipping a game. That they did it in just one year showed how skilled and in sync the *Heretic* team was. I felt good about the time I spent pursuing this deal, directing the game, and helping to get it across the line. It was well worth it and satisfied my goal of expanding id Software's business.

While there, I had to adapt our LAN and modem connection programs for *Heretic* since they were made for *DOOM* and *DOOM II*. I also updated my DM.EXE program to support *Heretic*. Testing my code and the game, *Heretic* really felt like an id Software game. It played great. I approved the gold master[†] as final, and the team and I celebrated with dinner before I flew back to Dallas. At 11 p.m. on December 23, 1994, I uploaded the shareware version of *Heretic* as HTICV1_0. ZIP from home. Like *DOOM*, *Heretic* shipped as shareware with a registered

---

[*]   A cross-development environment allows programmers to develop the game using a computer
      different from the one the game would run on. For example, games that run on an Xbox are created
      on PCs.
[†]   A gold master is the final copy of the game created by the development studio. The gold master is
      then given to publishing partners to create production masters, which are used for duplication.

boxed version available directly from us. Heretic sold half a million copies in its first year and generated a hefty return on id's investment of $500,000. Raven did an excellent job.

At long last, it was time for a holiday. They were never intentional, these January-to-Christmas development periods, but over the previous few years it just seemed to be the way it worked. The success of our games gave us the ability to give gifts like we were Santa Claus, and I loaded everyone up with presents, especially Michael and Steven, who loved LEGO. I got Kelly and the boys a new house, too. They were still in California, but we traveled back and forth as often as we could. Meanwhile, at home, Beth was doing well and was busy getting our house ready. Her love of cooking filled the air with smells of the holidays—cookies, cakes, and dinner roasts—and visions of starting work on *Quake* in the new year danced in my head.

As 1995 began, anticipation greeted us on our return to the office. I wondered if Carmack had done anything over the holidays. He and I both had the same tendency to work over breaks. Since he'd announced his desire to create a fully 3D engine, I had not been able to shut my brain off and had been doing a lot of research. I woke up, fell asleep, and dreamt thinking about *Quake*'s design and 3D gameplay. What possibilities would the new engine offer?

Nowadays, when game programmers start assembling the technology for a new game, the first question is often, "Which engine should we use?" It's a question as important as "What game should we make?" In 1995, we didn't ask this question, because there were no "off the shelf" engines to use—we crafted our own engines for our designs from the ground up, and that took a lot of expertise and time. If we wanted an engine that was high-speed, full-3D, texture-mapped, internet-aware, server-based, and capable of making *Quake*, we had to invent it. There was no engine that could do what we wanted it to do, and these were all the things we wanted *Quake*'s tech to be.

Our first task as a team was to explore the design and tech possibilities for *Quake*. Carmack and I sat down in his office to discuss it. These two primary pillars of id Software—engine and design—were inherently linked to one another in a Möbius strip. The gameplay design dictated the needs of the engine, while the engine gave potential to the game's design. Carmack and I were always pushing on those edges from the inside. From Carmack: "What if the engine did *this*? How might that affect gameplay?" From me: "If the engine could support *this*, I could get this gameplay." It worked in the other direction, too. The engine could constrain the design or the design could slow down the engine, but avoiding those issues was an unstated goal of ours. These conversations were always engaging negotiations and never edicts.

I had spent a lot of time thinking about the design of *Quake*, beginning with its birth as a character in our *D&D* campaign to its abandoned 1991 post-*Keen* incarnation right up through to today.* What, if any, gameplay features did we want to keep? What did I want to add? There were so many things we could do in 3D, and the trick was to focus on only those things that gave us the best gameplay and game design for the engine in question. Heading into the meeting, and knowing the engine would be 3D, I envisioned bringing these features forward from our 1991 RPG attempt:

- A main character, Quake, who was an all-powerful badass.
- A medieval world reflective of our D&D adventures, which took place mostly outdoors in rich settings.
- Quake's powerful hammer, which, when thrown, returned to him.
- A small extra-dimensional entity, the Hellgate Cube, that orbited Quake and attacked enemies. It also had the potential to go off exploring.
- Integration of a silver dragon, if only aesthetically.

Additionally, I wanted to focus on these new features to take advantage of and show off what Carmack had shared about his engine plans thus far:

- An action RPG with a fantasy aesthetic, where stats and stat management were not at the forefront and potentially not included at all.
- Continuation of Design Rule #8: If a level could be made in *DOOM II*, then it's not good enough for Quake. Design needed to be as cutting edge as our engine. Looking up and looking down needed be key pillars of our level design.
- Multiplayer gameplay that emphasized single, co-op, or deathmatch play between two or more players. The client-server model allowed us to have more than four players in the game, and I wanted to explore what we could do with this.

Beyond these features, there were too many dependencies between code and design to dig in deeper. As the design director, it was necessary to have a clear understanding of Carmack's key engine features, so I was eager to have our discussion. For game design well into the 1990s, this negotiation between design and code was a quintessential chicken-or-egg problem. When the engine is already done,

---

* In 1991, the game didn't get far. We created a crude overhead 2D map of a town with solid walls for walkways and buildings you could walk into. We realized that it wasn't going to be able to represent the game we held in our minds. It was two weeks of effort, and we learned how to fail fast.

as it is with today's Unreal Engine, much of the gameplay, or at least suggested optimum gameplay, is built into the engine itself, and the team chooses the best engine for a predetermined design job. The Unreal Engine, for instance, is used for many FPS games because it was originally built as an FPS engine. When there is no engine, though, it's a question of which comes first, the design or the engine? In our case, only the core of the engine came first (a 3D engine with a client-server model) and then grew by design from there. Carmack and I had a collaborative process so that one idea played off another.

It's a challenge to get across the complexity of this situation for people who were not developing games at the time, but this might help: look at the features in latest Unreal Engine. Now, get rid of all of them except the online and 3D bits. That's where we started with no idea of where we were going. Every idea Carmack and I discussed was balanced on every other idea to consider whether they might work together. The engine was still just an idea of a 3D space. Even fundamental stuff like movement, physics, weapons, and enemies didn't exist. The features that design scoped out affected code and vice versa. In essence, we were designing the world and what you could do in that world simultaneously, accepting benefits and trade-offs. It's a collaborative partnership where we want code to be just as excited about what it's building as design is about what it can create.

Sitting in Carmack's office, we were both looking forward to exploring *Quake*'s possibilities. We were still using NeXTSTEP workstations to develop *Quake*, and we were sticking with the C language, not C++, for speed (Objective-C was used only for the tools that I wrote). On the art side, we had a new workstation added to the mix, the Silicon Graphics Indigo, which we planned to use for 3D modeling. As always, game development is fluid, and I recognized that nothing we were here to discuss was promised or written in stone. However, I hoped to come away from this meeting with an understanding of the baseline design of the engine. Knowing how Carmack planned to architect it allowed us designers to make a more advanced game.

Carmack began with, "Okay, well, I'm going to base the engine on a new networking model where game clients connect to a game server. Multiple *Quake* clients will connect to a *Quake* server for single, deathmatch, or co-op play. If you're playing single-player, you will have the server and client running on the same PC. You could also host a multiplayer game on your PC and other PCs can connect to it."

The great thing about the client-server model is that players wouldn't be limited by the network speed of other *Quake* players that were connected to the same server. With *DOOM*, everyone who was in a multiplayer game ran at the speed of the slowest player's connection because they all had to be in perfect sync with each other. With *Quake*, that limitation was gone.[*] Players were going to love it. The client-server technology was new at the time. Our only experience with game network models was *DOOM*'s peer-to-peer model. The client-server model had not been used in an action game yet; it had only been used on mainframe computers for slow, primarily text-based games.

"Even better, there's no way to cheat because the server is authoritative," he continued. "The server is what runs the game code, and the clients are merely displaying the state of the game. They can only send commands to the server."

I was curious, though. "You're going to need to write that code first then?"

The order in which he wrote the code dictated what the design team was able to do.

"Yes, I need to get the networking architecture working so it's passing information between the client and server and simulating a game. Then, I can start working on the client architecture and the renderer."

I nodded. The success of the client-server code affected everything else he planned to write. We discussed the technical details of the architecture and imagined how it might affect gameplay, particularly deathmatch gameplay. Even though we were here to discuss *Quake*, new technology excited both of us, and we enjoyed these conversations. We were also eager to talk about the 3D engine because of the opportunities it afforded for gameplay.

"I've been thinking of a scene on a hilltop where the player is looking down at some enemy he wants to take out," I said. "Another player comes up behind him and—*SLAM!*—smashes him in the back of the head with their hammer, and the first player is falling forward down the hill and their entire view is rotating on that axis as it would in real life."

I was standing, waving my hands like a conductor. "Or imagine a central hub area where you can see into these other paths. One of the paths has some crazy huge monster patrolling in it, and the others are either empty or have some minor enemies milling around. Imagine feeling like Quake, all powerful, and you could just jump right into that shit, take on the boss and experience sheer terror right away! I want players to know that the game is hard-core dangerous, and that we're not trying to hold their hand."

We could see it and feel the potential experience. Everything else that was out there wasn't even close. *DOOM, Heretic,* and *Rise of the Triad* were 2.5D. Even games in development that we knew about, like *Duke Nukem 3D*, weren't close.

---

[*] With Quake's networking architecture, each player's PC was only going to be talking to one other PC, the server. With *DOOM*, each player's PC had to talk to every other player's PC. That's a lot of data moving around and slowed the game down.

Ultima Underworld was true 3D with six degrees of freedom, but it also had six degrees of slowness, and didn't fit with the fast-paced action RPG we were leaning toward. *Myst*, which continued to top the charts along with *DOOM* and *DOOM II*, continued to baffle us. We didn't understand the lure of an empty, slow-paced world. We knew players liked the story, but we were interested in creating games that let players make their own stories about amazing battles or deathmatch victories. Seeing the potential for *Quake* was an incredible place for us to be.

Carmack shared more about the research and work he had been doing thus far. Everything Carmack said about his code translated into a potential player experience in my mind.

"I'm really happy we're going to true 3D," I said. "No more sprites."

"Well, we will be limiting the use of sprites to UI elements only, I hope. The world will be textured, and we will have twice the light levels as *DOOM*. The lighting will depend on where you place lights in the world and how bright you make them."

Calculating the light in the level was a huge step forward for level design. Instead of meticulously specifying the light level of every area in the game, we were now able to put lights wherever we liked, with a brightness level for each light. In turn, the engine knew how to cast that light into the world and created wall textures that transitioned from bright to dark smoothly. In *DOOM*, the entire wall texture was always the same light level. In *Quake*, walls could now have complex lighting patterns depending on where the lights shone. In a nutshell, it allowed artists and level designers to create far more realistic and immersive environments.

"Can you imagine a Baron of Hell coming out of that darkness?" We didn't have enemies for *Quake* yet, so I substituted one of *DOOM*'s instead. I had never been so excited about the potential of a game.

"So, okay, thinking of those enemies, what are you planning to do for the video buffer? Are we still using 8-bit or are we going 16-bit color?" I asked.

The bit depth of the video buffer—either 8-bit or 16-bit—determined the amount of colors I'd have to work with. With 16-bit color, I had 65,536 colors at my disposal. With 8-bit, it was just 256. Carmack's answer determined whether I would be designing colorful creatures or mud monsters. In addition, 16-bit color mode would allow for smooth gradient shadows.

Carmack was writing the renderer, so he had a feeling 16-bit was too much data for current video cards. "We are going with VGA to start because the data size is one byte per pixel versus two bytes per pixel," he said, "and I want to be above 30fps (frames per second) frames per second and closer to 60fps."

That made perfect sense—drawing twice as much data takes twice as long and slows down the framerate. Getting close to 60fps was critical for movement to feel good. Future 3D video cards would be able to handle 16-bit color at a high framerate, but we weren't there yet. I wasn't at all disappointed. I just needed to know what I had to work with.

"With shadows, that means we will have fewer colors to use. How many levels of brightness will the colors have?"

I needed to know the levels of brightness to determine how many distinct colors were on my palette. If each color had four levels of brightness, for instance, that meant I had 64 distinct colors to work with since each of those four would be coming out of 256 colors total (64 colors x 4 levels of gradient each). However, I knew there would need to be more levels of gradient than that to get the effect we wanted.

"Well, yes, we will have fewer colors," he said. "I plan on having sixteen levels of brightness per color, so that would be a maximum of sixteen colors in the 256-color VGA palette," he said.

"Hmm, well, if *Quake* is a medieval game, the limited color palette will probably work. Lots of mud and rock colors." I laughed, "Plus red, of course."

"Medieval would work perfectly with that palette," he agreed.

"Since we're making *Quake*, and he has his huge hammer, this game could be about hand-to-hand combat, like, imagine completely obliterating something, smashing it and hammering it to gibs*," I mused.

"And don't forget the Hellgate Cube. It has a mind of its own!" Carmack laughed.

"Yeah, maybe it needs you to pulverize enemies to feed it? If you don't feed it often enough, it could get upset and leave for a while." I was into it. "But if it's happy, it can suck the souls out of your enemies. Also, you could have a devastating area attack if you slam the hammer into the ground, like if you get surrounded. Will we be able to have camera shakes for that?"

"Definitely, that will be easy with the way I plan on setting up the gameplay code. I'm going to write a simple C-like programming language so designers and coders can add whatever they like and see it work immediately. The server will just load the files and parse them quickly," Carmack said.

This was exciting. What Carmack was doing was separating the engine from the gameplay. The division between engine and gameplay can be tricky for those not in the industry to understand, so I'll explain it this way: Imagine the engine is an actual car engine. It has the basic rules by which it functions to turn gas into power. The gameplay is what happens when the player presses on the gas or the brake, changes gears, or installs a nitrous switch to supercharge

---

* Gibs (pronounced "jibs") is short for "giblets," the bits of meat that come packaged inside whole turkeys or chickens.

the fuel intake. All of these things affect the engine, but the engine needs to be specifically programmed to respond to these inputs. So, a game designer programs "press the gas" and Carmack programs the engine to respond to that gameplay. That's the basic idea, anyway. An engine might allow for the player to walk in the game world. The gameplay is what happens when a player steps on a trigger, thus opening up a monster closet, and takes a bunch of fireballs to the back of their head.

For designers, separating the gameplay from the engine meant we could make quick gameplay changes without needing to compile the whole engine. What was minutes now took seconds. Even better, modders could just write code to make changes to the game. They would not need the Objective-C tools we used to build the game or access to *Quake*'s source. With our previous games, each build process compiled the *entire* engine. The process was a minute or two, which may not seem like much, but it adds up quickly when you are making dozens and dozens of iterations a day. It also breaks design flow.

"Such a great idea," I said. "We could really increase our development speed."

I thought for a moment to explore an example of how this might work.

"Here's a test," I said. "Since combat will be mostly up close, how about Quake throws his hammer for distance attacks? He did that in the *D&D* campaign, and it was awesome!"

"Sure, that could be done in the new language," Carmack answered. "I'll just call the language QuakeC. QuakeC can do the camera shakes, the hammer attacks, enemy AI, and anything else we need for gameplay."

To the layperson, it may seem that separating the gameplay code from the engine would allow us to develop both of them quickly and independently. However, the gameplay QuakeC code could only do what the engine allowed it to do, so with the engine unfinished, there was less functionality in QuakeC. I'm getting ahead of myself here, but as an example, when QuakeC was first made, we could not put enemies in the game because the engine code didn't handle moving AI characters around or drawing 3D models yet. Later, when the engine supported AI pathing and drawing of 3D models, QuakeC was changed to allow the drawing and moving of 3D enemy models. This is how, over time, the functionality of QuakeC increased, and we could eventually control all aspects of what the engine could do from QuakeC. In a nutshell, it meant that real gameplay code couldn't be written until the engine was done—or stable, anyway. We could write parts of it incrementally, but not get a feel for how it all worked together, which is essential to game design and gameplay.

DOOM's engine took two and a half months, and while *Quake* was certainly more complicated, we didn't think it was light years away. Waiting for an engine to be developed was a necessity at id. We were also busy with plenty of other things. In the meantime, we level designers could experiment with QuakeC, but whatever we wrote was likely going to be tossed out with any big engine update or optimization.*

Next, we needed to pick a target CPU (central processing unit) to benchmark the game's performance throughout development. Getting the game running smoothly on the target CPU would help ensure the game played well on release. With a lot of Assembly language programming, the latest 75Mhz Pentium CPUs in 1995 were fast enough to deliver the game we'd dreamed of, and they were only getting faster. At least, we felt certain it was within the range of possibility. In addition, we were now able to use two times more memory than *DOOM*, so we could spend some of that memory on speed optimizations to reach our 60fps target framerate, and some more of it on the complex 3D levels we were going to make. Having this extra memory meant not having the super-tight constraints of the past. For example, PC games before *DOOM* used only 640K of memory, which is why they were so limited in scope. Before that, in the '80s, 8-bit computers typically had a *maximum* memory size of 64K—a tenth that of PCs in 1991. We still had constraints with *Quake*, of course, such as an upper memory size of 8MB, but on the whole, the extra memory allowed us to make a bigger, better-looking game.

I knew that with a move to a 3D engine, DoomEd, my long-serving level editor, was getting its walking papers. QuakeEd, like DoomEd, would be a tool to allow designers to create levels and connect objects we placed in the levels to QuakeC code for functionality such as enemy placement, torches, doors, item pickups, teleporters, and anything else we need. I'd need to code it from scratch to account for the new engine and our switch to 3D.

"I can't write QuakeEd until you get to the client and start defining the world data," I said.

"Correct. In the meantime, I'll set up a skeleton project for it so I can add code for a 3D renderer when I have time. After I figure out the basics of world construction, I'll define the data, and you can take it from there."

Once Carmack had those bits defined, I could move forward with programming QuakeEd. Everything we had discussed from 3D to QuakeC sounded great to me. We had a preliminary idea of what we wanted, and as we began the new year, we had to create all the tools and tech necessary to make an engine capable of building a full 3D world. Even nowadays, FPSs push engines and computers to

---

* Our early experiments in QuakeC, like American's "Spike Shower" and "Guided Fireball," didn't make it into the game as updates to the engine rendered some gameplay written in QuakeC obsolete.

their limit, and creating an engine, the tools to support it, and a design to show it off is a Herculean task. We'd done it three times before, but this engine was the most complex one yet. We guessed it to be about ten times more difficult than *DOOM*'s engine. This metric allowed us to estimate the time it might take, but in the end, it was only a guess. We were charting new territory.

It was as good a time as any to sync up about business, and so I jumped into it.

"While you're working on the engine, we're going to get started on the retail version of registered *DOOM*," I said.

Releasing a retail version of *DOOM* was long overdue. We had a deal with GT Interactive to put *DOOM* on store shelves, and I wanted to add a new episode, "Thy Flesh Consumed," to create value and entice players who already had the shareware or mail-order versions.

"I'm sure it'll reach way more people by being at retail," I told him. "American and Shawn are going to pitch in along with some mappers. I'm calling it *DOOM SE* for now, Special Edition. I'll update the codebase to v1.9 for it, and we can release a patch that upgrades our *DOOM* registered customers to it for free."

Carmack nodded. I knew he was ready to get back to coding.

"Oh, one more thing. Since *Heretic* has shipped, I'm getting Raven started on the sequel. I'm calling it *Heretic 2*, but we'll come up with a cool name later."

With that, we both had our plans for the next little while, and based on our conversation, the design of *Quake* expanded to include new elements. If we had written a press release for *Quake* as we did for *DOOM*, it may have listed these additional features:

- Explore a dark and foreboding 3D medieval setting full of devilish and diabolical enemies.
- Engage in hand-to-hand and hammer-to-head combat with your foes using Quake's devastating hammer.
- Rip enemies' heads off and take them to a sacrificial altar to power yourself up.
- New damage reactions—hits to the back of the head can result in you falling face-forward and tumbling into a cavern.
- Collect an array of thrown weapons to target enemies before they get too close.
- Use your hammer for new area-of-effect attacks.
- Slay enemies to power up your Hellgate Cube, which feeds on their souls.
- Watch where you look—if enemies catch you looking in their direction, they might just come after you.

I couldn't wait to get going on QuakeEd once Carmack determined the data structures, and, eventually, to get working on the game itself. Carmack returned to his work on the foundations of *Quake*'s 3D engine, and the rest of us got busy with *DOOM SE*, and I worked with Raven Software on the beginning of *Heretic 2*. Carmack was facing a massive programming challenge—building an engine from the ground up to do something neither he, nor anyone else, had done before—and I knew there was no place he'd rather be.

CHAPTER 16

Tremors

As *Quake* entered its R&D phase in earnest, we started to hold more meetings. Some were tech sync-ups where Carmack just wanted to excitedly share some discovery he made or let me know where he was with the data structures. Others were check-ins with American, Shawn, and Sandy to discuss our levels for *DOOM SE* and checking with the additional external level designers to see how they were progressing with their levels. I also got to work on my own map, E4M6: Against Thee Wickedly, which starts in the mountains and winds down to the entrance into a green subterranean castle.

There were lots of business update meetings that Jay Wilbur held to keep us apprised of the avalanche of opportunities as a result of our games' successes— potential movie deals, book deals, strategy guides, tech licensing opportunities, collaboration with Logitech on a new controller, quarterly income, and so on. I handled some of these business initiatives either because they required a degree of tech or design expertise or because we had no additional staff to help Jay. As owners, we decided things by unanimous democratic vote, and Carmack didn't want to bring extra people on to handle things that weren't directly related to the development of *Quake*. As Chris Lombardi put it in the July 1994 issue of *Computer Gaming World*, "When I stepped into the modest offices of id Software and saw how democratically and, often, anarchistically these 10 people ran their operation, and when I heard just how successful their games and their shareware marketing approach have been, I couldn't help but think that I had stepped back into the wilder and woolier days of the computer gaming Gold Rush."

Well, it wasn't broken, so we weren't going to fix it.

It's easy to see an argument being made to push past that limitation to allow the company to grow, to take advantage of our success and the IP we created, and to remove some of the pressure on our team. However, we had operated conservatively, and everyone who was at id Software, except for Donna and Jay, worked directly on the development of the games. I had the tech, design, and business knowledge to assist, and so I did. We were moving at the speed of light trying to stay at the forefront, and at this point, we didn't *need* money or *need* to grow. Deals that were software-related like *Heretic* or *DOOM SE* had a great one-to-many return and broadened the imprint of our two pillars—design and tech—and we voted them a worthy investment of my time. Deals like branded T-shirts and books or integrating someone else's tech or hardware into our pipeline? Less so.

Inspired by my work with Raven, Carmack initiated a similar deal with Cygnus Studios, a team of game developers in Illinois, who made *Galactix* in 1992. Carmack had been emailing their programmer, Scott Host, and was impressed enough by him that he suggested we bring their team down to create a game with the *DOOM* engine. Since Raven was working out well, we voted to go ahead and do a deal with them and install them in an office on our floor. Since it was his deal, we assumed Carmack would oversee their production and manage them the way I managed Raven. Cygnus was still finishing up a game for Apogee at the time, and given our proximity to Apogee, moving to Mesquite made sense. Jay arranged for a moving service and had an empty office prepared with new desks, lamps, and all the other things needed to start work when they arrived. A week later, they saw their new space and were suitably impressed, and happy to get to work.

In early January, outside of id, and unbeknownst to us at the time, something big was happening inside Microsoft in Redmond, Washington. All hands were on deck to deal with a technical issue that had happened over the Christmas holidays. The Windows 3.1 version of *The Lion King* multimedia CD-ROM, based on the WinG programming interface (the "G" was for graphics), had launched in December 1994 and was crashing on new holiday-launched Compaq PCs. *The Lion King* was one of Disney's biggest films, and an entire marketing campaign had been built around the game and specifically Windows as an operating system that was game-friendly. Companies like SEGA and Nintendo claimed the lion's share of the video game industry business, and Microsoft wanted in on that action. So when *The Lion King* was pre-installed on Compaq PCs and crashed on every last one of them, it raised a lot of eyebrows, especially since it was supposed to herald the power of WinG over MS-DOS. The event was so bad that *PCWorld* magazine listed it at number six in its list of "The 25 Worst Tech Products of All Time," stating that "few products get accused of killing Christmas for thousands of kids, but that fate befell Disney's first CD-ROM for Windows."

It turned out that Compaq had unilaterally changed their hardware without alerting WinG. In the industry, game developers started to raise concerns about plans to embrace Windows as the future for PC games and considered going back to developing for MS-DOS instead. They didn't want their games to be accused of killing Christmas, too. After all, the MS-DOS–based *DOOM II* played great without crashing, displaying the most advanced graphics and speed seen in any PC game, and proved the PC could compete with console platforms. Jason Robar, a Microsoft game technology evangelist, showed *DOOM II* to Alex St. John, the group manager of Microsoft's Multimedia Strategy. Alex saw *DOOM II*'s performance and knew that it was accessing the PC hardware at a high rate of speed—faster than the still-in-development Windows 95 allowed programs to access the hardware. This event was a significant catalyst for a direction change.

Alex and Jason needed to get game developers on board to support the launch of Windows 95 and to prove the PC could compete with game consoles from Nintendo, Sony, and SEGA in the game market. They knew getting *DOOM II* running on Windows 95 would be the key to wooing developers back. *DOOM II* used real-time hardware access in MS-DOS to run smoothly.

Alex, Craig Eisler, and Eric Engstrom decided Microsoft needed to develop a software development kit (SDK) that allowed Windows 95 this kind of fast access for games. Alex was working with Chris Hecker on the WinG SDK, which allowed fast graphics access, but *DOOM II* used all the PC's hardware, not just the video card. WinG was too limited in its scope. The new APIs would need to solve all the problems developers faced in making games for Windows 95, like sound effects, music, multiplayer connections, and input devices like joysticks.

Alex, Craig, and Eric ditched the WinG approach and built a small "skunk-works" team* to develop an SDK that allowed "direct" real-time hardware access for several components. The result of this project would go on to change the PC game industry forever, and *DOOM II* was the impetus for starting it. This project would eventually be known as DirectX, a permanent extension to Windows that enables all Windows programmers to make games as hardware intensive as *DOOM II*.

By mid-January, Carmack's work on the new engine had advanced to the point where he could render a test level, but the definition of "level" was still embryonic and displayed nothing more than a box. Still, it was an impressive box, a 3D box, and this representation allowed him to create *Quake*'s data structures and to experiment with how this 3D space might be stored in the computer's memory.

---

* A small team working on a project that may not be officially sanctioned.

Since there was no editor yet, American took time out from *DOOM SE* and was assigned to work with Carmack, as needed, to input the levels manually in text files. It was tedious, but these early test levels were necessary for Carmack to explore the engine's architecture. This got Carmack to the point where he could create the rudimentary framework for QuakeEd that integrated the basic building block of level creation, a textured 3D rectangle that Carmack named a brush. Once he got the brush in, he handed QuakeEd over to me.

I started designing and programming UI elements to improve the user experience of QuakeEd. Even if it wasn't a product we were going to release to the public, we believed that the quality and usability of the tools affected the quality of the output. If someone is struggling with a miserable tool, particularly when learning to design in 3D, they are not going to be inclined to create a masterpiece. We always worked directly with the tools and in the game. At id Software, we didn't use design documents on any of our twenty-four games, with the exception of *DOOM*, whose design document we didn't actually use. The game was the living document, and this worked well for us. Remembering details of a game's design wasn't an issue for me.

QuakeEd was critical for the level designers to start exploring 3D level design, and especially so for American to create more R&D levels for Carmack as he continued to develop the engine's architecture. Normally, I would be the one working hand-in-hand with Carmack on these prototype level designs, but American was assigned the job while I handled the programming of QuakeEd, the direction of *The Ultimate DOOM* (the new name for *DOOM SE*), *Heretic 2*, and the post-launch press and marketing antics of *Heretic* and *DOOM II*.

"We are the wind" may have been id Software's unofficial motto, but it felt like it described my day-to-day activity as well, as I ping-ponged from one project to the next to keep them all moving along, sometimes working on one game in the morning, another in the afternoon, and still another at night. It's impossible to describe how fast everything was happening. And on top of that, not a day passed when we weren't in the news, receiving dozens of calls from the media and potential partners, or inadvertently greeting fans in the parking lot, the lobby, at the grocery store—everywhere.

After getting QuakeEd up to date with the latest work from Carmack, I jumped in on *The Ultimate DOOM* with the goal of finishing episode four, "Thy Flesh Consumed," at the end of March. American, Shawn, and I were creating two levels each. Kevin threw together a new orange sky texture, a new world map screen (shown before starting to play a level), and a new credits screen. As the fourth episode in the series, it was designed to be tougher than the first three episodes. I finished up E4M6: Against Thee Wickedly, which I had been working on whenever I had time. It felt good and challenging to play from a pistol start, and it was a big level, too. For my second level in the episode, I decided to make E4M2. I wanted it to be tough as well but smaller in size, in keeping with where it fit in the episode. It came after American's E4M1, which was a perfectly small first level for the episode. Carried along by the intense current, perhaps, I wanted to see just how fast I could create something with a high level of production quality.

So, on a Friday night, I got ready. I didn't know how long it was going to take me, but what mattered most was that it was professional quality, fun, and difficult. My home NeXTSTEP workstation was all set, as was my PC. At the time, I was really into the just-released Mad Season album *Above*, so I had that looping. The level began as all levels do, with me leaning back in my chair, thinking, and trying to see the space in my mind.

The first thing I needed to do was visualize the player's path through the entire level. Usually, I don't know more than the first few rooms, but since this level was going to be small, and I was trying to go fast, I decided that I should be able to see most of the playable space from the player's starting position. With that decision made, I determined that the level's exit would also be visible from the starting point. In addition to the predominantly visible play area, I decided I'd have two side areas that were critical to the flow through the level, as well as some blocking pillars that the player needed keys to raise up. I'd place those keys in the side areas. At this point, I imagined the feel and play of this space, thinking my way through the movement of the level, and it felt good, at least to start. I grabbed my mouse and quickly created the bounds of the level, like roughing out a sketch, and made it playable so I could jump in, get a feel for it, and start creating. I decided the player would be on a raised platform inside a lava cavern, with enemies and items hidden in the lava below. I made the end area much higher up, with a sort of stairway they had to jump over to continue climbing toward the exit, except that a pillar blocked their progress. I locked the pillar until the player found the key to raise it and reveal the way forward up the stairway.

One of the most important decisions I made was how I wanted the level to start. With an open playable space, many of the level's enemies will be able to see the player at the beginning. I decided to place two shotgun sergeants in front of the player but facing away from them. Distant enemies would see the player and throw fireballs, and the player could move sideways and let those fireballs hit the shotgun guys and start some in-fighting right at the start. It worked beautifully and rewarded players who used this strategy.

My planned route through the level would have the player unlock the section on the left side, go through it, then teleport back to the start area to unlock the entrance to the right side, go through that, teleport back again, then the unlock the pillar blocking the path to the exit. After reaching the top, I made the decision to greet the player with a Cyberdemon!

Getting this level made on a condensed schedule came down to imagining the path through the level and then creating the level geometry as quickly as possible. When the geometry was there, I could start placing enemies and items, then tweak them until it felt good for a player using Ultra Violence difficulty (the second hardest difficulty setting) with a pistol start. I always balance my levels for that difficulty first, then scale it back for the easier difficulty levels and increase it for Nightmare.

I even added three secrets to the level so it felt complete. A third of my time making the level was playing it so I could get a good feel for it, then I tweaked balance constantly until the entire level felt good. I checked for texture alignment and any other possible technical glitches, and was done at 6 a.m. E4M2 was finished, shippable, and made in six hours. That's a speedmapping record for any officially published level in any *DOOM* game.

As the levels were finished, I did playthroughs to make sure that they felt balanced against one another and represented progressively more challenging play. When all were finished, we gave them their launch names. Sometimes, these names happened during development, but this was not the case with "Thy Flesh Consumed," probably because so much was going on at the time. Instead, Kevin compiled a list of Bible quotes, and we selected the names we liked. E4M2 became Perfect Hatred, named after Psalm 139:22, "I hate them all with perfect hatred; I count them as my enemies." *The Ultimate DOOM* was finished at the end of March, and GT Interactive got it on retail shelves by April. I did all the programming, updated the engine to v1.9 and handled project management to gold master.

By now, royalties were starting to come in from *DOOM II*, our first *DOOM* game sold at retail. Not everyone had access to a modem, so having a box on the shelves was a huge bonus. We knew from GT that *DOOM II* was selling "really well," but until we opened our first royalty check, it was hard to quantify what that meant. The day we got the check, Kevin, Adrian and I drove to the bank where we had our company account. I put the check in the drive-thru vacuum tube, and the teller's face looked puzzled when she saw the number of zeros on the check. Who were these three guys in their twenties, pulling up in a bright yellow '77 Chevy Blazer and depositing a check for $3 million? She vacuum-delivered the receipt to me, and we all laughed as we drove off. I don't know that moments like this ever felt normal. Most of us grew up without a lot, so even seeing a check like that was gratifying and rewarding but also incredibly weird. You don't know quite what to do with it, because you're used to being cautious and conservative. In my case, I had even been homeless as a kid and bankrupt as an adult. We did what we usually did—we kept it in the bank.

Meanwhile, the team at Raven was making good progress on the sequel to *Heretic*. The original was selling well, and we knew we would sell even more copies when we went into retail with GT Interactive, too. We had no doubts that the investment would pay off. I had a couple major design goals for *Heretic*'s sequel, the first of which was to increase the players' choice of character types from one to three: a spiritual cleric, a burly fighter, and a spellcasting mage. This pushed the game a little further in the RPG direction. Each persona had its own abilities and ultimate weapon to assemble throughout the game. My other goal was to devise a hub-level system. I imagined a central level that connected to multiple levels to have adventures and solve puzzles. Finishing the challenges in a level allowed the player to come back to the hub and discover new gates opening and new areas to explore.

The programmers for *Heretic 2*, Ben Gokey and Chris Rhinehart, were so good at using the *DOOM/Heretic* engine that they extended its design capabilities, figuring out a way for the doors to rotate open, like they do in real life, as opposed to *DOOM*'s doors, which went straight up. It was some tricky work, and they surprised me. They really understood the engine and made it do things we hadn't designed it to do. I hoped that they would be able to deliver the game before the end of the year.

In March 1995, Carmack and I held another meeting to advance *Quake*. Things were still tech heavy, as you might expect. At this stage in *DOOM*'s development cycle, its engine was finished, but *Quake* was proving a good deal more challenging than that. The discussion revolved around a problem: Carmack needed to find a way to light the world, and then, for all the textures touched by those lights, he needed to find a way to draw those textures quickly with the right lighting on them. Remember, depending on where the lights were, thanks to gradient lighting, a single texture could grow lighter or darker depending on how the lighting hit it, kind of like how light in the corner of a room casts light on the walls. Technically speaking, he needed to devise a fast method to display textures so that each polygon—the shapes that are part of every brush, character, weapon, and detail on the screen—looked perfect at every angle. This is called perspective-correct texture mapping and would require programming the floating-point unit for these calculations. Mastering perfect polygons was only half the challenge. The other half was ensuring the dots that fill a computer screen did so at a rate of 60fps so that the game would move smoothly. Nowadays, a 3D accelerator card would handle this. However, in 1995, no consumer-level GPUs (graphics processing units) existed. We were drawing every single pixel on the screen manually with our own calculations to determine what should be drawn at each pixel location based on what the player was looking at. Our screen was 320x200 or 64,000 pixels. At 60fps, we needed to draw 64,000 pixels sixty times per second for a total of 3.84 million pixels per second without any assistance from graphics hardware. We also needed to have enough CPU speed left over to compute which polygons to display, process player input, move the player(s) in the world, handle all moving objects including enemy AI, play sound and music, and move the network data in and out of the computer. It was a tremendous undertaking.

We discussed what it would take to program perspective-correct textures in Assembly language. Writing code in assembly allowed us to use the CPU at optimal efficiency beyond what a C compiler could do.* Then we would optimize the resulting code for speed. It's highly complex programming. With 3D accelerator cards, it's possible to take 3D animation and graphics for granted, but we shouldn't. It is a breathtakingly complicated feat to define and render a realistic-looking object on a flat screen, and that achievement becomes more complex when equally realistic characters can move around that object, impact and interact with the thing itself—moving it even—with each movement casting shadows, changing the quality of the light and the surrounding textures. And to do all that with no visible latency on the screen—even when you introduce multiplayer characters that arrive over a network with their own data-delivery issues? It's remarkable when you think about it. At id Software, we were used to taking on such tech and design challenges as well as the risks that came with them. We had to if we were going to stay ahead of the industry.

During one of our meetings, Carmack mentioned bringing in Michael Abrash, who he'd been exchanging emails with for a few months, to work with him on the engine. I was all for that. Abrash was the author of the book that helped Carmack achieve his side-scrolling breakthrough and wrote programming columns in *Dr. Dobb's Journal* for years. Given the complexity of 3D, it made perfect sense to get another Jedi-level coder to join the team, and up to this point, Carmack was working on the engine alone. So Carmack flew to Redmond, Washington, where Abrash was working at Microsoft. He had dinner with Abrash to convince him that joining the team to create *Quake* would be taking the first steps toward the metaverse as described in Neal Stephenson's 1992 award-winning cyberpunk novel *Snow Crash. Quake*, Carmack argued, would have a representation of independently controlled characters walking around in a 3D space, and it could be interpreted as one of the steps necessary to reach a metaverse or virtual world. Abrash was intrigued and said he was on board. He negotiated with Jay and came into id as a minority owner a couple of months later.

American continued to work with Carmack as his R&D level designer. There still weren't any actual levels to design or real gameplay to be had, but as Carmack was working out the engine tech, he needed someone to put together

---

* A C compiler doesn't know how to optimally interleave the CPU code with the FPU, floating-point unit, code to make those calculations as fast as they could be with the way our data was organized.

test locations. For the most part, it was building one box after another, but each of these boxes advanced or tested the engine he was trying to build. Things were progressing. Carmack succeeded in getting a 2D sprite—a golden ball—in the world to represent the player, and it was incredible: Our first look at something moving in our own 3D world.

American purchased a house next to Carmack, and Carmack, who was by now possessed by the problem in front of him and working constantly, took to visiting American at all hours to bounce things off him, all of which would have been well over American's head as a non-programmer, but American was a good listener and provided a sounding board, at least. Adrian and I used to joke that there was a tunnel between their houses.

Based on our past experience, I think we all expected that we'd be able to dig into building rudimentary *Quake* gameplay in a month or two. With *Wolfenstein 3-D* and *DOOM*, Carmack had gotten us working engines within weeks, but this time, the months passed. This engine was a massive technology jump. Not only were we raising the bar for 3D, we also wanted to connect players to one another through the internet. The internet is always on, so people could have *Quake* servers running constantly and connect to them to play any time they liked. We imagined players forming teams and playing deathmatch against other teams, like soccer. We were on the verge of seeing something new happen to games because of the internet, and *Quake* would be one of the first internet-aware games available.

To ensure we would have a proper focus on the highly important network code, we found a great network programmer that worked at Novell, a company specializing in file server software that handled many users at once over a local network. His name was John Cash. Before Cash joined, Carmack needed to program the engine to use the network data stream, a term used to describe how the network and the engine sent information back and forth. To set it up, Carmack wrote code that looked like the network drivers were working and delivering data, but it was simulated and just the engine talking to itself. John Cash's job would be to replace it with actual networking code. Cash would handle the network "plumbing"—all the programming that connects the game engine to the network device drivers and delivers data packets to and from *Quake*. Cash planned on joining in April, around the same time as Abrash. Bringing in these two expert-level programmers would, we hoped, take the pressure off Carmack and deliver the engine sooner.

Due to the significant technical challenge of creating a 3D engine, these hurdles meant the rest of us had to wait before we could start working in earnest on *Quake*. At this point, we had two full-time programmers on the game (Dave Taylor was working on audio) and Abrash and Cash planned for April, but none of them were assigned to gameplay. We understood that the engine had to come first.

Still, there was no shortage of work to do. We had grown a business that had gone nuclear as a result of releasing the most important games in recent memory, and that had benefits, for sure, but it also had trade-offs. When *DOOM II* launched, we set a lot of different things in motion to take advantage of our tech and to satisfy the overwhelming demand of our fans. GT Interactive sold through all we gave them, and fans never tired of it—they only wanted more. It seemed there was a new money-making idea around every corner. *Heretic 2* was in production and *The Ultimate DOOM* was close to launch. I was busy producing and directing both and programming QuakeEd and *The Ultimate DOOM*'s installation program. Kevin jumped in to create the packaging art for *The Ultimate DOOM* and worked with GT Interactive's marketing group on a campaign that would appeal to players. Jay, meanwhile, was the ringleader of 1,000 beasts, and there was simply no way he could do it all. If anyone wanted to contact id for a business venture, Jay was the first stop. The emails and phone calls never stopped. It was near overwhelming, but we were used to working hard by this point.

While Carmack's skill set was growing, the rest of us were also rapidly learning, going from the Middle Ages into the Early Modern Era of art and game design. Since the start of id Software, every element of our games was 2D. Even in *DOOM II* the enemies were *still* 2D. Breaking the 3D barrier was complex, and much of 1995 was dedicated to R&D. There was so much to learn from new software tools to new dimensions (literally) of player interaction, none of which we had done before.

Kevin was learning new technology to create the 3D models we would eventually get into the engine. He cut out the model-making middleman we used for *DOOM*, Gregor Punchatz, by creating models digitally on our new Silicon Graphics Indigo workstation and using its 3D modeling program, Alias Wavefront. Many people go to college for four years to grasp what Kevin was about to teach himself. His goal? To design 3D models in Wavefront, then use Deluxe Paint II to create the textures to cover his models. Putting textures on the 3D models was the new frontier. Because they would be attached to 3D objects, the textures needed to fit the models like a shirt fits a human.* This process is known as "skinning."

With a 3D character, you can rotate it and see all possible angles smoothly. The character animations in 3D were so much easier to create because it wasn't a matter of redrawing an entire character to make it look like it's running—we just changed the values of where the legs were at a certain time, and the game smoothly moved the leg from point A to point B, and the character looked like it was running. It was so much more fluid than our previous process of drawing a

---

* To make that look realistic, they needed their own new set of coordinates called u,v (as opposed to x,y) so the texture drawn in a graphic file can be adjusted to be in the correct location on the model's polygons.

set of individual sprites to account for movement. The work on these didn't stop with Kevin, though. Dave Taylor was writing a tool that would take Kevin's model and create a new graphic file that Kevin could then draw the model's texture on. Carmack's model-drawing code would use that graphic file to put the texture on every surface of the 3D model. Kevin's first character model had only two hundred polygons. It seemed like a low number at the time, but the texture drawn on the model had enough detail that it made the model look really good—we were surprised he didn't need more polygons to hit the detail level we wanted.

Adrian was busy designing textures for our first levels that would fit the medieval setting and its architecture, but he also had another important task: defining *Quake*'s color palette. From an entire array of colors, Adrian had to choose just sixteen colors. From these, each would have sixteen distinct gradients, because each color would go from fully dark to fully lit. It was a non-trivial undertaking that required a lot of trial and error.

As Carmack progressed on the engine, I updated QuakeEd so that everyone could both see and test their progress in-engine. I worked on the UI of the editor to enable us level designers to browse through all the textures Adrian was creating textures like stone, dirt, and grass for the ground, as well as ceiling textures, decorative wall textures, rock, wood, etc. I then needed to be able to put those textures on brush surfaces so that when someone placed a brush, it looked like rock and not like a gray rectangle. To create a mood and test the lighting, I added the ability to put objects in the levels, such as a torch that would light up an area. With QuakeEd getting more use, I improved the UI to simplify the process of compiling maps for use in the game. Our first R&D levels were made with these rudimentary rectangular brushes, which we could move around, resize, and put textures on. At the time, however, we couldn't create diagonals or perform other adjustments on them, so the earliest R&D maps were exceedingly rectangular, but we'd achieved full 3D. I continued to expand the editor over the next several months.

Sandy and American started using a rudimentary QuakeEd and Adrian's early textures to get acquainted with creating levels in 3D via a level editor. It was a huge creative conceptual jump and greatly increased the complexity and time to author. Making a simple room in *DOOM* could take about fifteen seconds if you were fluent with the editor. With *Quake*'s new method of using brushes to create spaces and lights to brighten up an area, it took several minutes to replicate the same room. Multiply that effort over the course of developing an entire level, and you can see how time-intensive each of *Quake*'s levels was. During this R&D phase, the complexity was even higher, because they were learning not only the tool but how to design in 3D.

We were feeling good about our progress, even if it was a lot of learning. It felt like the usual beginning of our games: lots of foundational work happening, tools being created, new technology being investigated, and everyone operating with a shared vision of the game we were trying to make. We knew we had to get the foundation right so the gameplay code, the meat of the game, could take advantage of this new tech. My intent in reiterating that "this was new" and "this was challenging" is not simply to contextualize that we were on the cutting edge but to emphasize that the edge we were cutting, so to speak, was revealing its complexity to us as we moved forward. The challenge was new, again and again, for code, art, and design. However, challenging as it was, we were having a great time. Learning new things and making new things—being ahead of everyone else—was exactly where we wanted to be, and we had enough financial security to allow it, particularly with our spin-off products bringing in revenue. Days in the office were shaped by conversations of discovery:

"This is so fucking cool."

"Come look at this."

"Holy shit, no one is going to believe this when they see it."

"I don't care that it's a sprite. It's a sprite moving in a 3D world."

Every night, we left excited. Every morning, we came in fired up and ready to do more.

A *DOOM II* strategy guide was in the works by Ed Dille. To help sell more copies, we thought including an interview with me about *Quake* might spark people's interest. We touched on our development process, which was:

JR: Totally loose. We don't ever have a design spec for a game. We all get together and say, "So what kind of game do we want to make?" We already have the technology and vision for the next game, so we know what the technology is going to be that will blow away the game we just did. Then we need to think of a setting and decide what kind of graphics we'll use. We try to get the graphics to go with the technology: What would be the best type of graphics and setting to go with this kind of technology so everything is as good as it can get? Then we think, "We have this kind of theme," so the artists start drawing what they think would look good. Then they start creating some monsters and we start creating some levels. And, of course, I have to start writing the utilities: the utility to create the world and that stuff. So we create some things and we get better with using that technology. We rework our tech from the ground up every time ...

By now, we were far enough along in our R&D phase that I felt comfortable telling people that it was going to "take a long time to do." We weren't beholden to what was written down in some design doc or milestone report, particularly if that might turn out to be the wrong thing to do or even impossible. There would be a lot of trial, error, doing, and re-doing. It was a familiar road of experimentation ahead:

> JR: . . . we'll have learned so much about the technology and the way the engine works. So we'll do a lot of development for the game, then probably throw it out about halfway through. That's how we learn and make cool games. We don't ever have a design spec where in Month Three we have to have the first three levels done, like milestones, and by the time the product's done a year later the first levels you did really suck, but you have to keep them because they're in the milestone. We never do that. We will not release a game unless it's cool. The first level of Doom was redone two weeks before it was released because the old one sucked. That's the way we design stuff. We don't stick to a design spec; there isn't any. It's just what is cool.

And then we talked about design. In the first third of 1995, the design was taking tentative shape, subject to tech development, as was our design process. In particular, I wanted to highlight Carmack's engine and explain that the world would be true 3D. I wanted the game world to be as amazing to explore as it was to fight enemies in, something later achieved by great games such as *World of Warcraft* and *Elden Ring*. I wanted to substitute a canned soundtrack for ambient sounds. I talked about how we would have a dark, creepy forest area, evocative of our early *D&D* campaigns, and introduced fans to a new mechanic we had discussed, a view trigger:

> Say you're walking into a forest . . . it's dark, and to the right you see this dark cave, or something. As soon as you look at that cave, something is going to happen. You'll hear some kind of low, evil kind of sound, and something will trigger, even just from your looking at this area.

Regarding combat in *Quake*, I discussed the differences between *DOOM II* and *Quake*, noting that I hoped for much more tactical and up-close combat between the player and fewer enemies, featuring, of course, Quake's hammer. With those enemies, I expected players would have to "work on it" to dispatch their foes. In a sign of my zeal for the game, I added:

> In the games you've played before, you're still kind of distanced from the death. You're pointing the shotgun at something, you're pulling the trigger, and it shoots and the thing is dead . . . In *Quake*, you'll have to

really kill things. You won't just press the trigger and hit it, you'll have
to really beat the living shit out of the thing until it's dead."

This early look at *Quake's* initial design got players excited about what we
were envisioning: You played as a badass named Quake, you had a hammer that
could be thrown to attack enemies that would come back, you could slam it into
the ground for a damaging effect to enemies around you, and you had a mysterious artifact named a Hellgate Cube that was happy when you fed it by destroying
enemies, and it would get upset if you spent too long not fighting. As payment, it
would suck the soul out of certain enemies. Clearly, for those who have played
Quake, the game vision changed rather dramatically, but up to this point, we were
aligned on this experience.

Of course, the engine was still in heavy R&D, so everything had an asterisk
after it: *subject to performance. Abrash and Cash had yet to join the team, and we
were eager for that to happen to get Carmack the much-needed support. We knew
it would be an incredible team, and once we knew what the engine was capable of,
these concepts would be tried, tested, and improved, and, if necessary, thrown out.

In the meantime, we level designers also entered our own period of hard-
core R&D, focusing on creating levels in our favorite styles. Just as Kevin had to
learn 3D modeling and all that went with it, we had to learn how to build in 3D. Up
to now, however, we were still making experimental 3D spaces. My expectation
was that we designers would get good at creating playable spaces to develop our
own styles so when tech was stable with the engine and ready to start work on the
actual gameplay, we would be fluent in true 3D level design and understand how
to create an amazing player experience.* The tying together of these styles would
likely be done in a central hub area, similar to *Heretic 2*. It wasn't clear yet because
the tech wasn't defined enough. For now, I wanted all the level designers, including myself, to start developing a style and understanding the possibility space.

As a level designer, the new 3D space offered so much creative opportunity.
I remember talking with Ben Gokey at Raven about *Heretic*: Ben figured out
that he could "look up and down" by vertically expanding the view. It wasn't
a true up and down view, but it did the job. With *Quake*, we could genuinely
look up and down, and it was amazing. We didn't have vertical mouse control
yet (it was a hard problem to solve), just keys to move your view slowly up and

---

*   Some game developers might wonder why we couldn't start making those levels right away. The level
     designs need to suit the core mechanics of the game: form follows function. So, a level design for
     an RPG in which the character possesses a huge hammer, is followed by a floating and wandering
     Hellgate cube, and performs area-of-effect attacks is going to be architecturally different than an
     FPS. At this point, we were not sure what we could do, and the engine didn't allow for 3D models
     beyond the basic rectangular brush.

down, but it was great to see this whole new dimension in more than just my imagination. Moving forward while looking straight down was a new sensation, as well as staring at the ceiling while moving forward. I imagined using this view to prompt the player to look down at grating with lava underneath all the while preparing to have an enemy fire on them from above. I knew we'd solve the looking-around interface problem at some point. It was important that we at least had a key to center your view back to normal, so Carmack added that. I set the look up and look down keys to PgUp and PgDn because I used the arrow keys for movement.

Our games remained red-hot, but we decided to keep our basic salary structure in place because it was always helpful to have a firm grip on predictable company expenses for long-term planning. We knew we had enough in the bank to last a few years, even if our sales suddenly dried up. As for our excess earnings, the founding partners were generous with ourselves and with the rest of the staff. Periodically, five people—Carmack, Adrian, Jay, Kevin, and I—decided what bonuses everyone in the company would get. Lots of money was flooding in monthly, so we cut some hefty checks, and we were flush enough that quarterly bonuses for the staff could be as high as $50,000 each.

In addition to sharing with people in the company, I got my father a house in Challis, Idaho. He had a great opportunity to join his best friend Pat managing a mining operation, work my father had done for a good part of his life. Pat was nearly an uncle to me, having always been a part of my father's life, and thus mine. Challis was a favorite camping spot of theirs.

Beth and I were still living in a small rented house in Plano. We began thinking about buying a home, since other people at id were doing the same, and we started looking around in the surrounding neighborhoods. When Beth and I got together, she knew everything she needed to know about me, and in a sense, I knew everything I needed to know about her. She knew that I loved games and programming, that it was my job but also my hobby and my passion, and now that I was in a start-up gone nuclear, she understood that it took considerable time to support our games and our business. The time we spent together was spent with my boys, Michael and Steven. Otherwise, our interests were quite divergent. She had no interest in games, and so was always doing her own thing. The search for a house united us, though, and we talked often of where we might like to live and what things we wanted in a house and in a neighborhood.

Eventually, Beth tired of the house search, and I moved forward on my own. In March, I learned of a new development north of Plano in Frisco called Stonebriar with an empty lot overlooking two golf fairways that I thought would be a perfect location to build a house. I found an architect and worked with him to design the house, my first experience at real-world level design. It would be a while before we could move in, though.

By April, Kevin had created some basic 3D models, and Carmack got them rendered on the screen. Seeing yourself running around as a 3D model instead of a gold ball sprite was a major leap forward for the tech team. Adrian had been working away on creating different texture sets, and each level designer had settled into using a specific set of textures for their levels. There was a set that looked like the interior of a building, with checkerboard floors and brick walls with stained-glass windows—Sandy decided he liked these textures. I liked the blue textures and black-crackle textures, and figured I could make some decent castles with them. American was using a brand-new Aztec-looking set of textures that Adrian just finished.

Even though QuakeEd was custom-built for *Quake* levels, it wasn't as full-featured and easy to use as a commercial product like Alias Wavefront, the software Kevin was using to build models. QuakeEd was evolving tech built on evolving tech, and it was slow to build levels because of the complexity involved in crafting and lighting all sides of a room as compared to *DOOM*'s method, which involved only drawing four lines and setting the simple information for the room. We got used to building levels in this slow way, and we figured out small ways to speed it up. But in the end, an entire level took quite a bit of time to build. Most of the time spent was getting the geometry and lighting done, but then it was a quick process to place the enemies and items.

In spite of the slow speed, building my medieval castle R&D levels with Adrian's new textures was inspiring and rewarding. They looked good and felt good to walk around, and I knew that more was to come since we were still in the early tech stages. With *Quake*'s levels, the ideas came readily, but building geometry took time, and innovative geometry took forever. For example, in the first level, E1M1, the first door the player sees is diagonally split in the middle and looks like future-tech. To build that one door, I had to create three pieces of geometry on the left side and two pieces on the right due to the complexity of their shapes having to be angled. Then, I had to create an object that consisted of those two groups of shapes and move them away from each other to look like the door is opening. This was the most complex door in *Quake*, and while it's certainly cool, we decided to make the rest of them easier: a rectangular texture that goes up, or a couple of rectangles that move apart.

Our *D&D* campaign was based in the medieval era, and we wanted to re-create Quake's world, game design–wise. Castles were part of the architecture that went along with outdoor rocks, rivers, and mountains. At this point, the engine was not yet supporting a character with a hammer because other engine features were top priority, so I waited until Carmack was done and could focus on the gameplay with me as we had in the past. Close-up, hand-to-hand combat required a different approach, level-design wise, and regardless of what kind of level one was building, testing out the play of it is essential, not just building the architecture.

Michael Abrash arrived in April 1995 to join the team, and he immediately mind-melded with Carmack in order to begin writing a high-performance renderer so we could reach a good framerate. Abrash's arrival was uplifting for everyone. He had to understand everything about the work Carmack had done so he could design an efficient solution to render polygons as fast as possible. Later in the month, Carmack changed the format of some of the graphics data over a weekend, and it caused Abrash to rewrite a large part of his code because it was heavily dependent on that data and its organization. Carmack was always looking for ways to improve his code, and sometimes those optimizations necessitated changes. A weekend of Carmack sometimes meant a rewrite of Abrash.

Abrash recognized that the process of writing *Quake*'s renderer was a once-in-a-lifetime opportunity and asked if it would be okay if he wrote about it—columns at first, and a compilation book of those columns. We agreed it would be a great thing to do. As programmers, we loved having easy access to information that would help us solve problems, and we liked to share our knowledge with others. Abrash had been doing that for years with his articles in *Dr. Dobb's Journal*, and his desire to write a book about how the *Quake* engine was made totally fit with our ethos.

As our level design R&D continued, the game's silent audioscape was replaced by whatever music we were listening to. For me, it was the latest Dokken album, *One Night Live*, or Alice in Chains's *Jar of Flies*. When it comes to designing levels, I feel it's important to tailor your environment to the level's atmosphere: I play music that evokes the feelings I hope players will feel. With *DOOM*, I played a lot of Queensrÿche and '80s metal. With *Quake*, I also had a set of atmospheric ambient tracks playing that helped me create the vibe I was going for.

American listened to a lot of Nine Inch Nails at the time and had *The Downward Spiral* playing on repeat, which gave him an idea. He went into Carmack's room to talk about it, then they both came out into the main room where I was talking to Adrian.

"What do you guys think about Nine Inch Nails doing the music for *Quake*?" American asked.

I wondered how their music would fit in our game, since I wanted ambient tracks to play in the background. Nine Inch Nails had an industrial metal edge and dark aesthetic that Carmack and American liked, and Trent Reznor's aggressive vocals reflected the '90s angst that some Gen Xers felt, but I didn't think *Quake* needed that kind of soundtrack. I felt like it needed something more atmospheric, with no vocals. But I figured if we could get Nine Inch Nails to make tracks in that vein, their sound would work well for *Quake*.

"They're great, but would they be able to make ambient tracks? We don't want music that takes your attention from the action, or lyrics playing either," I said.

"I'm sure they can make something like that, something disturbing," American answered, understanding the tone I was going for.

Together, we went to Jay's office to ask him if he could get in touch with Nine Inch Nails's management. The next day, to our surprise, it was done. Our agent at ICM Partners* was also the agent for Nine Inch Nails. The agent told Jay the band members were huge fans of our games and would love to connect and see what we could do. Trent Reznor and drummer Chris Vrenna planned on visiting a month later.

We couldn't believe it. They played *our* games? They were huge fans of *ours*? It seemed inconceivable. Because we were still insulated and the world was not yet in an immediate news cycle or hooked into social media, we didn't really have an understanding of the reach of our games beyond gamers. It didn't occur to us that the bands we listened to were playing *DOOM* on their tour buses.

After the mutual agreement to work together on *Quake*'s music, American was made the point person who would handle the deliveries of the music. He knew what I was looking for, and it was a job he relished. American went online and told fans on IRC (Internet Relay Chat) that Nine Inch Nails was making the soundtrack, and they erupted, as expected. *DOOM*'s music had always had a metal edge and inspiration to it, and this collaboration with Nine Inch Nails was a dream come true for many a fan.

It's worth noting here that we remained quite open as a company, sharing tech, design, and marketing plans, which was largely unheard of at the time and exceedingly rare today. Carmack or Abrash sharing tech information, me talking about *Quake*'s design, American sharing information about our audio plans—we felt that the open exchange of information was valuable. We were not concerned that others would take our ideas and run with them. No one could catch us anyway.

As the summer began and R&D continued. Carmack felt like experimenting with the way the player would look around in true 3D. It was something that was bugging him on a low level: He had taken great pains writing a true 3D engine, but he wondered, *Would players be able to really see it?* How would they control looking around? With *DOOM*, we were generous with the automatic aiming up and down to shoot enemies since you couldn't actually look up and down manually.

---

*   In early 1994, Hollywood decided that video games were going to be big, and they wanted a piece of the pie. Talent agencies cold-called several studios looking to see if they could represent them, their intellectual properties, and anything else of value. ICM Partners contacted Jay and we worked with them to secure *DOOM* movie options and get *DOOM* books written and published.

Controlling *DOOM* was easy, however, because the player only needed to move the mouse horizontally to look around, and they moved their character with the keyboard. We wanted to keep this ease of control for *Quake*, so I suggested an experiment: Try automatically looking up and down while you traveled up and down stairs. From a technical perspective, it worked well, but it also controlled where you were allowed to look—it wasn't free-form. It felt limited. So we tried another method. He bound the look up and look down functions to the mouse wheel, but it felt strange to turn by moving the mouse left and right while using the mouse wheel to look up and down. It wasn't smooth, and it wasn't consistent, either, since every mouse had different wheel mechanics: Some clicked into specific increments while some moved freely.

Great game feel is something players don't generally notice. It just feels right. The controls easily work their way into muscle memory or take advantage of existing affordances and give the player what they want without them having to really think about it. Bad game feel, or even just slightly off game feel, is something players notice instantly. Carmack and I both knew getting this down was important, but the core engine took priority, so we decided to revisit it later. We worked together to refine the feel of literally everything in all our games. I make design suggestions. He codes. I see how it feels. This cycle continues again and again until it's perfect.

Some team members were active on IRC and were talking about the game's design as it evolved.* Among the possible gameplay features: Injured players could leave blood trails behind them as they retreated, severed heads of enemies might fly off after you kill them, spells will be fireballs and lightning and magic missiles, and we might have AI where one creature would be a leader and other creatures would be followers. We were enthusiastic and hopeful that the engine could

---

* Contrary to what has been written elsewhere, the team clearly understood what we were trying to build and were talking about it frequently online. What we wrote was later compiled and published in 1996 in *QuakeTalk* (https://www.gamers.org/games/quake/quaketalk.txt). I believe this disconnect is due to two factors: (1) our "game as living design document" process, which we had used successfully for every one of our twenty-four games to date, and (2) among later additions to the team who were not programmers it was, perhaps, not clearly understood that some design decisions had to wait until the tech was established before those mechanics could be put into the game and iterated upon, the standard process when the game is the living doc. I did not want to dictate a design that depended on something that was still being developed, nor did I feel it was a good use of design's time to create a design that might all be for naught. The tech team was doing a great job, and going as fast as they could. It was the tech equivalent of creating Mount Everest: Design was making a plan to climb Everest, and then would climb it, but we needed the mountain, currently being created by tech to do that. For those not in game development, there are still teams as devoted to "game as living design document" as there are to "write a detailed design document." The bigger the team, the latter typically becomes a necessity, but in 1995, we were still small, and given our long history of the former, we did not deem docs necessary at the time. If you've made it this far in a footnote, you unlocked Achievement: Read the Longest Footnote.

support our plans. There was one comment by Dave Taylor that was contrary, where he stated that he thought the idea of the player using a hammer was "rather lame" and that he was trying to quietly destroy it. It was all good: We encouraged the team to express their thoughts openly.

By July, Carmack and Abrash had evolved the engine to the point where we did have a couple of 3D character models in the game based on our medieval design—a bat and a human—and soon Kevin got us a dragon. The programming team had just gotten the animation code for 3D models in, and had the test human character animated. The enemies would have their turn eventually. The enemy AI was gameplay code, and that would have to wait until the engine was finished, just like Quake and his hammer.

Even with the engine's progress, we knew Carmack was feeling the pressure. His brain was exceedingly taxed. He worked constantly, took no vacations, slept only when necessary, and had become occasionally irritated with those not directly working on the engine team. Just how irritated he felt became evident when we arrived one morning, opened our email, and discovered, of all things, this:

REPORT CARD

The report card listed each team member along with their assigned grade on *Quake*. I got a C.

"What in the hell is this?" I thought.

Let me provide some critical perspective here. Much has been written about our working relationship and our eventual breakup. It's written as if we were fifty-year-old Stanford MBAs who knew everything about business and not overworked, constantly crunching kids in our twenties with the whole world staring at us as we tried to do the best we could while creating a tech and a design that the world had never before seen. It's written in polarizing terms, "animosity" being a favorite, with one of us pitted against the other because that just makes for a better story. The truth is that Carmack and I were friends, and we cared about each other, and we still do. We talked, we laughed, and like all friends, sometimes we quarreled and took shots at each other. We made great decisions, good decisions, and downright terrible partnership-ending decisions. As you read through all that happened, keep these things in mind. As Carmack stated in a 2022 episode of Lex Fridman's podcast, this chapter of our lives certainly could have gone a different way if we'd been more mature and more experienced and not the twentysomethings we actually were, and I fully agree.

But in August 1995, looking at the report card, I was not concerned with my grade—I had done a ton of stuff that the *Quake* grade wasn't even taking into account—but I was concerned about him and why he had sent this to everyone on the team. Grades ranged from As to Ds. Carmack gave himself an A-. Since everyone could see one another's grades, I suspected some felt upset or humiliated. It put the focus rather glaringly on the individual rather than the team. I was especially worried about people in the company who didn't have an ownership stake. To them, this report card could seem like a prelude to a firing. The development process was already long and challenging. I didn't see how this helped. What about people who were waiting for the engine to be stabilized to do their work? Was it fair to penalize them when the proverbial text they needed to study for the test wasn't even done yet?

I walked over to Adrian and Kevin and asked if they had seen the morning missive. They nodded. We didn't bother discussing the individual grades.

"He's under a lot of pressure," I said.

That was obvious to all of us, and rather than give him hell about it, we decided to say nothing. For his part, Carmack also never brought it up.

Not talking about it wasn't the best decision. He sent that report card out because he needed something. That something wasn't our heads-down silence. What he wanted, I suspect, was for me to dump everything else I was working on—all of it, all the side projects that were bringing in income—and dive 100 percent into *Quake*. At the time, that would have meant jumping in on the engine to push it closer to gameplay. While the need was certainly there, the reality of our situation didn't exactly allow it. It would have meant breaking contracts we had signed and taken advances for. We had to deliver on those contracts. To offload all my stuff, like QuakeEd, *Heretic 2* and, prior to its release, *The Ultimate DOOM,* we needed to hire more people, but Carmack was strongly against this and had already shot the idea down before. It wasn't pretty, but it was the situation we were in.

We assumed that the report card was a onetime eruption from a person under incredible pressure and went on about our business.[*]

We needed something to lighten the mood and lift people up, and I had just the idea. We had always maintained a close relationship with our growing community, and based on the number of requests for screenshots, we decided to take some and release them to the internet. In August, I took sixteen screenshots of various levels we were working on, including five screenshots that showed a section of E1M5 from *DOOM* and the corresponding setting rebuilt in *Quake*. The difference was huge and served a threefold purpose—first, it got our fans excited about what we were making, and second, it showed that *Quake* was a phenomenal technological leap forward and helped to explain why *Quake* was

---

[*] How might I handle this today? I can't imagine Carmack sending a report card any more than I can image me not walking into his office and saying, "What's going on? Let's talk about this and figure something out." We had been through tough times before, and he and I had always pulled together and gotten it done. It makes me sad to think how he felt sending that and not getting a response.

taking longer than our previous releases. The screenshots were beautiful, and the lightmaps were in, making *Quake*'s shadows look incredible. I posed the dragon in the sky in one of the sixteen screens. There was no gameplay code yet, so the screenshots did not show off combat or other gameplay, and the dragon was only a model that wasn't even rigged to animate, but they were a massive hit with gamers, and they wondered how far along we were. The programming team estimated that the engine was about 75 percent complete. The third purpose was not for our fans, but for us. Releasing the screenshots let the team, who were by now feeling a bit worn down by the stress of the project and the recent report card, feel some excitement. Everyone loved the fan response. As they had when we announced our partnership with Nine Inch Nails, people went nuts. It was a deep breath of fresh air.

In August, after Kevin felt like he knew the rules for creating 3D models that Carmack could display, he was able to start working on some real action-RPG-style *Quake* models. I asked Kevin to create an ogre with an offbeat twist: It could launch grenades for a distance attack, chainsaw you if you got too close and laugh at your corpse. Despite leaving the taunting on the cutting room floor, the Ogre is perfect example of the dark humor we put into all our games. I was inspired by how awesome the spherical characters in 1994's amazingly violent 3D puzzle adventure game *Ecstatica* were—their sadistic personalities were all about punishing the player, beating you like a punching bag, dragging you around by your feet, hanging you upside down, and laughing at your dead body. I loved games that had an attitude, and I wanted *Quake* to have one as well. At this point, there was no gameplay to support any of the Ogre's intended attacks, but once the engine was completed and the programing team moved on to gameplay, the Ogre would be first in line.

In September, Sandy and Jay attended a European game conference to show off *Quake*. Journalists were able to experience the strange and novel "mouse wheel look up and down" feature, something no other first-person perspective 3D game had. Sandy did an interview with the legendary Finnish game magazine *Pelit*,[*] and he eagerly relayed some of the key details of our design that, even at this later stage, was still an action RPG. With his background is in pencil-and-paper RPG games, Sandy's enthusiasm was palpable. He shared details of *Quake*'s close-combat design, the hammer, the wide-area attack and its use for projectiles, and the magazine ate it up. He revealed that we would have spells, and monsters might go off and heal themselves, provided they could escape you. He also shared something particularly gruesome, but which we had not talked about much: the ability to take an enemy's head and sacrifice it at an altar for a power-up effect.

---

[*] *Pelit* started in 1987 and is the longest-lived computer game magazine in history.

Reporters loved it. Sandy's excellent interview gave readers insight into the kind of game we wanted to make.

By now, the engine had been in development for ten months, one month shy of *DOOM*'s entire development cycle, and gameplay programming had still not begun. We did not have a game. What we had was a technology still in development. Quake still had no hammer, and the things we had discussed with players and the press were not yet happening. This wasn't due to any fault of the programming team—quite the contrary. What they did and were doing was monumental and transformational. It was Carmack's most difficult challenge. He was doing what he had to do—making something incredibly awesome—and as a programmer myself, I knew it was going to take the time that it took. As the engine evolved, I steadily updated QuakeEd to account for its new features and to improve the experience for us level designers.

For a team that was dependent on iteration for its design process and progress, however, this was a problem. The engine may have been a technological marvel, but it was devoid of our intended gameplay. The process we had used for the last twenty-four games began not with a design doc but with defining our key feature set, developing an engine toward that, and programming the core of gameplay. We had barely started the latter. The code for gameplay would allow us to explore and refine the game's core loop—in this case combat and Quake's hammer—and experiment until we had something that felt good and worked, just as we had with the mouse looking up and down. It was the same process that led to us getting rid of dragging dead bodies in *Wolfenstein 3-D* and focusing on speed or jettisoning the opening of *DOOM* from the *DOOM* bible. We started adding more elements and tweaked them until they fit. Even if we had decided to write reams of design documents, they would have been of little use until we knew what the engine could support.

The game was the living design document, but we didn't have gameplay code. Some members of the team were growing restless.

CHAPTER 17

Quake

Heading into the last quarter of 1995, the slower-than-expected progress was wearing on the team members with the least amount of work to do: Dave, American, and Sandy. Making R&D levels with little gameplay or endlessly tweaking the sound engine was not inspiring. Worse, when their work had to be redone because of a necessary core engine change, their days could be actively draining. None of them had been through a full end-to-end engine development cycle with us before and didn't really know what to expect. They were frustrated with tech for not having a finished engine. They were frustrated that we couldn't finalize definitive gameplay. They were frustrated that their levels were still just R&D. At best, they were bored. It's easy to say "It's done when it's done" or "It takes the time it takes," except when it actually takes that time. Nevertheless, everyone wanted to push development of *something* forward in some way, particularly those who had received lower grades on the report card.

Sandy kept working away on R&D levels, developing his 3D level design style, but his normally cheerful demeanor was replaced by a sullen acceptance. American continued working on R&D levels, too. He tinkered around with QuakeC to make experimental weapons, but he needed our programming team to create the engine-side code for the weapons to work. Eventually, American turned to a part of the game that excited him: the music. He spent chunks of time in New Orleans watching Trent Reznor's music development and hanging out with Nine Inch Nails. While there, he even got Trent to make some sound effects for the player character just in case we needed them.

Dave's main job was to get a sound engine working, and it didn't take all of 1995 to do that. So, he decided to follow in our footsteps and try game studio ownership himself. He asked Carmack and me if it would be okay to start a studio in Austin, hire some coders he knew, and remotely run the team. As entrepreneurs ourselves, we knew it was an incredible opportunity and decided it would be fine, provided his work on *Quake* remained consistent and that he remained onsite in Mesquite. Dave ran with it and started Crack dot Com.*

The *Quake* team wasn't the only team drifting apart.

By now, Cygnus Studios was well established in our studio and working on *Strife* with our *DOOM* tech. Scott Host, the owner of Cygnus Studios, was in awe of Carmack and wanted to model himself after him. He admired Carmack's nonstop work ethic and thought that *Strife* could be shipped quicker if his team worked like Carmack. So, as we neared the last quarter of 1995, he extended his team's working hours well beyond the normal stopping time to get them focused on finishing the game faster. He even wrote a program to track their working hours and used it to evaluate their performance. That approach backfired spectacularly. The three guys on Scott's team were friends of his from Illinois, and none of them had made a game before. As new game developers, they were learning, and their speed reflected that. Scott got angry with them, and they returned that anger in spades. They came to our section of the office to talk to me.

"We're quitting."

"What? Why?"

They described the new schedule and the weaponized time-tracking tool, and it was obvious they weren't fans of it. More than once, they noted that they were sick of their game's name, *Strife*, describing their working conditions, too.

"We don't want to work with a dictator," they added.

I had a quick chat with Jay about the situation. I had expected Carmack to monitor the team as I had done with Raven, but work on *Quake* had kept him fully hands off. Even if he was aware of Scott's edict, he may not have seen it as a negative. After all, coding around the clock was normal for Carmack. We had spent almost $250,000 on *Strife* development, and we didn't want it to evaporate because of this. As far as I was concerned, Scott was the cause of the problem, and the best way to solve the problem was to cancel the game with Cygnus and move the game to the new start-up the three Cygnus employees planned to create and own. Carmack, Kevin, Jay, Adrian, and I met to discuss the situation, and they agreed with me. Kevin suggested we also add Sandy to their team as a quasi-producer to provide oversight. The discussions were difficult but straightforward. We told Scott the contract was canceled because of their internal issues, and Scott took his things and

---

*   He directed his team to make a platform-based shooter with impressive lighting called *Abuse*.

moved back to Illinois. The remaining developers gathered and prepared to move forward under a new name, Mutiny Software. The name seemed a little obvious and mean, so I suggested they change it. They decided on Rogue Entertainment instead. With a team of new developers, there were a thousand ways this could have gone wrong (which is true of any game), but this way seemed less likely to go wrong than the death march they were on. So, we worked to set them up for success. They just needed a coder to take over where Scott left off.

It just so happened that I knew a programmer who would probably be interested: James Monroe, the little brother of my high school girlfriend, Jennifer. Every time I went to Jennifer's house and got on her family's Apple IIe, James was watching. I'd show him what I was doing and try to explain it, but I think the most significant influence I had on him was showing him it was possible to make games on the computer he had at home. James was hooked and started to learn how to code. He finished high school in England, moved back to Texas with his family, graduated from Texas Tech University, and got a job at Origin Systems in Austin, the same company where I got my first game job seven years earlier. I called James and offered him the job, along with 25 percent of Rogue Entertainment. He took it immediately. James moved up to Dallas and got to work. Sandy, happy to be busy, was installed within the Rogue team to help manage things as they continued to develop *Strife*. This way, if other issues cropped up, we knew we had someone on the inside to spot them before they reached mutiny status again.

As we wound into late September, we knew that the engine was getting close to completion, and with that, gameplay code and realizing the design would begin in earnest soon. I still believed we needed to have a central hub area for players to practice playing in a 3D space. They were going to have to learn to navigate in 3D just as we had months before. Then, they could venture into one of the paths that took them into an episode. Since it was going to be the first thing players experienced, and representative of the whole of *Quake*'s gameplay and various level design styles, the hub needed be the last thing built in the game when we, the game's designers, had achieved a level of mastery with the tools and the possibilities of *Quake*'s design. I didn't want to create this central hub until we had reached that mastery level, until the engine was complete, until Quake's hammer and other core gameplay had been added, until we really knew what the engine could do, or else it risked both not being as good as it could be and not being representative (build your first level last). In our R&D levels to date, we had been establishing the scale of buildings and structures and experimenting with strategic ways to surprise, scare, and reward players. The development of our individual styles came down to defining the shapes of our world building blocks. This included stairs, doors, paths, walls, ceilings, and structural shapes of buildings but also things that rose from that architecture like traps, secret areas, and potential play progression. For instance, American liked to use thick blocks of iron and pools of lava, and I liked to build structures submerged in water with unexpected traps. We also considered organic shapes like rocks, rivers, trees, and mountains. All of these things were, of course, influenced by the textures that Adrian created. Each set of textures reflected a different possible use, and we ended up using them for different dimensions.

Adrian had just wrapped up an Aztec-inspired design featuring a full assortment of Aztec-style textures. He had put significant research into its development, and we were excited to see it come alive. From a design perspective, we believed that the starting point for the Aztec levels might be reminiscent of block-shaped pyramids, halls, and pit traps, and dive into some of the wilder ideas one might find in 1978's *Dungeons & Dragons* module *Tomb of Horrors*. The levels for this section were assigned to American.

After making levels in the Aztec style for about a month, American walked into my office.

"I'm just not feeling it with the Aztec stuff, John," he said.

"What?" I had no idea what that meant.

"It just doesn't get me excited. I'm not inspired to make anything interesting with those textures and that theme."

I couldn't understand it. The Aztec theme was quite literally my past. Growing up in Tucson, Arizona, in a Yaqui family, Aztec symbolism was everywhere, from our museums to our fabrics to the sun stones depicting the Aztec calendar (one of which still hangs in my mother's house). That said, if he didn't feel it, he didn't feel it.

"Okay," I said. This was new terrain. No designer had ever complained about a lack of inspiration from Adrian and Kevin's work, which had helped create the visual identity of id games.

"What I want to do is just have some really dark metal, like iron or black steel. Like a dimension that is completely made of heavy metal."

"Okay. I'll let the art team know. They are not going to be happy about it."

Later that day, I went to tell Adrian and Kevin.

"Are you serious?" Adrian asked. "He can't get excited about our textures, so he can't make anything? Really?"

"That's what he says. Let's just give him what he needs. It's creative and artistic. It's a challenge for you guys. I can totally see this fitting into the game, and American will do a better job."

As they always did, Adrian and Kevin delivered the goods: some dark, foreboding heavy metal textures. American used them to make magic. Being inspired transformed him. The Vaults of Zin, completed once the engine was done, is the second level in Episode 3 and displays a fully formed idea of what his style is all about. He used a distinctive set of heavy metal textures, and he constructed a set of puzzles strung together, one room or hallway at a time. The starting area lets the player explore a little before he releases an army of zombies behind secret doors. There is an exit from the zombies, but it's a tricky fall down toward a lava pool, and the player has to be cautious controlling their way down. Each new area reveals a new set of problems, and on the whole, the level shows a strong design aesthetic and a sense of humor. From the first playthrough, I knew American was happy with and inspired by the iron textures because it was apparent in the heavy-duty architecture he built with them. In the end, the Aztec texture set was never used.

Since we had multiple projects in the works and *Heretic 2* releasing soon, the pressure on our internal crew was building. It was obvious that Kevin, Jay, and I were stretched to the limit. To alleviate some of the pressure, we felt our self-publishing efforts could be the focus of just one person—a new person. Once again, we convened for a democratic decision. Carmack gave in and agreed to a new hire, and Adrian thought he knew the right person: Mike Wilson. Mike was a high school friend of Adrian's from Shreveport, Louisiana. Adrian had purchased a DWANGO franchise about six months earlier, and Mike ran it for him. Mike's office was on the floor below id, so moving upstairs would be easy. Adrian felt that Mike could help us in the marketing department for our upcoming games *Heretic 2* and *Quake* as well as other opportunities we were kicking around. Mike was hired in September 1995.

Mike saw that CDs full of *DOOM*, *Heretic*, and *DOOM II* levels scraped off the internet were selling like hotcakes. Mod packs like *D!ZONE*, *H!ZONE*, and *D!ZONE 2* cost nothing to develop and were sold at retail for pure profit. People were happy to buy a CD with thousands of levels on it because that meant they didn't have to spend their time downloading all those levels on their slow modems. By adding custom id-approved levels, Mike knew we could stand out from the crowd and viewed this as a major selling point. It sounded like a great idea, so I identified some of the best *DOOM* mappers, gave them direction, and paid them a flat rate for their levels. We ended up with twenty kickass, custom levels for *Master Levels for DOOM II*. Along with those levels, we scraped 1,830 levels from the internet—a mix of levels for *DOOM* (191 levels), *DOOM II* (1629 levels), and *Heretic* (10 levels)—and included them on the CD as well. I wrote an installation program for it, got the disks mastered, and we were good to go for a new product. We grouped the public mods under a *Maximum DOOM* banner.

Mike's next order of business was to find a great name for *Heretic 2*. It didn't take him long. Mike had a natural knack for marketing and selected the German name for "witch": *Hexen*. Ominously evil and starting with the same letter as *Heretic*, I thought it was a perfect continuation. I told Raven, the company creating *Heretic 2*, and they thought so, too.

Mike's biggest efforts, however, were reserved for an upcoming event dubbed Judgment Day, planned for October 30: a collaboration with Microsoft, which would see not only the release of *Hexen*, but the release of the *DOOM* port for the Windows 95 operating system and the release of DirectX, too. Mike wanted to send *Hexen* out into the world with a bang and came up with the idea of inviting the world's top *DOOM* players to a twenty-player tournament. It was likely to be nail-biting. On stage, these players would compete in the finals of Deathmatch 95.[*] While the event would generate a lot of attention for our games, for Microsoft, the stakes were even higher. They invited dozens of game developers to the event and were using it as an opportunity to highlight Windows 95 as a gaming and game development platform not just to us, but to other game developers, game players, and the press. The more I heard about the event, the more surreal it seemed. *Did I just overhear him talking about a Ferris wheel?*

By now, it was October 1995, and Carmack wanted to find a way to speed up our map processing times, since it was taking at least ten minutes to calculate the binary space partition and the lighting for each map, and this affected our development time. Carmack thought about buying a Cray supercomputer to solve the problem. Cray supercomputers were effectively the Ferrari of computers, many times more powerful than what anyone was using at home, and were typically reserved for government, research, or institutional use. They were even more powerful than mainframe computers. Carmack knew that the Cray could process maps at least three times faster than our Pentiums, if not faster.

Jay called Cray and asked them about doing a deal.

"If we put Cray-looking computers everywhere in *Quake*," Jay suggested, "would you give us a break on the price of a supercomputer?"

The Cray salespeople thought about it. By now, even if we hadn't fully grasped the extent of our reach, the people at Cray had. They agreed to sell us a Superserver 6400 (at a discount) for $500,000. We agreed and promised to show them all the places where we placed the computers so they could sign off on them. We agreed in principle and planned to sign off in several months, at which point we hoped to get the computer.

By now, we were receiving quarterly reports from GT Interactive on sales of *The Ultimate DOOM*. Three of the four episodes had already been released in *DOOM*'s registered mail-order version, but it was selling exceptionally well regardless. We decided that we would include four episodes in *Quake*'s registered release, too—one more than our previous games—to add incentive to buy the full version.

---

[*] The qualifying events for Deathmatch 95 were largely held on DWANGO servers from September 18 and October 20, 1995.

Overall, I was really feeling great about how the company was growing, from our *Softdisk* escape to developing our own line of original IP games like *Wolfenstein 3-D* and *DOOM* to the spin-offs like *Heretic, The Ultimate DOOM* and *Hexen*. The add-on level packs were growing both a community and a business, something that was important to me and the longevity of the games. It was one area where Carmack and I really differed, I knew. I wanted to grow the company and take full advantage of what we created, which, among other things, would insulate us against a bad game or a late launch as well as prime an audience for future launches. Carmack liked us as we were: small, with one main game in development. All this focus on revenue and releases might seem contrary to our goals as hard-core game players and game creators. It wasn't, though. While we clearly made games for love, money was necessary to keep the development train moving on *Quake*. Diversifying that income stream was (and is) critical to the long-term success of any company. While he didn't share my goals about expanding our business, all these projects were keeping our coffers flush. At id, we never had to make difficult decisions like laying people off or struggling to make payroll. The "it's done when it's done" development mantra requires a continuous money train to power it.

At long last, Judgment Day had arrived. While it had been hyped up, it was far more elaborate than any gaming promotion I'd ever heard about: There was a haunted house, a massive tent for food and drinks, and yes, even the rumored Ferris wheel. Thirty-five different developers had kitted out their own areas, and talk-show celebrity Jay Leno emceed the event. Even Bill Gates himself appeared, holding a shotgun in a *DOOM*-themed video to kick everything off. It was so far beyond anything that had happened before. Alex St. John's team at Microsoft launched DirectX, the platform for game development on Windows 95, as well as ports of *DOOM* and *DOOM II* and, of course, the MS-DOS version of *Hexen.* Expert-level players were flown in and deathmatched on a giant screen, turning our game into a spectator sport. The final match pitted Thresh, aka Dennis Fong, against Merlock, aka Ted Peterson, with Thresh emerging victorious and winning the ultimate prize: the right to battle me in *Hexen* over DWANGO.

As it turns out, I missed the live event. I was back at the id office in Mesquite, busy fine-tuning *Hexen* for its release on Halloween. I knew the game inside and out when I connected online with Thresh, which didn't exactly make for a fair fight.

Judgment Day wound up being a hit for id Software, and as the first event of its type, it was a prelude to how much of a cultural force games would become in

---

* Earlier in the year, Alex contacted us and offered to port *DOOM* and *DOOM II* to Windows 95 for free, and we would retain all publishing rights. Obviously we said yes.

the future. The event promoted our game, front and center, which would inevitably help our bottom line. At this point, I was happy with the new marketing for *DOOM* via Microsoft, because it kept revenue flowing. The timing was great, too, because the team at Raven had surprised me again, finishing the retail version of *Hexen* months before its targeted Christmas release date. They took my design direction and brought it to life, designing a fun game with lots of levels and an overall higher difficulty than our previous games. Like *DOOM II*, *Hexen* was a boxed retail release and entered stores in November.

The team fielded lots of questions about *Quake* and when it might be ready. We stuck by our old mantra of "it's done when it's done." Internally, the team felt certain that they were close to completing the engine, which meant that work on core gameplay would immediately follow. In a few weeks, I hoped, we would begin doing what Carmack and I always did when the tech was ready: work together to iterate the core of gameplay, in this case, Quake's hammer. The core was always a collaboration with me focusing on the design and him focusing on the implementation. We'd dial it in until it played great and was as performant as we needed it to be. Once that happened, I figured we'd need under a year to flesh out the gameplay code, iterate upon it, get the levels built, and get *Quake* out the door.

From the outside, everything at id Software seemed incredible. Inside, however, it was a different story. Just ten days before, on October 20, Carmack and I had our own judgment day. Tensions were flaring, and the frustration had reached a tipping point.

Carmack, Adrian, Kevin, Jay, and I were gathered in the conference room for our standard shareholder meeting. As Jay wrapped up the regular business, Carmack said he had something he wanted to talk about. I could tell from the sound of his voice that it wasn't going to be good.

"Romero is not doing enough work on *Quake*," he started. "You are spending too much time on other projects. So I want to issue a formal warning. And your bonus will be less to reflect it."

I couldn't believe what I was hearing.

"I'm working *constantly*," I said. "We have a ton of other stuff going on. *Hexen* is just about to launch." In addition to *Hexen*, *The Ultimate DOOM* released in March, *Master Levels for DOOM II* was in the works, and deals for two other products were pending. GT Interactive paid us advances on our new games before they even shipped. Our business was doing great, and these external projects were a ton of work.

I looked at Carmack. "I work *all the time!*"

Adrian and Kevin agreed. They knew how much I was working. Kevin had worked with me on every single project during *Quake*'s development.

Carmack doubled down. "You're not focused enough on *Quake*."

"The engine's not done! What do you want me to do? I have designed as many levels as Sandy and American, and I wrote the editor. I've done everything I *can* do on *Quake* until the engine's done."

At the time, I felt like he was blaming me because building the engine was harder than he'd thought it was going to be. I was irritated, too. He wasn't able to solve it quickly with his computer brain, it was blocking a whole team, and somehow, it was my fault. I didn't know what Carmack was expecting. I tried to parse it live in my head. Did he really think that it made sense to just sit there and endlessly tinker with R&D levels? As a level designer, those levels had to play upon the core of the gameplay. If Quake was going to have a hammer, those levels would be different than if Quake was just going to use one of the rudimentary weapons we made to test out multiplayer. My level design work was entirely predicated on the core of the game. It's like saying I wasn't doing enough work on a painting, but not actually giving me the brushes I needed or a prepared canvas to do it. I felt like he somehow forgot how we had worked on every single game we'd made together to date. The game required gameplay code, and we had yet to write that. I wasn't pressing him to finish the engine. I supported him. (And hold these thoughts in your head, because I'll come back to them in the next chapter.) The engine was complex, and it was going to take the time it took. In my mind, I was making the best use of that time by earning money for the company. My focus wasn't 100 percent on *Quake*, though, and that, it seemed, was all that mattered to Carmack.[*]

"When the engine's ready, you said we'll start work on Quake's hammer. In the meantime, I'm not going to sit there and do nothing. I am insulating the company. Can you imagine if we went two whole years without releasing a game? id Software? It would be horrible. That's forever."

Two years was forever in 1996 game development time, and it was forever++ in id Software time. We risked losing our leading edge and ownership of the genre we had created, crafted, and were about to redefine. We also risked losing the whole company without buffering our bottom line. Sure, we were bringing in a lot of cash *now*, but I'd seen multiple companies, including those I worked for, go out of business because they had failed to diversify with multiple income streams. To me, getting games like *Hexen* and *The Ultimate DOOM* out there was critical.

---

[*] In 2022, in an interview with Lex Fridman for his podcast, Carmack reflects on our division noting how I wanted to grow the company to have multiple products and that he wanted to focus only on *Quake*. He sees it differently now and recognizes the value of diversifying. Likewise, as this book makes clear, I see it differently, too. There were other ways this whole thing could have gone. We were young. To echo Carmack, there is no animosity in our relationship.

"*Quake* is our most important project, and I expect you to be working on it," Carmack said.

We were at an impasse. Carmack didn't value me growing the business. Instead, he viewed it as a lack of focus, and I didn't understand that. I was *extremely* focused on what I thought was best for the company during the engine's R&D phase. Likewise, he didn't understand why I couldn't just throw everything else out the window and start turning *Quake* into a game, but it simply wasn't possible without the programmers moving over to gameplay code. (Neither of us saw other options.) I thought back to the report card he had issued just a few weeks before. Not discussing that wasn't the right decision. This was clearly the next level. He didn't get the result he wanted from that, so he was escalating things.

"The design team also feels like there isn't enough direction," he added.

"The design team knows the direction of the game. Sandy just did a big interview on it. They don't have enough to do, and they're frustrated."*

A formal warning was at stake. On paper, it didn't mean much, but in practice, it showed just how fractured we'd become.

"I don't agree with the formal warning," Kevin said. "He's doing a lot of work."

Adrian felt the same way. The two refused to go along with it.

Carmack was angry. He realized that the formal warning wasn't going to pass, but he wasn't prepared to give up on the punitive bonus.

"Because of your lack of focus on *Quake*, you're going to get a lower bonus than normal."

"I don't think that's fair. I'm working hard."

Adrian and Kevin said nothing. They feared that if they did, Carmack might quit. He didn't say this, but he didn't need to. He had threatened to quit over business issues before, like if we ever decided to patent things, but fortunately that never came to pass. It was a standoff, and we knew it. It was him or me. He didn't get his formal warning, but I didn't get a full bonus. It was a relatively small concession to keeping peace on the team, and that was most important to me.

We didn't discuss the amount.

"Okay, then." I shrugged. "I guess that's what will happen, then."

There wasn't much more fight to be had.

---

* Years later, while reading another account of this meeting, I learned that Sandy went to Carmack shortly after receiving the report card to express his concerns about the lack of design documentation to which he had grown accustomed at a previous employer, MicroProse. Even though we had never used design docs at id (including *DOOM*'s, which we didn't use), Sandy was newly out of his comfort zone and probably anxious. Having something written down provided a feeling of security and a perceived sense of direction, even if that direction might not be practical or even possible. He expressed his concerns to Carmack, who listened, of course, but we didn't change direction to a "design doc" studio. I was never notified.

Before I go further, I want to address something. It has been reported that Carmack presented me with a list of my working hours at the beginning of this meeting, apparently from a program he wrote to track my work on my computer. While this meeting was difficult, that absolutely never happened. Rather, it was Scott Host who did this with the Cygnus Studios team. As I mentioned, Host felt he could make more progress if his team worked like Carmack did. He built a tool to track their time. I am not sure from whom the author got that story, but whoever told him conflated two stories. Carmack never programmed anything on my computer, a fact I've confirmed with him, nor did he give me a list of my hours. He didn't stoop to micromanagerial QuakeEd brush-tracking, as that would have only tracked a portion of the multiple projects we had going on. Further, he most certainly didn't accuse me of doing nothing. He knew the work that I did brought significant income to the company. Rather, he accused me of not being fully focused on *Quake*. That was true, by design and by necessity. From his perspective, this was a failing. From my perspective it was not only necessary given the engine development, it was necessary for the long-term stability and success of the company.

I have thought through this meeting a million times since. What an incredible, colossal failure this meeting was. There were so many other ways for this whole situation to go, and somehow—probably because of our inexperience—we just couldn't see the forest for the trees. Things that are so clear to me now just weren't then, and having talked to Carmack about this, most recently in November 2022, he feels the same way. Earlier, I said that I supported Carmack, and I definitely did. At the same time, though, I didn't. We didn't. Not in the right way. Real support would have been all of us saying, "This isn't working," listing the things that weren't working for everyone, and changing those things in a way that worked. Sure, Carmack was the critical path, but there were other things we could have done, other options we could have explored, and I wish we had done any one of those things. I'll discuss those in the next chapter.

More than anything, Carmack was under pressure and unhappy, and as cofounders, that's something we should have addressed. Our misaligned goals (me focusing on expanding our business with multiple projects and people, and him focusing only on *Quake* development and staying small) led to a lot of this tension, and work that wasn't on *Quake* was viewed in the same vein as vacation, particularly when, from his viewpoint, there was such a massive discrepancy between the hours he was putting in on *Quake* and everyone else. That doesn't mean we weren't plenty busy on other things, because most of us were, on business things that Carmack would, over time, come to appreciate. But right now, the engine was the bottleneck, and a lot of work was blocked until that engine was done.

But the failure, the total failure of this meeting, was that we came together and said, "It's not working!" And then, after tempers flared, we left the room, and everything was still not working exactly as it had not been working before. We remained committed to a development path that left some overworked and some without enough work to do, and we remained divided on our business priorities. Nothing changed, and *Quake* still had eight months to go.

CHAPTER 18

Aftershocks

Quake wasn't going to be shipping in the first quarter of 1996, so I needed to focus on generating sales for that quarter and the next. By this time, I knew the extent to which Carmack and I felt differently about sustaining our bottom line and growing the business. I hadn't realized *how* far apart we were until the recent meeting, of course, but that didn't change the fact that we'd have nothing new coming out and no new income coming in if I didn't get something rolling, and besides, the engine still wasn't ready.

Hexen was a hit with players, and Raven had been fantastic partners. Having worked with them on two games so far, I figured I could be relatively "hands off" on any new projects to appease Carmack. So, I got Raven to head down two separate tracks at the same time: First, I wanted them to create two additional episodes for *Heretic*. We would bundle those two episodes with the original three in a new big box, *Heretic: Shadow of the Serpent Riders*. At the same time, I got Raven started on the sequel to *Hexen*. I had some ideas about how to mirror *Dungeons & Dragons* more closely—adding another character class, going deep on how the characters increased their abilities—and I designed a more advanced level hub system. I decided to name the game *Hecatomb* (*Heretic* and *Hexen* started with an H, and I wanted to continue the pattern). Raven began on the games in early November 1995. Eventually, I figured we would also need a level pack for *Hexen*. On the spot, Sandy even came up with a great name for it: *Deathkings of the Dark Citadel*. His years in pencil-and-paper games paid off.

I truly believed that the huge success of *Heretic* and *Hexen* was because they were far and away the best, highest-speed, real-time representation of the feeling people experienced when they played *Dungeons & Dragons*. At the time, these games were as close as anyone had gotten to fast-action fantasy gaming. Sure, it was arcade-like in its design, but it had magic and swords and medieval monsters galore. Casting "freeze" on your enemies and shooting them into frozen bits had never looked or felt so good. These games delivered gameplay in a way *Ultima Underworld* couldn't.

Feeling good with those games heading down the pike, in early November, I discovered a post in a *DOOM* editing mailing list where people were talking about the imminent release of a thirty-two-level, full-replacement data file—a WAD, short for "Where's All the Data"—for *DOOM II* titled *TNT: Evilution*. It caught my eye. It had been created by a team of experienced modders, all with good reputations in the community, who were also known to have had good quality control, giving each other critical feedback to improve the playability of their levels. I felt like this could be a possible id game, especially since I knew that we needed more early 1996 releases. I immediately contacted the ringleader, a person named Ty Halderman. I told him I would love to publish *TNT: Evilution* in a box on store shelves, but he doubted he could stop the release—it was rolling like a freight train at that point. They had been working on the project for so long, and they were all excited to see it released on the internet for free. I convinced him that it would be far more helpful to his team if they were published by id Software and paid for their work. Also, they would be reaching a bigger audience. The people who bought their megaWAD would be those who didn't have much experience finding and downloading levels off the internet. Ty had an emergency meeting with the team, and they voted not to release their work, and allow me to take it to retail. We called it *Final DOOM*. I was delighted to add another relatively "hands off" game to the mix and to secure a continued income stream for the first half of 1996.

A week later, after eleven months of development, John Carmack and Michael Abrash declared the *Quake* engine ready. It was a Herculean engineering success. The pivot to gameplay code would now begin, and the plans for the game's design were finally going to become a reality. We knew we wouldn't be able to do *all* the things that were dreamt up, because when it comes down to actually implementing a game's design, there are always compromises. However, we would start work on the preestablished pillars: a medieval world, *D&D*-style enemies, Quake and his hammer. Of those, Quake and his hammer were the most important since the design of the levels was predicated on that play. After that, everything else would fall into place.

Designing in 3D is where most level designers start nowadays, but in 1995, all of this was new; our R&D phase gave us much-needed experience and mastery in building 3D spaces that provided opportunities for player exploration and challenge. We had learned to craft environments and use light in ways that showed off the game engine's innovative lighting, and we figured out what the scale of the world in relation to Quake was going to be. I was excited to see this design take shape in the engine.

In mid-November, we gathered in the big open area between our offices and had a meeting to discuss the direction of the game.

"Now we can get busy! We can finally do this!" I told the team. I wasn't cheerleading; I was genuinely full of excitement. "We can make an awesome game with this engine."

I didn't get an immediate response. I saw Dave and American looking at each other, then at me, and American said, "I just spent a year mostly making levels that I had to throw away, and these latest ones are good for a shooter, not a hammer-pounding game."

Dave followed with, "Yeah, really, I think the hammer is just cheesy."

I looked at Carmack.

"They do have a point," he said. "Most of the level work done up to now has been geared toward a *DOOM*-style game."

I didn't hold back.

"Right, because that's *all they know*. That's all they had to build with. We haven't done *any* experimentation with this new type of gameplay. We've been talking about the design *publicly for a year*. Playing as Quake. The hammer was on the cover of *PC Gamer*, for fuck's sake!"[*]

Much of our intended design was hardly a secret, and players were looking forward to it.

"Even *Hexen*'s sprite-based hammer is cool," I added. "And I know ours would take it to the next level. We need to put the effort into game design that we put into technology—that's how we create cool new things!"

Adrian agreed with me: "I'm with John on this. We can't keep making the same game."

I looked at Kevin.

"I can see both sides of this," he said. "We've made several shooters, and this new engine is an opportunity to try something different. But we've spent the equivalent of the entire *DOOM* development cycle creating *just* the technology. To get a game done faster, making a shooter and using the levels y'all have created seems less risky to me."

---

[*] The October 1995 issue of *PC Gamer* featured a hand gripping Quake's powerful hammer and touted a first look at *Quake*'s design.

This was such a wild moment. I had been looking forward to this day for a year, but never once did I foresee this conversation. This was the moment to pick up our shovels and dig in. Instead, people were leaning against the metaphorical walls and debating whether we should dig at all. id Software's games had always been defined by their technology *and* their design. We *had* to push the game design, too. I mean, Carmack just spent a year on the engine. Why didn't people want to give the design its due?

Carmack spoke up.

"I am on the fence regarding this point," he said. "I see the obvious benefit of doing what we already know and creating a shooter. It'll be better than *DOOM* because of the new engine, and it plays over the internet. I also see how trying something new could be a fruitful exercise as well."

Seriously? I don't know how I looked to others, but on the inside, I was wide-eyed with shock and surprise.

Sandy, sensing my growing frustration, chimed in. "I can go either way. I'm just here to make games."

American drove the nail in the coffin. "We're just burned out, John. We want to make this game and get it over with. We should just put *DOOM* weapons in the game and call it done."

The design team and art department had spun their wheels for the better part of a year. We had designed about fifty R&D levels during that time, and while the experience was critical toward building our understanding of crafting play in a 3D space, the levels themselves were essentially experiments that lacked the necessary gameplay code to make them useable in the version of *Quake* we envisioned. That work would need to be remade or abandoned since the engine had been under development and changing constantly. The code team was worse for wear, too. Michael Abrash had had to rewrite his highly optimized renderer eight times. John Cash had written a bunch of network code, some of which Carmack didn't like, and so Carmack rewrote it over a weekend. The team was brittle.

It wasn't a team that was ready. It was a team that was done.

At the same time, *I wasn't done*, and I couldn't believe what I was hearing. It was opposite of the innovation that had defined us. I'd discussed necessary explorations once the tech was ready: We had opportunities for characters to engage in melee combat, possibly in third-person perspective. I planned to explore using a first-person perspective for aiming and shooting a crossbow. I wanted to experiment with new ways of playing in a true 3D world.

Perhaps American, Sandy, and Dave were feeling that way because they hadn't been through a full dev cycle with us before. They didn't understand how exciting and dynamic it would be when Carmack and I got together to start working on the gameplay. In *Commander Keen*, in *Wolfenstein 3-D*, in *DOOM*, this collaboration resulted in amazing moments that defined a genre. American and Sandy advocated just sticking to our old *DOOM* combat formula.

"We don't need new weapons," Sandy said.

"Let's just make *DOOM III*," Dave offered.

Had we really come all this way to simply clone our own game?

The rebellion was in full effect. Sandy and American didn't have it in them to start again *again*. Despite their reluctance, I kept urging us to strive for an innovative game design. Why would we take a brand-new engine and reuse an old design? I couldn't wrap my head around it. It was so antithetical to the core of id Software, to the core of everything Carmack and I had ever done.

To me, this was a decision that the owners should make, but I didn't want to say that and make everyone who wasn't an owner feel called out. We had to make this game *as a team*. Telling them that their opinions didn't matter would not be helpful, and ultimately, their opinions *did* matter. Trying to get people to do something they didn't want to do would not make a great game. Still, I imagined how Carmack would respond if his tech plans were shot down by Dave, Sandy, or American. At best, he would ignore them and walk away.

After taking a whole year to get his programming vision together, Carmack was now entertaining talk about stopping any similar exploration of design using his engine. It was a painful moment for me. In that room, with everyone standing around, I realized that our shared vision was over. After five years of dedicating equal importance to his tech and my design—a formula that always pushed for equal innovation and absolutely worked—Carmack was listening to people who hadn't seen us go through a new engine cycle, and who were too burned out to put in the effort it took to reach for the stars. Merely copying design ideas of the past was not what I was here for. And with the loss of design's importance, id lost me.

I stood in silence for a moment to collect my thoughts. "As a team, we've reached a decision. I'll redesign *Quake* as an FPS and use as much of the game as we've made so you guys don't have to redo everything."

I knew this decision was necessary. I couldn't push for innovation with a burned-out team. We had to accomplish what they were able to accomplish, and an FPS design was something they could get excited about. Despite the loss I was feeling, from a game direction perspective, I knew everything there was to know about FPS design, and so I knew I could direct a great game, even if it wasn't as innovative as I had hoped it would be. I'd get to work and do what had to be done. I don't want to understate the grief I felt here, though. On the drive home that night, I rode in silence the whole way just thinking about it. Together, Carmack and I had built some great games and a lot of great memories. Now, our paths were beginning to diverge. When I got home, I sat in the driveway for a long time. I didn't want to talk about it once I was inside either.

The next day, I got to work. I had to pivot a team to work around a new FPS design. There was no point in sitting around and being frustrated about it. If this is what we were going to do, at least we were going to do it well.

My first task was to get an FPS design written up as soon as possible so the level designers knew what was going to happen with their levels. The enemies and weapons needed to be defined, too, so the art team had goals. Carmack and Dave needed plans for gameplay.

I spent the next week and a half assessing everything that had been created to date. I played through all the R&D levels to see what fit in an FPS, determined what needed to be edited or finished, and decided what was going to be left on the cutting room floor. We'd need some new levels to fill out the four episodes we had planned. When the level review was finished, I began the process of writing extensive docs to describe the map and item assignments for both the shareware and registered versions, in addition to writing detailed descriptions of every map in the game.

During this time, and to get things out the door quicker, we pulled Sandy back from his quasi-production role on *Strife*, and we decided to bring on Tim Willits, a level designer who was wrapping up work on *Strife*, too. Tim started coming in at night a few weeks earlier and was learning QuakeEd. By the time I was done the FPS redesign, he was on the team.

By now, a lot of the tension in the office had dissipated, and things were feeling if not normal, at least decidedly better. One night after work in late November, Adrian, Kevin, and I left the office together. We ended up sitting on the floor in the lobby of Town East Tower. We were shooting the shit about everything, and a lot of it was about the journey we had been on the last couple of months.

"Having the team sitting around for almost a year was a horrible decision," I said. "Of course, it's easy to see this *now*."

Adrian and Kevin agreed. None of us knew the engine would take as long as it did, and we didn't realize that having our team spin its wheels, making things only to abandon them with each engine upgrade, would hurt morale and performance as much as it did.

"I think if we had two teams, it would have gone better," I said. "Team one would be an engine team—keep American with Carmack, John Cash, and Michael Abrash, and maybe another programmer—and let them do R&D. Meanwhile, the rest of us should have been using the *DOOM* engine we already had to make a new game."

That way we would have been optimizing our resources and building a new release that would make money while the engine team spent a year creating the new *Quake* tech. We could have spared everyone almost a year of angst and divided our team *on purpose* instead of having it happen *as a consequence*.

Eventually, as the clock ticked past 1 a.m., Kevin, Adrian and I prepared to leave, having allowed ourselves a moment of reflection. In the years that followed, we'd read a lot of things, some from people who hadn't even been at the company at the time, saying we could have done this or should have done that. Surprisingly, some even commented on things as if they had been there since the beginning. But you know, we did the best we could at the time, and even if our goals weren't 100 percent aligned, everything we were doing was in—what we thought—the best interest of the company we had built from scratch.

In early December, I had completed my review and the new FPS design direction. Here's a summary of that initial write-up which was divided into an eight-level shareware episode with twenty-two registered levels:

The eight-level shareware episode contains:

- An intro Military Base level that leads to a second Base level, then the rest of the levels are medieval style.
- Two dimensional-teleporters called Slipgates that require specific keys to use them: an Amber element for one, and an Emerald element for the other. Slipgates were a new design element.
- Non-linear level progression with some backtracking to get the Amber element.
- A medieval level that has an Old One ("Shantak") imprisoned within a quantum gravity cage that is sapping its power.
- A Shalrath as an end boss attacking the player with mind-control rays; just before he's killed, he summons the Diabolord from the lava, and he disappears. The player must defeat the Diabolord to finish the game.

The twenty-two registered levels contain:

- Several more Slipgate elements to get: Chromite, Tektite, Onyx, and Malachite.
- Several keys needed to release Old Ones ("Yog-Sothoth," "Hastur," and "Ithaqua"): the Freedom Cube, Freedom Sphere, and Freedom Pyramid. These are found in levels connected to mini-hubs.
- A level layout with a lot of small hubs connected to two levels. Ultimately, progression is linear, but you need to visit every level that's not on the main path through the game.

- Shalrath as an end boss, who will take a ton of damage before morphing into his true form, Shub-Niggurath.
- Levels that are not separated into episodes, but they are grouped by designer, so all of my levels would be played, then American's levels would be played, then Sandy's levels would come right after.

We also needed enemies in the game, so I came up with a list:

- Military Base enemies (shareware): Guard dog, Soldier, Enforcer
- Medieval enemies: Ogre, Thrasher, Glop, Shambler, Garpike, Diabolord
- Registered enemies: Duke of Sheol, Mobula, Dracosaur, Vomitus, Shub-Niggurath
- Non-combatant characters: Shantak, Shalrath, Yog-Sothoth, Hastur, Ithaqua

Each character was researched quickly and then given a name based on its hopeful appearance and function. For example, the Diabolord rises up out of a field of lava, and he's a boss monster. So Diabolord sounded like a perfect mix of "diablo," the Spanish name for "devil," and "lord," appropriate for his status as a boss.

The team gathered in the meeting room to review the docs, and I explained the structure of the game, the levels, their ordering, and their assignment. People asked questions and made comments. As we read over the doc, some of that old familiar energy returned: people seemed happy with the new direction of the game and ready to work toward their goals. So, united around this new FPS design, we got to work. Between Carmack and I, we focused on what needed to be done. No previous design ideas were brought up—this was a new game, and we agreed it was the best route forward.

Things seemed to be settling into a rhythm for us, and people were excited to be moving forward. And you know? I was right there with them. As much as this pivot wasn't something I welcomed, in the end, I was making an FPS and making a game, and if making games is fun, making an FPS game is pure destructive satisfaction. During these days of creating production levels, I needed to make some rules to establish a performance and quality bar for the levels.

- Rule one: If any room in your level could have been made in *DOOM,* you need to keep working on it until it's uniquely *Quake.*
- Rule two: Look up. Your ceilings need to be interesting, and if you can see the sky outside, that's even better.

- Rule three: Try to place lights behind some geometry so it can cast shadows to look cool. This is a uniquely *Quake* design feature, so let's use it. Our levels will be instantly recognizable.

These rules are evident in my E1M1: The Slipgate Complex level, and even in the "Start" level where you choose the episode you want to play. In E1M1, the first room has an angled floor, platforms you can see under, a first jump that rewards you with secret armor, a complex base door that looks cool opening and closing, and quickly you find yourself outside, where you can see the sky and cross a bridge over a river. The rest of the level is all about showing the differences in *Quake* levels versus *DOOM* levels. I wanted players to get an immediate sense of innovation in the gameplay space.

We started taking over the sixth floor of the Black Cube in Mesquite, slowly easing out all the other companies (except for the dentist, because we liked him). Once we took over the old accounting firm's corner office, our corporate game of territorial acquisition was complete. Expanding into the rest of the sixth floor, we began demolition, pulling down the temporary walls and leaving electrical wires and network cabling hanging through holes in the ceiling where the tiles were missing. Our demolished corner office quickly looked like a barely started construction project.

In December 1995, Carmack wanted to move everyone into that area, call it the War Room, and enter crunch mode to finish *Quake* there: that's seven days a week, twelve hours a day minimum. We never had mandatory crunch mode at id before this, but we wanted to finish the game, and we knew being together in the same room would allow us to finish the game faster, so we agreed. In a sense, the War Room was a reflection of the team it housed. It worked, it did what it needed to do—but it was frayed and, well, wasn't what it used to be.

We kitted out the War Room with cheap forty-dollar tables and lined them up along the walls. Wires trailed all over the carpeted floor, and old sheets of drywall were exposed where facing sheets had been torn down.

The layout of the War Room was mostly a big L, with Carmack and me at the corner. Our proximity to each other allowed us to make sure design and tech decisions happened quickly with no need for meetings. To my left were level designers Tim, American, and Sandy, and to Carmack's right were Abrash, Kevin, and Adrian. John Cash set up a desk in the center of the room to be closer to American and Carmack. Alone on another wall was Dave Taylor. Most days, Carmack worked until after midnight and would come in around noon. The rest of us worked 10 a.m. to 10 p.m.—or later, if we were working on something we wanted to finish or push a little further. Every day, when I got to the office, I would play music on my stereo for everyone. I turned it off as soon as Carmack came in. Then, the office went silent, and we put on our headphones. All hands were officially on deck. Well, almost.

With *Quake* entering crunch mode, and Sandy back on our team, the *Strife* project struggled to wrap up. I was concerned about *Strife*, with its *DOOM*-era graphics, color palette, art style, and generic personality. The development problems and the team's learning curve took a toll on the game and delayed *Strife*'s release into 1996. Playing it through, it just didn't *feel* like an id Software game, and it would be up against strong competition: *Hexen, Star Wars: Dark Forces, Duke Nukem 3D, Heretic: Shadow of the Serpent Riders, Final DOOM*, and our own upcoming *Quake*. I just didn't see how we benefited from its release. Hoping to break even on our investment, Jay sold the game to San Francisco–based game publisher Velocity, Inc.* Playing the game now, I can see its merits, but in 1995, it was a liability for id Software. We needed every new IP to be forward-looking.

As the holidays neared . . . it didn't matter. We were in crunch mode and gave ourselves only Christmas Day off—no vacations. It was a tough time. We worked many long nights. We got the game together. Every single person on the team wanted to make *Quake* the best FPS it could possibly be—that was obvious—but that thing that we had, that comradery, the incredible fun we had in the long nights of *Keen*, or *DOOM*, that just wasn't there anymore, and I think we knew it.

I began to prepare myself to leave id. Only my desire to see *Quake* through, to make my last id game a great one, kept me going. I was determined to go out on an exceptional game, and I felt confident we had everything we needed to make that happen. Sometimes I considered staying. I'd think of how much I enjoyed working with this team, and all we had built together. When I thought about what we might make next, though I just didn't see myself in that picture. It was clear that design no longer had equal footing at id, and I didn't want to keep making games without innovative design. The team had begun to splinter. It was no longer a fun place to make fun things.

In late January, I picked up the phone and called Tom Hall.

"I'm done at id," I told him.

There was silence for a moment, and then Tom said, "*Whaaaaaat* did you say?"

"I'm done at id."

---

* Velocity, Inc. is defunct and the name is now being used by an aerospace company. To my knowledge, there is no connection between the two.

Another person might have thought my comment was a prelude to a rant about some momentary frustration, but Tom knew me, and knew id, having been one of its co-founders, and because of that, knew differently. At the time, Tom was still at Apogee, which had by then begun shipping games under the 3D Realms label. He had shipped *Rise of the Triad* and was working on his next game, *Prey*.

"What happened?" he asked.

"Well, the hope of doing new design R&D on *Quake* ended up with a burned-out team wanting to make another FPS like *DOOM*," I said. "I've decided to leave after shipping *Quake*. What do you think about joining me to start a new company where design drives the games? Tech will have to work with our design, not the other way around."

"That would be a dream," Tom said.

With that plan in my back pocket, I focused on finishing *Quake*. We remained in crunch mode, working twelve hours a day, seven days a week from December into June. As with previous id releases, I was responsible for the direction, design, levels, and getting the game out the door.

At the time, I was working on my first deathmatch-only level DM3: The Abandoned Base. I created one room that was filled with a mainframe computer. The mainframe itself is made up of a whole bunch of rectangular computers that the player can run around in, sort of like a maze. The plan was for me to change the computers to C-shaped Cray supercomputers when the deal with Cray was completed. The maze of hardware had buzzing overhead fluorescent lights, and I hid ammo and health below in the darkness. I imagined desperate deathmatchers hunting for those and hiding from their potential killer below the mainframe. I placed a super nailgun on top, and a tricky jump to a Megahealth around the corner. The room also had a path that ran along the walls so players could shoot anyone trying to hide in the shadows—anyone trying to survive.

As the team hit its groove, I did some calculations to see when we might be finished with the game. At our current velocity, the pace that we were creating finished levels and animated models, it would take the entire year to create all the game elements and figure out how to convey the story. Since story didn't work well with *DOOM*, it wasn't going to work in *Quake* as an FPS, either, so I decided to remove all the items that added complexity, particularly the legacy RPG-style ones. I removed the amber and emerald elements, almost all of the Old Ones, and I arranged the levels into distinct episodes, making them completely linear. This would be the way to get the game on a clear, simple path to completion in the shortest time possible. I sent these design changes to the team:

- Four distinct episodes with seven levels per episode. The first and fourth episodes have eight levels each.
- A Start map that connects to all four episodes, and an End map to finish the game is connected to the Start map, revealed only when the player finishes all four episodes.
- Specific bosses assigned to Episode one ("Chthon") and the final boss in the End level ("Shub-Niggurath")
- Some renaming of enemies as follows: Thrasher is now Fiend, Shalrath is now Vore, Glop is now Spawn, and Duke of Sheol is now Scrag.
- Enemies that are removed are the Dracosaur [the dragon people saw in the screenshot], Vomitus, and Mobula.
- Other characters (Old Ones) that you would have seen that are removed: Shantak, Yog-Sothoth, Hastur, and Ithaqua.
- Shub-Niggurath as the final boss is only killable by a telefrag in the End level.

Since we had four episodes, we needed to tie them all together. We were hurrying to get the game done, and the central hub area with the visibility into other paths would take too long. So I decided to make a small hub level whose only focus was to present the episodes of the game. To move from the hub to the episodes, I created a new design element: the Slipgate, a dimensional teleporter. This meant the different texture sets each of us designers had adopted would make even more sense, since our levels would be located in different dimensions. The hub level would have all four design styles in four paths that lead to those episodes through Slipgates.

Since *Quake* was now an FPS, and not a medieval splatterfest, we said good-bye to Quake and his hammer, and I turned the player into a space marine with guns. Sandy came up with a compelling story that an enemy codenamed Quake was using Slipgates to teleport into our bases to destroy our military and steal our weapons. Our scientists have determined that Quake is not from Earth, but from another dimension. The player is in charge of a new military directive, Operation Counterstrike: Find Quake and stop him. Tying the four episodes together would be done through military bases, so I asked Adrian for a Base texture set. We brainstormed for about ten minutes and came up with the various textures to create these bases.

In spite of the progress, the momentum we had felt around the new direction a month ago dissipated. It now felt arduous and like actual work. The pressure of working constantly, in a ruined room, no less, affected everybody. As we got closer to finishing the game, I wanted to keep everyone on track and focused. I understood the team's attitude. I was worried that any disagreements about the game could blow up and jeopardize *Quake* ever getting out the door.

We felt ready to get some external feedback and to test the networking code at scale, and so on February 24, 1996, we uploaded *QTEST*, a test version of our internet multiplayer feature with some early deathmatch-only levels: DM1 (Tim), DM2 (American), and my new DM3. Players marveled at how easy it was to connect to each other, and they loved the look of the game, the weapons, the movement, and deathmatch gameplay. Releasing *QTEST* was also exactly what we needed for team morale. All the hard work of getting the client-server architecture in place and functional, the hardest part of creating *QTEST*, worked well the first time it was played by a massive audience—tens of thousands of players. Although we had released only three deathmatch maps, we included all the weapons, and also accidentally included the models for some of the monsters from our single-player maps. Since *QTEST* had QuakeC with it, the modding community immediately jumped into action, and many mods for *QTEST* were created in the short time between March and *Quake*'s eventual June launch. This was a great indicator—people were modding our game, and it wasn't even released yet!

We were ecstatic about the results and decided to bring some deathmatchers on site to watch them play *Quake*. A few days later, seven highly skilled *DOOM* players came into our War Room around 8 p.m. and got on PCs with our *QTEST* version running. They reinforced what we'd collected from the online *QTEST* and sampled the single-player game, as well. Some weapon balance needed to be adjusted, but overall, they had a great time.

As the testers left that night, we heard the things we wanted to hear:

"We can't wait until it's released, man."

"Can I be in the next test?"

"That was fucking awesome!"

It gave us a much-needed boost. Even the news we got days later couldn't damper that feeling: On February 27, just as DM3 had made its player debut, Silicon Graphics, the company that built the workstation that Kevin was using for 3D modeling, bought Cray Inc. Our deal was now off, so *Quake* would continue sporting rectangular mainframe computers. We weren't disappointed that the computers wouldn't be in the level. Rather, we were disappointed they wouldn't be in the office. There was no time to dwell on it, though.

I remained *Quake* focused in full-on crunch mode even after another difficult shareholder meeting in March. At that meeting, Carmack declared that when a shareholder got fired, their stocks would lose 50 percent of their value (if the stock was worth $2, it was now worth $1). It was a bizarre idea. Our previously allotted shares were a done deal. Why would they lose their half their value? I shot the idea down on principle, and all the others agreed with me. However, it gave me pause. It was an ominous suggestion.

In March, GT Interactive offered $100 million to buy id, and we turned them down. It was a lot of money, certainly, but it was not an inconceivable amount of money compared to what we felt we could earn. We were in complete crunch mode and could not make any kind of rational decisions at the time. Discussions about selling the company would derail the fast track that we were on to finish the game. $100 million or not, we just wanted to get it done.

In April, Michael Abrash was having some trouble while testing his code. Occasionally, when he was moving around in the game, the screen would show a completely random view that was from a totally different location for a split second. He debugged all the way down to the exact instruction that was responsible, but determined it was impossible to get the calculation result that would produce that random viewpoint. Carmack looked over the code as well, and this error didn't make any sense. They were confident that there was not an error in the code. So Abrash called a friend who worked at Intel to come check it out. His friend saw the error happen, closely inspected Abrash's code, and noticed that a floating-point instruction was causing the trouble. He then asked Abrash what kind of processor he had in the PC. It was an overclocked 100Mhz Pentium. As it turned out, there was a hardware-level bug in the Pentium's floating-point divide instruction (FDIV)—if he divided certain pairs of numbers, it would return incorrect results. This calculation was responsible for the player's viewpoint angle. Abrash modified the calculation so it wouldn't run into that problem again. This Intel Pentium hardware error is known as the FDIV bug. It remains one of our favorite debugging stories.

Though we were feeling frayed, the game was shaping up well. We decided to focus on putting together a *Quake* beta, containing all the close-to-final levels we had, to test the flow and feel of the single-player game. We were gaining momentum, and the community was posting nonstop about the game's promise. I worked thirty-eight hours straight, without sleep, creating the beta. I was in the home stretch, at some point, I just decided to stay awake until it was done. We were nearing a major milestone and working extra-long hours seven days a week.

This was the first of three betas we needed to create to keep us focused on our launch target. The testing for these betas was internal only, but it was a great measure of our progress. We invited a collection of local players to the office and watched over their shoulders as the game came to life in front of them. At the time, we already had lists of what was left to do, and these betas helped us collect feedback, tie up loose ends and complete things faster.

One night in late April, I got a call from a friend at 3D Realms, Mark Dochtermann. He was wondering if I could swing by. It was only midnight, and I had done a lot of mapping that day, so I drove over and found three other developers at his place: Jim Dosé, Tom Mustaine, and Rob Atkins (a longtime friend of Adrian's). At the time, they were working for 3D Realms on *Duke Nukem 3D*. The shareware version had launched on January 29, and they wanted to start their own company after they shipped the full retail version. I told them I could help them out if they made a level pack for *Quake* as their first project. We talked until 4 a.m., laying plans for their company's founding, their first project, and possible ideas for the pack. It was the beginning of Hipnotic Software (eventually renamed Ritual Entertainment).

The next day, I brought it up to Jay, Kevin, Adrian, and Carmack. They were all excited about having an official map pack developed by a talented team, and Jay took over the communication from there. Their *Quake* pack would be named *The Scourge of Armagon*.

April was busy as we were wrapping up more levels, testing them, and adding more enemies. Since we were taking some of our early experimental level work and incorporating it into final production levels, I decided to pick one of my early *Quake* maps and make it part of the last level of my Episode 2 series, E2M6. Because the level was made before we had established the proper scale for the character in relation to everything else, I had to do quite a bit of reworking to get most of the level feeling good. Then, to finish E2M6 I added a couple of major new sections and a bridge that rotated as you progressed. One section is a submerged piece of a castle with jumping involved to get into it from the water. The last two rooms were designed as an homage to Disneyland's Haunted Mansion elevator—when the player gets in, bars slam shut, and the floor starts descending. Shamblers and other monsters teleport in while spikes are shooting into the room. At the bottom, two Vores, an enemy players hadn't encountered up to this point, start attacking with player-seeking missiles. The level had a good flow and a challenging ending.

Soon after finishing E2M6, I was at the office late and running through my levels. It felt to me that E2M6 needed to be a bit longer. So, I spent the next several hours making a new entrance that was dark and wound around an uphill cave system, ending in the room that was the original start. Playing the new beginning felt great, with just the right amount of challenge and puzzle solving. When I was finished, I looked at the file size. It was close to 2 MB. A few months earlier, however, we imposed a rule that levels could not be bigger than 1.4 MB, so they could fit in memory. It was clear that I could not keep this new level start, so I reverted back to the earlier version. It didn't faze me, because the creative process is full of moments like this. "Throwaway" work is never truly throwaway. I learn from the experience, and should I create something like it again, it may be even better.

The weapons were also evolving. I added a unique superpower for the lightning gun—if you fire it while you're in the water, all the damage you release will hit you and everyone in your view. It's *Quake*'s version of the *DOOM* BFG, but dangerous to you, too. American and I worked for a bit on sound effects. I added all the water and sky sounds; teleporter sounds; pickup sounds for the Quad, Pentagram, Megahealth, and other items; the gib sounds; and the leg-splintering sound when you fall too far. American created and added additional audio for the monster and weapon sounds. He also added the sounds Trent Reznor created for the player character.

A concept-to-launch development cycle is an endurance trial, especially when you're creating your own engine. It was particularly challenging for those experiencing it for the first time, and after some work on the sounds, American took needed time off. I got the other level designers to finish what was left of his levels. American was, and still is, an amazing level designer. Of all his levels in *Quake*, E3M4: Satan's Dark Delight is my favorite. It has a great sense of space with some great traps like an Ogre that comes down underwater on a lift. It has multiple floors that connect in interesting ways, and some great puzzles. You could sense the humor in American's designs, and that's something I've always valued.

In the end, *Quake*'s levels were divided among the four designers:

- American/Tim co-created: 1 level
- Sandy Petersen: 7 levels
- American McGee: 9 levels
- Tim Willits: 10 levels
- John Romero: 11 levels

It's a tremendous credit to the entire team that *Quake* was as great as it was, particularly given that it was redesigned from an action RPG to an FPS with just seven months to go. At this stage, the game felt *good*, there was no denying it. By now, we knew shooters, and I felt confident that each member of the level design team was bringing their best. I played all the levels, of course, and offered feedback. Others did, too.

One of the enhancements that fell by the wayside was a visual and atmospheric improvement I loved. I had long known that motion was an integral factor in making a 3D game feel real. When a player stopped moving, the small, 320x200 pixel static screen revealed the blemishes of our art—for example, images in the distance were not clear. Still, the player might not really notice the blurring while on the move because as they approached an object, its detail came into focus. I thought making the player's viewpoint move ever so slightly would have a realistic effect and would provide a cover for the clarity issue. Even if a player stopped, the screen itself would have a fractional ebb, like a faint breeze. I mentioned this to

Carmack, and he coded a sinusoidal function that created a smooth back-and-forth motion to make this happen. His demo set the movement rate higher than I wanted, so the movement wasn't quite as ambient as I'd envisioned, but you could see the concept would work.

"This is the idea," I said, showing the demo to Adrian, "but we can set the movement to just a fraction, so it is barely perceptible."

He looked at the screen for about five seconds. No doubt his mind was racing, knowing that whatever rate we decided on would mean more work; we'd still have to monitor every second of the game to make sure nothing looked off.

"That makes me sick, like motion sick," he said.

That was all I needed to hear. "Okay," I said. "I'll set it to zero."

As it turns out, the functionality is still part of the *Quake* engine, and I did sneak the slight motion into the game—it appears on the intermission screens after you finish a level and a player's time, secrets, and kill scores are listed.

As we headed into the home stretch, the atmosphere in the War Room was constantly tense. We tended to focus on what we had to do individually and tried to avoid talking too much, to just get through this game and move on to whatever lay on the other side of release.

As part of the process of fixing and polishing everything, mouse control needed to be fixed. Carmack and I talked about allowing the mouse to control not just left and right, but also up and down by moving the mouse in both axes fluidly. The idea would be to move the mouse around like you do on a desktop, but instead of moving a mouse pointer you would be moving your "eyes" in the game, looking in all directions. Moving the mouse left and right would look around like *Wolfenstein 3-D* and *DOOM*, but moving the mouse forward and backward would let you look straight up at one extreme and straight down at your feet at the other. Moving the mouse along each of those axes would feel like you're looking around in 360 degrees, just like in real life.

Carmack spent about ten minutes programming the new axis of control into the game. When it first got into the latest build it felt bizarre. It was dizzying to look around with the mouse while at the same time moving around with the keyboard—I wondered how players would ever get used to it. It felt like the right way to solve the problem, though. This was the birth of what's now called "mouse-look" and is a staple of all mouse-controlled 3D games. We kept the feature in but kept it inactive by default.

Around this time, my new house in Frisco was finally completed and ready for occupancy. We moved all our stuff from Plano and started decorating. I still remember the feeling of walking through the door for the first time. Two-story-high ceilings, giant fireplaces, a spiral staircase leading upstairs. On the one hand, it felt amazing to set foot in a house that I had designed. Everything was exactly as I wanted it to be. On the other hand, it felt like I was walking into someone else's life. No one I knew had a house like this—no one in my family, anyway. It even overlooked a golf course and waterfall! But I'd have to put off enjoying those things until later—right now I was focused on one thing only: delivering *Quake*. Everything else could wait. Beth was fine with my schedule, and she was busy doing her own thing. I don't think either of us realized it at the time, but we were growing apart, living our own lives in the same house yet separate from each other.

June rolled around, and *Quake* was nearing completion. We were exhausted in every conceivable way, but we could see the finish line. Almost all the levels were complete; the game flow worked so players could get through all four episodes in order, then access the final level from the start map. Saving and loading progress was tested over and over. Deathmatch on all our custom deathmatch maps was tested especially well, and the co-op mode worked great in the single-player levels. The final assets I needed to get in were the music tracks, which we didn't have from NIN yet. Jay got in touch, since American was gone, and pushed the legal licensing process through as quickly as possible. The problem was that twelve different signatures were required to clear the music through NIN's label, Interscope Records. Then, at the last minute, an unfortunate issue appeared: The music tracks could only be licensed as CD-audio tracks. This was a major setback, as the best way to play the music in *Quake* was as streamed songs installed along with the game. By limiting access to the music as playable solely on CD, only players who left the *Quake* CD in the drive would hear the music! Few people would leave the *Quake* CD in the drive, as it turns out. We had to scramble to get CD-audio playing code in the game and mapping the song tracks to the levels. It was the final holdup to releasing the game.

As we were wrapping everything up, the mood was somber. There weren't the usual exclamations of excitement when cool things were put in or long-term issues were fixed. We were just executing our work the way we knew how, almost like we were robots on autopilot. If the team was burned out at the beginning of crunch mode in December, we were dead at release. What should have been an exciting, thought-provoking, hard-but-fun process became one of the hardest grinds of my game-dev life, and that's probably true for everyone on the team. When the work on *Quake* was completed, nobody in the office really acknowledged it.

On Saturday, June 22, 1996, I came in to the office and was alone. The previous day, I told the team that since the game was finished, I'd be in the office the following day to upload the shareware version. *Quake* was ready to be unleashed, and none of the others were there. That's how burned out and disconnected we'd become. It was both surprising and sad. Every id release before *Quake* was a company-wide, sometimes industry-changing, event. It didn't matter if it was four in the morning, everyone was there to watch our games launch. Newsgroups and bulletin boards provided us with a live, interactive feedback loop. We could see the reactions. We'd celebrate.

I got on IRC and saw the #quake channel had hundreds of people in it, waiting for any news of *Quake*'s imminent release. Days earlier, I told people in the channel that Saturday was release day. As soon as I typed into the channel, it started flooding with people as word got out that it was time. Because so many people logged onto IRC #quake, the channel split several times to handle the load. Watching the screen, you could not tell what was going on, as hundreds of people all typed at once. It was madness. I told everyone I was working on getting *Quake* ready for upload.

In the end, it took me about three hours, for a couple of reasons. The first was that I wanted to be completely thorough—I was on my own, and I didn't want to upload something that had any issues. The internet never forgets, and any screwed-up version would become official and never disappear. The second was because *Quake* was the first game we created that had multiple folders and subfolders. All our previous games were contained in a single folder. As a result, I needed to run a compression program on *Quake*, but I couldn't use the highly popular PKZIP because of legal issues that were being raised at the time.* I found out that LHA.EXE could compress and decompress files in folders, but there was no manual for it, so I had to hack at it until I figured it out.

I knew it was going to be an important moment in time, and since the team wasn't there, I decided to call a friend to be there during the upload. I called Mark "NaTaS" Fletcher, an incredible *DOOM* deathmatcher and one of those who tested *Quake* back in February. Mark and I tested the game installation about five times on different computers to make sure everything was good, and we found no issues. I hopped on IRC and told everyone the upload was about to begin.

It was pandemonium.

I uploaded the game to our usual FTP location with no issues, satisfied the hordes, and played some deathmatch with Mark to celebrate.

Even with all of *Quake*'s development challenges, I was exceptionally proud of the FPS we had created. As a game designer, level designer, programmer, and hard-core player, I recognized that we had created something that would make players forget everything else for a long while, including our past games.

With all our previous releases, there had always been some sort of celebration, even if that was just us turning our chairs to face one another to talk about what we had done and what we would do next. The empty office was, in a sense, a

---

*   PKWARE, the maker of PKZIP and PKUNZIP, were being sued by the author of ARC, a competing compression method that did not approve of PKWARE supporting their compression method. Why buy ARC if you could get ARC compression and ZIP compression in the same program? We didn't want to get dragged into any legal mess, so I avoided using ZIP for *Quake*.

reflection of the energy we had left. It was unfortunate that no one else was there to celebrate the release of the game that would redefine the modern shooter. Truly, there was a lot to celebrate, with features like internet multiplayer, a true 3D world with fast perspective-correct texture mapping, level design that took advantage of the engine's capabilities, an in-game console for executing commands into the game, mouselook for viewing the true 3D world in a new way, and a programmable QuakeC language that allows modders to create anything they like in our game.

I took two weeks of vacation, relaxed, and enjoyed spending time in our new house. I was so exhausted, I have little recollection of it. When I returned, I was ready to master *Quake*'s retail shareware CD. This one was different, however, and a challenging job. Mike Wilson had the idea to store all our games encrypted on a single CD and then sell them all from the CD itself. This retail CD would be placed in every 7-Eleven store in the US. The shareware version was freely available on the CD, and the retail version, including all our other games, was unlocked via purchase from a unique interface designed for that purpose. GT Interactive was handling the retail big box, which contained only the full version of *Quake*.

The response was through the roof. Sales rolled in. Critics lauded the game. Here's one I especially like from *Computer Games Magazine*:

Satan, your game has arrived. It spits up blood and pisses vinegar. It sprouts horns from its head like the proud minion of evil that it is. It shoots lightning bolts, for cripes' sake. It's a game of pure evil, and even purer entertainment. It's also the best action game on the planet.

The week after shipping *Quake*, a couple of friends of Michael Abrash showed up at the office. They were starting a new game company and wanted to license *Quake*. The two guys were Gabe Newell and Mike Harrington, newly minted Microsoft millionaires, and their new start-up was named Valve Software. Abrash introduced us, and I spent several hours with them talking about building a team to create a game like *Quake*. I explained how the art and level design pipelines worked using NeXT computers and Silicon Graphics Indigo workstations. Most importantly, I told them they needed a lead game designer to manage a design team to come up with everything that the rest of the group would create.

They took lots of notes, we had a good, long chat, and they went back to Washington State with a *Quake* source code CD in their hands.

American returned to the office, refreshed. It was perfect timing. I was ready to discuss our next game, and so I held a design meeting with the level designers to talk about ideas for *Quake II*. The earliest ideas had gameplay taking place in extradimensional mines that players would Slipgate into. Since *Quake* established the franchise as an FPS, it would remain so. Although I planned to leave and was even looking forward to working with Tom again, I think a part of me also didn't accept that I was going to do that. My DNA was in id, and I felt as connected to it and what we had built as I did to some members of my own family. So, while I knew that we had reached a turning point, I think a part of me rejected that and kept going, id all the way. I didn't see the paradox.

After mastering *Quake*'s retail CD, I planned to start calling publishers to let them know that I was looking for funding for a new company I was founding with Tom Hall—Dream Design was the initial name we came up with. My first call was to Ron Chaimowitz at GT Interactive. I thought he'd be gung-ho to back me. id Software had just signed a deal with Activision to distribute all future titles; *Quake* was the last game Ron would get, so I figured he'd be looking for new partners. We talked about our initial plans—that I was looking to fund multiple projects, one for me and one for Tom, and I wanted to build a studio on new IP. Obviously, I asked for the conversations to remain confidential. Later that day, however, I'm guessing word got to id Software. Adrian was even called back from vacation for an emergency meeting that very day.

The next day, I walked into work and John Carmack demanded my resignation, accusing me of all kinds of things, denigrating my job performance and claiming I had hurt the company. Adrian, Jay, and Kevin didn't say a word; they looked somber. To me, it was a mind-boggling rewrite of history and my contributions to the company. I stood there, taking it in, thinking. I was surprised and angry. I worked seven days a week on *Quake* for seven months after redesigning the game around an FPS core. I created more levels than anyone else *and* I had reviewed all their levels, too, levels we made with my editor! I'd even shipped the game by myself and gotten the retail versions ready.

"Really?" I said. "I worked seven months in crunch mode and *I* am hurting the company?"

"That's where we stand," Carmack replied.

We stared at each other. I thought back to the division that had grown between us over the company's goals. I couldn't believe we had reached this moment.

(I remind readers that we were in our twenties, working around the clock for months at a time, and both Carmack and I agree this situation could have and should have had a different outcome.)

In assessing the power dynamic at the time, I suspect my cofounders knew that if they didn't agree with Carmack forcing me out, Carmack would likely leave the company. id Software was known for cutting-edge technology, and so they sided with him. As far as I was concerned, I was already on my way out—I made that decision back in January. I had already put the wheels in motion with publishers. Nonetheless, it was a horrible, painful moment, a moment that Adrian and I have talked about many times since then. He felt like I felt when we decided to ask for Tom's resignation. I didn't accept that I hadn't worked enough because I had worked nonstop before and after *Quake*'s pivot to an FPS. I'd even delivered millions into the company while its engine was in development. To me, it was too much of a coincidence that forcing me out took place the day after I talked to GT Interactive about leaving and publishing my next game (and to be clear, I'm not saying that anyone I talked to said something; it could have been anyone who knew of our plans).

I truly believe my working dynamic with Carmack was critical to the original id, and I think our collective ability with design and tech was responsible for our major advances. He trusted me because I also knew how to code, and we fell into an easy partnership. At the same time, I think it's fair to say I was the only one who ever argued with or challenged him. In development, our friction produced designs and technological advances that were perfect pairings. In business, I pushed to get Adrian an equal cut in the company. I continually advocated expanding id and handling our own distribution. I fought for Tom, demanding he get a second chance. I single-handedly pushed to develop *Heretic* and *Hexen*. The rest of the company kept their heads down and did the work. Now, with me gone, id was Carmack's company.

I left id on August 6, 1996.

Under the terms of our buy-sell agreement, I returned my stock to id Software immediately, and they paid me for it over the next five years. The stock price was calculated based on the collective sales the company had made over the previous 365 days multiplied by my percentage of ownership—for every dollar sold, I got a percentage. I'm grateful for the work I put into releasing products during *Quake*'s long development as it meant that there was company income to have a percentage of. I couldn't have known it at the time, but my desire to expand the business's bottom line and to ensure its security ended up ensuring mine. As it turned out, I saw no money from *Quake*.

Despite our team's fractured state, our arguments, and our overall solemnity, there is this undeniable fact: The incredible discipline we had as a team allowed us to create and publish thirty-two games in six years. Something malevolently magical happened between us, and I believe that my creative drive was the heart of Carmack's machine. We changed the world for the better.

As I write this, a quarter century has passed since I left id. Throughout the last couple of chapters, I mentioned that I would share some thoughts on what we might have done differently with *Quake*, with our divergent company strategies, and with our eventual irreconcilable differences. We know it didn't have to go as it did. Of course, that's the benefit of both maturity and hindsight.

Regarding *Quake,* Carmack recently suggested to me that he thought we could have split *Quake*'s technology advances into two games. The first game would have used the *DOOM II* engine with a new client/server networking model and a DoomC programming language. The second game would have been *Quake* with the true 3D world and advanced lighting. That idea makes a lot of sense to me and would have allowed us to progress more quickly. In a similar vein, it also seems that putting aside some new engine features and moving onto gameplay code at an earlier point would have allowed us and the rest of the design team to progress the gameplay much faster. Both of these methods would have kept everyone fully tasked *and* allowed for new products to come out. As I mentioned earlier, Adrian and Kevin agreed that we should have been working on *something* as a team, perhaps using the *DOOM II* engine, while the *Quake* engine was in R&D.

Regarding our misaligned company goals, I suspect it's obvious to readers that this difference only grew over time, and that *something* was going to give. We might have seen it, too, or managed it far better, if we hadn't been under extreme pressure, working constantly and caught up in some kind of success tornado. I believe we could have grown the business and had me on *Quake* too. As a hard-core programmer—and Carmack's programming partner for six years—we should have hired someone to take on all this extra work, particularly *The Ultimate DOOM, Heretic 2*, and maybe even QuakeEd, so that I could focus exclusively on engine code with Carmack and then exclusively on gameplay code and design. We had done that for all our previous games. Our collective expertise in tech and design pushed engines forward and revealed new forms of gameplay. It had always worked that way and worked well. That daily back and forth with another programmer fully immersed in the project would have been invaluable, not to mention having two full-time programmers on the engine. Bringing in that continued income was important. It gave id a good, long runway, created new IPs and made it so that we never had to make difficult decisions. I suspect my drive to strike when the iron was hot was also spurred on by having never had enough before. I couldn't accept that it wouldn't just go poof in short order because I'd seen that happen again and again in my personal and professional life.

Last, the homegrown development process that worked so great for us when we were small needed to evolve as we grew larger and our games became more complex. We were following a method that had served us well since 1990: The intended design is understood by the team, we put stuff in, take out stuff that doesn't work, and iterate toward perfection (or as close as we can get, anyway). It had worked great with *Wolfenstein 3-D, DOOM*, and *DOOM II*, not to mention all our games prior to those, and nothing was making us think, *You know, we really should consider changing this.* Adding a producer might have gone a long way toward alleviating the pressure and making sure people felt like they had enough direction and something to do. Communication is always important, and even more so as teams scale. You may be happy to know that today my games have extensive design docs, an absolute necessity as teams grow. I still believe in the game as the living doc, though. It holds the truth the documents cannot reveal.

Regarding the meeting where it all ended, well, by the time we reached that meeting, I don't know that there was another course. We'd missed several red flags at that point. Like Carmack said, "That is where we stand," and he was right. We had already built different paths without each other. It was only in that moment that those paths became apparent to everyone else. As much as I can't forget the past (literally), I can move past it. I recognize the incredible time that we had creating some of the coolest shit ever coded, and I am so incredibly grateful for it. We both are. Maybe that was all we were supposed to have. It was certainly enough.

In the years that followed, I have remained a supporter of id Software and its products, and become a part of the community itself, creating mods for *DOOM* and *DOOM II*, one of which id licensed for inclusion in its releases of *DOOM*. "SIGIL" was the unofficial fifth episode for *DOOM*, released in 2019. I am still friends with my fellow cofounders Carmack, Tom, Kevin, Jay, and Adrian. Our games will carry on.

EPISODE FOUR
POST LAUNCH

CHAPTER 19

Dream Design

First, I'd like to welcome those who turned directly to this chapter. It's a wild ride, most of it downhill. I've chronicled, to the best of my recollection, history as I lived it. As you read, you will likely note moments where I should have made a different decision or seen the writing on the wall, and you will not be wrong. I own the trainwreck that was Ion Storm. I learned a lot from it, and I certainly hope that in sharing and reflecting on the story of Ion Storm after nearly thirty years, you will, too. I offer some reflections at the end of its story.

On August 7, 1996, I hit the ground running with Dream Design, the company I'd pitched to Tom Hall back in January. I wasn't going to dwell on the past or on the negative. This was, after all, what I wanted to do, even if our plan was moving faster than we intended.

I walked into my home office, closed the door, and picked up the phone to call Tom.

"I resigned from id," I said.

"What? When?" I could hear the surprise in his voice. Tom was at work when I called, so I'd left him at a disadvantage if he wanted to ask more precise questions. He was surrounded by people who didn't know that we were planning to form a new company.

"Yesterday."

I recounted the story of being called into an empty office, of Carmack handing me my resignation letter, and told Tom the things he'd said. For the first time,

I was vocalizing what had happened—how Adrian looked particularly sad during the meeting, and what it felt like to go to my desk and pick up the photos of Beth and the boys, my CDs and headphones, and all the random pop culture things that game developers tend to collect on their desks. It's one thing *planning* to leave. It's quite another actually doing it.

All around us, the internet exploded with news of my resignation, which Carmack and I had independently announced in the most programmery way possible: in .plan files.*

From me on August 7: "I'm going to jump on this .plan bandwagon just this once. I have decided to leave id Software and start a new game company with different goals. I won't be taking anyone from id with me." I didn't want to be dramatic or air dirty laundry.

The day after I posted mine, Carmack wrote, "Romero is now gone from id. There will be no more grandiose statements about our future projects. I can tell you what I am thinking, and what I am trying to accomplish, but all I promise is my best effort."

Though our collective announcements amounted to only seventy-six words, tens of thousands more would follow—in magazines, books, and posts in news-groups. Everyone wanted to discuss our separation and offer their opinions, and some sought to build upon the polarization. We created id Software from nothing, worked together every day for years, and some of the best days of my life had been with my id coworkers. For my part, any "grandiose" statements I made were extolling the virtues of our company's tech and design. One would hope that someone speaking on behalf of the company would speak positively about current and future projects. I didn't quite understand his sentiment, and obviously, the time for discussion had passed.

On August 8, id issued a press release announcing my departure: "id Software's John Romero to Start New Computer Gaming Company":

> Mesquite, TX, August 8, 1996—id Software, developers of the hit computer games *DOOM* and *QUAKE*, announced today that co-owner and game designer John Romero will be leaving the company in an amicable split. Romero, who has been with id Software since the company was founded in February 1991, plans to start his own game company, tentatively named Dream Design.

---

* A .plan file is located in a computer user's home directory and is a text file that usually contains the status of the user. It was not uncommon for programmers to document their progress in .plan format.

"John has been integral to the incredible growth and notoriety of id Software," said Jay Wilbur, id Software's biz guy. "We wish him the best of luck and can't wait to see his creations."

According to Romero, "This new venture will allow me to focus on different types of games in addition to the first-person action genre. id has the most powerful 3D technology in the industry and I will definitely be licensing it. I plan on working with id first as a licensing partner; perhaps more in the future. I wish id well and will miss working with all my friends and partners."

And I genuinely did wish everyone at id well. I was leaving behind some great friends and great games I'd poured my soul into.

I told Tom that I would approach some publishers that day about a deal. We were planning a slate approach, which meant we'd have multiple internal teams working on multiple projects, something I'd wanted to do at id but achieved only via licensing of external projects like *Final DOOM* or through contracting of external teams like Raven. A slate approach insulated a company in the event of a project cancellation or delay—which is far more common than people outside of game development know—and allowed teams to share tech and resources. At id, the pseudo-slate approach I'd worked out effectively funded the team throughout *Quake*'s R&D period so that we didn't burn through all the *DOOM II* income. For Dream Design, our slate would be three games with budgets of $3 million each. Knowing we were bankable having just come off three of the biggest games in history, I also asked for a 40 percent royalty and rights to the IP we created.

I had already talked to Ron Chaimowitz at GT on Monday, and I planned to reach out to a couple of other publishers. I believed that having half of id Software's founding team would be a significant draw.

At the time, Tom was working at 3D Realms/Apogee on the game that would eventually become *Prey*. Talking to Tom about his work was like listening to a recording of myself a year earlier, and I could hear the frustration in his voice. The *Prey* team was building a 3D engine from the ground up with just a few programmers, so the engine was limiting design progress in the same way *Quake*'s engine had. While they waited for the engine, Tom was prototyping *Prey* levels in QERadiant, a *Quake* level editor. *Prey* would supposedly be able to draw levels in full 3D like *Quake*, so Tom only used QERadiant for prototyping, practicing 3D level design, and defining a unique style.

We both were excited to hang out again and finally get started on Dream Design, so Tom informed George Broussard and Scott Miller that he would be leaving in two weeks. With *Prey*'s engine still in development and the design stalled,

Tom leaving did nothing but save George and Scott some money. I told Tom that I'd cover his salary until we got a deal lined up.

Fortunately for us, that didn't take too long. Once my .plan hit the internet, interest in Dream Design was immediate. Activision called and scheduled flights for Tom and me to visit them the following week, and that same day, Mark Rein, who was now at Epic Games, emailed to discuss me joining Epic as a game designer creating a new IP. While it was both flattering and exciting, I declined, telling Mark that I was starting my own company with Tom. Otherwise, I would have seriously considered it. Mark, however, was not dissuaded. He and Tim Sweeney, the founder of Epic, flew to Dallas to discuss things in person. I knew Mark from his time at id, of course, and I'd previously met Tim in 1992 at the Shareware Industry Awards. He had just released *Jill of the Jungle* in June of that year. Tim was, and still is, one of the game industry's greatest coders. At the time, Epic was working on *Unreal*, which was clearly influenced by the design and tech of *Quake*. We talked long into the night about id, *Quake*, *Unreal*, and the plans they had for Epic. It was great to see how excited they were, but ultimately, starting a new company with Tom was more important to me. I told them that if they were interested in funding Dream Design and publishing our games, that I'd love to talk about it. Mark and Tim left the following day and agreed to discuss it. In the end, though, they weren't ready to fund another studio.

The following week, Tom and I headed to Activision. They put us up at the Beverly Wilshire Hotel in Beverly Hills, right at the intersection of Wilshire and Rodeo Drive. Both Tom and I were movie fans, and finding ourselves in such an iconic venue was exciting. We didn't walk around too much, however, because we were busy preparing for our meeting. Just before lunch, we met Bobby Kotick, Activision's CEO, in front of our hotel, and he drove us to the Ivy, telling us that it was a well-known Hollywood restaurant famous for celebrity sightings. Once inside, we were joined by Howard Marks, Activision's cofounder, and we sat down for lunch. While some of our fellow diners may have been hoping to spot a celebrity, for us the most interesting people were right across the table. We were impressed with Activision and were eager to discuss our plans and hear more about what they had to offer. After lunch, we headed to their office in Santa Monica. There, we were joined by Mitch Lasky, their in-house counsel, and they shared the story of how they purchased Mediagenic, a then-failing game company, and transformed it into Activision. It was obviously a lot of hard work that involved Chapter 11 filing and a reorganization. It had taken a lot to bring that company back from the dead, and they were once again publishing good games and had considerable plans for their future. We knew that the terms of the deal would be discussed soon, but first, Bobby wanted to give us a tour of their offices. They were, in a word, substantial— many, many times larger than id Software's space. There were empty areas where dev teams would be, and other areas that were already filled by teams working on *MechWarrior* and *Interstate '76*. The tour gave us confidence in Activision. It was obvious they believed in themselves and their vision and were investing significantly in success.

Bobby led us into his office and Tom and I each took a seat.

Bobby put a piece of white paper in front of him and started writing:

$1M JOHN'S GAME
$1M TOM'S GAME
$1M 3RD GAME

He spun the paper around and pushed it toward us.

"That's not enough money," I told him. "It's $3 million per game, not in total. We plan to have a decent-size team on each game, and I don't think $1 million is enough."

We went back and forth discussing different scenarios, but in the end, Activision decided to pass on our higher budgets. Though we left without a deal, it was an amazing whirlwind, and Tom and I were exposed to a new world of investment and opportunity. In our previous roles at id Software, we were self-funded, for the most part, aside from advances we'd taken for ports or for publishing rights. We hadn't been exposed to this side of the business as much, and so it was new, and new meant exciting. We may have been heading back to Dallas with a "no," but our spirits were higher than ever.

Making sure that our proverbial eggs were in more than just one basket, I sent an email to my contacts at Origin Systems, Virgin Games, Mindscape, and GT Interactive to discuss possible deals.

The road show continued. In September, I visited the Origin office to talk with one of my game development heroes, Richard Garriott, about publishing our games. Richard was the reason that I had wanted to work at Origin earlier in my career, and I had spent hours and hours exploring the worlds he created. Our paths never crossed when I worked in his company's New Hampshire office, and so I was in full fanboy mode when I met him, and Tom wasn't far behind. It was an incredible moment for me.

"Your games are so amazing. I played the hell out of them," I told him, fumbling for which of his games I wanted to talk about. In my hand, I held an *Ultima V* shirt and a Sharpie and asked if he would sign it for me.

Richard laughed, smiled, and held out a *DOOM* shirt in my direction. "Only if you sign this."

This was one of those moments that I wish I could summon my younger self to see through my eyes.

Richard gave us a tour around Origin's headquarters. It was even bigger than Activision—so big, in fact, that there was a road bisecting the two sides of the campus building, with an enclosed walking bridge joining the two. Art from Origin's games decorated the walls, and I just imagined the treasure trove of stuff they must have had locked away in their archives. We were kids in a candy store. Richard walked us through six different development areas where teams were working on games in development, but exactly what those game were was off limits.[*]

In Richard's office, I pitched our three-game plan. Though he looked like he already had a full slate, he promised to follow up with Electronic Arts (EA), which had purchased Origin Systems in 1992. He was interested, and Tom and I both knew it would be an honor to work with a legend whose career had shaped ours since the beginning. Richard walked us out, and we signed the shirts on the trunk of my car just before I drove back toward Dallas.

Plans for Dream Design were shaping up nicely. We had numerous irons in the fire, and time to contemplate and compare our options. We did need to get a third designer for the third game in our slate, though, and a chance encounter late in September led to that person.

I went to 7th Level, makers of the Monty Python games, to see Mike Maynard, an old friend of mine from *Softdisk*. He happened to mention that his boss was Todd Porter.

"Todd Porter who made *Knights of Legend*?" I asked.

Knights of Legend was an average RPG, a challenging genre to get right with its mix of so many systems—narrative, combat, magic, inventory, and character among them. I was curious to meet him, so Mike introduced us. Todd was a charismatic and energetic person. He was excited to meet me, too, and offered to show me the games currently in development, *G-Nome* and *Dominion: Storm Over Gift 3*, both 3D games. Discussing 7th Level, id, and Dream Design, I was impressed with Todd. Not only did he know about games, and game development, but in this conversation, it seemed to me that he knew a good deal about the games business, too. In particular, I was impressed with what I saw in his game *Dominion*, a real-time strategy (RTS) game. Aside from FPS games, RTS games were some of my favorites, particularly *Command & Conquer* and *Warcraft: Orcs & Humans*. The genre was really taking off.

A week later, Tom and I were having lunch. "What if we brought Todd on to design an RTS for us?" I asked him. "That could be our third team, and our slate would be good to go."

---

[*]   I later found out that all six games were canceled. It's not uncommon for companies to have multiple games in prototype, pre-production, or development, and not all of them survive.

I also liked the idea of the third game being a different genre than our others. Releasing three shooters meant that all three would be competing with one another. Whatever we made, I didn't want one project cannibalizing the prospective audience and sales of another. We approached Todd about joining our company, and he was all for it and was particularly excited about working on a 3D RTS. Even better, a few days later, Todd approached us about having his art director, Jerry O'Flaherty, join, too. Todd was currently working with Jerry on *G-Nome* and *Dominion*. They had a good working relationship, and since we needed an art director, we felt fortunate that he was interested, too. Both Todd and Jerry planned to join us later in the year, once we were official.

By October, talks were intensifying with our prospective partners, and we hoped to get things rolling soon. We met with a couple of other companies, but they didn't feel like a fit for us or what we hoped to do. Some seemed like sinking ships, challenged by the monumental transformations taking place and unable to keep up with the industry's tech and design momentum. In their offices, we saw the struggle of those who were stuck in the 2D era trying to code their way toward a 3D engine without a Carmack or a Sweeney to guide them. Others were replicating a game design that had worked for one game with the hope that it would work for all. They looked at me and Tom as possible life preservers to save their companies and bring in an infusion of cash from external investors.

The more I spoke our company name aloud, the more I felt that it was too soft. Dream Design was a better name for a mattress brand than a company planning to make video games. We knew we needed a name that embodied all the genres that we planned to make, a name that would immediately catch the attention of players, publishers, and press alike. Tom and I met Todd and Jerry for lunch to get their thoughts. As we ate, we spent time thinking about the most respected names of the game industry, like Sony and Nintendo. We listed company names we thought were cool and evocative: Blizzard, Epic, Square. We wanted something that was short and intelligent sounding and infused with meaning.

"How about the word 'ion,'" Tom said.

"Yeah, I like that." Its definition fit perfectly with the process taking place in the company formation, but the domain wasn't available. So, we started to think of words that might go with "ion." Todd and Jerry were busy thinking, too. Eventually, Tom came up with four pages of possible name combinations. We gathered for another meeting.

Kee Kimbrell, the coder from DWANGO, was considering joining us, and phoned into the meeting. Out of the blue, he said, "The competition better watch out, or they are going to get caught up in an *ion storm!*"

I laughed. "That's it! We're done here."

We weren't actually done until we checked the trademark and registered the domain, but both of those were in the clear. Ion Storm was to be our new name.

By early November, Tom, Todd, Jerry, and I were meeting regularly to hash out ideas for who would do what in the new company. Things were going well between us, so we decided to bring Todd and Jerry on as partners, giving each of them an ownership stake in the new company. As we tossed numbers back and forth, Todd insisted that he and Jerry own the company 50/50 with Tom and me, and if we weren't interested in an equal partnership split, we could forget it. Neither Tom nor I agreed, but it was a tricky situation; we had already started talking to prospective partners. I thought back to the beginning of id Software and our unequal share distribution. I'd fought then for everyone to have an equal stake since we were all a key part of the games and the company we were creating. If we split 50/50 now, at worst, if we disagreed on a company direction, we'd stalemate.

With that decision made, Ion Storm was officially founded on November 15, 1996.

Todd found a great starter space for Ion Storm in the Quadrangle, located in Dallas's Uptown area. It was a good fit for a twenty-person team, smaller than what we'd need when we hit full steam, but since there were only four of us, it worked well for the time being. By this point, résumés had started to come in from people looking to work with us. Tom and I had reached out to a few folks, and gradually word got out that we were making 3D games and looking for level designers. It snowballed. We weren't even sure where some people got the address from. One guy moved to Dallas, lived in his friend's closet, and made a level to send to me. I ended up hiring him. It was a good level!

In November, we traveled to Acclaim Entertainment's New York offices. Comparatively speaking, Acclaim's space was as large as Activision's, and they even had a motion-capture studio, which we were informed with a great deal of pride, was an industry first. While there, we met with Greg Fischbach, cofounder and president, and Russ Howard, director of artists and repertoire. We joined Russ in his office to discuss Acclaim: how they worked as a publisher, and what games they had in the works. In the end, though, neither Tom nor I felt that Acclaim was the right fit for us. They didn't ask about our plans for Ion Storm or our games, and we felt the meeting was more a "meet and greet" than potential partnership discussion.

While in New York, Tom and I stopped in to talk with GT Interactive. My last meeting with GT in August had been the suspected catalyst for great upheaval, with word somehow getting back to id about my new company plans with Tom in fewer than twenty-four hours. This time, we talked with Jim Perkins, their new biz guy. I knew Jim as the owner of FormGen, the company that published *Spear of Destiny* and held the publishing rights. GT was after those rights and still gathering as many id games in their portfolio as they could. So, it was no surprise that they were eager to work with us. We didn't have a good feeling about GT, though. Looking at their catalog, it seemed they were investing in some bad games.

"My concern is that they will go out of business before our games get finished," I told Tom. We decided to pass.

By now, the media circus around my departure from id was dying down, and Kevin Cloud took over the management of products that I used to handle. In November, he contacted me to see if I was interested in providing some photos for a new product to commemorate the early days of id: An anthology box filled with collectibles and a book about our history from our formation right up through *Quake*'s launch. It was written by the talented Marc Laidlaw, who wrote a *Wired* cover story about us just before I left, and would later go on to write the stories for *Half-Life 1*, *Half-Life 2*, and the unreleased *Half-Life 3*.

Richards Group R&D was handling all the creative aspects of the package, so Tom Hall and I met Kevin at their office. Tom brought a ton of photos, and I carried in collectible items like floppy disks, drawings, and my own photos. Kevin brought a bunch of Adrian's sketches for all our games, and we had a great time sitting around choosing the things that could be plastered across the pages of the book. The design of *The Book of Id* was going to be mostly photos, with writing along the edges as if typed on a manual typewriter.

Sifting through everything and flipping through funny photos stirred up memories of the magic we'd made. As a team, we'd been really close. We were so in tune for those years, and we were focused. As we reminisced, I was a little melancholy. On the one hand, there was a pull to return to id and the knowledge that we could sort our differences if we had tried, but on the other hand, the tracks were already set for my next venture with Tom.

The Ion Storm road show continued. Touring office after office—from Activision to Origin to Virgin to Acclaim—was useful for us. I picked up on the presence that the spaces conveyed. At id, when I left, we had wires hanging from the ceiling, unfinished walls, and ceiling tiles missing to reveal ductwork, cabling, and concrete above. No one cared, least of all us, because we didn't need to impress anyone. That was certainly true for id, but the industry was growing. Publishers and studios with multiple games in development had spaces that conveyed both creativity and confidence. When prospective employees entered an office, first impressions mattered. They wanted to see a company in creative control, investing in its space and its teams, and providing a good working environment.

Of all our prospective suitors, it was Eidos Interactive that interested us the most. After a few preliminary conversations in December, we met with the president of Eidos, Mike McGarvey. Eidos had just published *Tomb Raider*, an action-adventure game, which was making loads of money for them. It was a great twist on the explorer/archaeologist theme featuring Lara Croft, a strong lead character that everyone wanted to play. No wonder it was both a commercial and critical success. The tenor of our meetings was different from other publishers, too. Eidos was coming from a position of power, having a hit game on their hands, but they were also keenly interested in what our plans were, and repeatedly said that they wanted to be involved. We were introduced to Charles Cornwall, the owner of Eidos, who expressed complete confidence in McGarvey. During our meetings, I also discovered that Ian Livingstone, cofounder of Games Workshop, was the chairman of the board, and that gave us confidence that an actual game legend was running things. Talks progressed quickly with Eidos, and we agreed to the following deal: $3 million for each game plus $4 million for console rights for a total of $13 million. Eidos also negotiated options for three additional games, meaning that they had right of first refusal on the next three games we developed, which upped the deal to $22 million. Tom, Todd, Jerry, and I were delighted with the terms and ready to get to work in the new year.

Back at id and through the grapevine, I heard that the culture was both somber and challenging. Even deathmatching had been entirely banned, which made it difficult for designers to test their levels. I had been talking to Shawn and Mike on and off since I left, and in January, they joined our team, setting up their desks in the Quadrangle office. Shawn came on as a programmer, something he'd been wanting to do but hadn't been able to at id. Mike joined as CEO and was eager to get going and start his business relationship with Eidos.

Tom, Todd, and I got to work designing our various games. Tom started work on *Anachronox*, Todd started on *Doppelganger*, and I got to work on *Daikatana*. This stage is often one of the most fun and creative periods for me—thinking of the experiences I want players to have, experiences that innovate within the genre while providing the pillars of the experience that players have come to expect. In starting *Daikatana*'s design, I was influenced by *Chrono Trigger*'s time-travel narrative and the way Link's sword becomes more powerful as you progress through a *Zelda* game. I decided to integrate RPG elements so players could increase their personal stats, as well as those of their sword—the titular Daikatana—when they gained a level, and added sidekicks to make the adventure more interesting. Instead of the player being alone in the game, they would be responsible for two other characters. I planned to weave them into the story in such a way that they were not always together or with you all the time. To keep it interesting and to give the sidekicks their own sense of agency, I had them go in and out of the player's gameplay. The player might have both of them at the end of a level, but in the next episode, both are gone. Eventually, the player might cross paths with one again. It made them more believable characters with their own will. Hiro Miyamoto was *Daikatana*'s player character and a tribute to Shigeru Miyamoto, designer of *Super Mario Bros.*, *Donkey Kong*, and many other seminal titles. The content plan behind *Daikatana* was to have new content show up in every level, with four episodes that were from different time periods. Each episode has between five to seven levels plus all-new enemies and weapons. To further individualize the episodes, I planned to have different styles of music composed to specifically reflect the individual time periods.

As we worked, Todd suggested we bring on a chief operating officer (COO) to keep operations running smoothly while we focused exclusively on our games, and we heartily agreed. As game directors, Tom and I knew that it was critical for us to spend as much time on our games as possible. Todd suggested that his lawyer, Bob Wright, might be just the guy for the job. After all, Bob had helped Todd with the sale of his previous company, Distant Thunder, to 7th Level for $1.5 million. We met with Bob, discussed his background and our corporate plans, and decided to move forward. Eager to work with us, Bob joined Ion Storm near the end of January. In our conversations with him, Bob came across as an experienced businessman, which would be beneficial to the media perception of us as an emerging company.

With all three games underway, our teams ramping up, and a new CEO and COO on board, Tom, Todd, Jerry, and I were as optimistic as we could be for Ion Storm's future.

CHAPTER 20

Ion Storm

Unbeknownst to us, a small warhead was headed in Ion Storm's direction. 7th Level, Todd's previous workplace, sued Ion Storm, alleging Todd and Jerry left the company in a bad position with both *G-Nome* and *Dominion* unfinished. As a part of the suit, I was deposed by 7th Level's lawyers. How long had I known Todd? How long had I been planning to bring him on as a partner before he joined the company? Did I know any of 7th Level's employees? The questions went on for three hours. We weren't worried, though, because we hadn't done anything wrong, and fortunately, they dropped the suit. It wasn't a great way to start the year, but we shrugged it off and went back to work on our games.

As the highs and lows of January rolled into February, I started looking for people to join my team.

"I'm starting work on my new game," was how I started each email. From there, everything was customized and targeted toward level designers or programmers whose work I had played and respected. On the level design side, I started with popular level designers like John Anderson, who made levels for both *The Ultimate DOOM* and *Master Levels for DOOM II*, as well as Matt Hooper, who worked with Hipnotic Software on *Scourge of Armagon*. I also reached out to Steve Rescoe, who was a good *Quake* level designer, making Shadow Over Innsmouth, and Sverre Kvernmo, a *DOOM* mapper who worked on *Eternal DOOM* and the *Master Levels for DOOM II*. All four joined the team. On the programming side, getting a lead coder was my top priority, and so I hoped Kee Kimbrell would join us. I had one concern, though—his boss and founder of DWANGO, Bob Huntley.

Bob had a good history, and I didn't want to crater his company by approaching his number one coder. As it turned out, Bob was actually okay with it. The availability of the internet was displacing those using traditional dial-up, and if I took Kee, it would save him a lot of money. Kee joined the team in February.

With critical members of the team starting to fall into place, I targeted a late-1997 completion date for *Daikatana*. Rather than roll our own—creating a new engine from scratch—we planned to use the *Quake* engine. The advantage was clear. First, I believed it was still the most advanced engine on the market, and I knew it would be a while before something more advanced came along to take its place. Second, it would relieve the team of the all-tech upheavals that so many companies were facing by creating their own engines. Last, I knew everything there was to know about how it worked, and we could start developing gameplay immediately. I contacted Jay at id, asked about licensing the engine, and got a quick reply: $500K. We agreed—it would have cost far more to develop our own tech—and they sent over a CD with all the source code on it.

I anticipated the team would be at thirty people by the time we were fully ramped up, and I calculated the number of assets I hoped to include, how long it would take to create those assets, and how long it would take to integrate them into the game with code. I felt confident that with a team of thirty *and* a finished engine, we could hit my target completion date at the end of 1997. I didn't expect to do any engine modifications, so what was ahead of us was gameplay programming and asset creation. Things felt like they were coming together.

In early March, shortly after we closed the deal with id, Jay left for Epic Games. I gathered from Jay what I had heard from others—that the mood had turned somber and dark after I left, and it wasn't fun for him anymore. In addition, Mike Wilson being gone meant he was the sole business person again, and he did not want to deal with the crushing demands that the newly released *Quake* had brought, similar to the deluge we faced after *DOOM* and *DOOM II*. id was not going to hire more people in business, so he had enough of that and quit. I wished Jay well, and I was sure that both Mark Rein and Tim Sweeney were delighted to have Jay join them. Jay remains at Epic to this day. On my side, there wasn't any gloating over people leaving id. I knew that the company would survive, and as a cofounder, even if I wasn't there, I still wanted to see it succeed.

At Ion Storm, we remained both excited and focused. I finished the *Daikatana* design document and talked over its design with Tom. I felt that it was ambitious, but at the same time, its content roadmap was what I felt the FPS genre needed to mature. While we had deprioritized story in *DOOM* and *Quake*, as design director I felt a better story could be told when a game felt like an exciting rollercoaster, where the player discovered new content constantly and felt that their actions led to that.

As I said to Tom, "Why am I fighting the same enemy in the last level as I fought in the first level? Why aren't there new enemies throughout the game?" Moreover, why wasn't there a narrative design to pair with the game design?

I felt that narrative design was an area where FPS games fell behind their peers in other genres. At the time, shooters were still emerging, and the "graphics arms race" was on. Teams were competing to produce the best-looking and fastest shooters, with id being the clear front-runner. Some games, like *Duke Nukem 3D*, were pushing forward character design. Games like Eidos's own *Tomb Raider*, while not a shooter, showed how some components of a shooter could be married with narrative and character design to create a richer experience. For *Daikatana*, since we were using a licensed engine, it was imperative we differentiate in design. As a part of that, I wanted an epic storyline with time travel, fleshed-out characters, and many twists and turns. Feeling secure in the design and excited about the narrative's innovative potential, I hoped the industry would take note. While we still had yet to bring on a writer, I figured the story would require a body of assets to carry it, and so I planned for sixty-four monsters, twenty-four levels, and twenty-five weapons.

As the design gelled and the teams started to build, Mike Wilson came up with his first marketing plan, a "No Excuses" press tour where we would talk about our promise: If we screw this up, there were no excuses, because we were getting as much money and time as we needed to create the best games we could make. The primary goal was to get us in the media more, to elevate awareness around our new brand and the games we were making. It was a bold move, sure, but Mike had success with bold moves like id's Judgment Day, and we trusted him and his intuition. The No Excuses press tour landed us in some major magazines, including *TIME* and *Newsweek* later in the year.

Seeing ourselves in their pages, Tom and I felt the first pangs of concern. The June 23, 1997, *TIME* article proclaimed, "Everything Game Designer John Romero Touches Turns to Gore. And to Gold." It covered my history with id, our breakup, and touted all the things we thought would be great about *Daikatana*.[*]

"It's way too early for this," I said.

Tom looked up from *TIME* and nodded. "Yeah."

"I need to focus on making the game."

While we felt confident in our designs, and we had strong track records, there were a thousand ways for things to go wrong in the execution. Beyond that, companies close, relationships crumble, health fails. Coders at our core, we knew there were far too many variables to be flying our flag so high.

---

[*] To his credit, in the same article, Carmack predicted we would never make our shipping window, and he was right.

Looking at the magazine open in front of Tom, I added, "I can't believe I wore fucking shorts. Stupid."

The hype train was just warming up as we headed into April. In another attempt to build awareness for the company and embrace the hard-edged nature of first-person shooters, Mike thought we needed to make a huge statement before the Electronic Entertainment Expo, better known as E3. The expo was the see-and-be-seen event of the game industry calendar, with companies setting up booths to show off their current games and to announce their upcoming releases. GT Interactive had a huge *Quake* booth in 1996, the year after the show first started. E3 was closed to the public and open only to members of the press and industry, and it drew tens of thousands of attendees to the Los Angeles Convention Center each year. Mike contacted Richards Group R&D, the same group that worked on id's advertising, and we were fortunate enough to land Sasha Shor, the ad executive who created the *Quake* packaging, font, and logo.

Mike was thrilled at the advertisement she created. I suspect readers already know what the advertisement was.

John Romero's About to Make You His Bitch.
Suck It Down

Mike brought the ad to me. It was evident that he was hyped by what he saw. I looked at the ad, blinked, and leaned back in my chair. I laughed, a weird uncomfortable laugh.

"I mean, that's not something I would say, if that's what you're getting at."

"You say all kinds of shit when you're deathmatching!" he replied.

"But I wouldn't say that. I don't think people reading the ad will think it's cool or funny. It's insulting and makes me sound like an asshole. I wouldn't say that."

"Don't be a pussy," Mike said.

"It's my name on the ad."

I scrolled back through Mike's advertising campaigns in my head. He thought outside the proverbial box, and I had to admit that his efforts got results.

"I wouldn't say something like that," I repeated.

The look on Mike's face said only one thing: *It's fucking awesome.*

I begrudgingly agreed. "Okay, marketing is your job, so I guess I'll let you do it." Mike left the office, ecstatic.

As the Bitch ad made its way toward publication, more buzz about Ion Storm appeared in *Computer Gaming World*, then the number-one publication for the game industry, the *Wall Street Journal*, and *Fortune*. *TIME* put me in the magazine *again* and named me one of the fifty Cyber Elite. *Fortune* called Ion Storm one of the country's twenty-five "Cool Companies." On the one hand, it was great to see that people had such interest. It certainly helped with our recruiting for prospective team members. On the other hand, Tom and I felt it was too much too soon. We should be making games, not press, especially since the "No Excuses" line had been drawn in the sand. We'd already had plenty enough time in the spotlight.

Not everyone, it seemed, felt that way. Todd wanted to be promoted in ads, too, so he asked Mike how that could happen. Mike contacted our PR firm, TSI Communications, and they workshopped a few ideas before landing on a series of "image ads" of the Ion Storm top level team: Mike, Bob, and us four founders. The image ads looked like film strips with three to four photos of us on each strip.

Seeing the proofs, I felt it was ridiculous and said so. "Why are we doing this? We're not advertising our games. It just looks pretentious."

Others pushed back. "It's new. Don't worry about it. No one's done it before, and it's cool."

It was new, and no one had done it before, that was true. But was it necessary? An argument was made that Tom and I were so closely associated with id that we needed to establish our own brand as a company, and, as I understood it, Todd didn't want Ion Storm to be known as just "John and Tom's" company. I didn't buy that.

"I think the game is the brand, and if the game does well, people will know about the people behind the game," I said.

As founders, our goals were split. Tom and I were not comfortable with Todd's apparent vision of what we needed to be focusing on at the start, particularly the image ads. All the hype in such high-profile places created more pressure for us than pleasure. I thought about the EA "We See Farther" advertisement from 1983, which featured eight game developers who created games published by EA. To me, that ad was an exception. The ad was selling EA as a company in an attempt to lure other software artists to join them. That made sense. This? Less so.

We believed press and players were interested in the games we were developing, and so returned to that as our focus. In April, we announced via press release that Tom Hall was working on his new game, *Anachronox*. It began, "Ion Storm isn't just playing around." The press loved it, but news of the company itself was still center stage. Ken Brown at *Computer Gaming World* called Ion "the most exciting new company in computer gaming."

And then the "Bitch" ad dropped.

It was like a needle being scratched across a record. The reaction was swift and visceral. Entire armies of online fans pivoted into righteously angry mobs typeshouting, "Who the fuck does John Romero think he is?" Game developers who once respected me turned away. Pissed off op-ed pieces appeared on fan sites and forums. The ad hit as far off marketing's mark as possible. I felt terrible, of course, but there was no coming back from it. No amount of "Yes, that was a dumb idea" and "We shouldn't have done that" was going to save it. (I'll share some reflections on this later.)

In spite of the swirling "Bitch ad" mayhem, we pushed forward with hiring for our three teams. I planned to staff mine mostly from the mod community. At this point, I already had three modders on the team, and I was on the lookout for even more. I knew the mod community was passionate about making levels—after all, they made levels for free for the pure pleasure of it. We had received a ton of résumés and sample levels, and I was busy playing through those while also taking note of modders getting a lot of attention in the growing *DOOM* and *Quake* communities.

Daikatana was designed to have four episodes: "Future Japan," "Ancient Greece," "Medieval Norway," and "Near-Future San Francisco," and we were moving forward on their designs. The level designers were up to speed with the level editor, QERadiant, and we decided to focus on making a map in episode three, the Medieval Norway Plague Village. Kee had spent a month learning the *Quake* codebase and was changing the menu system to *Daikatana's* look as we approached our upcoming E3 demo milestone in early June. It was a short time frame between the start of the game's development and its E3 debut, but we were determined to make as good an "early look" showing as possible. We included explosive barrels, a crossbow, a snow weather effect, and made sure all the movement felt like a fast-action FPS.

With our three games—*Daikatana, Anachronox,* and *Doppelganger*—on track at Ion Storm, Mike approached us in early May with an idea to grow the company. He wanted to start a publisher, and he even had a name for it: Ion Strike.

"We already have a deal for six games with Eidos," I said. "That will keep us busy for at least four years. It doesn't make any sense to start a publisher right now."

Mike wasn't so sure. He thought if we hurried up and got through our initial three games, we could start making games and publishing them for ourselves. The funding model in the game industry traditionally looks like this: Publishers put up the money to develop, publish, and market the game, usually dividing up the development payments over many performance-based milestones. In return for their investment, they recoup a multiplier of that money via game sales, usually two, three, or even four times their investment. Once that's recouped, developers start seeing royalties on sales. From a financial standpoint, publishers take the lion's share of the risk, and due to this also take the lion's share of the revenue

Regardless of the perceived potential upside, we didn't have the means, money, or manpower to start a publisher at the time. Publishers also had active accounts with all the big box retail and distribution companies, something that was critical back in the mid-1990s before there was widely available digital distribution on platforms like Steam. I appreciated his initiative, but it wasn't something we could do. It just didn't feel like a cool move to create our own publisher to compete with a publisher that had just committed $22 million to our development studio.

It wasn't a decision we could dwell on because we were all hands on deck for our first trip to E3 to show off *Daikatana*. There's no way to overstate the spectacle of E3. Every major publisher has a booth set up, each with banks of monitors showing off the latest games. The audioscape is sometimes deafening, with multiple games competing for attention across expansive aisles. Company representatives are handing out T-shirts, headbands, posters, and press kits while meeting rooms are available to give hands-on, private demos to select media. While the show floor is open during working hours, the dinner meetings, post-dinner meetings, and the after-hours networking go on late into the night. Mike had arranged for us to have a massive *Daikatana* booth—funded by Eidos but ours alone. The booth was constructed of an open metal frame with a large gray-and-auburn wall behind it. Multiple machines allowed people a chance for hands-on play, and TV monitors were hung high so others could watch. There were even character standees in the booth for people to pose next to and get their picture taken with.

After three months of work using the *Quake* engine, we were happy to give people their first look at *Daikatana*, albeit one without any monsters—just a snow level with weapons and barrel explosions working. The goal was to let the press see that we were in active development and give them a feel for the environmental design of the game and to discuss plans for its overall game design. (By the standards of any other game, showing off *Daikatana* at this early state was highly unusual, but we had also been open about the start of its development, and our marketing had been aggressive in getting knowledge of our company and games out there.)

During a break, I took a tour of the show floor, looking at games that were on display from other companies. I was, of course, particularly curious to see what id was showing, and headed over to their booth. Even from ten feet away, I could see that something different was on the screen, and everything else faded into the background. It was *Quake II*.

It looked amazing—next-level amazing. After a year of development, *Quake II* featured colored lights and showed off 3D acceleration. Comparatively speaking, *Daikatana* looked bad in software-rendered mode. *There is no way I can release* Daikatana *in 1997 with* Quake *tech*, I thought. *It would look ancient in comparison!* I decided right then to delay it so that I could use *Quake II*'s engine. Obviously, I'd have to talk with id about it, but no matter what, *Daikatana* couldn't go out the door looking like it was from the last tech century. I complimented Kevin on the engine improvements, told him I was blown away, and that I'd follow up about the license after.

The show continued. There were a lot of interviews, and I saw lots of other games, but for me, E3 was really about *Quake II*. It's as if I had seen only one game and talked to only one person.

Our teams were growing, and we needed to get a bigger office space than our current twenty-person box in the Quadrangle. Mike was out searching for spaces, and in late June told us he'd found a perfect spot for our growing company: the fifty-fourth and fifty-fifth floors of the Chase Tower. Seeing the space was breathtaking—it sported a panoramic view of Dallas and the fifty-fifth floor even had a glass ceiling. It had also never been occupied before. It wasn't usable as an office yet because it was all cement floors with glass walls and ceilings, but it was a beautiful space. Nonetheless, I was hesitant. I recalled the offices I had visited during our pitching tour. Activision's and Origin's offices were grand, and they definitely made an impression, which from a marketing point of view was important. As a development company, though, I wasn't sure we needed that. I expressed my hesitation, not just about the scope of the place, but about its price tag and the amount of money it would take to turn the space from its current state into something functional for game developers. Even my rough mental estimates were far above what we had budgeted. Mike assured me he would get Eidos to foot the bill for the rent and for renovating the space, and true to his word, he actually did.

He crafted a proposal for Eidos to build out the top two floors of the skyscraper. They agreed to it, enthusiastically even, because they didn't have a true flagship office to compete with other publishers. The Ion Storm office would be that office, towering above Dallas with a commanding view of its skyline, 360 degrees around. In addition to having the option to hold key meetings there, Eidos planned to house their QA under Ion's roof. With Eidos on board, we temporarily moved into Chase Tower's thirtieth floor. It was a substantial office space and necessary with all our new hires coming in. We began working with an architect to get the fifty-fourth and fifty-fifth floors designed, with an estimated move-in date of January 1998. At first, it seemed impossible that we would fill the space, but as our teams began to grow, we knew it was certainly possible.

In early August, Todd heard rumblings that 7th Level was in trouble. Rumor was that they might go bankrupt, and with that, Todd's former team would be out of their jobs. Seeing a potential opportunity, Todd said he wanted to approach 7th Level about buying *Dominion*. Purchasing the game, he figured, would get his game done much faster than if he fully developed *Doppelganger* from scratch. Plus, it would keep people in jobs. From his perspective, it was a win-win-win.

I remembered seeing *Dominion* when I first visited 7th Level. "How much do you think it will take to finish it?" I asked.

He thought for a minute about where the game was when he last worked on it. As best he could figure, it would take a couple months and $50,000. The game was close to being finished.

Mike was all for it since it got us closer to creating our own publisher. In his eyes, purchasing *Dominion* "burned an option quickly" if we were able to get it done in just three months.

"I don't care about 'burning options,'" I said. "If *Dominion* has a chance of succeeding soon, then let's get *Dominion*, but I don't want to get *Dominion* for any other reason."

I still wasn't interested in Ion Strike, nor was I ready to move to a publishing business. In fact, I enjoyed working with Eidos because they really believed in us, put up lots of money, and deserved to be rewarded for that. Starting a publishing company would most certainly splinter our focus and derail our efforts to make great games. I also suspected Eidos would kill the deal if we formed a publisher that competed with them, even indirectly.

Todd was confident that he could reach a deal with 7th Level and get *Dominion* done before returning to work on *Doppelganger*. Given that the last we heard from 7th Level was via a lawyer and a lawsuit, I was dubious that they'd agree to anything, must less welcome a conversation on it. However, in the end, they did. 7th Level sold us the game for $1.8 million and allowed us to bring on the team. Given that we received $3 million to make the game, it seemed like a wise business move. Particularly if Todd finished the game in the time he stated.

A few months after E3, I reached out to Kevin as promised to discuss the *Quake II* engine for *Daikatana*. He wasn't sure when they would ship exactly, but he hoped it would be by Christmas. All signs were that they were on track, and he thought that we would have the tech in our hands by early 1998. It was ironic to once again be waiting for *Quake, albeit Quake II*, but the wait was going to be more than worth it. In the meantime, the *Daikatana* level designers were working in the *Quake* engine to build out the levels. Once we got *Quake II*'s source, we would move the levels over into its editor and adjust the levels to show off the new lighting. It would be a bit more work, but we certainly weren't blocked. We were already seeing the improved lighting in our imaginations.

During this time, Jeff Wand, an artist on the team, got word from a friend of his that the entire Austin office at Looking Glass Studios had been cut loose. That friend had been an artist there. I'd long been familiar with Looking Glass, of course, which was cofounded by Paul Neurath. Years earlier, I had a chance to cofound a company with Paul, when both of us were at Origin. He left to start his own studio, Blue Sky Productions, and I left to start mine. In the years since, Blue Sky Productions had flourished, and their early game, *Ultima Underworld*, had become a landmark game for RPG players. *Ultima Underworld* brought the studio a lot of success and renown. Warren Spector, a longtime producer at Origin Systems who worked on everything from *Ultima* to the *Wing Commander* series, had left Origin to join Paul at Blue Sky Productions. Eventually, the company merged with another, and its name became Looking Glass Studios, but Warren continued doing what Warren does, making great games. He produced *System Shock*, which launched in 1994, and became general manager of Looking Glass Austin. In spite of its successes, however, Looking Glass was falling on hard times, and the studio was cutting Warren and his team loose. I knew Warren and knew of his reputation. I wasn't exactly sure how he got great things done, but I did know that when he was at the helm, games turned out great.

I talked to Mike and Tom, and then called Warren and asked if Mike and I could come down and pitch him on joining Ion Storm.

"I'm just about to sign a deal with EA," he said. He laughed and added, "Literally. I am holding the pen, and the contract is in front of me."

"Don't sign it!" I said. Of course, he was free to do whatever he wanted, but I hoped I could delay his decision. "Let me pitch you on what we can do for you at Ion Storm."

He agreed, and we wasted no time hitting the road.

Three hours later, I arrived at his Jollyville office and saw his team sitting outside on the steps—ten game devs including Warren. They represented all disciplines and were interested in hearing what we had to say. I wasn't sure why we weren't going inside, but I suspected it was because Warren wanted his entire team to be a part of the decision, and they didn't have a meeting room large enough to hold us. It was a nice day, anyway, so none of us seemed to mind.

At the time, they were working on AIR, the "Austin Internet Roleplaying Game." They were using the *Dark Project* game engine. Looking Glass planned to take the source and assets and send it back to the home studio to complete. It's a somber thing to lose your game, whether it's canceled, moved to another studio, or, sometimes, released and pushed out the door before it's ready. Creating a game is a massive effort. You put so much of your creative energy into it, and having that game taken away is painful. I could see that pain on this team's faces.

I pitched Warren and his team on what we could do for them. Most importantly, I promised Warren he could have the right-size team, a long enough development timeline, and run his own office in Austin, separate from the Dallas office.

"You can do whatever you want, and I will make sure no one gets in your way. You'll have enough money and enough time. I trust your process."

He looked at me like he was looking at a unicorn.

"Seriously?"

"Seriously."

"Are you . . . I have your word? Are you sure? You realize what you're saying."

Warren has recounted this moment in many interviews, when he was given not just a green light but a blank check and all the runway he needed.

"Yes, I trust your process."

"Well, okay then." He laughed and looked around at his team. They'd gone from the lowest game-dev low—out of a job and having their game taken away from them—to a great high. I really did believe in Warren and his team. I knew that Warren could make a great game if he had the right conditions for success. When I left, Warren and his team were creatively excited and wildly exhausted from the roller coaster they'd been on that day. I was elated that he and his team agreed to join us. I felt like Looking Glass had dropped a diamond in Austin.

Shortly thereafter, Mike headed to the UK for a trade show and, while there, met up with the Eidos execs to lay out our current development plan and trajectory. Eidos had signed us to three games with options on an additional three. In doing so, their expectation was that we would work on three games, and as one neared completion, we would pitch another until our six games were finished. *Daikatana, Dominion,* and *Anachronox* were currently in development. Warren's team at Ion Austin was now working on *Deus Ex*, then called *Shooter: Majestic Revelations*. *Doppelganger* was also still in development, though it was put on pause so Todd could finish *Dominion*. The last game on the second slate of three was *Daikatana 2*. According to *Masters of Doom,* Mike told Eidos, "Here they are. Take them or leave them."[*] This put Eidos in a tricky spot. It seemed that Mike hoped they would say no to funding five games simultaneously so that we would be free of the second slate commitment and could move into publishing our own games. Paying for the simultaneous development of five games was a huge investment of cash for Eidos, but also a risky proposition for a new game development studio. Developing three games simultaneously was tricky enough for a new studio. Five was nuts. To add rain to the river, *Daikatana* had just been delayed, and *Dominion* wasn't going to make its hoped for two-months-or-so deadline either! Yet, if Eidos passed on any game, we were free of that option.

Eidos was backed into a corner. After discussing it internally, they called Todd Porter to complain about Mike's stance. It was obvious they were not pleased. Todd called a meeting of the owners and relayed what he had been told. I think everyone took a moment to take it in and think. We were all concerned about upsetting the sole funder of our games and the ramifications it could have. By now, we were

---

[*]   I was not at the meeting, and so trust this retelling.

around fifty people including the Austin office, and we wouldn't have done anything to jeopardize everyone's employment by pushing our publisher into a corner. I certainly wasn't interested in losing Eidos. I really liked working with them, and I wanted to stick with them through these first games and then the second slate. It made no sense to me that he would allegedly offer them an ultimatum on the last three games just to "burn those options," particularly since we had decided against forming a publisher. When Mike returned from the UK, Todd and I met with him and told him to stop upsetting Eidos. As owners, we wanted to stick with them, and we didn't want to do anything to jeopardize the company. We knew Mike was eager to start a publisher, but now was not the time.

At home, things were good. Beth was still busy setting up our new home and enjoying the space it provided. It was unlike anything either of us had lived in before, something I had designed and had custom built. There wasn't a day that I didn't come home and think, *I live here?* I had a large office where all the game stuff was—my PCs, consoles, pinball machines, and even a pool table—so that it was out of Beth's view. While she enjoyed the spoils that games brought, having games all over the home was another matter. It was also at this time that we got some wonderful news—she was expecting. We hadn't been planning on having a child, but we were delighted. Our baby was due in May.

As we headed into the fall, the first visible signs of discontent in the teams began to emerge. While we had had our disagreements as owners, sure, morale in the various teams seemed okay. However, Mike let us know otherwise. He took me and Tom out to lunch and told us point blank: Our teams did not like Todd.

"Our teams? How are they even interacting with Todd?" I asked.

Mike shared a bevy of complaints, most of which took us by surprise. Todd, it seemed, was allegedly a military-style leader, referring to people on his team as units, soldiers, or troops, and ordering them around accordingly. I heard that he apparently called my producer, who initially put him on speakerphone, but quickly muted the call as soon as Todd started yelling. The team also had lesser issues with Jerry and shared concerns about how the art department was run. I was hearing all these complaints secondhand, of course, but in a nutshell it was clear that people didn't like how they were being treated. The complaints filtered through the teams, and the sentiment turned against them. Truth be told, Tom and I were not big fans of Todd at this point either. There had been lots of minor clashes and differences of opinion over leadership styles and management boundaries. So, we considered our options. The weight of these complaints, our own misgivings, and *Dominion*'s delay all pointed toward an exit sign.

"So that's it, then?" I said.

Mike and Tom nodded.

"Okay, then. Next week, I'll let him go."

Over the weekend, I thought about what I'd say to Todd, how I'd break it to him. While I trusted Mike's information, at the same time, I felt Todd deserved a chance. After all, we hadn't talked to him about any of these issues, and felt it was only fair to allow him an opportunity to improve. Beyond that, Todd was an owner, and it would take a lot to change the ownership structure of the company. *If I fire him, how will Eidos take this?* I wondered. I felt it was best if we stayed the course. On Monday, I met with Todd to express our concerns and to say the obvious: that people didn't like a dictatorial style of communication, and that being mean is no way to get a game made. At this point, things were feeling somewhat frayed at the leadership level, except between Tom and me, of course.

"I need to be working on the *actual game*," I said to Tom.

"And not playing a turn-based strategy game in, you know, the company," he said.

"Exactly."

In December, a friend from Ritual Entertainment contacted me about a fax he'd seen regarding investment in a new publishing company called God-Games. According to the fax, GodGames, which I'd never heard of, was formed by Harry Miller, then-CEO of Ritual Entertainment, and Mike Wilson—our Mike Wilson! My contact shared that Harry had been spending a lot of time talking to Mike lately.

I was livid. *Had he started his own publishing company without our knowledge? While still working for us?* We knew Mike was eager to start a publishing company, but it wasn't the right time for Ion Storm to do it. *If he'd so desperately wanted to do it on his own, why didn't he just quit Ion Storm and then do it?* I was blown away that this happened behind our backs. *How long had this been going on?* We held an emergency meeting, and we unanimously agreed on the next course of action.

I drove Mike to our lawyer's office and fired him there.

Tom and I were so incredibly sad, shocked, and disappointed. We really liked Mike. At best, it seemed uncool. At worst, it was a possible breach of contract with both Ion Storm and with Eidos. We never saw it coming, though in retrospect, Mike was always driven, so maybe we should have.

It was a difficult time. Mike was a trusted part of the team at the leadership level who was responsible for everything from advertising to finding our office space, and I had worked with him since he entered the industry. Lots of people on the team loved him. He was fun to work with, and he cared about people, too. Obviously, in wanting to start a publisher, Mike was determined and knew what he was after. Years later, he would have massive success with Devolver Digital, a publisher that provides a platform for many independent game developers. He's helped a lot of people along the way. The start at GodGames, however, was problematic for us. When we broke news of his departure to Eidos, not surprisingly, they were relieved. Mike and Ion Storm issued a joint press release in which he discussed his excitement, and I wished the best for him in his new role.*

Quake II launched on December 9, 1997. What I'd seen at E3 was still mesmerizing me, and I couldn't wait to get the game installed and check it out in action. I spent hours exploring its levels and cataloging the differences between *Quake II* and its predecessor. All of these were things I needed to consider for *Daikatana*. I contacted Kevin to congratulate him on the launch and on the incredible reception. It was all anyone was talking about online and even at Ion Storm. I could tell that Kevin was pleased, and by extension, everyone at id. It felt odd to see a series that I had co-created going on without me, sure, but it also felt fantastic to see it *going on*. There are other ways any of these games could have gone, and I'd rather someone be advancing *Wolfenstein*, *DOOM*, and *Quake* than leave them sitting on a repo to collect dust. The id team had done a fantastic job with *Quake II*, and I was sure that Carmack was pleased with how it turned out. I couldn't help but wonder what his next innovation would be. True to id's pattern, they released a game, then a sequel, and then Carmack started work on a new engine. This would be the first time that I wouldn't be there on day one.

Kevin let me know that id would provide us with the *Quake II* source early in the new year, so I talked it over with the team before we broke for the holidays. To my surprise, the team didn't like the idea of switching engines. They were worried about losing progress and the amount of things that would need to be changed to work in the new engine. I understood their concerns. No one likes to redo work again and again, but I explained my reasoning.

"*Daikatana* is using last-gen technology. If we don't switch engines, *it* will look ancient in comparison, and *Quake II* is what everyone will be comparing it to. This gives us a huge advantage."

I demoed the games next to one another. Looking at *Quake II* next to *Daikatana*, the team understood why it was critical to switch engines and got on board. We made plans for how we might move our existing game over to the new technology.

As 1997 wound to a close, everyone was ready for a break. The year had been a challenging one, between the inner-company squabbles, the teams not liking

---

* The press release can be viewed on the Blue's News archives: bluesnews.com/archives/dec97-1.html

their leadership, and most of all, Mike leaving. In all the twists and turns of the year, there was a bright spot, of course—Ion Storm Austin. Warren and his team had begun work on the game that would become *Deus Ex*.

I could not wait to enjoy some time with the boys, my family, and some games. By now, Michael and Steven were nine and eight, respectively, and we enjoyed playing games together, particularly *F-Zero*, *Super Mario World*, and *Street Fighter II*. They looked forward to welcoming their new baby sister, Lillia. My mom and stepdad visited from California, and I had a blast showing my mom around the local hot spots, and we treated her to a shopping trip. I wish she would have really treated herself, but my mother is, above all things, practical, and so even at my insistence to the contrary, all she got herself was a new pair of shoes.

Closing the door on 1997 was a necessary transition. We were looking forward to the new year and the things that it had in store for us as a company.

In January, we moved into the top floors of Chase Tower. The build-out cost Eidos $2.5 million. It was an incredible space—22,000 square feet across the two floors. Designed by a well-known firm, it had arcade machines, a pool table, a Ping-Pong table, a full THX movie theater, a locker room and shower, a motion-capture stage, and model display cases. The floors in the lobby were custom inset terrazzo. While it was far more elaborate than I expected to be, it wasn't too far from other flagship spaces I'd toured.*

Still, walking through the doors for the first time, I felt incredibly anxious, the same way I felt when I first drove my Testarossa. I was worried that I had to be not just successful, but *hugely* successful to pay off the renovations on top of all the other money we were spending on products in development. Even though Eidos agreed to fund the space, it was reasonable to assume that they would want a return on that investment from Ion Storm, currently the sole tenant. Watching the team walk in, the concerns momentarily faded. Everyone was smiling as they passed through the doors. It was genuinely a beautiful space, a space you'd feel good about working in. Everyone moved in with their boxes of figurines, picture frames, and memorabilia. My team was on the fifty-fifth floor on the north side; the *Anachronox* team took up the south side. The *Dominion* team was on the fifty-fourth floor's northeast corner. The first few days were a honeymoon, of sorts, with everyone eagerly checking out the space, playing pool, and taking in the incredible views of the Dallas skyline, especially at night.

---

* Most flagship offices today also have a theater for employee meetings and for screening builds and game cinematics, a gym, and motion-capture spaces. If anything, Ion Storm's office was only missing a full canteen and a gallery. We certainly didn't expect it to be as amazing as it was, and we felt amazed that Eidos had kitted it out as much as they had.

Unfortunately, it became apparent almost immediately that the space had not been designed to suit a technology company.

"I can't see what's on the screen."

An artist on the fifty-fifth floor pointed at his monitor. The sun blazed through the glass roof. Whatever was on his screen was washed out.

"I can't work like this," he said.

He was right. I couldn't believe that in all the details of designing the space, from the pool table to the theater, this had been overlooked. Sure, the design firm had crafted canopies over the tops of desks, but the canopies didn't do the job. We contacted them, and they arranged for huge blinds to be installed along the entire glass ceiling of the office. Even *these* weren't opaque enough, and so the space was still bright. The blinds had cost a fortune, however, and Eidos was done paying for solutions. We had to figure out what to do with what we had, and that meant, at least in the short term, getting felt to cover the cubes of people affected by the light. Sadly, this became the long-term solution. What was once a state-of-the-art flagship office was now, at least in part, a tent city.

With Mike gone, we appointed Todd CEO. *Dominion* was by now complete and on its way through the process of duplication and distribution. It wasn't a decision of opportunity as much as it was a decision of necessity. More than anything, I needed to focus on *Daikatana* and Tom needed to focus on *Anachronox*, not on running the company. Neither Tom nor I were too worried about anything going seriously wrong. After all, any big decisions still required board of director approval.

In February, we got the source for *Quake II*, and I was eager to dig in. I was surprised that the codebase had changed so much from *Quake*. I knew there were some changes to lighting and rendering, but the changes to its core tech ran deeper than that. The programmers got it compiling on their PCs, and once everyone had had a look at it, we gathered to plan for our tech and art transition from *Quake* to *Quake II*.

Before I could say it myself, Kee spoke up. He had been working on *Daikatana* as its lead programmer since the beginning and had spent months learning the *Quake* codebase.

"It's massively different," he said. "It's going to be a lot of work."

We itemized the work in a spreadsheet to quantify "massively." Clearly, this was a sign that the project wasn't going out the door as quickly as we hoped. There's no such thing as a simple conversion from one engine to another, and this was to be my first hard lesson. Still, as a team, we knew we had to do it or risk having *Daikatana* look like the game version of Steve Buscemi in *30 Rock* saying, "How do you do, fellow kids?" So, we stuck to that plan. We discussed the challenge and problem with Eidos, and they were supportive. We converted our original budget of $3 million per game to a run-rate model that came in at $1.2 million per month and covered all one hundred employees working across our various games. This allowed us more flexibility in our budget to get the games across the line. In spite of the hiccups, there were signs that things were going well in other areas, and we were close to releasing our first game: *Dominion: Storm Over Gift 3*.

When Todd originally pitched us on acquiring the game, I recall he was sure it would sell a half million units. Its combination of science fiction and military themes was popular among gamers, and he was confident that he could pull off a hit game (or at least a good one). I didn't have a reason to doubt him—not then, anyway—and builds of the game seemed promising. If anything, I felt we were fortunate to get the game for $1.8 million, particularly considering that Eidos had given us $3 million to make it. The delays took their toll, however, not just on the game itself, but on its ballooned budget and its release date: May 31, 1998. The new release date meant it would launch two months after *Starcraft*, which was advertising a March 31, 1998, launch date. That concerned us. *Starcraft,* by Blizzard Entertainment, looked fantastic in every preview, and they had a history of greatness. After all, *Diablo* and *Warcraft* had owned their genres. Todd and his team continued to work toward their gold master.

Meanwhile, Tom was filling out his *Anachronox* team with programmers, artists, and designers, some of whom were shared between my team and his. His team had a chill vibe because Tom himself is a laid-back guy, something his team loved about him as a leader. Progress on *Anachronox* was steady.

Warren and his team had finally outgrown the office I'd seen when I pitched him and had moved into a much bigger space elsewhere in Austin. He even added a reception area like we had in the Dallas office. I visited soon after Warren's team settled in, and I got to meet his latest hire, lead designer Harvey Smith, who had just come off the game *Fireteam*. Harvey seemed like a confident, intelligent, and experienced designer. I was happy Warren did such a great job at hiring. His team was learning the Unreal Engine technology while building out *Deus Ex*.

It's around this time that I received an email from an old colleague and friend, Ben Gokey. He was still at Raven, and he let me know that the *Heretic/Hexen* team wanted to leave and make games together. Once I left id, the control of the team at Raven was out of id's hands, and the various members were split apart and spread out onto three different teams at Raven. The reasoning, Ben told me, was that they made winning games, and if they put some of that "win" onto every team, they might get three winning games out of it. However, that magic was in the original group itself. They really liked working together, and since they couldn't do that at Raven, they wanted to do it somewhere else. Ben wondered if I had any ideas or opportunities. I gave it some thought.

The opportunity to secure a proven, experienced team for a future project seemed too good to pass up. I talked with Eidos, and we agreed to get started on a prototype for *Daikatana II*, hoping at some point we might have another game for them to start on or an in-house dev team for them to support. The start-up costs were $250K, and I arranged it. With that in place, they were able to leave Raven and form Human Head Studios.[*]

In the end, Eidos decided not to continue development on a *Daikatana II* prototype, and Human Head began work on other projects. The initial funding got them off the ground, though. I'll always be grateful to them for their work on *Heretic* and *Hexen* and for allowing me to play a small part in the studio's founding.

With lots of things swirling in the air around Ion Storm, my personal life was becoming more settled. I purchased a house for my boys and their mother, Kelly, in McKinney, Texas, and they moved from California. I felt so content having them so close to me. Instead of having to pack in as much as possible over a weekend or on a trip, we were able to spend much more time together. The boys were still into SNES games at the time, and Michael wanted to try out an RPG. I debated which RPG to introduce him to since he was only ten. I didn't want it to be too systemically complex. So, I started him on *Super Mario RPG*. He loved it, and so we decided that *Chrono Trigger* was next. As I mentioned, it's among my favorite games of all time, and it had the same effect on Michael. Years later, when Michael was twenty-six, I was able to introduce him to Hironobu Sakaguchi, the supervisor of *Chrono Trigger*, and the look on his face will always stay with me. In that moment, Michael met his hero. While Michael and I played *Chrono Trigger*, Steven was engaged in early experiments in level design using LEGO. He had a seemingly endless supply of them, and we built castles, manors, machines, and monsters, each with its own story. As a family, we were all looking forward to Lillia's pending arrival.

She was a beautiful baby, my first girl, and both Beth and I were delighted and grateful. I was planning to take some time off from work to support Beth and spend time with my new daughter. Ion Storm, however, had other plans, and the day after her birth, my team held a meeting with our then-COO Bob Wright. It seems the team had had it with how people were being treated and reportedly shared some patterns of unacceptable behavior and choice phrases Todd had used, more concerns about how Jerry ran the art department, and their frustration that I didn't do enough to address their issues in the first place. They'd lost faith that I would. I suspect the general state of *Daikatana*, its delays, and *Dominion*'s poor reception

---

[*] Human Head went on to do many great games, including *Prey* and *Rune*. In 2019, Human Head closed its doors and reopened with the same team and Roundhouse Studios.

exacerbated everything. They gave me an ultimatum: If Todd and Jerry didn't go, my entire team threatened to leave. I thought of Mike who had raised the red flag months earlier. Now, the situation had reached a head at the most inopportune time for me personally, but I also understood that they wouldn't have taken this step if they didn't feel they had to. Bob asked them to put it all in writing, and then I was told that he did something which still shocks me whenever I think of it. Rather than calling Tom and me to say he had a team emergency on his hands, he instead allegedly suggested that he could help set them up somewhere else if they quit or were fired.* When Tom got wind of it, he gave me a ring to let me know what was happening. I excused myself from Beth's room in the maternity ward, took a deep breath, and called Tom back.

"I can't believe this shit," is probably what I said. I don't recall precisely, but the gist of it was that Ion Storm felt like a company that made problems, not games. I fired Bob immediately, and he was formally dismissed on May 19. Bob sued Ion Storm and its partners alleging breach of fiduciary duties on May 22. *Masters of Doom*, the book by David Kushner, remembers it this way:

> On May 13, Sverre, Will, and six other members of Romero's team asked Bob Wright, Ion's chief operating officer, whom they had perceived as an ally back when he was working closely with Mike Wilson, to join them for lunch. They had an ultimatum for Romero, they said—Todd and Jerry had to go or they would walk out the door. Bob urged them to put their complaints in writing.
>
> Word about the meeting leaked back to Tom Hall—Bob had told the guys that he could help them to finance their own company if they did quit or get fired. Tom called Romero . . .
>
> "What the fuck?" Romero screamed when Tom told him about Bob's interference. "That's it. Bob fucked with my team. He's gone." Bob was fired the next week.

---

* Bob Wright disputed this version of events in a January 14, 1999, article in the *Dallas Observer*: "On the morning of May 13, Jonathan Wright, the programmer responsible for the artificial intelligence in *Daikatana*—making the computer characters smart—invited Bob Wright to lunch with eight other employees, mostly *Daikatana* team members. According to seven of the 10 who were at lunch, the *Daikatana* team was seriously disenchanted. (Two did not respond to requests for interviews, and one, Shawn Green, supports [Todd] Porter's version.) They wanted some changes, or they were ready to leave. 'I told them to be very concrete and to present their problems in writing to their supervisors,' recalls Bob Wright. 'I didn't think any more about it. On Friday, Porter comes in and confronts me, and goes off on how I've supposedly incited a riot . . . On Monday, when I came in, rumors were circulating that I was gone.' In the same article, Porter said, 'We fired our COO,' insists Porter. 'We fired him because he'd gone to [the *Daikatana* team] and told them that he could start another company with them.' "

The weight of the corporate struggles was taking its toll. I'd heard plenty of game-dev war stories by this point in my career, but I had a strong feeling that Ion Storm was setting a new low. We had a caustic environment on our hands, and we needed to protect the teams, but as equal owners, we couldn't just show Todd the door. Tom and I didn't have the shares to vote him out (our ownership was 50 percent to Todd and Jerry's 50 percent), and the company couldn't afford to buy Todd out, either. Tom and I realized that we'd made a critical mistake in handing over 50 percent ownership to Todd and Jerry. So we tried an approach that had yet to succeed—we talked to both Todd and Jerry, more sternly this time, and told Todd to fucking cool it. The situation was causing a lot of damage. I came into the office the next day and met with my team. They were so pissed and frustrated. They wanted something done, and I explained that we were going to do everything we could, but that pledge, as I'd soon see, wasn't really enough. As game modders and developers, their reasonable expectation was that they would spend their day making games, not hearing an owner yelling at their teammates. The *Anachronox* team started keeping to themselves more, keeping their heads down, trying to just stay out of the firing lines. News of the increasing instability in Dallas reached Ion Austin, of course, but Warren did what Warren does: He just kept making games, shielding his team via the geographical distance.

Into this maelstrom came *Dominion*'s retail release. Arriving just two months after the launch of *Starcraft*, it was doomed. Every review compared it unfavorably to *Starcraft*'s many strengths, and in light of the poor reviews, we heard that distributors were getting cancelations or changes to larger orders. Sales would certainly be affected. Todd planned to take the *Dominion* team onto *Doppelganger*, but Eidos pumped the brakes. There was no way they were going to put any more money into a Todd Porter game after *Dominion*'s poor showing. The *Dominion* team was split across the three existing teams—*Daikatana*, *Anachronox*, and *Deus Ex*. As it turned out, unfortunately, *Dominion* received no good reviews that I recall. For a team that was already feeling down, *Dominion*'s release was a nail in a morale coffin.

The media and Ion Storm's fans started to wonder what the hell was happening. The loss of senior leadership roles, a lawsuit, and now a poor release? People started to ask questions and point fingers. Forums sprung up to mock Ion Storm, our games and, of course, me. It was humiliating, but I understood that it was par for the course we were on.

Later that month, the Ion founders met with Eidos to see if they were interested in purchasing a part of the company. In spite of our challenges and rocky first release, Eidos held out hope for our future games. We had been in discussions for some time, but with recent happenings, Tom and I were more eager to finalize it than we had been. By now, Ion Storm had spent $15 million in development across all our games. As is normal in the industry, we would have to recoup a multiple of the $15 million development budget in sales before we would see any royalties. We discussed a deal to give Eidos 19 percent of the company in exchange for forgiving the $15 million development costs. Eidos pushed back, wanting majority control. Obviously, we'd see no money from the deal either way, and it would dilute each owner equally, but it would put the company on better footing. Talks advanced, but in the end, Eidos decided to stay the current course.

Before long, news of the potential deal, as well as its collapse, leaked to the press. Todd took it upon himself to talk to IT and to trace people's email activity to see who was talking.

"You've already got everyone on edge. That's not going to help," I said.

"And it's an invasion of privacy," Tom added. "I don't think that's cool."

Todd insisted that it was well within our rights to search people's work email, and, he insisted, wasn't the leak an invasion of *our* privacy?

"C'mon. No one is going to send a leak from their work email," I said. "We employ intelligent people. What's done is done. Declaring martial law isn't going to make anything better."

After the leak, the press could smell blood in the water, It was to be the beginning of a long and storied bad news cycle. *Dominion*'s failure and *Doppelganger*'s cancellation were newsworthy tidbits, and various outlets began openly wondering where the much-hyped *Daikatana* was, predicting its demise as well. Internally, some employees, disgruntled at the general state of affairs and unable to solve institutional problems the normal way (they had brought them to us in management multiple times by now), started to feed the flames. Dallas was such a small scene and mostly a first-person shooter scene, so news traveled quickly through the whisper networks. People were leaving regularly, and I had to fire a senior member of my team who stopped making progress and seemingly spent his days tossing cans over his partition wall and into the space between it and the glass window. (Eventually, he filled the entire space.) It turned out he had started a company on the side months earlier and was spending most of his time working on that. Each loss hit the team hard, as it always does, and it hit me, too, because he was a friend, but he'd left me no choice.

Tom and I felt like we were in freefall, having gone over the edge of a cliff many months ago, an edge that we somehow didn't see (I see plenty in hindsight!). Our only choice was to keep our eyes open for a branch to grab on to or a safe landing spot for the team and the games. I would have killed for a "reload from your last checkpoint" option. We knew what we *needed to do*—work on our games and address the team's demand to get certain individuals out of the company—but we were not able to vote them out or pay them off, not at the current company valuation, anyway. It felt like an all-around no-win situation. We believed then that bringing our concerns before Eidos risked getting *everything* canceled, so we decided not to do it.

What I wish I could do at this point in the story is to begin the redemption arc and tell you how we found a solution and pulled victory from the jaws of defeat. I want to tell a story that is inspiring, a story where people banded together and saved a company. But Ion Storm's road leads nowhere but downhill. I learned a lot from it, and I will share some reflections in the coming pages. At this point, though, let me just say that a lot of great people passed through Ion's doors—for many, it was their first job—and eventually two great games would launch. As for me? Failure—especially public failure—brings with it a few gifts. The first of these is resilience. Though this period of my life was exceedingly difficult, it taught me that I can get through anything (and that my friendship and recurring partnership with Tom Hall is bulletproof). It's also shown me the incredible power of humility. You are only as good as your last game, no matter who you are. This was a lesson I needed to learn.

In August, I separated from Beth. Our house was large, and we had a baby, so I moved into my home office. We tried counseling a few times, and both of us thought we worked better apart than together. Five months later, once we had things sorted and stabilized, I moved out, and did right by Beth and our daughter. I supported and cared for both, and today, Lilia lives a few blocks from me here in Ireland.

The same month we separated, a report that I was murdered, by a headshot no less, spread like wildfire on the internet. Stories were everywhere: "Romero Buys the Farm" was one of many headlines. I had done a photoshoot for *Texas Monthly*'s "Top Twenty Texans" issue, and the resulting photograph was obviously convincing. Because of the genre of games I'd made, the photographer thought a picture of me as a corpse on a steel table in a morgue would be perfect. A makeup artist even added a gunshot wound. Somehow, that photo found its way online. I was at work late at night when the news came in, and it was scary to see the reaction from the internet. Some people thought it was just a publicity stunt and were pissed. Others were truly afraid that I'd been shot in the head and killed. I am sure that more than a few jokes were also made, but because the picture was so realistic, the concern was genuine. I found out when a reporter called the office to ask us for a statement.

"I'm not dead," I assured him.

"You only wish you were," Tom said later.

Those who hadn't yet published articles on my death adjusted their headlines and stories, and they appeared regularly throughout the end of 1998.

With team members shifting around between the projects—and me still very much alive—things were starting to move forward on *Daikatana*. A new lead programmer joined the team, and he jumped straight in, getting both weapons and enemies working. He had expertise in AI, and it gave everyone on the team a lift. We knew we wouldn't ship this year, particularly with the move to the *Quake II* engine, but things were progressing. We gave out bonuses to thank people for staying the course and to give a bit of a morale boost to the teams who had, by now, weathered a bad launch, a project cancellation, and upheaval at the senior level, not to mention the shitshower of bad press. Despite our repeated earlier talks, our failure to take action on previous team concerns meant we continued to receive complaints about Todd here and there.[*]

To let Warren run his office without interference, I visited only occasionally. I didn't want him to feel like we needed to watch his every move, but each time I went down to Austin he was always able to show off some great-looking graphics and fun and interesting gameplay. *Deus Ex* was turning out to be something special. I was particularly impressed with Harvey Smith. Harvey had the ability to really see a story through gameplay and craft the narrative and game design in such a way that players felt fully immersed in the game's world. Back at home base, *Anachronox* was also looking impressive. Tom had a complex camera system built for his writing team to create elaborate cinematics, and they were truly some of the best I had seen in real time in a PC game. Things seemed to be stabilizing for us, but that stability was really just my own blind optimism.

On November 20, 1998, eight people on my team received an email from Mike Wilson. It read: "The monkey has landed." Mike had just cashed the check Todd had sent him to settle his partnership taxes from Ion Storm. The email was the sign the group had been waiting for. They called me into a meeting in the main conference room. All eight were gathered around the table. One acted as spokesperson. He told me that they couldn't continue working under the current conditions with Todd and Jerry in their positions, and that they were leaving that day to form Third Law Interactive and would be working with Mike Wilson at Gathering of Developers (GodGames). They left once they delivered the news.

---

[*]   As *Masters of Doom* describes it, apparently Todd thought I "was too nonconfrontational" which is fair, and "despite knowing that his own aggressive style could alienate those around him, [Todd] felt obliged to get the *Daikatana* team back into shape."

It was a lot to take in. I was genuinely sad to lose such a decent group of people with whom I'd worked for a while. I was pissed at and disappointed in myself. They had spoken up time and time again, so it's not like I could say I didn't see it coming. They gave me a chance, and I hadn't done what needed doing because I just didn't see a way around it. Doing nothing, however, was clearly the wrong answer. Mike gave them the opportunity to get out, and they took it. What Mike did, what they did, was just good, common sense.

I was resolved to rebuild the team, assess the game, and figure out how to go forward. It was horrible news, and I hoped that maybe this unintended changing of the guard might allow me to bring in some fresh, senior people to accelerate development. I started hiring coders and designers right away and began a full product assessment. I played through every level in production from beginning to end, the finished ones and the in-progress ones, and assessed their gameflow and construction. Many needed to be reworked. I stayed late revising episode one maps for weeks. I had to take some gigantic levels and cut them into pieces or just make them far smaller. I promoted Andrew Welch from the original *Dominion* team to be my lead programmer, by now the third one. He was level-headed and professional. He was the best lead programmer we had yet on the team.

On December 10, it was *DOOM*'s fifth birthday, and a celebration dinner was held at a restaurant in Addison with Jay Wilbur, Shawn Green, Tom Hall, John Carmack, Adrian Carmack, American McGee, Sandy Petersen, Dave Taylor, John Cash, and me all in attendance. After all Ion Storm had been through those last few months, it was nice to have a bunch of laughs with old friends. We had a great time. There was no animosity, and we got along well.

In January, I hired Chris Klie to be lead level designer. Chris had most recently worked on LucasArts's *Outlaws* and was a well-respected *DOOM* community level designer. He and I worked together to reassess the existing levels beyond episode one, both the new ones made in the *Quake II* engine and the older ones that had been brought over from *Quake*. Digging into the levels, we came to the realization that, as in episode one, several of them needed to be remade due to poor technical construction. So much time and work had been put into them. Although they played well (I had liked them when I did reviews with the previous level designers), but once Chris and I looked under the hood, they were built in a suboptimal way that choked the map-processing tools. What should have been a one-hour process took all day. Having Chris Klie was really helpful for identifying the issues and setting us on a path to fixing them.

At Chris's recommendation, I hired Stephen Ash from LucasArts to be my new lead programmer, the fourth one, after the third one left. Stephen turned out to be far and away the best programming hire we made. Volumetric fog was added to the engine, and the levels started to look better due to Chris and Stephen's work.

The new team finished moving the game completely over to the new *Quake II* engine, and on March 12, we released a multiplayer-only demo of *Daikatana*. We felt great about it. The players really liked the movement, air control, weapons, and levels. But even more than that, after the trials we faced over the last year, we felt like the Blues Brothers when they finally arrived at Daly Plaza—their car may have fallen to bits, but they got there.

CHAPTER 21

Columbine

The biggest shock of this entire time period came not from within the team or even the game industry, but from an incredibly tragic and senseless mass shooting in a school in Littleton, Colorado. Like everyone else, we watched the news in horror. It was wanton, senseless violence and destruction. Work stopped as people tuned into CNN, which was, by now, carrying live footage from the scene. Despite living in Texas at the time, I was not a fan of guns. I had already lost one family member to murder.

After the perpetrators committed their atrocity, *DOOM* became an unwitting scapegoat for their behavior. Dave Cullen's well-researched book, *Columbine*, mentions the game at least seven times, suggesting that, at age eleven, one of the perpetrators basically graduated from playing imaginary war games in the woods to *DOOM*. He "found the perfect virtual playground to explore his fantasies" with the game, Cullen writes. "His adversaries had faces, bodies, and identities now. They made sounds and fought back. [He] could measure his skills and keep score. He could beat nearly everyone he knew. On the Internet, the triumph of thousands of strangers he had never met. He almost always won . . ." That changed when he met his co-conspirator. According to Cullen, "They were an even match."

Cullen paints one of the perpetrators as obsessed with *DOOM*. He writes that he "hacked into the software and created new characters, unique obstacles, higher levels and increasingly elaborate adventures." It's a powerful description, and even more so without added context: Thousands and thousands of *DOOM* fans were doing the same thing—modifying the game, not "hacking" it, because id

Software encouraged fans to do exactly that. It wasn't unique behavior. Rather, it was a normal activity that produced only fun results for many. Here, however, the association was truly horrifying. To use anything—pencils, paper, software—as a pretext for mass murder was appalling.

The killers left behind a series of video tapes in which they discussed their lethal plans, which Cullen evidently watched. These "basement tapes" have never been fully released, but some clips have been made public. In one, the duo engage in a racist rant and name students they hope to kill. Then one of the killers, toting a gun, says: "We need a fucking kickstart. If we have a fucking religious war—or oil—or anything. We need to get a chain reaction going here. It's gonna be like fucking *DOOM*, man—after the bombs explode. Tick, tick, tick, tick . . . Haa! That fucking shotgun"—he kisses his gun—"straight out of *DOOM*."

DOOM was one of the many things they mentioned, from the LA riots to the Oklahoma City bombing to WWI and Vietnam. "Maybe we will even start a little rebellion or revolution to fuck things up as much as we can," one of the killers said. "I want to leave a lasting impression on the world."

I felt nauseated. I broke out in a literal cold sweat. I could not believe what I was hearing. They were obviously incredibly unstable, dangerous young men. I was horrified to even hear them mention *DOOM*. My shock at hearing *DOOM* in the discussion paled, of course, in comparison to the general sense of horror I felt—that we felt. I had two kids in school at the time. It's a tragic reality that school shootings are sadly not uncommon in the US now. When Columbine happened, however, it was supremely shocking, cataclysmic, and worldwide news. And to be clear, when a school shooting happens, it is still supremely shocking and cataclysmic, even if it no longer makes worldwide news.

With quotes like theirs, *DOOM* and the massacre were intertwined in the minds of the general public, news commentators, and US senators, who by now had already put video games in their censorship lists many times. I was horrified that this was even a part of the discussion. Ten years later, an academic friend of mine sent me a 2009 essay, the result of research into the writings of one of the killers by Dr. Peter Langman. The essay echoes a lot of the findings in Cullen's book, namely that video games, and *DOOM* and *Duke Nukem 3D* specifically, happened to be in the wrong place at the wrong time. The themes the killers repeatedly discussed were weapons, power, hatred of people they perceived hated them, and violent control.

I do not believe that video game violence causes real-life violent events. Multiple studies bear this out. As someone who endured physical assaults as a kid and lost a family member to murder, the discussion strikes me as well intentioned but not fruitful. There was a clear and obvious dividing line to me. Playing *Duck Hunt* and *DOOM* is quite different than firing a real gun at a real human being. I have played practically every video game on the planet. I've never even so much as spanked my children; I am a gentle father, friend, and husband. Images of violence have been everywhere for generations, in movies, on TV, in books and paintings. Blaming video games for sociopathic and psychopathic behavior in a society rife with violent imagery, guns, and mass shootings strikes me as problematic.

Years after the Columbine massacre, I met Brooks Brown, an insider who knew the killers and played *DOOM* with them. He let me know that there was so much more to the story and that our game was not responsible. It did not create the killers' break with reality and, ultimately, mortality. His book, *No Easy Answers: The Truth Behind Death at Columbine* chronicles his chilling experience. Brooks and I have become friends over the years, and him sharing his experience was both generous, courageous, and important. He believes *DOOM* had nothing to do with inciting their deranged behavior. As his book and Cullen's make clear, Brooks could easily have been a victim.

All this discussion, of course, is purely academic. Tragically, fifteen children died that day and a further twenty-four were injured. It remains one of the darkest days of my life, and like the rest of the world, I felt and still feel so incredibly sorry for every single person who lost their lives or lost someone they loved that day.

CHAPTER 22

Hitting Bottom

E3 kicked off in May 1999, a month earlier than normal. We were prepared to show off the latest work on *Daikatana* at the huge Eidos booth that featured all their upcoming games and recent releases. As always, E3 was a spectacle of sound, light, and just pure, endless energy. David Bowie even performed at the Eidos party! Members of the press and those in the trade looked forward to seeing what was on offer, and as game developers, we were eager to see what the competition was up to. Our section of the booth included a giant statue of Hiro Miyamoto, and computers were set up so we could give press attendees a chance to play the latest build. The game looked and played okay, but it wasn't a standout. The further we got from *Quake II*'s release, nearly eighteen months earlier, the older it looked. Still, we were making progress and moving forward, which, all things considered, was a minor miracle. We told the press to expect the game in January.

Deus Ex looked great, and several environments were shown off along with gameplay that included the various ways players could identify interactive objects and open hatches, crowbar crates, and use computers. There was a lot going on in their E3 demo, and the press was duly impressed by it. Warren was doing plenty of interviews extolling the features of his game and emphasizing that the team wanted the player to be able to decide how they approached the game's challenges: total action or quiet stealth.

Anachronox's awesome in-game cinematic camera was shown off as well, with shots swooping through several of Tom's worlds accompanied by detective-movie-style saxophone music in the background. Players got an idea of the scale of the game from this E3 demo, and people loved the *Final Fantasy*-style fighting system.

Daikatana's latest build was showing fine, and the press were excited to get some time with it. On the second day of the show, we received a new build of the game via FedEx. I'd been expecting it—the level designers wanted to add more action in the environments, and we really wanted to make as great a showing as possible. We'd reviewed their plans level by level before I left for California. Excited to get a look at it, we immediately began installation and fired it up. My excitement turned to confusion and then anger.

"What the fuck is going on?" I said to the computer. The game was chugging, practically skipping as I tried to move forward. "What the fuck is going on? What the fuck happened?" I couldn't understand what I was seeing. We had made our plans so carefully. Why was the game fucking crawling? What changed? I was so upset I don't even remember who I asked to reinstall the stable version of the build.

I called Chris Klie, the lead level designer. I trusted Chris implicitly. He was exceptional and detail-oriented, and he knew how important this show was for us. Both he and Stephen Ash, *Daikatana*'s fourth lead programmer, had worked their asses off to deliver a stable build for the show. As it turned out, once I got Chris on the phone, I realized that he was fuming, too. Apparently, Todd had presented him with a list of changes to be included with the E3 update build.

"What the fuck?" I said. I didn't want Todd *anywhere* near my game, and I'd certainly provided him no such direction. To make matters even worse, once Chris made the changes he thought I requested, Todd took the CD to FedEx before the VIS process on the levels was completed. That more than explained why the maps were running slow: Without VIS, the game was trying to draw the entire map every frame.

Chris Klie was so pissed that he ended up going to John Kavanagh, vice president of development at Eidos, who by then had been installed in our office to keep an eye on things, to complain about Todd's meddling.

For me, this was the straw that broke the camel's back in half. When I got back to Dallas, I wasted no time going straight to John Kavanaugh myself. Granted, it should have happened sooner—the eight people who left to form Third Law Interactive made that more than clear—but I was officially done with Todd.

I laid out the problems, starting with our most recent issue, the E3 build, then put the long litany of complaints out there on the table, things I had experienced myself as well as those which had been relayed to me from people who were still at Ion and those who had left. It was all uncalled for, and this moment was long,

long overdue. I explained that we had tried everything we could think of short of this measure, and that nothing had worked. There was no other choice: Todd needed to leave Ion Storm.

Seeing the writing on the wall, John arranged a meeting with Charles Cornwall, the owner of Eidos, at the Four Seasons Hotel in LA the following month. Until that time, we kept plans for the meeting under wraps.

In June, Todd, Jerry, Tom, and I flew to LA, took cabs to the Four Seasons, and got ourselves set up in the conference room for the big meeting with Eidos. Todd started to talk about the buyout he believed Eidos called us there to discuss. Charles Cornwall took a deep breath, and let Todd know point-blank that a deal was not in the cards. "We're here because we're concerned about Ion Storm's leadership," he said.

I started talking. "I'm trying to make a game, Tom is trying to make a game, and it's been nothing but problems." While it wasn't the most professional way to put it, I added, "Either Todd goes, or I go. There's always some kind of bullshit going on. Screwing up our E3 showing is just the latest."

I went on to discuss the changes that Todd asked Chris to make.

Tom talked about how people in the company perceived him. It was his opinion that Todd wasn't well liked and had treated people poorly. Jerry, suggesting some kind of amicable arrangement, wondered if we could perhaps give Todd his own project to work on.

Charles looked toward Tom and me and, as I remember it, said, "The only reason I invested in Ion Storm is because of John. I do not know who Todd Porter is, and I do not care."

I don't recall Todd addressing our issues. Rather, I recall that he collected his thoughts and calmly indicated that it was going to cost us some money.

Charles didn't acknowledge the money comment. Instead, he told him not to bother returning to the Ion Storm office once we were back in Dallas. It was decided that both he and Jerry would leave.

With that, it was finished. I'd never felt so light in my life. I knew it wasn't the end of the road with him, but at least the hardest part was over. I felt for Jerry, but we didn't see any other way.

We returned from LA and informed the team that Todd and Jerry were gone. It seemed as if people were surprised and relieved. It felt like a weight had been lifted. Outside the company, it only fanned the flames of Ion Storm's *Titanic*-like storyline. Behind the scenes, Todd was negotiating the financial terms of his departure. As a shareholder in the company, he had to be paid to relinquish those shares. By July, however, Todd hadn't been paid yet and started saying he'd come back into the office. We took his message to mean, "The sooner I'm paid, the sooner I'm gone and won't cause any problems."

Recruiters had started circling the company looking for talent, and knowing that *Daikatana* wasn't going to be the career boost their résumés were looking for, I lost both Chris Klie and Stephen Ash. I didn't begrudge them. I'd never been on a more challenging project myself. I promoted Shawn Green, who by now had been programming in the engine since 1997, to be my fifth lead programmer, which may be an industry record. Having seen everything at id Software, he had excellent discipline, and his experience in the engine made his progress smooth. *Daikatana* was coming together, and though it wasn't the game I'd hoped it would be and was certainly not the game that was hyped, it was a miracle that it was in playable shape, considering everything it had been through. Putting out one fire after another, I wasn't able to spend enough time on it, but with the leadership changes made, everyone agreed that things were so much better.

In September, Eidos bought a majority stake of the company in exchange for development costs paid to that point and the cost of buying out Todd and Jerry (the amounts they were paid are confidential, of course, but they were substantial payments). Of us four owners, they were the only two that saw any money from Eidos. We were just grateful to have peace, and I am sure they were grateful to receive those checks.

As the year came to a close, we kept our heads down and kept working on *Daikatana, Anachronox,* and *Deus Ex.* Things were productive and sometimes stressful. We were working a lot of hours, and the firestorm in the media and on forums had only heated up. Heading into December, we knew we weren't going to make the January launch of *Daikatana,* but we held the "not launch" party anyway in the Rotunda of the Chase Tower, since Eidos had planned it for months and too many people's calendars were scheduled around it. The party was a big affair, and around one hundred people came. It was the first chance we'd had to celebrate in our entire existence as a company.

For the first half of 2000, the *Daikatana* team put their heads down to get the game ready to go out the door. In March, it hit beta (all the content was in), and we furiously fixed all the bugs we could find. Through April, we tested the game over and over for weeks. Every four days, we made a new build, and a new release candidate. Inevitably, we'd find another bug, usually a serious one. We worked and worked to fix that, too. By mid-May, we were at Release Candidate 18. It was not the game we hoped it might be, but we had run out of time. Eidos deemed it good enough to launch.

On May 22, *Daikatana* appeared in stores in the US. Those who believed the hype were heartily disappointed when it didn't live up to it. Those who did not believe the hype took pleasure in pointing out just how hard it had failed. One reviewer even said I should be punched in the face for it—in print no less. Not surprisingly, it got mostly negative reviews, with many knocking it for its poor sidekick AI (which dramatically affected play), a host of remaining bugs, and its dated look. By now, *Quake III* had been out for five months. I also decided to make the first level super challenging, but players didn't like that either, something that would surely be revealed in today's focus test–driven development. Reviewers had expected a game better than *Quake*, and it was certainly not. (Today, the unofficial community patches have addressed the core issues of the game, and its gameplay is closer to what it should have been at launch. It even has a following and active community.)

In contrast to *Daikatana*, *Deus Ex* released June 23, 2000, to amazing reviews. We were thrilled for the team, and I was grateful that Warren got the chance to make it and make it at Ion Storm. *Deus Ex* went on to win several well-deserved Game of the Year awards. As of May 2022, series sales for *Deus Ex* have reached twelve million units. It was a breakaway success story where everything went right, and Eidos easily earned out its investment in Ion Storm on *Deus Ex* sales alone. Some did criticize *Deus Ex* for dated graphics, but I feel that this was not uncommon in this era of the graphics arms race, where sometimes graphics took precedence over gameplay. The team took a break after shipping it and returned to work on a patch to fix the noted issues. Once that was done, they began preproduction on the next game in the series.

After a break, I started to work on my next FPS, then titled, simply, *Game X*. I worked with the art team and created some environmental concepts so that we could visualize the world, and we began to experiment with a new program, Bryce 4, a terrain generator that created fractal landscapes. For *Game X*, we installed and were getting familiar with Unreal Engine. It was different than *Quake*'s engine, obviously, but exceptionally powerful and being used by a number of developers to make FPS games. The main character used a first- to third-person camera that transitioned smoothly between those modes. To my knowledge, it was the first FPS to do this, although the game was never released.

The *Anachronox* team buckled down, and we worked together to both determine and solidify only the maps with which *Anachronox* would launch. In September, the team started to work longer hours, under pressure to get the game out the door. Eidos asked me and my *Game X* team to join forces with the *Anachronox* developers. The levels needed some help, and I took control of the game location and map compilation tasks and also aided in scripting everything that wasn't done yet, for which Tom was grateful. After the *Daikatana* and *Deus Ex* launches, we really wanted *Anachronox* to be closer to the *Deus Ex* end of the spectrum, so we did whatever we could to ensure that everything Tom needed was in the game.

Anachronox hit retail shelves on June 27, 2001, and, fortunately, it was well received, garnering positive reviews from critics and even a "Best Use of Humor" award from *Computer Gaming World*. Unfortunately, Eidos barely supported it through advertising, and most players came to it via word of mouth or reviews. Development had taken a full year longer than *Daikatana*, and in order to recoup some of their investment, Eidos limited its marketing spend.

A month earlier, rumors on the internet surfaced to say that Ion Storm was shutting down. I talked to Stan Herndon, our then CFO, who was in daily contact with Eidos. He'd just received the news himself and was planning to talk with me. The rumors were true: Eidos was planning to close the studio in the next few months, as soon as *Anachronox* shipped. It was not unexpected, but it was certainly tough news. Of paramount importance to me was making sure that the team knew right away so they could prepare for their futures. I wanted to plan a shutdown, and not have them stuck in an instantaneous scramble. I negotiated with Eidos to give us a month after *Anachronox* shipped so our people would have time to get new jobs. To their credit, Eidos agreed, and to the team's credit, everyone stayed until the end.

July 31, 2001, was our last day at Ion Storm. Tom and I rolled carts of our stuff from the office into the parking lot and loaded up the trunks of our cars.

"See you tomorrow?" he asked.

"Yeah," I said. "I'll see you then."

Daikatana and Ion Storm are cautionary tales of a game that still somehow made it out the door and of a company that could not survive its many challenges. People have asked me for years what went wrong. The answer, in a literal word, is me. If nothing else, writing this book has been a transformative process. It has allowed me to see patterns that have followed and defined me, patterns I may not otherwise have seen. As a child, when things got bad, out of necessity, I stayed quiet and waited for it to pass. When Carmack sent out his report card, I stayed quiet and waited for it to pass. When people were upset at things happening within Ion Storm, I stayed quiet and waited for it to pass. Everything that happened at Ion Storm is a direct result of that flaw in my character. Had I taken action, had I talked to people, had I prevented issues from developing when they were just emerging, so many things in my career and in my life would have been different and so many people would have been spared the difficulties this flaw created.

In particular, at Ion Storm, I should have taken action regarding the team's issues with people in positions of leadership when people first asked me to, instead of letting it go on. In the end, that caused the teams a lot of stress and cost me a lot of time away from *Daikatana*. Both paid the price. I also never should have approved the notorious Bitch ad or allowed the hype train to leave the station.

While comparing notes, Tom and I reflected on a lot of difficult moments at Ion Storm, but we shared a lot of beautiful ones, too. To this day, the *Anachronox* team still meets up for dinner every year at the Game Developers Conference. They're close. *Deus Ex* is regularly named "Game of the Decade" and always appears on "greatest games of all time" lists. I remain good friends with most everyone who was at Ion Storm, people who are still changing the industry through their visionary work even today. And it bears repeating that many people got their start at Ion Storm. I think Henrik Jonsson, former programmer on *Anachronax* who is currently an investment scout for the game industry, put it best: "The young people who got together at Ion Storm learned massive amounts about game development, and went on to do great things: I doubt that Epic Games would be the same if not for people like Lee Perry, Jay Hosfeldt, Chris Perna, and Josh Jay, who grew into their own at Ion Storm. *Gears of War* and *Fortnite* would be very, very different, or even not exist, if it weren't for some Ion Storm people. You liked the writing in *God of War*? Matt Sophos and Richie Gaubert, the writers of *GoW*, both grew up at Ion Storm. Joey Liaw, who saved Healthcare 2.0 "Obama-care" website? Ion Storm programmer. The list goes on. It's hard to overstate the importance of Ion Storm as a breeding ground for exceptional talent." Not surprisingly, Jerry O'Flaherty, who even then showed a lot of talent in spite of everything happening around him, went on to become the Art Director at Epic Games.

While I wish it had not been as rocky as it was, I am grateful to everyone who was there, however briefly, and to those who stuck with it as long as they did. I'm also grateful to the fans who send me emails, sometimes apologetically, like they're admitting to a crime, "I actually liked *Daikatana*." I am sure they also like it more now that fan-made patches fixed the AI and other issues. I'm grateful for the lessons I learned, including the hard ones. If I had to sum it all up as a business lesson, this is it:

> Don't let problems magnify; deal with issues as soon as they arise. Problems always magnify over time.
>
> Don't hype what you don't have.
>
> Never insult your fans, even in jest.
>
> Trust your gut instinct. If you think something is wrong, there's probably a reason, even if it's not obvious. (Though in the case of the Bitch ad, it was obvious).
>
> Make sure people are treated well; games do not make themselves.
>
> Focus on the fun; games do not design themselves.
>
> Surround yourself with good people and give them what they need to make something great.

Find a way to support someone, like a video game publisher, who wants to make something else great, even if that something else is without you.

Vet your founders because you will face highs, lows, and challenges together.

Fail gracefully. Failure is a part of games, a part of life, and a part of success. Accept your flaws, reload your save and try again.

CHAPTER 23

Open-World Exploration

I was ready to explore.

For the past thirteen years, I had been making first-person shooters, from *Hovertank One* through to *Daikatana*, and I felt I had explored the highs and lows of shooter design. Likewise, I had experienced the best and the worst of company dynamics. My "eureka moment" at *Softdisk* with *Dangerous Dave in "Copyright Infringement"* led to the formation of id Software, while Ion Storm had been a roller coaster of challenges.

I thought about all of this in that last month as Ion Storm wound to a close as well as what opportunities were on the horizon. As we walked out of Ion Storm, Tom and I knew we wanted to continue working together, and there were numerous options to consider. The game industry had gone through so many changes, just in the last few years. Japanese role-playing games (JRPGs) dominated the awards with *Chrono Cross*, *Final Fantasy IX*, *Dragon Quest VI*, and *The Legend of Zelda: Majora's Mask* each taking a Game of the Year award from various outlets in 2000. *The Sims*, designer Will Wright's game about simulated humans, created a new and interesting genre. *Deus Ex* managed to take home a BAFTA Interactive Award for Game of the Year, giving us a reason to celebrate.

In considering our next steps, we didn't want to start another big company.

"I just want to code," I said. The best times I ever had in game dev involved me coding for hours and hours and hours. "In my dream scenario, that's all I'm doing. You design whatever it is," I said to Tom, "And I'll code it."

I also wanted a break from the calamity of management.

At the time, the PC world was just getting off MS-DOS and onto Windows, and then a new kind of gaming platform emerged: the mobile phone. Early mobile phones were far from the smartphones that we have today, which are powerful computers in their own right with screen resolutions and processors capable of delivering exceptional play experiences. In the early 2000s, mobile phones had much smaller screens and most were two color, black on a green, gray, or blue screen. As primitive as they were, I knew that playing games on the go was going to be a massive segment of the industry soon, and I wanted to get in on the ground floor of the new mobile revolution that I was sure was about to take place. A hand-held/mobile company was perfect for a small team, and it also put us in what we believed was an emerging market.

JAMDAT, a new company founded by Activision veterans in early 2001, was leading the mobile gaming charge. The hardware was beginning to improve, with faster processors and bigger screens, and soon the handheld PC market emerged. The most popular handheld PC was Compaq's iPAQ. Compared to the limited mobile devices of the time, the iPAQ had a great-looking color screen, exceptional audio, a fast processor, and even early on had some decent games. That was the handheld we targeted for our first game. I was excited to code again full-time and learn C++, the Win32 API, and the iPAQ hardware (learning C++ was relatively easy since I was fluent in C, a language I adhered to because it was more performant, and working on shooters required every ounce of performance).

On August 1, 2001, the day after things with Ion Storm wrapped up, Tom and I founded Monkeystone Games along with Stevie Case, a level designer from Ion Storm. Tom handled design, I handled code, and Stevie handled business. As our first project, Tom designed *Hyperspace Delivery Boy!*, a top-down Zelda-style puzzle adventure game where the player takes on the role of Guy Carrington, a courier in training. Guy embarks on several dangerous missions in four differ-ent locations—all full of Tom's signature brand of funny characters for players to interact with while solving puzzles and attempting to deliver various items. *Hyperspace Delivery Boy!* also had an action mode so the player could attack enemies as they solved puzzles and Panic Zones that gave the players thirty sec-onds to escape or die trying.

I was looking forward to writing the tools for Tom to make game levels, writ-ing our game engine in C++ and the gameplay code in Lua. My last real program-ming stint was in 1995, using a NeXTSTEP computer and working in Objective-C. I also had to write all of the tools to collect and bundle game data, write a new level editor, build the game, and do a deep dive into Pocket PC hardware so I could put the game on it. It took me three weeks to write our tools in Windows, and another three weeks for the game engine—which was designed to function on both Pocket PC and other platforms, so we could sell it in multiple markets. We finished the game in four months, on December 23, 2001. Next up would be ports for Game Boy Advance, PC, Mac, and Linux. *Hyperspace Delivery Boy!* was critically successful and attracted a good following, but it wasn't a breakout hit.

We moved from *Hyperspace Delivery Boy!* to *Congo Cube*, a match-3 game designed to be more action-based and wild than the current market leader, *Bejeweled*. *Congo Cube* hit high on my personal fun meter and joined hundreds of other games on RealArcade, a PC game store that released about a dozen games a week. Discovery, the process by which people find games, then, as now, was a challenge for game creators. Market leaders like PopCap Games had captured an audience with hits like *Bejeweled* and were able to advertise to that audience to promote new games. Others needed to spend significant money to advertise in those existing channels to attract players. It was an expensive proposition for most of us developing at that time. Mind you, this was years before the iPhone and the App Store combined to create the biggest casual gaming market on the planet.

Our next project was to develop a port of *Red Faction*, a PlayStation 2 game, for the Nokia N-Gage, a unique phone-game console hybrid with a button-like joystick. Its shape—a rectangle with one long rounded side at the bottom—earned it the nickname "taco phone." *Red Faction* did something new for mobile games in 2003: It was the first fully 3D cell phone game with deathmatch played over Bluetooth. Up to three phones in the same room could deathmatch head-to-head. Looking back, I only wish this innovation had been on a platform that had more players! We were proud of our work, though.

There were plenty of exciting technical and design opportunities in the Wild West of the early 2000s mobile market, but were likely too early in the space to make a big splash. The market was microscopic compared to what it is today, and phones and handheld devices of the time did not have good input mechanisms to allow intuitive gameplay. Regardless, as a programmer and a designer, working on a new platform and learning a new language in C++ was captivating.

In 2003, Tom and I decided to move on from Monkeystone to work in the console space. Both of us had had our games published on consoles or ported to them, but we had not worked natively in the console space except for that brief and unexpected three-week marathon coding session for *Wolfenstein 3-D*'s port to the SNES. By now, the console market was well diversified. The PlayStation 2 (PS2) arrived in 2000, and the original Xbox entered the market in 2001. Working on consoles offered the tremendous benefit of platform uniformity. Where PC games and mobile phones had many different operating systems, device drivers, and performance capabilities, consoles presented a uniform target for developers to hit. I had enjoyed that aspect of Monkeystone the most—learning new tech, platforms, and design patterns. Through the grapevine, I learned that Midway Games in San Diego needed a game designer to steer the latest *Gauntlet* game. Midway originally brought *Space Invaders* and *Pac-Man* to the US, so I was familiar with their history. I loved San Diego, its climate, and its easy access to authentic Mexican food, and I felt ready for a move to explore entirely new horizons. As a bonus, Kelly and the boys were now also in California, so I would be closer to them, too. After some back-and-forth discussion, I signed on. As a computer-first developer for the past twenty-four years, I was eager to get some console-first development experience. Tom signed on to work in the company's third-party division providing creative support for Midway's studios.

From a design perspective, I jumped into the world of console certification requirements. Those in development already know what many players may not—there's a reason that the user experience of all console games feels somewhat similar. It's by design. The shared wisdom of design and user experience in the TRCs (technical certification requirements) was incredible. Technically, the consoles were likewise impressive. To develop on consoles, developers use a "dev kit," which is specialized hardware designed by the console manufacturer to allow developers to run pre-release builds on the machines. As a designer, I ran the game via dev kits, too, but didn't get into the code side. I left Midway shortly before *Gauntlet: Seven Sorrows* shipped. The game was heading for a "get it out quick" trajectory to compensate for some other games slipping, and Midway no longer had the need for the deep game design. It was great to get some console experience under my belt, though. As most games aim to do, *Gauntlet* shipped simultaneously on both PS2 and Xbox to take advantage of the biggest potential audience.

After I left Midway,* I decided to take a few months off, the first time I had done so since receiving the Apple II as a kid. This period of exploration, from mobile to console, was energizing to me. In the early days of my career, exploring machines and new languages was as consuming as a good game. I stayed up around the clock working on something not because I needed to but because I *wanted* to. Sometimes, games were released that had a similar effect, and I studied them like a writer studied a great piece of literature. While I was still at Midway, for example, *Half-Life 2* came out. The expert use of physics for interacting with the environment, and the inclusion of physics puzzles gating progression was brand-new for shooters. This sequel was better than the original, and that was a tough act to follow. As of this writing, I believe it's one of the best shooters ever made, and at least for me, it stands the test of time.

A few weeks later, *World of Warcraft (WoW)*, a massively multiplayer online game, released. A brand extension of the longtime favorite role-playing strategy franchise *Warcraft*, the new game took the characters and the setting and placed

---

* Tom would eventually leave as well to work for KingsIsle Entertainment in Austin.

them in a vast monster-filled world with millions of players running around with swords and axes on quests to kill those monsters (or anything else, for that matter). There was a huge social element that allowed players to form friendships and guilds. As a gamer and game designer, I was awestruck by the concept and the execution—the world size, graphical polish, orchestral score, and sophisticated, transition-less engine took things to a new level. As a game industry veteran, the business model and subscription rate left my jaw on the floor. At the height of its popularity, *WoW* had a reported 12 million players, each paying $15 a month. The game was making $180 million per month, or $2.1 billion a year. Of course, dozens of new MMOs were announced, all planning to take some of *WoW*'s market share. The second round of the MMO gold rush was on.[*]

Knowing I'd be taking a break from work, I decided to wait to really sink some time into *WoW*. I started as a rogue Night Elf (an Alliance character race) named Deathtruck. There were other players running around learning the game as I was, in training areas that taught players how to use weapons, fight enemies, loot corpses, and turn in quests. The entire area was situated on top of a massive tree named Teldrassil. Finding my way to the edge of this zone, I peeked over the canopy of the tree and saw for miles down to the ocean below. Up until now, I had been largely immune to the pull of MMOs, but my goodness, did *WoW* ever hook me. I played for fun, I played to learn, I played to escape, and I played to hang out with friends. As a designer, I took notes, compared its systems to systems in non-MMO games and in other MMOs. It was obvious to me that *WoW* had done something exceedingly right. Game designers immerse themselves in successful games to learn. Games are our texts.

Working on an MMO appealed to me. I started exploring opportunities for design gigs in that space and connected with a couple of other individuals looking to do the same—Rob Hutter and Bhavin Shah. Together, we founded the company that was to become Gazillion Entertainment. While there were multiple opportunities in the space, what attracted me to Gazillion was its focus.

"How about making an educational MMO for kids?" Rob said, telling me about the company's focus. "A game that will provide the same kind of interactions you get with *World of Warcraft* but integrated with stealth education components."

I'd seen firsthand the ability of tech to transform lives, my own included, and likewise, I knew what a powerful educator games were. In a sense, all games teach players how systems work and reward them for their success and their progress. I believed an edu-MMO focused on math could be done in a stealthy manner,

---

[*]   The first round of the MMO gold rush was launched by *Ultima Online* in 1997. While other games certainly predated *Ultima Online*, its success captured the attention of the more mainstream developers. By then, more players had access to an internet connection, allowing them to partake in the world of online gameplay.

where the learning was integrated into the game in such a way that players would have no idea they were actually learning something. My hope was that when they encountered certain math concepts in school, they'd have a leg up, because they would have mastered a similar method of thought in our game. I'd seen my own kids rattle off world leaders thanks to the game *Civilization,* and Michael knew Pokémon better than the periodic table of elements. In creating this game, I hoped kids would find math fun in school, because the same "puzzle solving" in our game was rewarding. Their path to a STEM career was made a little easier.

I got to work on the design and hired a capable team to build the game, which we named *Project Redwood.* In addition to programming, art, narrative, and level design teams, I also created my first-ever learning design team composed of teachers and designers with experience creating physical toys and educational materials for kids. This team was composed of veterans of the classroom and from *LEGO MINDSTORMS,* LeapFrog, and other educational toy companies.

What I wished for was this: to make an intriguing, fun, role-playing game for kids. *World of Warcraft,* as the name suggests, is scary. I wanted to flip *WoW* on its head and make an MMO that was just as amazing looking and safely social for kids, but as far as quests and challenges went, not scary at all. The big challenge, as I saw it, was to develop a game mechanic that was as fun as combat in MMOs but wasn't combat at all. My solution was to fill the *Project Redwood* universe with animals kids could tame. The primary taming tool I designed was music played with a variety of instruments. If the player confronted a huge ten-point stag, I thought, instead of hitting or trapping them, the player tamed them with music or helped them in other ways to establish a bond. In this way, the game was almost idyllic and gentle—the complete opposite of *DOOM.* The learning team presented stealth learning within this world in the form of puzzles or progression. Most players, for instance, are unaware that experience point curves are sometimes exponential, while level curves are often logarithmic.

I loved what we were doing. We created a global advisory board of math education experts to evaluate our work every six months. We focused on introducing basic math concepts partly because we wanted to encourage kids to work in STEM fields, but also because math is a global language. The feedback from the advisory team was better than expected. They loved it. They thought it was intensely fun, encouraged repetition, and exposed mathematical concepts in a fully integrated, transparent manner. They said we had come up with representations of math concepts they'd never seen before and were thoroughly convinced that this was a new, engaging way to get kids excited about math.

We continued on, building and crafting our big world. Four years into development, however, rumblings on the tech team about problems with the licensed MMO engine began to surface. The engine was having difficulty supporting content at the scale it had been advertised as capable of handling. Our decision to license a game engine developed by a third party wound up being *Project Redwood*'s fatal flaw: The engine simply couldn't do the job we needed it to do. We spent some time trying to retrench, to see if there was a way to save the vision. We even hired a specialized technical director to assess the entire tech ecosystem, but the engine technology components had major problems working together at scale. Blizzard had spent five years building the engine behind *World of Warcraft*. The tech director delivered a verdict that it would take at least a year to fix the client software and tools, or a year moving everything we had built to a different engine, a process I knew would take far longer. In the end, we assessed that the risks were too great and the additional investment unlikely to provide the return the investors hoped for. The project came to an end, but many of the learning concepts carried on in other games. It was a somber time—the end of an exceptional team and of a game we believed held huge promise. Overall, though, in 2009, Gazillion's outlook was healthy. We still had five other games going, including two based in the Marvel universe. The takeaway lesson for me was this: Always license tried-and-true tech.

During the early development of *Project Redwood*, my father passed away on his fifty-seventh birthday. His death was not unexpected, but was nonetheless incredibly painful. His struggles with addiction had progressed, as they have a tendency to do. In early 2001, my brother, Ralph, and I flew to Boise, Idaho, to rescue him from a precarious situation. I paid off his debts and brought him to Dallas, where we checked him into rehab. I purchased a house for him to live in, and Ralph even moved in to help out. After a few years, though, he just up and left and moved back to Grandma Suki's in Tucson. She welcomed him back, and unfortunately, he went back to drinking hard liquor.

So much of who I am comes from my father. Not just my appearance—I look just like him—and my name—I am named after him—but also my sense of humor, adventure, and desire to play games competitively (he bet, won, and sometimes lost cars playing pool). He was proud of his time singing with Mariachi Cobre, and I am blessed to have inherited his voice as well, though I only sing while coding, as several of my coworkers have noticed. He was incredibly proud of our Mexican and Yaqui heritage, taught me to be, too, and every dish I make comes from him having taught me to cook and cherish the dishes and flavors of Mexico. I still listen to our traditional music every day.

I flew to Tucson for his memorial. Family from both sides of the border were there, and everyone had good things to say about him. Everyone loved him. I loved him. While alcoholism and addiction defined his death, it did not define his life. He was so many things to so many people. When he passed, he had very few possessions. Among those, however, was a single beige folder. Inside was only his résumé, his GED papers, and an article about "mi hijo" who made *DOOM*. He always told me he was proud of me. Te extraño y te amo, Papá.

With *Project Redwood* coming to a close and people moving on to other projects, I was ready for my next exploration. As it turned out, friends and family who had never played games were suddenly interested in a game called *Farmville*, and they wanted to know if I had played it, too. The volume of these requests both in person and on Facebook caught my attention. What exactly was drawing in people who had, until now, never cared about playing games? By now, I was dating another game developer, Brenda Garno, who was working at social game company Slide at the time, and she and I started talking about the design patterns in these games. Slide published a game called *SuperPoke! Pets* where players created, cared for, outfitted, and customized a home for virtual pets. It was extremely light touch—players didn't need to learn any specialized controls beyond point-and-click and click-and-drag. Further, the play was shallow—players didn't need to retain information session-to-session or strategize about grand plans or short-term tactics. All the social games integrated the player's friend network as a core component of play and a means of spreading the word about the game itself. Players asked for and gave gifts. It was about as far from first-person shooters as one could get, but nonetheless, I was fascinated with the design of these games. It was a form of asynchronous play that involved a player's entire friend graph, giving new meaning to the term "shareware."

As you might expect, game designers in a relationship spend an inordinate amount of time talking about games. Like me, Brenda is from the Apple II days, and she has an appreciation for game history and a lifelong love of game design. We had originally met at Origin in 1987 and stayed in touch throughout the years. I spent some time with her at Slide, with founder Max Levchin's permission, taking in what was happening and discussing the business model with him. An original member of the "PayPal Mafia," Max is one of Silicon Valley's greatest technologists, founders, and investors, and we enjoyed discussing tech, both games and consumer products. These social games brought tens of millions of new players to games.

While we dabbled in casual games at Monkeystone, the rise of Facebook and release of *Farmville* kicked off the huge social gaming movement. The technology behind the games wasn't interesting to me, but the game design for this new audience certainly was. In addition, the asynchronous play and shallow game dynamics presented an interesting design challenge, much of it running counter to traditional methods of game design, where we worked to build a mental model of the game in players' heads to get them thinking and keep them thinking for hours at a time. This form of game design required us to come up with designs that captivated players who weren't used to playing games and teach the necessary mechanics to progress further. Even more exciting, this audience was predominantly women in their thirties and forties, a demographic that traditional games had yet to cultivate or expressly design for. I was excited by the challenge and the diversity in the games and their audience. The more I learned about it, the more I wanted Gazillion to enter the space, too, but my cofounders and the board wanted to stay full speed ahead on MMOs.

I left my day-to-day role in Gazillion to join Brenda in making social games. By then, she had moved on from Slide to a smaller company that was, as they all were, looking for the next big thing. Working as a consultant, I spent three days doing nothing but studying the design patterns of the most successful games, in particular *FrontierVille* by Brian Reynolds, which had just released. Now I needed to come up with a cool game design, something that was going to make the social gaming world sit up and go, "Wow!" *FrontierVille*, like *Farmville*, was basically about growing crops as a pioneer out West. I wanted a totally different environment. And that's when I thought back to the things I loved as a kid and teen: *Don't build a farm, build something fun—like a fun fair!*

After a three-day deep dive into social gaming, *Ravenwood Fair* was born. It came to me all at once: the build-your-own fair idea, the gameplay events that would compel players to spend money incrementally and consistently. I mapped out the game for my small team of four programmers, an artist, and a producer.

It took fifty-seven days to build, and release, *Ravenwood Fair*. Within three weeks of its October 19, 2010, release, the game had four million players and earned $1 million in revenue for the company. Over the next six months, the game grew to 25 million monthly players, and the company grew from 30 people to 130 people. It was a huge hit. I got a lot of personal satisfaction from *Ravenwood*'s success, and offers to join companies and make games for them, too. It was such a wild time. In the end, however, *Ravenwood* was the springboard for what would be my next company, solely focused on social games. Brenda and I founded Loot Drop in 2010, with the goal of having four teams creating four separate games. Tom Hall joined us, too. Over the next two years, Loot Drop grew to forty developers, and we made games for everyone from Zynga to Ubisoft and worked on prototypes for big publishers looking to get into the space. In 2012, the social game bubble popped with Facebook's change to the way game notifications worked. Namely, people were annoyed with the game messages spamming their feed, and so Facebook curtailed the practice, and with it, curtailed the ability for games to take off. It was a great ride for Loot Drop and for our time in the social and casual space. We released three games during that time—*Ghost Recon Commander*, *Charmcraft Hollow*, and *Pettington Park*—and built many more prototypes. One thing I'll always find interesting about this time is that *Ravenwood Fair* was arguably as successful in terms of player numbers and revenue as *DOOM* was in its early days, but because of its platform, demographic, and market, it is still relatively unknown. Of those who do know about it, most are surprised to find that someone known primarily for violent video games made it.

By this time, Brenda and I had been together for years, and we got married in October 2012. We decided to get stealth-married in one of our favorite places in the world, Disneyland in Anaheim. Tom Hall got ordained as a minister to marry us, and along with his wife, Terri, we, our families, and closest friends got in line at the Mark Twain Riverboat in the afternoon. After the boat left the dock and rounded the corner, Tom began the ceremony. Eventually, all the other riders on the boat, including Disney employees, knew what was happening. People clapped and congratulated us, and we went to eat at the Big Thunder Ranch BBQ. Brenda's three young kids were my kids, too. Maezza, Avalon, Donovan, and I all got on really well. When she was just ten, I introduced Maezza to *Chrono Trigger*, and as I had with Michael, we played through the game together. She was soon my *WoW* buddy, and she even started to learn C++. Avalon had an early interest in cooking, and together she and I cooked my family's traditional cheese tacos, tamales, and taquitos. Donovan, Avalon's twin brother, played games with me, narrating my play like he was telling a story. He took an early interest in game design, too, and wrote entire game designs in notebooks, "playable," so to speak, from beginning to end starting when he was just five years old. Lillia, who was fourteen at the time, had been raised as an only child to this point, and found the family she always wanted.

Following Loot Drop, I worked mostly as a consultant, a tried-and-true road followed by a good number of game designers. I worked with mobile companies, traditional game companies, TV shows looking to expand their audience, and movie studios who were sitting on juggernaut IP that had major game potential but hadn't yet been picked up. My interests outside of work, or perhaps orthogonal to my work, were also occupying a larger part of my life.

Because of my work on *Project Redwood*, teaching kids to code was becoming a real passion project for me. Programming is transformative, not just for tech, but for people's lives. Because of code, my life was transformed from one of poverty to one of privilege, and I wasn't going to take it for granted. I spoke regularly at schools in the area, particularly to Latino and Indigenous students in nearby communities whose backgrounds were most like mine. I volunteered to work with kids who had a tough start in life and who reminded me of myself, giving lots of in-person and online talks and mentoring kids who showed interest. I ended up writing a booklet for kids to teach them how to code in Lua and donated it to Pinnguaq, an agency that works with Indigenous youth in Canada.

I was also becoming increasingly interested in preserving game history through my work with the Strong National Museum of Play in Rochester, New

York, and the Computer History Museum in Mountain View, California. In particular, I realized that many game archivists didn't have the ability to interview early coders about their process if they didn't also have an understanding of assembly language, the tools, or the computers of the time. I began interviewing designers, including Sid Meier, Will Wright, Nasir Gebelli, and even Ralph Baer, about their early processes. I hosted an event at my house, another Apple II reunion party, and invited technology historian Jason Scott to interview people while there. Among others, Jason interviewed Margot Comstock, the cofounder and editor of *Softalk* magazine.* Capturing these oral histories is so incredibly important.

Through work with museum conservationists, I was becoming aware of the importance of my own archives. Every day, we lose critical materials that are historically significant as they are tossed out, recycled, or deleted. Design documents and disks full of uncompiled code represent the foundation and building blocks of the most important cultural medium of modern times. My own archives were substantial, containing everything I had ever worked on, including while at id Software. There are things that I have from early id Software that even id Software doesn't have (unreleased game assets or early builds, for instance). These materials, as well as the materials of other game creators, have critical historical significance. Believe or not, they're still tossed out every single day.

I began to get my archives in order just as our family headed to New York City for a bit of vacation and a consulting trip. We had just moved into our new home, which had a unique room, an actual hidden room—the perfect place to store my archives.

---

* While working on this chapter, I received news that she had passed away. Margot was the glue that held the Apple II community together.

CHAPTER 24

The Grass Is Greener

On July 13, 2013, Brenda called me while I was meeting with a client in New York.

"The house is flooded," she said.

Thinking of the brownstone where we were staying in Manhattan, I wondered how on earth that might flood, and so I answered simply with, "What?"

"The house. In California. Michael went to check on it and . . ."

She meant our *new* house in the Santa Cruz Mountains, the one we'd just filled full of boxes and furniture before heading off on our trip. The one that contained all my games, career notebooks, floppy disks, and id Software archives. Flooding and landslides are always a possibility in the Santa Cruz Mountains. My mind started to race. Was anyone hurt? What state was the house in? What state were our archives in? Unless you've experienced this nightmare, it's impossible to convey the emotions.

So many things you think you might care about are forgotten in an instant: All I could think of was the collection of boxes stored in a secret room on the bottom floor of the house. To access the room, one needed to go into a small auxiliary closet in our bedroom. On the back wall, there was a hidden half-height sliding panel that revealed the entrance to the room. It was the only way in, and to us it was one of the selling points of the house. We felt secure putting our archives there, knowing that any successful burglar first needed to bypass the alarm system and then develop an unnatural interest in the back wall of a closet to reveal the secret panel. I suppose any fan of id's FPS games might have looked for a push wall, but I wasn't expecting any of you to break in.

Those boxes, probably twenty of them, contained my entire archives, every-thing from 5.25" Apple II floppy disks to the letters I wrote to magazines as a kid hoping to get my games published. In one box, there was the original *Dangerous Dave in "Copyright Infringement"* disk Carmack and Tom had left on my desk at *Softdisk*, as well as the original drawings of the *DOOM* logo, the original *DOOM* bible, hand-drawn screen perspective tests for *DOOM*, and the only videotape in existence of our *Quake* design meetings. Really, these items just scratch the surface. With the exception of one small box that someone lifted twenty years prior, every single piece of paper and every line of code I wrote in my entire career was in that room. In addition to my personal archives, hundreds of boxed games were there, too—sealed games from id Software as well as dozens of mint-condition early Apple II games that I treasured, some of them signed by Nasir Gebelli.

In a flash, I imagined that room in one of two states: waterlogged with boxes floating around or pancaked in a flattened house that I feared had taken a slow ride down the steep hillside to the creek below. Most of our things were in plastic bins, but water finds a way. I feared the worst.

"What happened?" I asked Brenda.

"Michael was going to check the house. He couldn't get the back door open. So, he pushed and pushed, and finally, he got it open enough so that he could squeeze through. The floors were all warped and wet. He said it was like a sauna in there. He went downstairs and the ceiling in our bedroom was collapsed."

"Collapsed?" I couldn't believe what I was hearing.

"The ceiling is on the floor. There's water everywhere."

Our bedroom was the room next to the secret room.

"Do you know where it's coming from?"

"Yes, it's the fridge. The line that goes to the ice maker and water dispenser," she said.

The house was built on a hill, and our bedroom was on the lower level of the house directly underneath the kitchen.

"Michael said he heard something that sounded like it was hissing coming from behind the fridge. So, he pulled the fridge out some, and there it was."

"That's a tiny hose!"

"Give it three weeks, and it's enough to wreck the house."

"Do you know whether—"

I didn't need to finish my question. "No, I don't know if the water got to the archives," she said. "I called David to see if he could come over to figure out where the shut-off valve is."

David was the real estate agent who'd sold us the house. Since we were there only five days before heading east to New York, we didn't have time to meet any of our neighbors. David was the only person we knew in the whole of the Santa Cruz mountains. Fortunately, he came right over and showed Michael where the valve was. That evening, as we sat in New York talking to David and then to Michael in California, we learned the full extent of the damage.

The house was likely going to be condemned, David told us, and within a week, signs to that effect were placed on the doors. David kindly connected us with everyone we needed in order to deal with the situation.

"Should I come back to California?" Brenda asked. "John has a month or so before he's finished up, but I can come back."

"There's no point. You don't have anywhere to live." The words hit us like bricks. "It's best to let the remediation experts handle it from here," he added.

Over FaceTime, Michael walked through the house to show us the damage. Every room was wrecked. The wood floors were warped, the ceilings were collapsed, and the sheetrock walls on the ground floor and lower level were soaked.

"Can you go in the closet in our bedroom and check that room?" I asked.

Michael pushed the clothing aside, found the secret wall, and poked the phone and a flashlight inside.

Expecting the worst, we couldn't believe our eyes. The secret room had escaped the disaster. Unbelievably, *everything* in that room survived. The ceiling and walls were intact. I still can't believe our luck. We directed Michael to the most critical boxes, and he took those home with him that night.

This near-fatal brush to my archives brought me face-to-face with its historic value, and shortly thereafter I donated and continue to donate parts of it to the Strong National Museum of Play. Today, the collection that remains in my possession is stored in fire- and waterproof containers in an offsite location that is itself monitored against all forms of calamity. It doesn't have push walls. I've also talked with many other game developers, encouraging them to donate or at least make available their materials to museums like the Strong or to universities so they can be copied or preserved for future generations and researchers.

In the weeks that followed our home's destruction, we stayed in New York. We were fortunate that the insurance company covered all our losses and the cost of reconstruction. Sometimes, we had interesting conversations with the insurance adjusters over the value of the few game items that didn't escape the water, things like a ruined, original *DOOM* "Wrote It" T-shirt, a shirt made exclusively for members of the development team that is now a rare collectable. The insurance company appraised it as "Tee shirt, $3." An original *Commander Keen: Aliens Ate My Baby Sitter!* box that had been left out on my desk was valued as "Old software, $10." Fortunately, I had another shirt and a duplicate game.

Finally back into our home, the kids settled into a normal routine for the first time in months. I worked on some personal projects, like cataloging my archives, learning new programming languages, and catching up on recent research. I became interested in the Lua programming language again, largely because it was accessible and easy to learn, and I thought it would be perfect for students at the college level but also for kids at the high school and grade school levels, too.

Donovan, who was just nine, became curious about Lua and asked me to teach it to him. I don't remember a time when Donovan wasn't all about games. From when he was a little boy, he talked a nonstop stream of games and game design. My coding lessons with Donovan always started the same way:

"What game do you want to make today?"

Granted, we weren't going to make a full game, but at least it gave him something to wrap his head around while I taught him Lua.

"*Gunman Taco Truck*," he said.

"Yes!" I laughed at the sound of it and the possibilities it brought to my imagination.

We spent an entire Saturday working on code, getting a taco truck up on the screen, getting the truck moving, and mounting a gun to its roof. That night, as Brenda and I were hanging out, Donovan came bounding into our room.

"Mommy, Mommy. I know what the game is about."

Like a proud game-dev parent, Brenda grabbed her phone, told him to wait, and started recording.

"You're this Mexican gunslinger who runs a taco truck," he began. "You're trying to get through the wasteland to kill all the mutant animals, and once you do that, you finally get to the resisting safe bases. Every time you get to a resisting safe base, you get more money for selling tacos!"

"So you go to the bases and you serve tacos with your truck?" I asked.

"Yes. Randomly generated. There's just . . . infinity, so it's an endless game."

I wanted to make sure I had it right. The kid had a solid core loop.

Brenda posted the video on Facebook. Donovan made her promise to add that players were able to purchase upgrades with income earned from their taco truck. He was quite serious about it. By morning, a few of our friends were excited about it, too. George Broussard, a longtime friend and a cofounder of Apogee Software, gave Donovan an enthusiastic thumbs-up.

"Even wasteland bandits need tacos! Best idea ever. Good job, Donovan!"

I decided to make the game with him. I'd help him with the code, but the design needed to be all his.

As Donovan and I kicked off our project, Brenda was finalizing the details of what would become a life-changing adventure: a three-month research trip to Ireland, the result of Brenda winning a Fulbright Specialist award. A prestigious United States government program designed for cultural and academic exchange, the Fulbright agenda took her all over Ireland to visit universities and meet with game developers and government ministers.

For Brenda, it was a no-brainer and a fantastic opportunity. I thought I might like to come along, too. Although I'd lived in England as a teen, my family never crossed the Irish Sea. Brenda, whose ancestors came from Ireland, had also never been. Since neither of us were tied down to a commercial game-dev project, the runway was clear.

Donovan and I met for one last game jam before our trip. He didn't want *Gunman Taco Truck* to sit idle while I was away, and neither did I. I had a plan.

"Let's focus some on the design and the art assets for the game. Players can upgrade their truck, right?"

"Yes. They can purchase better guns and rockets and more ammo! And more trucks."

"Exactly. So here's what I want you to work on."

I put four stacks of paper on the table, each with ten sheets. Each had a place to write a name, an area for drawing, and an area for a description.

Pointing to the first pile, I said, "On these pages, I want you to draw the different trucks. Name them and tell me exactly what their properties are. Then, move on to the mutant animals, the truck upgrades, and finally, you can figure out what the tacos are."

It was a lot of work for Donovan to do in that time, but if he had it all done when we came home, we would be in a good place to begin development of his game.

We arrived in Dublin on August 20, 2014, and Brenda started her Fulbright. It's true what they say about Ireland—it's embarrassingly beautiful and lush, particularly to someone like me who comes from the desert. In the countryside, especially in Counties Kerry and Donegal, the sights are breathtaking: tiny roads carved through lush, green mountain passes unlike anything I'd ever seen. Irish people are as friendly, welcoming, and funny as they are said to be, and we felt at home everywhere we went. On the weekends, when Brenda didn't have responsibilities tied to the Fulbright, we traveled as much as we could. The more we traveled, the more I felt similarities to my family's Mexican culture: All gatherings were about fun, food, and music. In fact, you'll see it on pub signs everywhere: "Craic agus Ceol," Irish for fun and music.

Three months were over before we knew it. Back in our home in the Santa Cruz Mountains, we couldn't wait to see the kids, and we shared the goodies we collected for them and talked about how amazing the trip was. Though we hadn't said anything to each other, I think we knew even then that we were going to move to Ireland.

Donovan was glad to receive his gifts, of course, but what he really wanted to talk about was *Gunman Taco Truck*. He handed me a binder.

"It's all done," he said.

Michael, now twenty-six, happened to be at the house, too, and we looked over Donovan's drawings with a mix of admiration and affection.

Everything was just what I asked for. I was so proud of him in that moment, of both of them, really. Michael's career in the game industry was taking off. He was now working with Tom Hall as a programmer, and every job he was in, he worked hard and delivered constantly shippable code.

"Are you going to make Donovan's game?" Michael asked.

"We are. Thinking of a game jam. You want to join us?"*

"Just let me know when!"

I invited Ian Dunbar, an outstanding student in the UC Santa Cruz master of science in game development program, to join us, and contracted Paul Conway, an artist we met in Galway, to create pixel art for Donovan's game. We met regularly to work on the game and shared great fun and food. After some time, the game was really starting to come together.

In March, Dean Takahashi, a reporter for *VentureBeat*, called us. He'd heard about Donovan's game from Brenda's Facebook post and wanted to write a story about it. The resulting article, "A 10-Year-Old Designs Gunman Taco Truck with Help from Legendary Gaming Parents," opened a floodgate of interest. In April, the *Wall Street Journal* sent a reporter and photographer to our house and ran a great article about the power of video games to inspire kids to learn to code. It was great coverage for kids and programming, but we wanted to keep Donovan's focus on the game. He joined us in the game jams, playing the game, designing the world map, and helping out where he could.

Brenda was nearly finished with her Fulbright report.

"You know, the goal of this report wasn't to convince me that we should move to Ireland, but that's what it's done," she told me. "We can live anywhere in the world. Why not Ireland?"

When you're here as a tourist looking at the amazingly beautiful scenery, you might not be thinking about Ireland as a tech hub, but it most certainly is. As I write, Ireland is the second-largest exporter of software in the world, and nine of the ten largest software companies in the world have their European headquarters in Ireland.

I was in. Before long, the kids were, too. We decided to settle in Galway, on the west coast of Ireland. Something about the city's charm got to us. Judging by the amount of times it has ended up on various tourist "top ten" lists, it seems it's gotten to others, too. It's creative, artistic, and weird in all the right ways. When we asked Irish people where they liked to vacation, Galway was the answer. We made plans to move in the summer of 2015.

---

* Game jams are events where game developers come together, form groups, and try to create a game in a constrained space of time, usually over a weekend.

Coming to Ireland changed the course of our lives for the better, and we are grateful to Bob Jackson of the Institute of Technology Tralee and the Fulbright Program whose idea kicked this whole thing off. We felt welcomed as part of the tech community in Galway and in Ireland as a whole, and my Yaqui and Cherokee heritage is celebrated here (I even appeared on RTÉ, Ireland's national broadcasting network, to discuss Irish donations to the Navajo Nation). My only regret is that we did not move here sooner.

As it turned out, I wasn't the only id Software alum in the country. Adrian Carmack had purchased The Heritage, a five-star hotel in Killenard, County Laois, in 2014. During the move and while we searched for a house, we stayed at The Heritage and Adrian and I spent lots of time talking about our shared past as well as my plans for the future.

CHAPTER 25

The Road to Hell Is Paved with Good Intentions

Adrian and I had been in touch throughout the years, but we really reconnected in 2014 while Brenda and I were driving cross-country from California to New York. We stopped at QuakeCon in Dallas, where Adrian still lived, and had a fun, laugh-filled evening. We spent hours talking about our time at id (by then, he had left, too), our plans for the future, and the current trends in games in general and, of course, FPS games specifically. We shut the restaurant down, and continued talking in the parking lot until nearly 4 A.M. We connected again in Ireland a month later while we were staying at Adrian's hotel, The Heritage. We talked about everything under the sun, but it was the first time in a long time that I'd had extended conversations on FPS design specifically.

I had been thinking about the next big thing—not just for games, but for me. It had been fifteen years since my last first-person shooter. I still loved the genre. When I played games, more often than not, an FPS is what I was playing. I was just waiting for the right idea, the right design, the right moment. Retro-style shooters were picking up steam, but I didn't want to design a retro shooter, exactly. I wanted a modern shooter that was cutting-edge, like the games we had made at id, with classic elements that would remind players of how fun and visceral these games could be, and that younger players could discover for the first time.

Although I was getting excited about designing a new FPS game, it wasn't my top priority. I had to move it to the back burner to deal with everything that came with a move to Ireland: new schools for the kids, finding a place to live, getting our visas sorted. Only when the dust from our move had settled and we'd leased an office for our newly created company, Romero Games, did I finally turn my thoughts back to designing a first-person shooter.

I had a futuristic design percolating, but before I designed something new, I needed a warm-up.

As fall gave way to Christmas, I shared exciting news with Brenda: I was going to make a new *DOOM* level.

We both realized this was a big deal. I hadn't made a map for *DOOM* since *The Ultimate DOOM* in 1995. On top of that, every map I'd made for a *DOOM* game—*DOOM*, *DOOM II*, and *The Ultimate DOOM*—had been part of a shareware or commercial package. This time, I would be making a *DOOM* level as a member of the community I had helped create back in 1993. That year was key. Most *DOOM* modders make maps for *DOOM II*. It has more weapons, enemies, and power-ups. I had my sights set on the first *DOOM*, though, and for good reasons.

First, before I designed a new FPS from the ground up, I wanted to get back in the right creative headspace by returning to a style of level design I knew and loved. *DOOM* was the perfect choice. I know the engine inside and out, and building maps in Doom Builder 2, a free editor written and maintained by Pascal van der Heiden, is fast and easy. Second, the development of *DOOM* was the best sort of chaos. John Carmack was writing the engine, and I was juggling DoomEd, level design, and gameplay. When you play a *DOOM* map, anything that happens in that level—a lift that moves, a lever that flips, a button that glows when pressed, lava or toxic slime that burns you, a light that flashes on and off, a ceiling that crushes the life from you—I'm the one who designed and programmed it. I made every map in episode one of *DOOM*, "Knee-Deep in the Dead," except for a small bit of level four, which Tom had designed before he left id, and the episode's final level. I turned that job over to Sandy. He was a great choice: He worked quickly, pounding out smaller maps every couple days at his peak. That freed me up to focus on DoomEd and our distribution plans.

In 2015, I saw an opportunity to end episode one the way I would have ended it. It's not that there was anything wrong with Sandy's E1M8 map. On the contrary, I really like it. He made a gloomy, claustrophobic map that focused on pitting players against a small amount of enemies before an encounter with the "Bruiser Brothers," the Barons of Hell waiting for them in the boss room. I loved the sight of twin doors opening to reveal the Bruisers, and the two of them striding forward as they roared like tyrannosaurus rexes. I would keep that setup, but I planned to make that showdown even more epic. If I had a criticism of the map, it was that, for a final map it was too small.

Looking back at episode one, every level was bigger than the one before it. The moments, the encounters, the weapons, the map designs—everything escalated, pushing the player toward a confrontation against the biggest demons they've yet faced. That's what I had in mind for E1M8b, which I called "Tech Gone Bad." This was the final level, so I wanted to take the player on a long, grand journey that culminated in an epic boss fight. I applied the techbase theme I used for E1M1 through E1M7, keeping the continuity of the episode's environments, and made "Tech Gone Bad" the largest map in the set.

Throughout the map, the player moves in and out of interior rooms and outdoor regions covered in slime. This forces them to adapt as they navigate between safe and hazardous floors, and to fight enemies from different vantage points. Occasionally, the player reaches high positions that give them a view of the level, driving home its scale and letting them scout for regions they haven't explored. Eventually, the player realizes they've been running on top of passageways they haven't explored yet, and they need to find a way to enter them to progress. It's as if the level is a puzzle box, and making progress opens more avenues of exploration to you.

Of course, everything leads to a battle against the Bruiser Brothers. Sandy's level has players race down a short hallway and jump onboard a lift that raised them into the arena. The first things players see are two closed doors. You know something bad—two bad somethings—are hiding behind them, and moving forward triggers them to open. My goal was to amplify that cool factor tenfold.

E1M8b's boss room is a chamber with just enough room for the player—and, inevitably, the Bruisers—to maneuver when the fight breaks out. Players enter by way of a narrow ledge set high above. Stepping onto it causes the ground to break away, lowering the player into the arena like fish bait set on a hook. That was thematic. Whereas Sandy's E1M8 has a lift that raises the player into an arena, I wanted the player to descend. Below, the walls are made from computer terminals, sticking with the map's theme, but the rest of the room has a distinctly ominous vibe. Glowing red cracks line the floor, snaking out from two gigantic red portals with steps leading to each entryway that dominate the center of the room. I hoped the sight was so terrifying that it gave the player pause. *What the hell is going to come out of those?* Move a little closer, and the Bruiser Brothers appear, kicking off the most epic encounter in "Knee-Deep in the Dead."

Despite using someone else's map editor, I found designing maps for *DOOM* as natural as it had been more than twenty years earlier. However, everything about my environment had changed. For one thing, DoomEd was written on the NeXTSTEP operating system, so I couldn't use that. The original *DOOM* code doesn't run on Windows, so I used a source port named GZDoom. I ran Doom Builder 2 on a 2013 Mac Pro with 128 GB of RAM, a terabyte solid-state drive, and two 3D graphics cards. Doom Builder 2 isn't compatible with Mac OS, so I ran it through a virtual machine (VM) that had Windows 10 installed. As I designed

E1M8b, I dropped new versions of other files I needed into a Dropbox account and retrieved them in the Windows 10 VM environment. Doom Builder 2 and GZDoom ran at full speed with no slowdown, because I wasn't emulating either program. My Mac Pro ran on an Intel processor, giving me access to GZDoom in sixty-frames-per-second glory.

In short, designing E1M8b was easy and felt like going home. I didn't develop a test level first. E1M8b *was* the test level, and the version you play was my first draft, created in about twenty hours over two weeks. Every time I sat down to Doom Builder 2, I felt things coming back to me. It was muscle memory, with no gap between 1995 and 2015.

On January 16, 2016, I uploaded E1M8b to my Dropbox and tweeted out the link. To set the mood for my take on episode one's final level, I wrote a story in a text file that accompanied the map:

After exiting the Computer Station, you knew the worst was up ahead. You still hadn't reached the place where the demons were coming from. The steel door shuts behind you as you realize you're there; you're at the Phobos Anomaly. Cracks from hell are all over the place as seepage from the portal invades the entire installation.

Now it's time to find the portal and stop the demons from coming through. You know UAC had hundreds of scientists working at a high-tech lab somewhere in this area, and the portal must be connected to it somehow. Time to lock and load.

I'd hoped the community would be excited about my first *DOOM* map in more than two decades. As it turned out, that excitement extended far beyond just the community. Within hours, gaming outlets like *PC Gamer*, Polygon, IGN, Shacknews, and Eurogamer had written stories about it. Soon, mainstream tech outlets like *PC Magazine* covered it, too. Within ten minutes, the map had been downloaded thousands of times, and players were already sharing their thoughts with me on Twitter, in forum posts on doomworld.com, and in playthroughs live on Twitch and uploaded to YouTube. Word of my return to *DOOM* went beyond the gaming sphere, as well: "New *DOOM* level released by game creator John Romero" read a headline by the BBC.

Behind the scenes and out of the spotlight, I had already started concepting my next game, a new first-person shooter. At the time, Kickstarter was established as a viable means to fund a game, and I decided that was the way to go. E1M8b was the confidence boost I needed to feel that gamers would embrace a new FPS from me.

While I worked on the new shooter and its Kickstarter campaign, I was itching to create more maps for *DOOM*. I decided to strike while the proverbial portal to hell was still hot. Once again, I was more interested in replacing a map from episode one than creating a level disconnected from the original game. Tom Hall had started E1M4 before leaving id. I had stepped in and re-textured it, adding things like weapons, power-ups, and enemies to balance the map flow on every difficulty setting. My issue with E1M4 was that there was only one thing special about it. Near the end, you use the blue keycard to access a maze. Tom did a great job on this part: It's darkly lit, and the walls of the main artery are so tight, the ceiling so low, the player almost feels like they'll have to crawl on their belly to get through it. Side passages unspool from the main path, and each passageway leads to supplies, or dead ends, or a fight against imps and pinkies. The maze is memorable, but the rest of the level felt like yet another futuristic lab.

E1M4b, Phobos Mission Control, is my vision of episode one's fourth level. My goal was to do something that none of *DOOM*'s original maps had done—to build a map of layers. At the start, players think the map is small. Every button they press, every switch they flip, and, in some areas, every step they take peels back layers. Elevators come to life, stairs rise to let them reach previously inaccessible terrain, and walls drop to show new paths. Every new path hits the player with a surge of excitement as they move deeper into unexplored terrain. E1M4b is especially fun to play in deathmatch, because bringing down walls reveals things like openings players can shoot rockets through to gain a tactical advantage over their opponents.

I dropped E1M4b as a surprise on April 26, 2016, just over three months after E1M8b, and one day after launching the Kickstarter for *Blackroom*, the new FPS I'd been working on over the last few months. The release timing of E1M4b was no coincidence. In my tweet, I described it as more of the classic FPS gameplay I promised to deliver in *Blackroom*. Fans could download it from my Dropbox, along with a readme file on how to play the map and a story to get them excited:

> With the Toxin Refinery in the rearview, you make your way to Phobos Mission Control, where the computers crunching the data from the Phobos Anomaly are located. You need to use them to gain access to the Phobos Lab—but you remember hearing that the computers were tied into all areas of the installation and that you never knew when the environment around you would change. You need to keep your eyes alert to all movement—this place is not what it seems . . .

I was still in a groove from "Tech Gone Bad," so the development of E1M4b flowed similarly. It was a few hours in my spare time over two weeks, between working on the design and Kickstarter page for my upcoming FPS. My goal was to take what I knew about level design and give fans a style of map they had never experienced in the original game.

The positive reception to "Tech Gone Bad," the unveiling of *Blackroom*'s Kickstarter, and the surprise announcement of another free *DOOM* map was a triple whammy of positivity for me. *DOOM* fans were ecstatic to experience new levels made by the game's original designer, and the hype around those was transferred to *Blackroom*'s crowdfunding campaign.

CHAPTER 26

Blackroom

Virtual reality was around long before I began making games. The first machine of its type was patented in 1962. The field has made great strides over the past decade thanks to breakthrough technologies such as those from Oculus and Valve Index, more affordable hardware like Sony's PlayStation VR, and popular games like *Half-Life: Alyx* and *Beat Saber*. But despite VR's growing presence, many players wondered when the tech would become the present rather than continue to be hyped as the future.

Around the time I returned to *DOOM* maps, I asked myself a different but related question: What would it be like to work on the far future of VR, years or even decades after the technology had become as ubiquitous as PCs and smartphones?

It's a question I attempted to explore in *Blackroom*, an FPS concept I'd been fleshing out while working on E1M8b. I coupled what I thought might be the far future of VR with the possibilities of advanced artificial intelligence.

Blackroom was envisioned with design and story at its core. In the game's world, VR doesn't require the player to wear a headset. They stand in a massive space called a Blackroom, and a simulation comes to life around them. It's room-scale VR, but in a coliseum-size room. In the game, the player takes the role of technologist Dr. Santiago Sonora, the chief engineer employed by Hoxar, Inc., creators of the Blackroom tech. These simulations differed vastly from today's real-world VR, however. In *Blackroom*, it's more than just fancy visuals. The Blackroom tech dropped users inside a solid simulation. They climbed over walls and crawled under things. Most importantly, the simulation allowed for "effect persistence":

any wounds inflicted on the player in the simulation could be carried over into real life. If they were shot in the Blackroom, they would be wounded in real life.

Like any good (bad) corporate entity in the world of video games, Hoxar flew too close to the sun when it experimented with advanced AI. It started as a simple and even moving request—to have simulated conversations with deceased loved ones in an environment modeled after a childhood home, a favorite hangout, or somewhere completely fictional. The AI's responses weren't just the canned, impersonal dialogue spoken by virtual AI assistants. Hoxar's advanced AI deployed machine learning in real time, based on the user's memories, to create characters that acted and responded in ways that felt real. The value of Hoxar's technology was obvious for entertainment, educational, and military purposes. The company could simulate anything and adjust that simulation in real time based on the user's actions and thoughts.

As one of Hoxar's engineers, the player's job was to enter the simulation, analyze its performance, and address any issues as they arose. Santiago was, in that role, not unlike *Half-Life*'s Gordon Freeman, a well-trained research associate at Black Mesa. Santiago had a variety of tools at his disposal such as a Boxel, a device worn on his left arm that let him analyze and change the simulation in real time, as well as a drone that allowed him to see parts of the simulation he couldn't access in person.

During a routine mission, Santiago noticed subtle anomalies in the simulation—things he could neither identify nor correct. Over time, these anomalies in the AI and its algorithms transformed the simulation into something extremely dangerous, even lethal. Instead of generating realistic simulated environments for the the sim user's entertainment, the algorithms began to simulate fears as well. Even worse, when he entered the Blackroom with his Boxel, he discovered that the AI had begun to protect itself against his ability to fix whatever was going on. Meanwhile the AI, driven by its rogue algorithms, continued to go further astray.

Writing about *Blackroom* now, nearly seven years later, I see issues at the core of the concept. With games in *early* concepting, there are rough spots, things that seem interesting to the game's designer, but which will certainly change throughout development. I think the core concept of an advanced virtual simulation with a rogue AI is interesting, but at least in its initial and unrefined state, it was not the game people wanted from me.

The levels in *Blackroom* were, in essence, an analog of game development. When I made *DOOM* maps at id and again years later as a solo designer, I playtested them constantly before they were finished to see how objects were looking and to decide if I liked the placement of this imp or that shotgun. *Blackroom*'s simulation (the one in the game's story) worked similarly. Some simulations the player explored were complete. Others were simulations in development by Hoxar or broken because of bugs created by the rogue AI. As the player made their way through the simulation, they saw things like messed-up textures and regions that were impassable. In those scenarios, they controlled a drone to fly through walls, the ceiling, or the floor, to scout out what was going on elsewhere. The player's camera allowed them to see these unfinished and mangled levels from any vantage point. The AI corruption manifested in many ways, such as weird creatures that weren't programmed into the simulation. I wanted to create an atmosphere of tension and dread, amplified by the solidity and the real consequences of the virtual world. Some corruption couldn't be disabled with your Boxel, further raising the stakes for your character.

Blackroom was supposed to be the ultimate meta expression of technology, with an atmosphere and world that posed a threat to the player's character. One of the joys I had concepting it, which I wanted to pass on to players, was this idea that they were seeing things in the simulation that they weren't supposed to see. In *Blackroom*, you lived in a world of tech gone bad, and you had to fix it while it was trying to kill you.

It was an ambitious setting and concept that I hoped would push design forward. For *Blackroom* to really land, I needed an artist who was as passionate about visual direction as I was about game mechanics and storytelling. Adrian Carmack was the perfect choice. He was more than a friend and fellow cofounder of id Software. *Wolfenstein 3-D*, *DOOM*, and *Quake* were all seminal games, and his artistic choices on each game were inspired, but they were arguably most important in *Wolfenstein 3-D* and *DOOM*. Those games were pioneering efforts made by pioneers, and Adrian was the visionary who defined their look—and by definition, the look of the FPS.

By the time Brenda and I moved to Ireland in 2015, the concept of *Blackroom* was taking shape, and I was excited to talk to Adrian about making video games together again. He accepted my offer to become the art director, and together we formed Night Work Games Ltd. Adrian started working right away. He created a brilliant logo with huge, bold letters. The animated version seen in our Kickstarter video was an extension of *Blackroom*'s themes and setting. It's quick and looks like a graphical glitch, the letters fuzzy before they coalesce into the *Blackroom* title. From there, he moved on to the glitch creatures stalking through *Blackroom*'s corrupted worlds. Some of his concept art, also seen in our video, showed a wide range of settings that manifested in the simulation, such as gothic ruins.

The pitch video is a crucial component of any successful crowdfunding campaign. You can write all the marketing copy to describe your idea and the rewards tied to it, but videos are more accessible. Some ideas, especially for audiovisual mediums like games, are better communicated in a video (if the game itself is not yet playable). To craft our pitch video, we hired 2 Player Productions, a video production company based in San Francisco dedicated to generating content rooted in games and game development. 2 Player had been involved in projects made by both AAA and indie companies, and had even made a documentary that chronicled the making of *Double Fine Adventure*, a Kickstarter game made by Tim Schafer and his team at Double Fine Productions, the first game development studio to fund a title on Kickstarter.

Our first collaboration with 2 Player Productions was a teaser video inspired by *Star Wars: The Force Awakens* that we spun off from our full pitch video. *The Force Awakens* ends with Rey scaling a mountain and extending a lightsaber to Luke Skywalker, who had been conspicuously absent from the film until that point. It was a fantastic cliffhanger that teased the return of a beloved character fans had been waiting decades to see again. Our idea was to film part of the pitch video in Connemara, a rugged, beautiful coastal region in the west of Ireland, that revealed our return to the genre we had helped to create. The teaser, titled "The Return," opened with Adrian looking nervous as he began his climb at the foot of the mountain. He hikes to the top and finds a hooded figure, but wearing jeans, sturdy footwear, and a thick jacket in place of Luke's brown robe. Dramatic music swells to a crescendo as the figure turns slowly and lifts his hood, revealing yours truly. Wordlessly, Adrian hands me a keyboard and mouse. I take a breath. The camera pans out to show us standing across from each other, and then the finale theme—a nod to John Williams's epic score—kicks in, promising an announcement on April 25, 2016.

"The Return" was a hit with fans, and with Adrian and me. We had a blast making it and felt it was the perfect way to get fans even more excited than they were when I released E1M8b. We filmed a second promotional video, working with prolific filmmaker Tomek Ciezki, who had founded production company Heavy Man Films in Galway, Ireland. "The Return" was imitation as flattery, but our video with Tomek was more lighthearted. We got Tim Schafer to do a mockumentary-style interview where he thanked me for killing adventure games—referencing how "*DOOM* clones" had nearly made every other genre extinct in the '90s—because it freed up time he could spend doing other things. Most of the video summarized my history in the industry, based on sit-down interviews I recorded. Other industry luminaries such as Gearbox founder Randy Pitchford, who got his start as a level designer on *Duke Nukem 3D*, and Richard Garriott were kind enough to make appearances and talk about my history in the industry. But the best guest appearance may have been my mom, who reminisced about my creativity as a child and praised me for being "such a good boy" growing up. "He never shot at his mom," she said.

The bulk of our Kickstarter pitch video made with 2 Player Productions focused on discussion of *Blackroom* as a concept. They shot footage of me walking around Ireland as castles and other scenery flickered into view, giving the impression that I was walking through an advanced simulation where I had the tools and ability to manifest anything, even entire structures. It took around a month to put the full Kickstarter together. During that time, heading up to the campaign's launch, Adrian and I asked our consultants whether or not we should have a demo. The answer nowadays is an obvious "Of course!" but surprisingly, it wasn't the de facto approach in 2015.

Kickstarter-funded games were going through a transition at the time. In 2012, Tim Schafer and Double Fine created a campaign seeking $400,000 in funding for *Double Fine Adventure* and wound up taking in more than $3 million—all without a demo. Game developers took notice, and Kickstarters sprang up left, right, and center. With this glut of Kickstarters came some success stories, but others failed to live up to their promises and some were even outright no-shows. Gradually, those who pledged the games became more discerning with their investments.

Surveying the current crop of Kickstarters, Adrian and I felt that a demo was the way to go, and we certainly had the means to fund it. Our thinking was that we should be able to back up the concepts shared in the pitch video so players could see that the game was more than just an idea and a lot of striking concept artwork. However, our consultants felt differently. They pointed out that the recently launched and successful *Bloodstained*, a 2D "Metroidvania" made by Koji Igarashi, most famous for working on *Castlevania: Symphony of the Night* as an assistant director, writer, and programmer, didn't have a demo. Igarashi described *Bloodstained* as a return to the look and game design of *Symphony of the Night*, and his Kickstarter reached and exceeded its funding goal without a game demo. More than anything, our consultants pointed out, we didn't *need* one. Everyone knew we could make FPS games, and I had released E1M8b, which players loved, by then. I was also working on E1M4b and planned to release it during the Kickstarter campaign to generate even more excitement.

Together with our various consultants, we decided to launch without a demo.

The date was set. On April 25, 2016, *Blackroom*'s Kickstarter went live. We set a launch goal of $700,000 and gave ourselves thirty-two days to reach it. In four days, we raised just north of $131,000. Fans in the comments section thought the game had potential but questioned why we didn't have any gameplay to show. The concept itself was too far from what Adrian and I were known for, and prospective players were confused. Funding started strong then slowed dramatically. On April 29, we canceled the project, and all money raised went back to the backers.

There is a lot of data behind whether or not Kickstarters will succeed. The first forty-eight hours are critical, and all the data strongly suggested we didn't have a hope in hell. The way we phrased it externally was that we wanted to "press pause" on the campaign and develop a demo that would show the game's groundbreaking direction. It was not a decision any of us took lightly, least of all me. There were many reasons for pausing, and each came with an invaluable lesson.

The most important takeaway was, of course, to have a demo. It seems obvious. People need to see or test what they're buying. Back in the 1990s, demos were called shareware. You could play a nice chunk of *Commander Keen, Wolfenstein 3-D, DOOM,* or *Quake,* and know exactly what the full game promised: the demo, but more of that. At a minimum, prospective Kickstarters needed a video of the demo so players could understand how the promises of the marketing video and the pitch translated to actual gameplay. The initial concept of a VR simulation and AI gone rogue sounds fun, but it's also conceptual and difficult to grasp. If we'd had footage of a demo, or even a video people could get their hands on, players would have understood the game's goals better.

Shortly after ending *Blackroom*'s Kickstarter, I collaborated with expert graphics programmer Keith O'Conor and virtuoso game artist Warren Marshall to build a gameplay demo that communicated the coolness of the game's setting and play mechanics. Our goal was to build a slice of the game that showed off a cool environment, its tech-gone-rogue aesthetic, and its enemy encounters. Our goal was to combine the demo with Adrian's concept art and voiceovers to set the scene for aspects of the game we hadn't developed yet. Everything would come together in a pitch video we could shop to publishers, starting with the annual Gamescom event in Germany set for mid-August 2016.

I've never talked publicly about the pitch or the gameplay video until now. At every event, I'm asked, "Where's *Blackroom*?" Here, finally, is the answer. The demo and video have not been released publicly.

The pitch video opens with Santiago, our engineer-turned-hero, receiving his assignment. One of Hoxar's holosims, their term for simulations, is experiencing anomalies. Santiago needs to enter the holosim, diagnose the issue, and repair it. He steps into the Blackroom, an open space with blue grid lines mapped over black walls, ceiling, and floor. A voice announces that the Blackroom holo sequence will initiate in three . . . two . . .

As the viewer watches from Santiago's point of view, the simulation loads in like a wave. A realistic environment spreads like water being poured: blue grid lines fade and are replaced by rocks, trees, and uneven terrain. The player is now outside Ravenscroft Manor in one of Hoxar's most popular holosim games, "The Curse of the Ebon Raven." Its title appears in the sky ahead as, in the distance, the sprawling estate flickers and then solidifies as it finishes loading into the simulation. As Santiago makes his way along a dirt path bordered by large rocks and foliage, he keeps up a dialogue with his partner using the Boxel. He's not the classic space marine character we popularized in *DOOM* and *Quake*, known for inarticulate grunts when hunting for secret rooms hidden behind walls. He's an inquisitive, intelligent technologist, and he chats with his partner as she informs him that she has marked instances of bizarre activity for him to investigate.[*] The Ravenscroft Manor holosim starts at night, and although Santiago doesn't realize it yet, he's going to have to fight for his life in that manor. The eerie ambience of the game's soundtrack sets the mood perfectly—for players, and for the publishers we wanted to pitch our game to in just a few months.

Ravenscroft Manor is a sight to behold, with wrought-iron fences, towering columns that appeared carved from white marble, and torches set in iron sconces. Santiago makes his way up a curving marble staircase to the front entrance, which is locked. This presented the perfect opportunity to showcase Santiago's skills in these virtual worlds. The view reverts to the blue grid lines over a black background—kind of like Detective Mode in the *Batman: Arkham* games—only the simulation maintains its three-dimensionality. Santiago is still looking at stairs, trees, and marble pillars; they are just black and covered in a grid. The exception is the door, which the Boxel has registered as a dynamic object. Information about objects appears in the player's view, similar to scanning the environment with your visor in *Metroid Prime*. A text box for the door lists it as a dynamic object locked by the Key of Despair. Players can use the key, but it's hidden in the catacombs beneath the nearby town of Rankleton. (These names were placeholders.)

Santiago doesn't have the key, and since he's under some time pressure, he uses his Boxel to remove the door (remember, he's an engineer who works for the company that makes these simulations, not just a Hoxar client going through them). This process takes a few seconds. Although the demo didn't come right out and say so, it invited the audience to imagine scenarios where time was the critical resource: Maybe something huge and terrifying is chasing them and they come to a dead end—a locked door. The player doesn't have a key. They can use a tool to modify the environment, but it takes precious seconds, while they're sweating up a storm, hoping against hope that the door will vanish before the monster catches up to them. They could also run away or turn around and fight.

In the case of the demo, the door was programmed to always disappear. Santiago switches back to the simulation view and steps into a foyer with oak-paneled walls lined with bookcases and stairs that take the player up to walkways bordered by a wooden railing. Off to one side is a pair of sofas placed near a stone

---

[*]   I intended for players to be able to play as either Santiago or as his partner, Maria.

fireplace set in the center of one wall. A painting is hung above the mantel, and light fixtures on the walls and chandeliers overhead give the manor a stately if spookily quiet feel. It's a setting that would look right at home in a *Resident Evil* game, but there are worse things than zombies waiting for this player. The first sign of the abnormal activity Santiago was sent to diagnose is the statue in the center of the room. It's a carving of Arthur Ravenscroft, a singer whose descent into madness spurred him to build Ravenscroft Manor. The statue flickers and fades, giving off a fuzziness like a bad TV signal. Switching to the grid view gives the player information about Arthur, along with a troubling message—STATUS: GLITCH DETECTED, written in blood-red text. Santiago reports this to his partner, who asks him to record what he's seeing. Ominously, she isn't seeing the same thing from the control room.

In the demo, Santiago wanders over to the fireplace. One of the sofas flickers in and out of place. Scanning it displays the same STATUS: GLITCH DETECTED message. Before either character can say anything else, the computerized voice reports that an anomaly has been detected. "What the hell?" Santiago says as a monster charges at him from the side. This is the player's first look at a glitch, a four-legged beast that bull-rushes you like pinkies and has glowing eyes set deep in its skull-shaped head and spikes jutting from its body. *Blackroom* is a first-person shooter, so naturally Santiago equips a double-barreled shotgun. However, the player doesn't juggle weapons the way players do in other FPS games. "Military ordinance enabled," the voice says as the gun materializes in the player's hands. Remember, this is a simulation. With a mere thought, Santiago has summoned his weapon from the simulation's database. He lets fly with both barrels, and blood sprays with every hit. He circles the monster as he fires. Little effects cement the audience in *Blackroom*'s setting, such as the statue blinking in and out of existence as Santiago and the beast do battle. When the shotgun doesn't seem enough to get a job done, it fades away in a flash and is replaced by a futuristic rocket launcher. Santiago maneuvers to the stairs and rocket-jumps up to the second floor, where he fires one more rocket. It's not a direct hit, but the splash damage it inflicts on the floor is enough. The beast growls as it collapses. Its body pulses with digital runes. Santiago switches to the grid view, but his Boxel lists the entity as unknown, explaining that it's not registered in Hoxar's database. "Analysis reveals procedural merging of multiple Predictive Memory personas. Highly dangerous."

When Santiago asks if his partner is getting all this in control, she replies that she's registering multiple anomalies, but what she sees looking at the simulation from reality isn't the same as what he sees from inside it. Exploring the second floor, Santiago comes to a dead end when he notices a glitch in the wall. It manifests as something dark, almost like television static, and it looks like it's crawling beneath the wallpaper. Scanning it reveals that it's a sliding wall that can be opened using a switch. A glowing blue line unfurls along the grid: It's a trail the player, as Santiago, can follow if they want to get to the next area of interest right away. As he follows the line, the robotic voice rattles off another node number, and another four-legged monster appears out of thin air. Santiago puts it down. "Santiago, what's happening?" his partner asks. He reports that he's found and killed another monster and is detecting multiple glitches in the area ahead. This is another tool, a way for players who are diligent about scanning their surroundings to be prepared for monsters to attack.

The line stops at a bookshelf. Scanning it shows a book, glowing orange, that's actually a switch, one of the deranged musician's secrets that will open a passageway when pulled. Sure enough, it causes the glitchy wall Santiago found earlier to slide open. He has to backtrack to get there, but he can move in gliding bursts—one of many abilities at the player's fingertips as an engineer with almost total control over simulations—to cover ground faster. Entering the secret passage, Santiago finds a rug containing a glitch, and a mysterious portal at the end of one corridor. As he moves toward the opening, the walls, floor, and portal flash and flicker rapidly, signaling the worst glitch he's encountered yet. Through the portal, he gets a view of a colorful fantasy world—something he absolutely should not be seeing. He steps through, and the haunting music is swapped out for an intense metal track, signifying a change in tempo and setting. His partner panics and informs him he's disappeared from the "Curse of the Ebon Raven" simulation. He reports that he's in a completely different, unknown holosim.

Before she can respond, the computerized voice calls out the presence of another node. In Santiago's periphery, the wings of the biggest monster yet beat at the air. The screen fades to black, and the *Blackroom* title appears. The demo was over, and so was Santiago, if the player didn't handle that situation well. Now the pitching process could begin.

Keith, Warren, and I were thrilled with the demo, and with the video walkthrough of it we put together to show it off. I traveled to Gamescom and gave our *Blackroom* presentation to multiple publishers. Publishers liked the demo, and few of them were very interested. Talks went back and forth, but none panned out. In the end, it came down to the game having already failed publicly in its Kickstarter.

Behind the scenes at game development studios, ideas are a dime a dozen. Sometimes, those ideas make it to concept and demo phase, like *Blackroom* did. Sometimes, they make it past that and go on to development and release. There's a figure I sometimes hear kicked around in the game industry—for every ten games started, one makes it to completion. I suspect its actually more games started than that, like for every one hundred games pitched in demo form, one makes it to completion. Even that estimate might be generous. Kickstarter gave people outside of game dev a chance to see behind the scenes: a game concept coming to life, getting a demo, but ultimately not succeeding. In a sense, it wasn't much different than the original attempt at *Quake* in 1991. We had a demo for it, but we decided not to go forward. With *Blackroom*, the decision to not go forward wasn't exactly ours, but it was definitely the best decision in the end.

In the weeks and months after halting the Kickstarter, we received inquiries from countless outlets who wanted to know what was happening with the game and where we planned to take it next. We decided its public story would end there. Perhaps there would come a point in time when we would tell it, we reasoned. This is that time. *Blackroom* was a concept that became a demo, and that's all it was destined to become. It was time to focus on other games.

CHAPTER 27

The Icon of Sin Returns

I had expected E1M8b and E1M4b to make news in the gaming scene, but I never could have expected how long of a tail *DOOM* had. Gaming, like all technology sectors, moves at the speed of light. New games come out and are forgotten in a heartbeat as players move on to the next new thing. *DOOM* fans, on the other hand, visit the old levels as if they are coming home.

In late 2017, *DOOM* fans were still uploading playthroughs of my recent *DOOM* maps to YouTube, still commenting on videos, still tweeting at me about them, and still asking questions about *DOOM*'s development and legacy. It is such an incredible and dedicated community. Amid all the comments and video uploads, some players posed a good question: "When will you make a full episode?" In *DOOM*, modders can build and release a single map, or they can release a pack of maps, called a megaWAD. Other fans went on doomworld.com and asked the same question in forum threads. It just so happened that I was being asked that question over and over in late 2017, when I realized *DOOM*'s twenty-fifth anniversary was one year away.

The timing seemed perfect. I decided to celebrate a quarter-century of *DOOM* by releasing a megaWAD. I could build a megaWAD in my spare time, when I wasn't working on company projects.

There were lots of questions to answer. What did I want the megaWAD to be about? What should it look like? What theme and gameplay features should guide its design? At that moment, none of those questions had answers. There was a single idea: Make a new episode of *DOOM*—eight regular levels and a secret map.

As I thought about the episode, it started to take shape. E1M8b and E1M4b had been techbase levels because those fit the theme of episode one. Since I was making a brand-new episode, I wanted to design it using a theme I'd never used when we were making the game: hell. Sandy Petersen designed every map in episode three, "Inferno," while I was laser-focused on building DoomEd—Sandy was fast! I'd dipped my toe into hell in E1M8b, painting the glowing cracks along the floor of the first room right through to the boss room where you fight the Bruiser Brothers. This time, I wanted to take you to hell and keep you there for nine levels.

Choosing hell as a theme helped me decide where to place the episode within the other episodes. Back in 1995, we made episode four, "Thy Flesh Consumed." It's by far the toughest chapter of *DOOM*, but I set out to change that. My episode would fit between "Thy Flesh Consumed" and *DOOM II*. I chose *SIGIL* as the title. A sigil is a symbol of magical power, and I wanted to extend that definition to serve as the theme of these levels. When I was thinking about where the episode could take place, I went back and played the final map of "Thy Flesh Consumed," Unto the Cruel. I noticed that the final teleporter has some weird texture issues. That was something we didn't catch before shipping *The Ultimate DOOM*. I wove that glitch into my story: When you step into it, it doesn't transport you back to earth, where hell has invaded. Instead, a mysterious sigil causes the teleporter to malfunction, transporting you to the deepest, darkest, hottest pits of hell.

The thing about *DOOM's* third and fourth episodes is that even though they take place in hell, the satanic imagery we used was kind of light. I wanted to push the envelope, so Brenda and I hunted for artwork that evoked Satan and eternal damnation. She found artist Christopher Lovell's painting of Baphomet, a bipedal deity with the head, horns, and legs of a goat, and the wings of a demon. Lovell's painting, particularly the colors and textures he used, would look right at home on the cover of an Ozzy Osbourne album from the '80s. But the best part of it is a detail you might miss unless you look closely: In the center of Baphomet's forehead is "666," the mark of the beast, but the numbers are twisted so they almost resemble the symbol for atomic energy. It evokes terror, heavy metal, and pure evil—just the cocktail of elements I wanted to imbue *SIGIL* with. I worked Baphomet into my story: The teleporter in Unto the Cruel did not malfunction by coincidence. Baphomet sabotaged it by placing a sigil inside it.

We reached out to Christopher to see if the piece was available. As it turned out, he was a huge *DOOM* fan and was as excited about his piece being selected as I was about Brenda finding it! For the cover of the box, I decided I wanted the artwork to appear without a logo. I didn't want anything to obscure Christopher's work, which was, I felt, the perfect complement to what I had in mind for episode five. Everything was coming together.

The word "sigil" resonated with me in other ways, too. I liked that it was one word, like many of my other games: *DOOM, Quake, Daikatana*. It was also versatile. I could build an entire brand around it: *SIGIL*, the name of *DOOM*'s unofficial fifth episode, and then, later, *SIGIL* followed by a subtitle—a way to let fans know that what they were seeing was part of the *SIGIL* brand. In order for the brand to generate excitement, though, I needed more than a cool name and a wicked piece of cover art. I needed a fresh gameplay hook.

When *SIGIL* entered development, *DOOM* had been around for nearly a quarter century. Players had made tens of thousands of maps. Coming up with a style of gameplay no one had seen seemed impossible at first. Then I thought of the evil eye symbol we included in *DOOM* and *DOOM II*. It's an eye floating in midair and set in the center of a pulsating green triangle pointing to the right, almost like an arrow, and ringed by a green circle. The artwork was awesome, but we didn't use it much. That gave me an idea: *What if the evil eye was Baphomet's eye?* It could be more than just a piece of décor. Normally, players make things happen in *DOOM* by opening doors, flipping switches, and walking over line triggers. However, there's another progression mechanic in the *DOOM* engine called a gun-action trigger, and we didn't use it much, either. The first instance can be found in the secret maze of computer terminals in E1M2. The player comes to a corridor with a light that fades in and out. Two imps guard a green armor vest, and shooting the wall behind the vest opens another secret area—a secret within a secret—that leads to the chainsaw.

My gameplay hook was coupling Baphomet's eye and gun action trigger to make something happen when you shoot the eye. From a game design perspective, it's important to teach the player something, and verify that they get it before moving them on to the next mechanic so they don't get frustrated later on. In E5M1, Baphomet's Demesne, I taught the player about the eye—the sigil alluded to in the megaWAD's title—right away. The level has the player coming in hot: They start in the middle of a pentagram surrounded by imps and a spectre. The immediate task is to kill the demons and look around. There doesn't seem to be a path forward. Then, the player hopefully notices an ammo clip near a wall with a window in the middle. Looking through that window reveals the sigil, and the ammo clip functions as a clue for what to do with it—I gave you bullets, so you need to use them. Players shoot the sigil, and the wall raises to reveal a cavern filled with lava and bordered by bodies and severed heads impaled on spikes. As they walk forward, part of the wall in front of them slides open to reveal another sigil. Players blast that and raise a bridge to their right that takes them further into the cavern.

The next couple of sigils are harder to find: They're set back within walls and visible through vertical slits. The player has to position themself just right to shoot through them to hit the sigils. Each eye is a breadcrumb in a trail players follow to the exit, a massive symbol of Baphomet that ends the level when players touch it. By the time they enter E5M2, they are equipped with more than weapons—they have a firm grasp on how the eyes work.

E5M2, Sheol, builds on what players learned in the first level. As they play, they may notice an eye set back in a wall just enough that it's easy to miss. Players don't need to shoot it to finish the level, but if they do, it reveals a secret. Now they knew two things: that shooting the eye made something happen, and that something could be a way forward *or* a secret. Interestingly, the gun-action trigger only responds to weapons using bullets or shells. That means that players have to use the pistol, chain gun, or shotgun to activate them, which meant I had to give them a steady supply of bullets and shells. The goal was to balance each map with Ultra-Violence difficulty mode and pistol start in mind, the same goal used as we made the original *DOOM*. Because it was the fifth episode, I knew it had to be difficult, just as if the player had rolled into it from episode four in 1993. As I designed *SIGIL*, I updated a progression list detailing which maps would get certain weapons and which ones would have a weapon hidden in a secret area.

I was feeling devious when I designed E5M1, so I created a triple-nested secret—a secret within a secret within a secret—the first such sequence of that type I'd made. In summary, after shooting the first eye and entering the cavern, players shoot the wall dead ahead and raise two bridges (an obvious one in front and a secret one behind them).

E5M1 shows off another design hook. We designed *DOOM*'s levels to be playable in single-player as well as in deathmatch and co-op games. That's why there are spawn points, weapons, and ammo that only appear in multiplayer. The problem is that some of those maps were too big for deathmatch. Shooting friends and strangers with rockets is fun, but having to hunt down an opponent between frags ruins the excitement. With *SIGIL*, I wanted each map to be a Trojan horse—a single-player level and a multiplayer level, but not the same terrain. Load any *SIGIL* map into an editor, and you'll see that it's two maps in one. There's the area players access playing solo, and an entirely separate area built with multiplayer in mind. I came up with this idea on February 18, 2018, and was convinced I was the first *DOOM* mapmaker to do it—until I found *REKKR*.

REKKR is a megaWAD by Matthew Little, known as Revae, that replaces all four of *The Ultimate DOOM*'s episodes with four brand-new ones. The day *REKKR* came out, I was reading reviews and learned that Revae had built a separate deathmatch arena into each map. I couldn't help laughing. *REKKR* ended up releasing first, and I gracefully surrendered the honorific "first" title. It made me happy to see others still trying to innovate within *DOOM*, too.

I needed to add something new to the deathmatch experience to see if I could one-up *REKKR*, and figured some players might like to play deathmatch in the single-player maps. I solved that by adding a way for players to connect the single- and multiplayer sections of each map as they played. In a deathmatch session, each player must flip two switches, which are set far apart, at the same time. After throwing the switches, both players must go through teleporters that transport them to the single-player section. This implementation forced both players to agree to expand the terrain where they're playing. If one player wanted to stick to the deathmatch area, they just didn't flip one of the switches. Also, knowing that some of those single-player areas would be too large for a good one-on-one deathmatch, I added some new walls to constrain the space a little on each map where needed.

E5M7 was *SIGIL*'s first designed map, and originally, I intended it to be its fifth. But by the time I finished with it, it was, to that point, the largest map I'd ever designed, and it ended up being the largest in the episode. It's got a nest of secrets to discover, and it's brutally difficult. To open the episode in E5M1, the first room I made was also not the starting room. It was the lava cavern players entered after shooting the sigil to leave the first room. Players were on bridges bordered by lava. If they fell in, they would have to scramble to climb out. Full of shotgunners and imps, players had to be mindful of their footing as they dodged fireballs, or they would strafe right off the bridge into the lava.

I approached the design of levels for *SIGIL* the same way I approached levels for *DOOM*, *DOOM II*, and *The Ultimate DOOM*. First, I imagined an opening scene. The first thing the player sees or hears in a level sets the tone and pacing for the rest of the level. Next, I created an area that players would visit multiple times—a landmark they would come to recognize as they opened up parts of the map and discovered how everything connected. Finally, I kept the design of each map tight. I don't do sprawling levels. They get too chaotic and distracting. I want my levels to feel like roller coasters—high points of excitement broken up with exploratory lulls for the player to get their bearings. While I am making a level, as always, I play through it hundreds of times. Even the smallest change necessitates a replay to see how it feels.

I listen to music while I work. During the development of *DOOM*, I was at my keyboard with the tunes of Queensrÿche and Lynch Mob flowing into my ears. On *DOOM II*, it was Alice in Chains and Vince Guaraldi. While I made *SIGIL*, I listened to Buckethead's music nonstop. Buckethead is one of the most creative musicians around, and I've been a fan since he started in the late '80s. I mentioned to Brenda once that I wished I could use Buckethead's music in *SIGIL*. Having listened to his music constantly throughout development, I just couldn't imagine *SIGIL* sounding any different.

"Why not ask?" she said.

She had a point. The worst that could happen is he would say no, and that would be no different from where I was without his music. Why not? I sent him an email, and after a couple of months, his representative answered. It turned out Buckethead was a *DOOM* fan! This had happened once before, when Trent Reznor and Nine Inch Nails told us they played *DOOM* on their tour bus between shows and would love to write the soundtrack for *Quake*. Buckethead was gracious enough to let me license any songs I wanted, but the cherry on top was he wanted to write a brand-new song for *SIGIL*. I had no idea what it sounded like or what it would be called until the day I got a link to it. As a huge Buckethead fan, words fail to describe how I felt listening to a song that the virtuoso had composed for my game. Even writing about it now, it feels unreal. I was honored by his generosity and made his new track, "Romero One Mind Any Weapon," the background music for E5M1. For the free version of the game, I worked with musician James Paddock. Paddock was already well known in the *DOOM* community, and his work is excellent. Like Buckethead, I selected scores from Paddock's existing work that best fit the levels and the feeling I was going for.

Licensing to Buckethead's music was one reason I needed to consider all the source ports of *DOOM* that have sprung up since John Carmack released the game's code in the late '90s. The larger reason was that *SIGIL*'s map design was incompatible with certain versions. All versions of *DOOM* can be sorted into two categories: those that adhere to the same rules and limits of *The Ultimate DOOM*, and those that have bells and whistles, such as allowing for more line segments. In *DOOM* parlance, this is known as limit removing—literally removing the limit of how many lines you can have in a level. Some older *DOOM* source ports support them, or let you enable or disable them, but many don't. I released two versions of *SIGIL*, one for each generation. The "older" generation complies with the original game's compatibility, such as a MIDI soundtrack by James Paddock, while the "new" generation's release uses MP3s and supports added complexity in the map design.

Really, I was working on three WADs at once. There was the *SIGIL* mega-WAD, the music WAD, and another WAD called "SIGIL_compat" for the old generation. As an example of compatibility, the old generation of *DOOM* cannot register any episode beyond "Thy Flesh Consumed." Running "SIGIL_compat" on any old-gen release will replace episode three, "Inferno," with *SIGIL*. (You can still play "Inferno," just not while you're running the *SIGIL* megaWAD.)

There are all sorts of technical issues in *DOOM*'s engine. The only people who know about them are people who have analyzed the source code, and people like John Carmack and me, because we wrote it. That knowledge gave me the advantage of understanding *DOOM*'s tech at the deepest, lowest level. It's like the difference between a high-level programming language like C and a low-level language like Assembly. If you're fluent in Assembly, you can get down into the guts of a computer's hardware and manipulate it in ways that add incredible amounts of performance to your software. Looking at *DOOM*'s source code reveals a hybrid of C and assembly language. That combination made *DOOM* fast, sleek, and cutting edge.

Another example of compatibility challenges can be found in E5M6, Unspeakable Persecution. The map's defining feature—the landmark architecture—is a maze patrolled by a Cyberdemon. I'm thrilled with how the area came together. There are monsters all around the maze, and the player's goal is to climb to higher ground above it while avoiding fireballs thrown by the Baron of Hell, camped in a nearby tower. The Cyberdemon stomps around the maze like the minotaur in Daedalus's labyrinth from Greek mythology. It is utterly terrifying as a player to know the Cyberdemon is seeking you out while you try desperately to escape.

But as cool as the maze turned out, I also enjoyed crafting the area before it. Like many regions of *SIGIL*, E5M6 is a dark level—it is the depths of hell, after all. There are places so dark that the best way to fight monsters is to wait until they walk across a lighted area or a light source, such as a torch. The area before the maze is a river of blood that inflicts damage as the player wades through it. Three Barons of Hell teleport down there to hunt them, and the only way out for the player is by finding lifts that raise them onto safer terrain. Those lifts are deceptively complex. They ascend and descend, but they're constructed with lots of vertices and line segments. The challenge was that *DOOM*'s engine was written to process a maximum of eight line segments intersected by the player's hit box—a rectangle. That meant I had to simplify the line segments that made up those lifts, or they would be unusable.

I didn't mind striving for compatibility at all. The reception to E1M8b and E1M4b assured me that millions of players welcomed more *DOOM* levels, and I was determined to meet their expectations.

Before releasing *SIGIL*, it needed to pass through its own gauntlet. Even though I've been making *DOOM* maps since the beginning, my maps are never perfect out of the gate. Every game goes through testing, and *SIGIL* was no different. Boris "dew" Klimeš, Xaser, Michael "UberGewei" Schaap, Flambeau, and Keyboard_Doomer were my play testers for *SIGIL*, and their feedback was invaluable.

Even before play testing, my process was iterative. Sometimes I'd come up with an idea for one map while I worked on another, or I'd think of a hook for a deathmatch arena that I felt was so cool I had to go back and make sure it was in all of them. In designing a game, I expect my early maps to be altered during the development process as I come to understand the aesthetic of an episode. It's why

I make my first level last. It's the first thing players will see, and by then, hopefully, I'll be at my best.

Most times, my iterations come from seeing the level as a player. I work on a level for a minute or two, play it, and explore how it feels. Designers can't know how the adjusted hallway, or the change they made to a weapon's damage, will affect the flow of their level and the player's perception of the space or a game's systems without testing it over and over and over, long before anyone else weighs in with feedback. So often during *SIGIL* I moved through areas before adding any monsters because I had to know how an area looked, how it felt to interact with and be in that space, before thinking about encounters. By the time a level was truly finished—no more adjustments, no more play testing—I had played it hundreds of times. I code the same way: code, test, code, test.

My launch plan was staged depending on what players wanted. As a collector of big-box PC games, I wanted *SIGIL* in a big box, too. It was for that reason that we had licensed Christopher Lovell's Baphomet. I planned to release the megaWAD for free online with James Paddock's excellent MIDI soundtrack. If people wanted the licensed Buckethead soundtrack, they had to purchase the version that included it. Many players knew *SIGIL* would be released for free, and most of them were content to wait for the free version. I knew that, too, and was fine with it.

Limited Run Games was enthusiastic about entering into a manufacturing and distribution relationship with us. Up to that point, they had specialized in curating physical editions of retro or indie console games and games that had only been published digitally. *SIGIL* would be their first PC game. We devised a roadmap that offered two physical versions of *SIGIL*. The Beast Box was positioned as a top-shelf item for collectors, featuring an oversize box inspired by the *id Anthology* box and boasting Christopher Lovell's artwork. Each box was individually numbered and signed by hand. Inside the box there were some great collectibles, including a USB drive shaped like a 3.5" floppy disk, an art print signed by Christopher Lovell, a large pewter statue of my head on a spike as a wink and nod to *DOOM II*, a T-shirt with Baphomet on it, and lots more. The second box, called the Big Box, was much less expensive and came with fewer collectibles, but would satisfy any *DOOM* fan who experienced sticker shock at the Beast Box's price tag. It also featured another of Christopher Lovell's pieces on its cover.

We announced *SIGIL* on December 10, 2018, the day *DOOM* turned twenty-five. That same day, we announced a two-week window to order the Beast Box and Big Box physical editions. We sold thousands of boxes, making *SIGIL* an instant success for us and for Limited Run Games. On May 31, 2019, we finished manufacturing and shipped all the products to our customers. When everyone had it in their hands, I released the megaWAD for free online. It has since been downloaded more than a million times.

Fortunately, positive reviews and comments flooded in. Every fan who tweeted their review to me, streamed the game, or took the time to share their opinions about the game on forums meant the world to me. As *Daikatana* taught me, there are a million ways for things to go wrong, and I was truly feeling emotional seeing people say things like, "Romero's still got it," or "A typical Romero level," followed by a discussion of how *SIGIL* was punishing and diabolical, both of which I took as high praise. A highlight was spending hours on Twitch watching players experience *SIGIL* for the first time. For game creators, the opportunity to watch your audience experience your product in real time is invaluable. I ended up altering a couple of things because of those plays, too. Among the first was the E5M4 crusher maze. It was too difficult for players and ruining their experience. So I made it easier. I also addressed most of speedrunner extraordinaire Zero Master's exploits.

At the end of the year, I was honored when doomworld.com named *SIGIL* a runner-up for a 2019 Cacoward, annual awards given out to the honor the best *DOOM* levels, WADs, and total conversions released that year. In their write-up for the Cacoward, they described it as "the most anticipated, previewed, played, pored over, replayed, analyzed, praised, and shat-on release of the year." In 2016, they had awarded E1M8b the best of the year. But the review that meant the most to me didn't come from critics. After Bethesda and id Software rereleased *DOOM* and *DOOM II* in 2019, I got an email from Kevin Cloud. I hadn't talked to him since QuakeCon in 2014, and it was great to catch up, but he wasn't emailing just to say hello. I was floored when he explained that the team had curators looking for megaWADs to release as free content, and they would love to feature *SIGIL*. *SIGIL*'s availability through an official *DOOM* release felt like coming home. It had been welcomed as an unofficial/official fifth episode of *DOOM*, one twenty-five years in the making.

The release of *SIGIL* provided me with an education of sorts. The positive response let me know that people still had as much fun playing my levels as I did making them. Fans started asking for a sequel megaWAD to *SIGIL* right away, and I plan to release *SIGIL II* for *DOOM* in time for *DOOM*'s thirtieth birthday on December 10, 2023. A megaWAD for *DOOM II* is also underway, and I've already published a teaser. As a show of support to Ukraine following Russia's invasion in 2022, I released *One Humanity*, a single-level WAD for *DOOM II* that is part of an upcoming thirty-two-map megaWAD. *One Humanity* costs five euros, and 100 percent of it goes toward the Red Cross and UN Central Emergency Response Fund. As of the date of this writing, just over €40,000 has been donated.

As for the rest of the upcoming megaWAD for *DOOM II*, I'm going to take a page from id Software's playbook and say, "When it's done." All of these projects are made in my spare time, when I'm not designing my main project.

In July 2022, Romero Games announced that we partnered with a major publisher to develop my next first-person shooter. It's not a megaWAD, it's not *Blackroom*, and it's not a retro-style shooter. It's a modern shooter that pairs modern tech with a combination of old-school and contemporary design sensibilities.

First-person shooters have undergone major evolutions since we created and popularized the genre in the early 1990s. For most of that decade, the "FPS genre" did not exist, at least under that name. Everyone called them "*DOOM* clones," and that's what they were: imitators that looked to us as the pioneer in tech and game design. Now there are more subgenres than I can count: military sims, tactical, arena, battle royale, competitive, retro, multiplayer online battle arena (MOBA) shooters, hero shooters—the list goes on. Developers now have access to tools Carmack and I would have killed to have when we were getting id Software off the ground. AAA shooters have deep analytics that tell developers everything they could ever want to know about who's playing their game, and how, and when, and what they like most and least. Live-service FPS games require around-the-clock maintenance and a constant flow of new stories, characters, weapons, and mechanics to keep players invested.

Today's technology is light years ahead of what we had at our disposal in the '90s. As technology advanced, player expectations rose. For an FPS to succeed, it has to go beyond the minimum effort of meeting those expectations. It has to do what id Software did with *Commander Keen, Wolfenstein 3-D, DOOM*, and *Quake*—it has to find and define a space.

When will my next shooter be released? When it's done. Until then, the response to *SIGIL* has made one undeniable statement: The Icon of Sin is back, back to making games in the genre I pioneered, where I feel most at home, and where the community is the best. It will take more than a few rockets to the head—or a spike impaled through my brain—for me to leave.

Epilogue

When I was a kid, all I wanted to do was wake up and make games every day for the rest of my life. How lucky am I that this has happened? Entering my fifth decade as a game developer, I am eternally grateful that this wish, this dream, has been realized. I wish I could go back and tell young me all the amazing things he'd see along the way.

In writing this book, I put everything I could think of into it, except where it was necessary out of respect or request to leave some details or individuals out. I purposefully focused on the positive and did not dwell too much on the negative, except to explain the facts about a situation with the hope that people might learn from my challenges and see that anything can be overcome. I believe I am a lucky person, and so when faced with seeming difficulty, I tell myself that there is a reason for it—an upside. Growing up poor meant few toys, but it also meant that I had to learn to make my own fun. Contracts canceled and business difficulties paved the way for new opportunities. While the game industry has many colorful characters, people make mistakes and bad decisions, me included. On the whole, though, I have nothing but gratitude for my life in games and for the people I have worked with and for. Everything that happened has gotten me here and given me experience and perspective.

I've tried my best to share my passion for this incredible industry, for the beauty in games, game design, and code. I hope those starting out in game development find something here that is of use. From that first moment you start working on a game, you are one of us. Seek out game development communities online or join a local game jam. Working with other developers to create and finish a game gets you on your way. Early in my career, I worked on multiple games at a time. Start small and get some practice. Try remaking a classic arcade game to get a feel for things before you attempt to make a giant RPG. Carmack, Tom, and I had each been making games for ten years before we started working together. It was another few years before we made *DOOM*, and that was my ninetieth game. Give yourself time to get good, and don't be dissuaded by setbacks. Game development is like gameplay. Load your save and try again.

Likewise, I hope those who feel like they are struggling or are the odd one out see themselves in the various ups and downs of my life. I deeply believe that technology is transformative, and it can take someone from nothing to something. The game industry is a culture created by the outsiders—the kids who didn't fit in, the ones who listened to and loved Black Sabbath, Judas Priest, *D&D*, and *Aliens*. Today, the bands, games, and movies may be different, but the feeling is the same. We outsiders are unique, and our perspective leads to innovation. The continued diversification of the game industry can only bring with it more good things. I hope you find a way to success through code and creativity, too.

Along those lines, the industry has taught me some exceptional lessons.

Failure is a part of games: Innovation is not certain, and sometimes you are not going to hit the mark. Failing means you're trying and taking chances. The biggest lessons I've learned come from having tried and failed. Some of those lessons you know about, and others were fixed before they ever saw the light of day. Irish writer Samuel Beckett got it: "Ever tried. Ever failed. No matter. Try again. Fail again. Fail better." Don't be afraid of failure. It's a risk that's necessary to innovate.

Resilience: Saved games are there for a reason. Game developers expect you to take a shot now and again. In life and especially in game dev, it's no different. Get up and do it again. That said, if whatever you're doing is not going according to plan, if it feels like you're taking one too many knocks on the chin, leave and find a better place or start another game.

Execution is everything: Success is not defined by an idea. It is determined by your ability to execute on that idea. Surround yourself with good people who know when to compliment you and when to give you a critique.

Give credit where it is due: Thank you for reading my book and thank you so much for playing my games.

Acknowledgments

DOOM Guy wouldn't be what it is without the help of a great many people. First and foremost, my profound thanks go to the original id Software team who form such a big part of this story: Tom Hall, Adrian Carmack, John Carmack, Jay Wilbur, and Kevin Cloud. We were all in the right place at the right time at the *same time*, and our lives are forever entwined because of the games we made together. We had so much fun, learned so much from one another, and created some incredible games that have left a legacy on the artform of games. Even in our most difficult times, we released something that was great, which is a testament to what we could do. Thanks also to the current id Software team for keeping the games alive. I was genuinely misty-eyed seeing a reference to "King Ormero, the father." Thank you so much for this. Keep ripping and tearing and never, ever let it be done.

My family has supported me throughout my career. My mother, Ginny, did her best for me through thick and thin and showed me how to stay positive through anything. My father, Alfonso, gifted me with a devious sense of playfulness that certainly comes across in my level design. My stepfather, John Schuneman, recognized my early interest in programming and got me the Apple II that transformed all my waking hours into a hopeful career. For that, I am forever grateful. My brother, Ralph, played all my games and was a constant fan, even when the games weren't good. My wife, Brenda, encouraged me to tell my life story and helped me to write and edit these chapters into something that resembled a story instead of a listing of hyperthymestic ROM dumps. My kids, Michael, Steven, Lillia, Maezza, Avalon, and Donovan, are my pride and joy. They've been raised in a culture of game dev and have supported the oddities and ups and downs that come with that life. Three of them have even followed me into game dev (Michael, Maezza, and Donovan). My extended family—my aunt Yoly, and my many cousins on both sides of the US-Mexico border—have supported me throughout the years, particularly my grandma Suki, during the times that my mom and I had so little. Amo a mi familia.

Early friends like Rob Lavelock and Christian Divine opened creative worlds for me, shared my love of tech and design, and together, we set ourselves on paths that crossed again and again. Tom Hall, before and after id Software, is my life mate and closest friend. We picked each other up when we crashed and celebrated our wins. Shawn Green is likewise a great friend; we deathmatched, sang metal, and made it through shipping *Daikatana*. I'm grateful for our adventures together and our lifelong friendships.

My agent, Markus Hoffman of Regal | Hoffman & Associates, championed the book from the start, seeing in its pages an extraordinary journey against the odds, believing that there was something unique in my life of games and code. Markus helped me find a perfect home for this book. Abrams was that home. Connor Leonard at Abrams was exactly the editor this book needed—a gamer and a fan of my games. He asked the questions and got the answers that added much substance to this book. Connor encouraged me to tell an authentic story, was understanding when game dev got in the way of chapter dev, and celebrated when we crossed the finish line. Thank you, Connor, for your part in getting this story out there. Working with the team at Abrams—including Annalea Manalili, Devin Grosz, Taryn Roeder, and Sarah Masterson Hally—has been an absolute honor and a pleasure. Thanks are also due to David Craddock, the foremost chronicler of the FPS history, for your review and feedback on critical chapters; Katie Gardner, who provided feedback on the manuscript; and to Seth Kaufman, whose aid and assistance in the early stages of this book is appreciated.

And that leaves me to acknowledge the most important person of all: *you*. Seriously, you. I don't expect everyone to read every word of this book, but there are the superfans, the *DOOM* fans, the *Quake* fans, the *Wolfenstein 3-D* fans, the *Commander Keen* fans, the id Software fans, and as unlikely as it is, here you are still reading to the end of the acknowledgments. I don't know of any community that is more dedicated than ours. So, thank you for your support, your emails, your messages, your DMs, your mail. Thanks for being a part of our community, and thanks especially to the mods of that community. Thanks for playing my games. Whether your comments were positive or negative, you took the time to share your thoughts with me, and I appreciate it. I read every single one. It's down to you that I have the life I dreamed of as a kid—to wake up and make games every single day. I could not imagine anything better. I hope my games have brought you a little bit of the same joy that you have given me. Emag eht niw uoy.